LUKE

God's Word
for the
Biblically-Inept™ SERIES

Joyce L. Gibson

CARTOONS BY

Reverend Fun
(Dennis "Max" Hengeveld)
Dennis is a graphic de-
signer for Gospel Films and
the author of *Has
Anybody Seen My Locust?*
His cartoons can
be seen worldwide at
www.reverendfun.com.

STARBURST PUBLISHERS®

P. O. Box 4123, Lancaster, Pennsylvania 17604

To schedule author appearances, write:
Author Appearances
Starburst Publishers
P.O. Box 4123
Lancaster, Pennsylvania 17604
(717) 293-0939

www.starburstpublishers.com

CREDITS:
Copyedited by Chad Allen and Deb Strubel
Cover design by David Marty Design
Text design and composition by John Reinhardt Book Design
Illustrations by Mark Ammerman and Melissa A. Burkhart
Cartoons by Dennis "Max" Hengeveld

First Printing, March 2002

ISBN: 1-892016-47-8
Library of Congress Number 2001097841

Printed in the United States of America

READ THIS PAGE BEFORE YOU READ THIS BOOK . . .

Welcome to the *God's Word for the Biblically-Inept™* series. If you find reading the Bible overwhelming, baffling, and frustrating, then this Revolutionary Commentary™ is for you!

Each page of the series is organized for easy reading with icons, sidebars, and bullets to make the Bible's message easy to understand. *God's Word for the Biblically-Inept™* series includes opinions and insights from Bible experts of all kinds, so you get various opinions on Bible teachings—not just one!

There are more *God's Word for the Biblically-Inept™* titles on the way. The following is a list of available books. (See page 350 for ordering information.) We have assigned each title an abbreviated **title code**. This code along with page numbers is incorporated in the text **throughout the series**, allowing easy reference from one title to another.

God's Word for the Biblically-Inept™ Series

CHAPTERS AT A GLANCE

PART TWO: Miracles, Teachings, and Actions

PART THREE: Betrayal, Death, and Resurrection

ILLUSTRATIONS

INTRODUCTION

CHAPTER HIGHLIGHTS

(Chapter Highlights)

Welcome to ***Luke—God's Word for the Biblically-Inept*™**, another in a series that makes the Bible easy to understand. This is not a traditional Bible study! It's a REVOLUTIONARY COMMENTARY™ designed to uncomplicate the Bible and change your outlook on this book forever. I want to help you Learn the Word™ so that you will turn to it often for enjoyment and instruction.

To Gain Your Confidence

Luke—God's Word for the Biblically-Inept™ is for you if you want an easy walk-through of the book Luke wrote to introduce people to Jesus Christ. In writing about Luke's account I have tried to fill you in on historically correct background information, but mostly I have kept the focus on Jesus Christ, as Luke did. The Bible was written for you, so you'll want to read Luke's words, which we have included throughout this book.

What Is The Bible?

When you hold a Bible in your hand you see one book. But it's really a collection of sixty-six books written by a number of authors over a long period of time. You'll find a list of those books in the front of the Bible. You'll also notice that the books are listed under two headings: Old Testament (thirty-nine books) and New Testament (twenty-seven books).

Many years after the Bible was written, scholars took the books and divided them into chapters and verses. Today when you see a reference, such as Luke 19:10, you can find it quite easily by locating first the book, then the chapter, and then the verse.

Let's Get Started

(Let's Get Started)

> **Luke 19:10** For the Son of Man . . .

(Verse of Scripture)

inspired: *influence or guided*

(What?)

The Bible was written by ordinary people, but the Bible is not an ordinary book. God himself was the source of their writing. These ordinary people wrote what God **inspired** them to write. God gave them the wisdom and insight to write what he wanted. That's why we call the Bible the Word of God.

Why Study The Bible?

One good reason to study the Bible is that it is the only book that has God's message for us. As you turn the pages of your Bible, you'll see again and again—more than 2,600 times—that the writers claimed that they were recording what God said. In other words, these writers put down what God told them to say.

Another reason to read the Bible is that it tells you the truth—about God, about the world we live in, about you, and about how much God loves you and wants you to know him. And the truth in your Bible has power to change your life—far more than you may think—because the living God speaks to you through its pages. You can get to know God as a real, living Person when you believe what you read and do what he says.

What Others are Saying:

(What Others Are Saying)

Lois LeBar: It is not enough to know about the Lord; we must know him.

It is not enough to believe our beliefs; we must *believe him.*

It is not enough to take the Word as God's; we must *take God at his word.*[1]

Why Study The Life Of Jesus Christ?

Actually, Luke is one of four Bible books that give us the life of Christ. Those books are Matthew, Mark, Luke, and John. You may wonder why the first four books of the New Testament are devoted to the life of one person. When Jesus came to earth, he came as the focal point of all history!

All the years from Creation to the end of the Old Testament were years of preparation for Jesus' coming. God was at work in the nation of Israel to prepare them for the arrival of his Son to be the Savior of all people. The first four books of the New Testament tell about Jesus'

- birth,
- three years of ministry,
- death on the cross,

- resurrection from the tomb, and
- return to his Father in heaven.

The rest of the New Testament tells how Jesus changed the world by taking his followers and forming the church. He gave the apostles power to lead many others to have faith in him. Today the church is still growing all around the world.

Who Wrote The Four Gospels?

God chose three Jewish men and one Greek to write about the life of Jesus (see GWLC, pages xvi–xviii). These men were convinced without even the slightest doubt that Jesus is the Son of God, the **Messiah-King** promised by Old Testament prophets, the Savior of the world who will come again as King.

Let's look briefly at the men who wrote three of the books: Matthew, Mark, and John. That will help us see how Luke's Gospel account is unique. Matthew was a tax collector before he met Jesus. Matthew directed his Gospel to the Jewish people. He quoted Old Testament Scriptures to prove that Jesus was the Messiah they were looking for.

John Mark (also called John or Mark) traveled with Peter, one of Jesus' disciples. In his Gospel Mark recorded what he learned from Peter's close association with Jesus. He wrote for the Romans.

John was a fisherman who arranged his Gospel thematically and included lengthy conversations in which Jesus revealed his true nature. John wrote for everyone and showed Jesus as the divine Son of God.

Why Study Luke's Gospel?

Luke was Greek and was a doctor. He must have loved to write too. When we count the actual number of verses, he wrote more of the New Testament (in Luke and Acts) than any other writer.

Though Luke never met Jesus in person, he did thorough research and must have conducted in-depth interviews, because through his Gospel he clearly reveals Jesus' great heart of compassion, and he includes parts of Jesus' life and teaching that are not in the other Gospels.

Luke addressed his book (as well as the Book of Acts) to an individual—Theophilus, thought to be a Gentile official of some kind who believed in Jesus. Luke wanted him to have an "*orderly account*" of Jesus' life, which would give him confidence that he had heard the truth about Jesus (Luke 1:3–4).

FAST FORWARD

(Fast Forward)

Messiah-King: Hebrew for Christ, God-sent deliverer

(Fact or Fiction)

Though Luke never mentions himself in his Gospel, he leaves the distinct impression that he loved Jesus as the Son of Man—completely human as well as completely divine. He understood that Jesus came as a servant *"to seek and to save what was lost"* (Luke 19:10). In his Gospel account he shows how Jesus went out of his way to reach out to ordinary people, especially to those who were ignored or despised by the religious leadership of his day.

What Others are Saying:

☞ **GO TO:**

Luke 9:51; 24:25–27 (give his life)

(Go To)

Larry Sibley: Luke's Gospel has several main themes. Christ is presented as the Savior of the world; the friend who stands with the poor and powerless, the sick and the brokenhearted. Luke emphasizes the urban setting of Jesus' life and work. Women play a prominent role in this gospel. The Holy Spirit is given an important place. Most important of all is Jesus' purpose to <u>give his life</u> in Jerusalem for the sinners he called to repentance.[2]

 PHYSICIAN'S PERSPECTIVE—Dr. Luke must have shared some of Jesus' deep understanding of people's heartaches because he shows amazing insight as he notes again and again how Jesus related to people, especially those who had needs: women, children, the sick and disabled, the poor, and the oppressed. Luke also makes special mention that in addition to the twelve disciples who traveled with Jesus, there were other followers, including women, who used their personal funds to pay the bills as they moved from place to place. Luke's care in telling about specific individuals not mentioned in the other Gospels—widows, children, and babies—points to him as a heart specialist, a doctor of the soul.

(Physician's Perspective)

Feelings Flow

Luke wasn't a stuffy academic-type doctor. He wasn't afraid of emotions. God's love for all people—not only the Jews—flows through the pages, both in Jesus' actions and in the stories he told. Because of that love, the spirit of joy brightens Luke's book. In one form or another the word "joy" appears more than twenty times. Praise to God pervades Luke's accounts of the birth of John the Baptist and Jesus. He includes four songs in his first two chapters:

- The Magnificat (Luke 1:46–55)
- The Benedictus (1:68–79)
- The Nunc Dimittis (2:29–32)
- The Gloria (2:14)

The Language Of The Gospels

The Jews in Jesus' day were trilingual! That's what archaeologists and Bible students tell us (see GWLC, pages xix–xx).

1. Aramaic was used in everyday conversation.
2. Hebrew was used in the synagogues and the Temple, but was also spoken in everyday conversation.
3. Greek, however, was the universal language. Most Jews spoke it fluently. They used it for communication with Roman authorities and foreign traders. Jews in Israel used spoken and written Greek.

The writers of the New Testament used common Greek so that their books could be read by people all over the Roman Empire.

Why Use The New International Version (NIV)?

Most of us cannot read the Bible in the language in which it was originally written, but we do have a number of Bible **translations** and **paraphrases** in English. I use a number of these regularly for my personal study, and I consulted them as I prepared this commentary. For this book we used the New International Version (NIV) of the Bible.

How To Use *Luke—God's Word For The Biblically-Inept*™

Sit down with this book and your Bible.

- Start the book at chapter 1.
- As you work through each chapter, read the specified verses in your Bible.
- Use the sidebars loaded with icons and helpful information to give you a knowledge boost.
- Answer the Study Questions and review with the Chapter Wrap-Up.
- Then go on to the next chapter. It's simple!

This book contains a variety of special features that will help you learn. They are illustrated in the sidebar of this introduction. Here are the features, with a brief explanation of each.

Something to Ponder

(Something to Ponder)

translations: conversions from original Hebrew and Greek

paraphrases: restatements in another form

Study Questions

(Study Questions)

Sections and Icons	What's It For?
CHAPTER HIGHLIGHTS	the most prominent points of the chapter
Let's Get Started	a chapter intro
Bible Quote	what you came for: the Bible
Commentary	my thoughts on what the verses mean
GO TO:	other Bible verses to help you better understand (underlined in text)
What?	definition of a word (bold in text)
KEY POINT	major point of a passage
What Others Are Saying:	if you don't believe me, listen to the experts
Illustrations	a picture is worth a thousand words
Remember This . . .	don't forget this
Something to Ponder	interesting points to get you thinking
Fast Forward	linking Bible times with today
Fact or Fiction	Looking at ideas people have to see if they are true or not true
MORE INFORMATION	additional information from other Gospel writers
PHYSICIAN'S PERSPECTIVE	the passage from a doctor's point of view
Study Questions	questions to get you discussing and studying
CHAPTER WRAP-UP	recap of the prominent points

(More Information)

A Word About Series Cross-References

To aid you in studying various topics, biblical characters, and Bible passages, we have included cross-references to other books in the *God's Word for the Biblically-Inept™* and *What's in the Bible for . . .™* series. These references are scattered throughout the text of this book. The references will look similar to this: (Read more about Abraham in GWMB, pages 13–28). The four-letter code "GWMB" refers to the title of the book, in this case *Men of the Bible*. The page numbers that follow the title code tell you exactly where to look in *Men of the Bible* to find more about Abraham. Use the chart on page xvii to understand the four-letter title codes.

A Word About Words

There are several interchangeable terms: Scripture, Scriptures, Holy Scriptures, the Word, Word of God, God's Word, Gospel. All these mean the same thing and come under the broad heading called the Bible. I may use each of these terms at various times.

Title Code	Book Title
GWAC	*Acts*
GWBI	*The Bible*
GWDN	*Daniel*
GWGN	*Genesis*
GWHN	*Health & Nutrition*
GWJN	*John*
GWLC	*Life of Christ, Volume 1*
GWLC2	*Life of Christ, Volume 2*
GWLK	*Luke*
GWMK	*Mark*
GWMB	*Men of the Bible*
GWPB	*Prophecies of the Bible*
GWRV	*Revelation*
GWRM	*Romans*
GWWB	*Women of the Bible*
WBFC	*What's in the Bible for . . .™ Couples*
WBFM	*What's in the Bible for . . .™ Mothers*
WBFT	*What's in the Bible for . . .™ Teens*
WBFW	*What's in the Bible for . . .™ Women*

The word "Gospel" may refer to one of the four books written about the life of Jesus, of which the Gospel of Luke is one. Or "Gospel" may refer to the good news about Jesus.

One Final Word

As you read Luke, you'll see God's love for the Jews and how that love extends to the rest of us. You'll see Jesus' wisdom and compassion for all. You'll see how Jesus willingly gave his life for us. God promises that when we acknowledge our guilt and trust Jesus as Savior, God will forgive our sins and make us his own children.

When you open your heart to God and ask him to speak to you, he will. Ask God to speak to you as you read Luke, and you'll be amazed how wonderfully the Bible will enrich your life!

KEY POINT

If Jesus had not died, he could not be our living Savior today.

(Key Point)

Ken Gire: The words He speaks are words of life. That is why we must reach for them, receive them, and respond to them. Whatever they may say, however they may sound, whatever implications they may have for our lives, the words that proceed from his mouth offer life to our world.

Those words are how our relationship with God grows.
Living reflectively is how we receive them.[3]

What Others are Saying:

Bible Quote: This is where you'll read a quote from the Bible.

James 1:5 If any of you lacks wisdom, he should ask God, who gives generously to all without finding fault and it will be given to him.

Decisions, Decisions: In Or Out?

James, the brother of Jesus, is writing to the new believers who were scattered about the Roman world (see GWBI, pages 213–214) when they fled from persecution. James knows that godly wisdom is a great gift. He gives a simple plan to get it: if you need wisdom, ask for it. God will give it to us.

Up 'til now we've concentrated on finding the wind for the sails of your drifting marriage and overcoming marital problems. But you may be the reader who is shaking her head, thinking that I just don't understand what you're going through. You can't take the abuse any longer; you've forgiven the **infidelity** time after time; and in order for you and your children to survive, you see no alternative but divorce.

So let me [...]
husband [...] get out a [...] your abuse sec [...] nues, [...] ing to you; they are [...] eep the [...]most are not only damaging to your children's physical and emotional state.

When you feel you've depleted all of your options, continue to ask God for wisdom in order to have the knowledge to make the right decisions. Wise women seek God. God is the <u>source</u> of wisdom and wisdom is found in Christ and the Word.

Commentary: This is where you'll read commentary about the biblical quote.

"What?": When you see a word in bold, go to the sidebar for a definition.

infidelity: sexual unfaithfulness of a spouse

Go To: When you see a word or phrase that's underlined, go to the sidebar for a biblical cross-reference.

☞ **GO TO:**

Psalm 111:10 (source)

Remember This . . .

What Others are Saying:

Gary Chapman, Ph.D.: Is there hope for women who suffer physical abuse from their husbands? Does reality living offer any genuine hope? I believe the answer to those questions is yes.[6]

Give It Away

You don't have to be a farmer to understand what the Apostle Paul wrote to the Corinthian church (see illustration, page 143). A picture is worth a thousand words, and Paul is painting a master-piece. He reminds us of what any smart farmer knows: in order to produce a bountiful harvest, he has to plan for it.

What Others Are Saying: This is where you'll read what an expert has to say about the subject at hand.

Feature with icon in the sidebar: Throughout the book you will see sections of text with corresponding icons in the sidebar. See the chart on page xvi for a description of all the features in this book.

MEN OF POWER LESSONS IN MIGHT AND MISSTEPS 9

127

Part One

BABYHOOD, BOYHOOD, AND MANHOOD

REVEREND FUN

BIRTH CERTIFICATES

"Jesus, Wonderful Counselor, Mighty God, Everlasting Father, Prince of Peace" is a bit long for this form . . . you might want to just use "Jesus."

LUKE 1: VISITORS FROM HEAVEN

CHAPTER HIGHLIGHTS

- A Reliable Account
- An Angel Visits the Temple
- Meanwhile, in an Obscure Village . . .
- Mary's Song
- Birth of a Messenger
- A Father's Song

Let's Get Started

Welcome to a true story about encounters with a heavenly being! But this heavenly being didn't come without prior notice. For years **prophets** told people about God's promise to send a **Messiah**, a king from heaven, and everybody had high hopes for him. They hoped he would rescue them from the domination of foreign powers. They hoped he would establish a kingdom of justice and prosperity. How they yearned for this promise to be fulfilled in their lifetime! But God had been silent for four hundred years. Was he still coming? Had God forgotten his promise? Some of his people, the Jews, had become weary and indifferent to the promise. But in the hearts of the faithful, anticipation lived on.

At the beginning of the first century an incredible series of events began to unfold, and the Messiah—Jesus Christ—was sent to earth. Jesus bewildered the religious authorities because many of the prophecies that foretold his coming (see GWPB, pages 64–66) and purpose were not fulfilled as they had expected. Nevertheless, Jesus changed the course of history, and even today our lives are touched by his thirty-three-year visit to our planet.

prophets: *people who declare a message on behalf of God*

Messiah: *"anointed one" whom God would send; the Christ*

A RELIABLE ACCOUNT

> **Luke 1:1–4** Many have undertaken to draw up an account of the things that have been fulfilled among us, just as they were handed down to us by those who from

> the first were eyewitnesses and servants of the word. Therefore, since I myself have carefully investigated everything from the beginning, it seemed good also to me to write an orderly account for you, most excellent Theophilus, so that you may know the certainty of the things you have been taught.

This One's For Theo

Read a book's dedication or the personal comments in the preface and you'll discover at least some of the author's motivation for writing. Most authors have a purpose that fuels them throughout the often tough and painful process of writing. Luke is no exception.

The birth of Jesus Christ and his life on earth caused such a stir that many of Luke's contemporaries wrote accounts of Jesus' life to get the truth out. We have four of these in the Bible—the Gospels—written by Matthew, Mark, Luke, and John, each having a distinct emphasis.

Luke made it his responsibility to investigate all aspects of Jesus' life. Though Luke was not an eyewitness to Jesus' life and teachings, he did thorough research. Some think he interviewed Mary (the mother of Jesus) and others who knew Jesus personally. He organized the material chronologically and highlighted particular themes, keeping in mind the needs and interests of his main recipient, Theophilus, and other Gentiles.

To this day Theophilus is somewhat of a mystery man. His name, which means "lover of God" or "dear to God," was common. He seems to have been a Christian Gentile, recognized as an official of some kind. Luke addresses him as *"most excellent,"* a title he quoted the **apostle** Paul as using in reference to <u>Felix</u> and <u>Festus</u> (see GWAC, pages 275–288).

apostle: Christ's ambassador sent out; Jesus' twelve disciples, Paul, and other New Testament missionaries

☞ **GO TO:**

Acts 24:3 (Felix)

Acts 26:25 (Festus)

What Others are Saying:

disciples: learners, students

Paul N. Benware: In the introduction to his gospel, Luke explained his purpose for writing. He wrote to present a historically accurate and chronologically correct account of the life and ministry of Jesus Christ. He wanted his readers to be well grounded in their faith.[1]

The Gospels were written by four of Jesus' twelve **disciples**. Fact or fiction? Fiction. Here is what is generally understood about the writers:

Matthew does not identify himself, but tradition holds the book was written by the <u>tax collector</u> whom Jesus called to be one of **the Twelve**.

Mark was written by John Mark, who was not one of the twelve disciples. He was, however, a close associate of <u>Peter</u>, who was an original disciple. John Mark also traveled with Barnabas and Paul on their first <u>missionary journey</u> (see WBFT, pages 76–79 and GWBI, pages 220–222).

Luke was written by a Greek physician who worked closely with <u>Paul</u>. He was not one of the twelve disciples. Luke also wrote the Book of <u>Acts</u>.

John was written by one of Jesus' inner circle of disciples and was recognized as *"the disciple whom Jesus loved"* (John 13:23).

So, two of the Gospels, Matthew and John, were written by original disciples, but the other two, Mark and Luke, were not.

☞ **GO TO:**

Matthew 9:9–13
(tax collector)

1 Peter 5:13 (Peter)

Acts 13:1–5
(missionary journey)

Colossians 4:14;
Philemon 24; 2
Timothy 4:11 (Paul)

Acts 1:1–2 (Acts)

the Twelve: original group of disciples who traveled with Jesus and were taught by him

PHYSICIAN'S PERSPECTIVE—Luke wrote from the perspective of a physician. Throughout his books of Luke and Acts you'll find medical references that are not included in the other Gospel accounts. He gives insight into his own heart when he writes about Jesus' compassion for those who were sick or in special need.

AN ANGEL VISITS THE TEMPLE

Luke 1:5–10 In the time of Herod king of Judea there was a priest named Zechariah, who belonged to the priestly division of Abijah; his wife Elizabeth was also a descendant of Aaron. Both of them were upright in the sight of God, observing all the Lord's commandments and regulations blamelessly. But they had no children, because Elizabeth was barren; and they were well along in years.

Once when Zechariah's division was on duty and he was serving as priest before God, he was chosen by lot, according to the custom of the priesthood, to go into the temple of the Lord and burn incense. And when the time for the burning of incense came, all the assembled worshipers were praying outside.

Just Doing My Job

lots: *devices used to determine God's will, much like drawing straws*

incense: *resin that emits a fragrant aroma when burned*

altar: *a stone or metal construction used for offering sacrifice*

☞ **GO TO:**

1 Chronicles 24:7–18 (divisions of priests)

1 Chronicles 24:5 (custom)

Meet Zechariah, a model citizen and devout follower of the Lord. Both he and his wife, Elizabeth, were serious about obeying all God's laws. They were faithful in this practice, even though God had withheld the gift that their hearts ached to receive. They were childless! Their voices must have choked when they sang the old Hebrew song, *"Sons are a heritage from the Lord, children a reward from him"* (Psalm 127:3). Still they remained faithful, even though old age had crept up and all hope of having a child had long since faded.

Zechariah was also faithful in his professional life as a priest, honored to perform duties at the Temple in Jerusalem. Many years before, King David had set up twenty-four groups of priests from the sons of Aaron. These <u>divisions of priests</u> were assigned duties for one week twice a year. Zechariah was born into the division of Abijah, the eighth division, and as part of a long line of priests he followed the job descriptions set up by David hundreds of years before. According to <u>custom</u> the priests drew **lots** to determine who would have the once-in-a-lifetime honor of entering the Holy Place, an inner room of the Temple (see illustration below), to offer prayers for the nation and to offer **incense** at the **altar**.

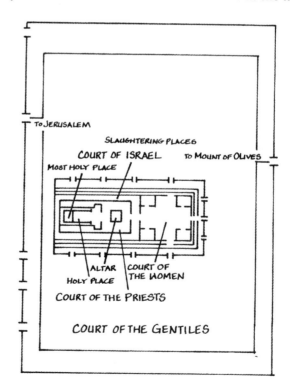

TO JERUSALEM

SLAUGHTERING PLACES

COURT OF ISRAEL   TO MOUNT OF OLIVES

MOST HOLY PLACE

ALTAR   COURT OF THE WOMEN

HOLY PLACE

COURT OF THE PRIESTS

COURT OF THE GENTILES

Temple Diagram

This diagram shows the Temple as it appeared in Jesus' day.

Zechariah and Elizabeth lived with embarrassment and humiliation. In Bible times children were viewed as evidence of God's blessing on the parents. Many people probably assumed their barrenness was the result of some hidden sin. Zechariah and Elizabeth also lived with anxiety. Children and grandchildren were expected to provide for the elderly in their declining years. Who would care for Zechariah and Elizabeth when they were no longer able to care for themselves?

Today many couples seek every possible medical means to become parents. The longing to bear a child is inborn and comes from God. Parents seldom count on their children to take care of them in old age. Rather they depend on pension plans, insurance, and government benefits to provide for their needs.

No matter how times have changed, certain truths have not changed. Children are still a _gift_ from God, and children are to _honor_ their parents throughout their lives. (Read about other women who struggled with infertility in WBFM, pages 49–66.)

The Bible Knowledge Commentary: [Zechariah and Elizabeth] were both well along in years and thus had no prospect of children. This fact was a constant embarrassment to Elizabeth as is evident from her statement later on (verse 25). God's allowing a barren woman to have children occurred several times in the Old Testament (e.g., the mothers of <u>Isaac</u>, <u>Samson</u>, and <u>Samuel</u>).[2]

> **Luke 1:11–17** Then an angel of the Lord appeared to him, standing at the right side of the altar of incense. When Zechariah saw him, he was startled and was gripped with fear. But the angel said to him: "Do not be afraid, Zechariah; your prayer has been heard. Your wife Elizabeth will bear you a son, and you are to give him the name John. He will be a joy and delight to you, and many will rejoice because of his birth, for he will be great in the sight of the Lord. He is never to take wine or other fermented drink, and he will be filled with the Holy Spirit even from birth. Many of the people of Israel will he bring back to the Lord their God. And he will go on before the Lord, in the spirit and power of Elijah, to turn the hearts of the fathers to their children and the disobedient to the wisdom of the righteous—to make ready a people prepared for the Lord."

FAST FORWARD

☞ **GO TO:**

Psalm 113:9 (gift)

Exodus 20:12 (honor)

What Others are Saying:

☞ **GO TO:**

Genesis 21:1–7 (Isaac)

Judges 13:1–5, 24 (Samson)

1 Samuel 1:1–20 (Samuel)

Zack Is Taken Aback

Zechariah was performing his priestly duty when suddenly an angel appeared at the right side of the altar when he was offering incense (see illustration below). He was more than surprised—he was gripped with terror. Ironic, isn't it? Zechariah had given his life to serving God and speaking for God, but when God actually appeared to him in the person of an angel, godly Zechariah responded with absolute terror!

The angel quickly assured him that he had come with good news. God had heard his priestly prayer for the nation and was about to answer it in an amazing way. God had also heard Zechariah and Elizabeth's prayers for a child. He was about to bestow on them the gift they had so earnestly desired. Elizabeth—even in her old age—would bear a son, and his name would be John.

This child would delight his parents' hearts. He would also be infused with the spirit and power of **Elijah** to fulfill a God-given mission of leading many of his people back to the Lord. He would have the special role of preparing the people for an awesome event that God would orchestrate.

Elijah: Old Testament prophet whose messages and prayers were accompanied by miracles

What Others are Saying:

J. C. Ryle: Prayers are not necessarily rejected because the answer is long delayed. Zechariah, no doubt, had often prayed for the blessing of children, and to all appearances he had prayed in vain. At his advanced age he had probably stopped mentioning the subject before God long ago and had given up all hope of being a father. Yet the very first words of the angel show clearly that Zechariah's prayers of long ago had not been forgotten: "Your prayer has been heard" (verse 13).[3]

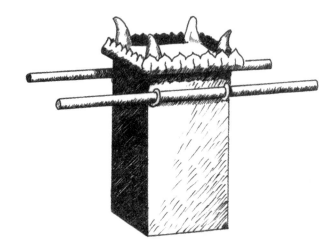

Altar of Incense

Pictured is an altar like the one that Zechariah may have used in Luke 1.

> **Luke 1:18–20** Zechariah asked the angel, "How can I be sure of this? I am an old man and my wife is well along in years."
>
> The angel answered, "I am **Gabriel**. I stand in the presence of God, and I have been sent to speak to you and to tell you this good news. And now you will be silent and not able to speak until the day this happens, because you did not believe my words, which will come true at their proper time."

Gabriel: high-ranking angel who appears in both the Old and New Testaments

Gabe Sets Him Straight

Zechariah was stunned, but not speechless. Filled with doubt, he asked how this incredible miracle could be accomplished. After all, it was humanly impossible for Elizabeth to bear a child. Zechariah recognized that his visitor was a heavenly being, but when the messenger spoke, his response was based on earthly information. His questioning heart left no room for faith.

The angel responded with authority. He gave Zechariah:

HIS NAME: Gabriel

HIS CREDENTIALS: Gabriel stood in the presence of the living God and was sent with a specific message from God.

PROOF OF HIS MESSAGE'S AUTHENTICITY: Zechariah would be unable to speak until the birth of the promised son.

KEY POINT

God never forgets our prayers of faith, though he may not answer them as we desire.

R. C. Sproul: Zechariah would not have missed the fact that the angel was quoting from the book of Malachi. . . . The angel's announcement links the <u>last promise</u> of the Old Testament with the first promise of the New. Zechariah was given the message that he and his wife would be parents of the prophet who would announce the Messiah![4]

God decided when it was time to send the Messiah. Perhaps we can get a better understanding of God's timing by looking at first-century society. Rome provided roads that enabled relatively easy travel. Greece provided a language that was widely understood, and the faithful Jews were looking for the Messiah to be sent. The time was ripe to launch the Messiah's mission!

What Others are Saying:

☞ **GO TO:**

Malachi 4:5–6 (last promise)

Remember This . . .

> **Luke 1:21–25** Meanwhile, the people were waiting for Zechariah and wondering why he stayed so long in the temple. When he came out, he could not speak to them. They realized he had seen a vision in the temple, for he kept making signs to them but remained unable to speak.
>
> When his time of service was completed, he returned home. After this his wife Elizabeth became pregnant and for five months remained in seclusion. "The Lord has done this for me," she said. "In these days he has shown his favor and taken away my disgrace among the people."

A Long Silence

It's hard to imagine the scene outside the Temple as the people waited for Zechariah to appear. What was going on in there? What was taking Zechariah so long? And when he emerged from the Holy Place, they probably looked at each other in bewilderment. Why couldn't he speak to them? Why didn't Zechariah offer the usual benediction that followed the burning of incense?

It's even harder to imagine the scenes in Zechariah's home when he returned unable to speak of his awesome encounter with Gabriel and Elizabeth discovered she had become pregnant. Elizabeth must have poured out her joyous thoughts to Zechariah, but all he could do was gesture and write notes. This **miracle** was not random good luck in a game of chance—it was God invading Zechariah and Elizabeth's life with loving-kindness. Though Zechariah could not articulate the thoughts and feelings that welled up, they must have drawn closer to each other as they opened their hearts more and more to the Lord.

miracle: an occurrence that cannot be explained apart from the power of God

What Others are Saying:

Darrell L. Bock: Zechariah teaches us that God occasionally instructs saints through difficult times. Sometimes underestimating God is as dangerous as rebelling against him. Our sin may not be a matter of doing overt wrong but of being hesitant to pursue righteousness and to trust fully in the Lord.[5]

FAST FORWARD

Zechariah doubted God's promise to give him the child of his hopes and dreams. Abraham, Isaac, Moses, and many other Bible heroes also doubted God's promises. Unbelief began in the Garden of Eden when Eve questioned God's Word.

Let's avoid looking down on these individuals, as if we're su-

perior (see GWRM, pages 25–36). Like them, we doubt God's promises sometimes. The old washing machine gives up and the car breaks down—again. We complain, "Why me?" instead of trusting God to supply our needs. Rumors fly around that the company is going to downsize. We panic instead of believing that God is in control. A family member hurts us deeply. We write "hopeless" over the situation rather than trusting God to change hearts on both sides of the relationship. God still speaks today. Are we listening? Do we believe and act on what he tells us?

MEANWHILE, IN AN OBSCURE VILLAGE . . .

> **Luke 1:26–33** In the sixth month, God sent the angel Gabriel to Nazareth, a town in Galilee, to a virgin pledged to be married to a man named Joseph, a descendant of David. The virgin's name was Mary. The angel went to her and said, "Greetings, you who are highly favored! The Lord is with you."
>
> Mary was greatly troubled at his words and wondered what kind of greeting this might be. But the angel said to her, "Do not be afraid, Mary, you have found favor with God. You will be with child and give birth to a son, and you are to give him the name Jesus. He will be great and will be called the Son of the Most High. The Lord God will give him the throne of his father David, and he will reign over the house of Jacob forever; his kingdom will never end."

An Astounding Encounter

In the village of Nazareth, within a small region in northern Israel called Galilee, a young woman, actually a teenager, was engaged to be married (see also WBFT, pages 71–76). Mary's engagement had not been heralded in the social observations of the more elite Judea to the south. For her, village life was simple and predictable. Her daily tasks involved cooking, cleaning, visiting the village well, and preparing for marriage to Joseph.

Suddenly, like a bolt of lightning, the angel Gabriel appeared, piercing and forever shattering the tranquility of Mary's life. When Gabriel greeted her, he told her she was highly favored by God, who was actually right there with her, knowing her every thought and motive!

Naturally Mary was astounded. Immediately, the angel assured her that she did not need to be afraid. God favored her so much he chose her to give birth to a child who would be unique in every way.

- The child would be called the Son of the Most High—equal with Jehovah, whom Mary worshiped. This would be **blasphemy** if Mary had thought of this without the angel's prompting. How could her son be equal with God?
- God would give him the throne of his ancestor King David. A throne? What poor village girl would ever have aspired to such a privilege for her son?
- He would rule over the house of Jacob forever—as king of the nation Israel. How could this be when the Jews were then being ruled by the hated Romans?
- His kingdom would never end. What mystery was this? A mother has dreams for her child's well-being for a lifetime—but forever?

The angel was saying that Mary had been chosen to give birth to the Messiah, the one who had been promised throughout ages past. Could it be true? For her?

This was no time for theological debate. Hundreds of years before, the prophet Isaiah had written, *"Therefore the Lord himself will give you a sign: The virgin will be with child and will give birth to a son, and will call him **Immanuel**"* (Isaiah 7:14). Whether Mary knew this or not, the fact was there: God had chosen her, a virgin, to bear a son who would be both God and man.

blasphemy: *treating God with contempt, bringing him down to human level*

Immanuel: *name meaning "God with us"*

> **Luke 1:34–38** "How will this be," Mary asked the angel, "since I am a virgin?"
>
> The angel answered, "The Holy Spirit will come upon you, and the power of the Most High will overshadow you. So the holy one to be born will be called the Son of God. Even Elizabeth your relative is going to have a child in her old age, and she who was said to be barren is in her sixth month. "For nothing is impossible with God."
>
> "I am the Lord's servant," Mary answered. "May it be to me as you have said." Then the angel left her.

Angelic Explanation

Mary could have raised a number of panicky questions. "What will Joseph do to me?" "How will my parents handle the disgrace that I will bring on them?" "What will the village leaders say?" Instead, Mary asked a perfectly logical question as she prepared her heart to cooperate with God's plan for her: "How can this be?" No matter how honored she was to be the mother of the long-promised Messiah, no matter how convincingly the angel Gabriel had spoken, the practical question arose: How could a virgin possibly give birth to a son? Further, how could a human give birth to a child whose father was God?

Gabriel was not caught off guard. The answer was ready. The conception of Jesus would be an act of God. The Holy Spirit would come upon Mary and his presence would perform a unique miracle—once and only once in the history of humankind—so that she would give birth to a "holy" child, the only child ever born without sin of any kind. To bolster her trust in God's ability to do the impossible, Gabriel informed Mary that her elderly relative Elizabeth was already in her sixth month of pregnancy—another miracle of God.

Mary's response to God's plan for her has remained one of the most beautiful statements ever expressed: *"I am the Lord's servant. May it be to me as you have said."* She did not argue or question. She submitted to the will of God for her and for the son she would bear.

A Study in Contrasts

Both Zechariah and Mary were visited by the angel Gabriel, who delivered God's promise of a child (Luke 1:19, 26). Note the contrasts:

Zechariah	Mary
A man *"well along in years"* (1:7)	A teenager engaged to be married (1:21)
A priest with temple duties (1:8–10)	A peasant girl who lived in the small village of Nazareth (1:26)
Responded to angel *"startled and gripped with fear"* (1:12)	Responded to angel filled with wonder at the meaning of his greeting (1:29)
Doubted: How can I be sure? My wife and I are old (1:18)	Asked: *"How can this be, since I am a virgin?"* (1:34)
Because of his unbelief, made unable to speak until birth of son—proof that God had given the promise (1:20)	Believed the message and submitted to God's will (1:38); was articulate, filled with praise to God (1:46–55)

A virgin gave birth to Jesus Christ. Is this fact or fiction? Students of the Bible have long wrestled with this question while skeptics have laughed it off as utter fiction. However, it is a question on which hinges everything else the New Testament tells us about Jesus. If his virgin birth is fiction, then how much else in the New Testament is fiction?

If we believe Gabriel's statement that *"nothing is impossible with God"* (verse 37), then we can accept as fact that Jesus was born of a virgin and that he was actually God in human form.

Much as Mary had to have faith to believe that she, a virgin, would conceive a son, so we must have faith that the conception actually occurred as stated in the Bible. Will we respond to God's Word as Mary did—with reverence and acceptance—or as Zechariah did—with doubt and disbelief?

What Others are Saying:

Gilbert Bilezikian: The significance of the virgin birth (or, more accurately, the virginal conception) of Christ is twofold. It demonstrates Christ's complete identification with the human race and his uniqueness as the Son of God.[6]

Incarnation: the eternal Son of God becoming a human being

Charles C. Ryrie: The virgin birth was the means of the **Incarnation**. The Incarnation, once accomplished, is a lasting state for our Lord. It began at his birth and continues (albeit in a resurrection body now) forever. The virgin birth was an event that lasted only a matter of hours.[7]

Something to Ponder

Mary's submission to God's will was not something she piously expressed, hoping to impress the messenger from heaven. She spoke spontaneously from her heart, revealing an attitude that was there even before the angel appeared.

MARY'S SONG

KEY POINT

We should respond to God's Word with simple faith and a readiness to do whatever he says.

Luke 1:39–45 At that time Mary got ready and hurried to a town in the hill country of Judea, where she entered Zechariah's home and greeted Elizabeth. When Elizabeth heard Mary's greeting, the baby leaped in her womb, and Elizabeth was filled with the Holy Spirit. In a loud voice she exclaimed: "Blessed are you among women, and blessed is the child you will bear! But why am I so favored, that the mother of my Lord should come to me? As soon as the sound of your greeting reached my ears, the baby in my womb leaped for joy.

> Blessed is she who has believed that what the Lord has said to her will be accomplished!"

Kindred Hearts

Of all the people Mary knew, one would understand her experience better than any other. Elizabeth, her elderly relative (possibly her cousin), was also to be the mother of a miracle child. She was already in her sixth month of pregnancy.

Mary hurried to the town where Elizabeth and Zechariah lived, assured of a welcome. She could hardly have anticipated, however, the joyful, Spirit-guided reception Elizabeth gave her. As soon as Mary greeted her, Elizabeth felt her baby leap within her. Instantly Elizabeth sensed that her unborn child recognized that Mary was the mother of the yet-to-be-born Messiah, and she herself acknowledged that she was favored to be visited by Mary, whom she referred to as *"the mother of my Lord."* Mary's heart must have welled up with thankfulness for the confirmation that she was indeed blessed by God and that he would reward her obedience.

Paul N. Benware: When Mary arrived at her home, the Holy Spirit in an instant revealed to Elizabeth that her relative Mary was to have that exalted privilege of being the mother of Messiah. Before Mary could reveal one thing about her own experience, Elizabeth declared prophetically Mary's special and wonderful place in God's plans.[8]

What Others are Saying:

Luke 1:46–56 And Mary said: "My soul glorifies the Lord and my spirit rejoices in God my Savior, for he has been mindful of the humble state of his servant. From now on all generations will call me blessed, for the Mighty One has done great things for me—holy is his name. His mercy extends to those who fear him, from generation to generation. He has performed mighty deeds with his arm; he has scattered those who are proud in their inmost thoughts. He has brought down rulers from their thrones but has lifted up the humble. He has filled the hungry with good things but has sent the rich away empty. He has helped his servant Israel, remembering to be merciful to Abraham and his descendants forever, even as he said to our fathers."

Mary stayed with Elizabeth for about three months and then returned home.

Impromptu Concert

Mary was so eager to express her praise to God that she burst into song! Her song is so remarkable that it is still celebrated as "**The Magnificat**." Her words are amazing when we remember that she was a young teenager living in a quiet village that had no resources for enrichment in the fine arts. Her song is somewhat like <u>Hannah's song</u> in which she praised God for giving her the son for whom she had prayed.

Mary begins by expressing her desire to **glorify** the Lord and rejoice in him as her Savior. She praises him for his favor on her, such favor that future generations would call her blessed. She then turns her focus on God. Her lyrics are lavish with references to the Old Testament as she praises him for his mercy, mighty deeds, power, loving-kindness to the humble, his faithfulness in keeping his promises to Abraham and his descendants.

Luke records that Mary stayed with Elizabeth for about three months, probably returning to Nazareth just before Elizabeth gave birth to her son.

Larry Sibley: Mary's words are called "The Magnificat" from the first word in the Latin translation. Her praise was couched in phrases drawn from the Old Testament. . . . Her mind was saturated with Old Testament language. When she spoke her praise, it was largely with words that were already part of the Bible.

When one realizes that Mary had no personal copy of the Old Testament it is clear that she must have listened very carefully to synagogue readings.[9]

Mary's song has 131 words, as translated in the New International Version of the Bible. The opening 48 words relate to her personal wonder and joy in the amazing blessing the Lord had given her, and the remaining 83 words express praise to God for who he is.

If we examined our contemporary songs, I suspect we'd find the reverse—one-third exalting the Lord and two-thirds relating to ourselves and how we feel. If you were to write a song to the Lord today, what would its content be?

MORE INFORMATION—Matthew, who records these events from a different angle in Matthew 1:18–25, gives us some interesting information. Soon after Mary returned to Nazareth, she must have told Joseph the news. Understandably he was distraught. His engagement to Mary was

---

The Magnificat: the liturgical name given to Mary's song of praise

☞ **GO TO:**

1 Samuel 2:1–10 (Hannah's song)

glorify: to praise God for who he is and to submit to him in worship and obedience

What Others are Saying:

FAST FORWARD

legally binding, yet it would appear that she had been unfaithful. To avoid seeing her publicly disgraced, he decided to seek a quiet divorce from her. But God sent an angel, perhaps Gabriel, to assure him of the truth of Mary's message. Joseph's heart was open to God. He accepted the news and immediately took Mary to be his wife (see WBFC, page 272).

The Bible Knowledge Commentary: In Jewish culture a man and woman were betrothed or pledged to each other for a period of time before the actual consummation of their marriage. This betrothal was much stronger than an engagement period today, for the two were considered husband and wife except that they did not live together till after the wedding.[10]

BIRTH OF A MESSENGER

Luke 1:57–66 When it was time for Elizabeth to have her baby, she gave birth to a son. Her neighbors and relatives heard that the Lord had shown her great mercy, and they shared her joy.

On the eighth day they came to circumcise the child, and they were going to name him after his father Zechariah, but his mother spoke up and said, "No! He is to be called John."

They said to her, "There is no one among your relatives who has that name."

Then they made signs to his father, to find out what he would like to name the child. He asked for a writing tablet, and to everyone's astonishment he wrote, "His name is John." Immediately his mouth was opened and his tongue was loosed, and he began to speak, praising God. The neighbors were all filled with awe, and throughout the hill country of Judea people were talking about all these things. Everyone who heard this wondered about it, asking, "What then is this child going to be?" For the Lord's hand was with him.

Beth Wins The Name Game

Excitement surged through a little town in the hilly area near Jerusalem. Word spread quickly that Elizabeth had just given birth to a son, and just as quickly people praised God for his great mercy in giving Zechariah and Elizabeth a child in their old age.

A celebration was held on the eighth day. Obeying God's law, they performed the rite of circumcision, which set the baby boy apart as a Jew. Then came the naming of the child. Friends and relatives assumed that custom would be followed and the child would be named Zechariah after his father Zechariah, whose name meant "Yahweh remembers." But Elizabeth spoke up, correcting them. The child would be called John!

Surely Elizabeth had made a mistake! No relative had that name. So they turned to Zechariah. To everyone's amazement he wrote, *"His name is John."*

What was the significance of giving the baby the name of John, meaning "Yahweh is gracious"? When Zechariah agreed with Elizabeth, he was obeying what the angel had directed, *"You are to give him the name John"* (1:13) and demonstrated his faith in God. Immediately his ability to speak was restored, and understandably his first words were praises to God.

Everyone in that town and in the surrounding area could not stop talking about what was happening. Surely John was a child to be watched as he grew up, for it was evident that God's special blessing was on him.

What Others are Saying:

The Bible Knowledge Commentary: Word then spread through the whole hill country (in the Jerusalem area) that this was an unusual child. The people continued to note that the Lord's hand was with him. Years later, when John began his preaching ministry, many went out from this district who no doubt remembered the amazing events surrounding his birth (Matthew 3:5).[11]

A FATHER'S SONG

Luke 1:67–75 His father Zechariah was filled with the Holy Spirit and prophesied: "Praise be to the Lord, the God of Israel, because he has come and has redeemed his people. He has raised up a horn of salvation for us in the house of his servant David (as he said through his holy prophets of long ago), salvation from our enemies and from the hand of all who hate us—to show mercy to our fathers and to remember his holy covenant, the oath he swore to our father Abraham: to rescue us from the hand of our enemies, and to enable us to serve him without fear in holiness and righteousness before him all our days."

Zechariah Lets Loose

Zechariah's joy could not be repressed. During his months of silence he had opportunity to reflect on both Gabriel's words to him and on the Old Testament Scriptures he had loved for so long. Now he was filled with the Holy Spirit and burst out in a song that was full of praise to God for his faithfulness in keeping his promises to Israel. His hymn focused not on his newborn son, but on the one John would be introducing to the world, the Messiah.

Zechariah's reference to Israel's *"horn of salvation"* (verse 69) was significant. The <u>horns</u> of an animal, such as an ox, were symbolic of his strength. A horn was filled with oil, which was used to <u>anoint</u> kings. Zechariah was picturing the power of the Messiah, the horn of <u>salvation</u>, who was coming to bring salvation and to fulfill God's promise that the Messiah would save them from their <u>enemies</u>.

☞ **GO TO:**

Deuteronomy 33:17 (horns)

1 Samuel 16:1, 13 (anoint)

Psalm 18:2 (salvation)

Psalm 132:17–18; Jeremiah 30:8–9 (enemies)

> **Luke 1:76–80** "And you, my child, will be called a prophet of the Most High; for you will go on before the Lord to prepare the way for him, to give his people the knowledge of salvation through the forgiveness of their sins, because of the tender mercy of our God, by which the rising sun will come to us from heaven to shine on those living in darkness and in the shadow of death, to guide our feet into the path of peace."
>
> And the child grew and became strong in spirit; and he lived in the desert until he appeared publicly to Israel.

Praise For A Precious Child

Zechariah also sang of the mission his son would fulfill. John would become a prophet of God to prepare the way for the Messiah. Through his preaching many people would turn to God for forgiveness and thus would be prepared to welcome the Messiah, who would come as the *"rising sun."* Centuries before, **Balaam** had prophesied of the Messiah, saying a <u>star</u> would come. Malachi, in the last Old Testament book, prophesied that the Messiah would

Balaam: a practitioner of the occult through whom God gave a prophecy

☞ **GO TO:**

Numbers 24:17 (star)

☞ **GO TO:**

Malachi 4:2
   (sun of righteousness)

KEY POINT

God's actions draw forth praise from true believers.

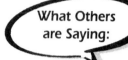

come as the <u>sun of righteousness</u>. Those living in the darkness of sin and death would welcome John's message that the Messiah was coming to bring light and life.

Under the watchful eyes of his parents, John grew both physically and spiritually. Gabriel had announced that John would work *"in the spirit and power of Elijah"* (verse 17). It was fitting that when John grew up and was preparing himself for his work, he lived briefly in the wilderness, as Elijah had done so long before. In the silence of those lonely surroundings, John discovered the message he was to bring—a message Israel had not heard for many generations.

Stephen Fortosis: We worship the same God Zechariah and Elizabeth worshiped. Yet sometimes we actually imply to God, either directly or indirectly, that we don't believe he can act in supernatural ways. We should never underestimate God's ability to do anything he wills. His grace and power have no limits.[12]

Study Questions

1. After four hundred years of silence, how did God set in motion his timetable for sending the promised Messiah?
2. God sent Gabriel to give announcements to Zechariah and Mary. In what ways were Zechariah and Mary alike in their responses? How were they different?
3. What did God say would be John's unique mission?
4. What purpose was served by Zechariah's inability to speak throughout Elizabeth's pregnancy?
5. Why is it important for you to accept and believe in the virgin birth of Jesus Christ?
6. What events led the people to see that *"the Lord's hand"* was on John?

CHAPTER WRAP-UP

- Luke wrote his Gospel to give Theophilus and others a carefully researched and organized account of Jesus' life on earth. (Luke 1:1–4)

- Though Zechariah and his wife, Elizabeth, grieved because they were still childless in their old age, they followed God's laws and lived without blame before God. Zechariah faithfully performed his duties as a priest. (Luke 1:5–10)

- An angel told Zechariah that Elizabeth would bear a son whose name would be John and whose mission would be to prepare people for the arrival of the Messiah. Zechariah questioned this possibility, and God took away Zechariah's ability to speak until John was born. God kept his promise: Elizabeth became pregnant; Zechariah became dumb. (Luke 1:11–25)

- Gabriel was sent by God to announce to Mary that she had been chosen to be the mother of the Messiah. Though Mary was a virgin, the conception would take place through the Holy Spirit overshadowing her. She would give birth to Jesus, the God-man. Gabriel assured Mary that *"nothing is impossible with God."* (Luke 1:26–38)

- When Mary visited Elizabeth, the Holy Spirit gave Elizabeth insight to see that Mary would be the mother of God. Mary burst into a song of praise that exalted God, first for his favor on her, and then for his favor on all her people in showing mercy, mighty deeds, power, loving-kindness, and faithfulness in keeping his promises. (Luke 1:39–56)

- When John was born, people rejoiced, acknowledging that God had given Zechariah and Elizabeth a son in their old age. The people were in awe in the way both Elizabeth and Zechariah confirmed that their child would be named John, and Zechariah's speech returned immediately afterward. (Luke 1:57–66)

- After nine months of silence, Zechariah expressed praise to God in a song. He praised God for his faithfulness in keeping his promise to Israel. He also acknowledged that John would grow up to be God's prophet who would prepare people to receive the Messiah. (Luke 1:67–80)

LUKE 2: BIRTH AND BOYHOOD

Let's Get Started

One birth is celebrated today with far more joy and pageantry than could have been imagined when the actual birth occurred two thousand years ago. There's a great contrast between the humble arrival of the Son of God and the lavish displays of Christmas decorations that compete for our attention and entice us to spend money on merchandise that is not remotely related to the one whose birth we celebrate.

Dr. Luke, ever a realist, did not garnish his account of Jesus' arrival with tinsel and glittering lights. Instead, he causes a hush to come over our hearts as he takes us into what really happened that holy night when God came in the person of his Son to live among us.

THE BIRTH OF JESUS

Luke 2:1–5 In those days Caesar Augustus issued a decree that a census should be taken of the entire Roman world. (This was the first census that took place while Quirinius was governor of Syria.) And everyone went to his own town to register.

So Joseph also went up from the town of Nazareth in Galilee to Judea, to Bethlehem the town of David, because he belonged to the house and line of David. He went there to register with Mary, who was pledged to be married to him and was expecting a child.

☞ **GO TO:**

Micah 5:2 (Micah)

Caesar's Census

Through his prophet <u>Micah</u>, God had announced that Bethlehem would be the birthplace of the coming Messiah. (The word "Messiah" comes from the Hebrew word for "anointed one." The word for "anointed" in Greek is *christos*, from which we get the title "Christ.")

Mary, however, lived in the Galilean town of Nazareth—a village ninety miles north of Bethlehem (see appendix A). So, how did God relocate Mary in time for Jesus' birth? He used the Roman Emperor's census (see GWLC, pages 21–22). The custom was for people to register for the census at their hometown, and Joseph's hometown was Bethlehem.

Why did Caesar Augustus take a census? He needed money for the imperial treasury. The best way for the emperor to get money was to increase taxes. The best way to increase taxes was to take a census.

FAST FORWARD

Most people resent being forced to reveal personal information, especially to a government that is going to use the information to levy taxes. Imagine being required to travel almost a hundred miles to provide this information to the oppressive Roman government.

Today census takers work by mailings or discreet house calls, assuring us that the information we give will not be passed on to anyone who would misuse it. As for taxes, politicians talk themselves hoarse assuring us the government will use all funds for our benefit and provide judicious tax cuts for our advantage. Today we pay our taxes by payroll deductions, checks in the mail, credit cards, or computer. Though our government is hardly as oppressive as the Roman Empire's, we still know something of the tax burden that Joseph and Mary shouldered all the way to Bethlehem.

FACT or FICTION

Artists show Mary riding on a donkey to Bethlehem. Fact or fiction? Luke makes no mention of a donkey, so we shouldn't claim this as fact. Mary was pregnant, however, and we know from other Scriptures that Joseph did his best to look after her. So it's certainly possible Joseph provided his pregnant fiancée with a donkey or some other means of transportation less toilsome than walking.

> **Luke 2:6–7** While they were there, the time came for the baby to be born, and she gave birth to her firstborn, a son. She wrapped him in cloths and placed him in a manger, because there was no room for them in the inn.

Birth In Bethlehem

Because of the influx of census registrants, there was no room for Mary and Joseph in the inn. The Son of God was born in unsanitary surroundings with only Mary and Joseph and a few animals to hear his first cry.

Was Jesus born in the muck and grime of an animal stable? Though this isn't explicit in Scripture, most Bible students conclude such, because Mary laid him in a **manger**. Was the newborn baby surrounded by soft lights, sweet-smelling hay, the rhythmic munching of cattle, and the soft cooing of doves? Probably not. Typically a first-century "inn" was a series of stalls where guests built fires and cooked the food they had brought with them. They could look out toward a cave or common area where animals were tethered. If this was the case in Bethlehem, Mary and Joseph could not find an open stall, so Mary gave birth in less-than-pleasant surroundings among animals.

FACT OR FICTION

manger: feeding trough for animals

R. Kent Hughes: If we imagine that Jesus was born in a freshly swept, county fair stable, we miss the whole point. It was wretched—scandalous! There was sweat and pain and blood and cries as Mary reached up to the heavens for help. The earth was cold and hard. The smell of birth mixed with the stench of manure and acrid straw made a contemptible bouquet. Trembling carpenter's hands, clumsy with fear, grasped God's Son slippery with blood—the baby's limbs waving helplessly as if falling through space—his face grimacing as he gasped in the cold and his cry pierced the night.[1]

What Others are Saying:

PHYSICIAN'S PERSPECTIVE—Dr. Luke gives particular emphasis to the birth of Jesus, providing details that may have come from personal interviews with Mary herself. As he notes the place where Mary gave birth to her son, we can almost sense his sympathy for the shattering disappointment Mary and Joseph must have felt when there was no room for them in the inn.

As Mary placed her newborn son in the manger, Dr. Luke notes that she followed the common practice of their day, called "swaddling." She wrapped his whole body in long strips of cloth, as the medical profession recommended (see GWWB, page 104). People of that day thought the snug wrapping helped ensure straight limbs and prevented broken bones.

ANGEL ANNOUNCEMENT

Luke 2:8–14 And there were shepherds living out in the fields nearby, keeping watch over their flocks at night. An angel of the Lord appeared to them, and the glory of the Lord shone around them, and they were terrified. But the angel said to them, "Do not be afraid. I bring you good news of great joy that will be for all the people. Today in the town of David a Savior has been born to you; he is Christ the Lord. This will be a sign to you: You will find a baby wrapped in cloths and lying in a manger."

Suddenly a great company of the heavenly host appeared with the angel, praising God and saying, "Glory to God in the highest, and on earth peace to men on whom his favor rests."

On A Night Like Any Other Night

Just like always, shepherds were out in the fields near Bethlehem. Just like always, they were keeping track of the sheep that huddled around them in the darkness.

Suddenly the silence was shattered and the darkness was pierced by an unearthly light. An angel appeared to them and the heaven's glory shone around the trembling shepherds. They were terrified, but the heavenly messenger assured them they had no need to fear. The angel came with good news for them and for all people. A Savior had been born in Bethlehem. They would find the newborn *"wrapped in cloths and lying in a manger."*

The startled shepherds listened breathlessly as the angel was joined by a huge choir of angels that filled the sky, praising God in heaven and blessing people on earth.

Who Is This Newborn?

The angel spoke of the newborn as Savior, Christ, and the Lord, names that spoke volumes.

Savior: the one who would deliver his people. Though the shepherds would not have known it, the name confirmed what both <u>Mary</u> and <u>Zechariah</u> had acknowledged in their songs.

Christ: the Anointed One of God, the promised Messiah, for whom faithful Jews had waited for many generations.

The Lord: God who became one of us in a human body.

Who were these shepherds and why did God choose to give them the heavenly announcement of Jesus' birth? These were humble men not highly thought of by the law-keeping religious leaders of their day. Their outdoor duties of caring for sheep prohibited them from observing rigid ceremonial rules demanded by the orthodox Jews. Still, they probably were sincere in their faith in God. Some scholars of this period believe shepherds tended sheep that would be offered in temple sacrifices. Perhaps, uneducated as they were, they understood the significance of their roles as shepherds of such sheep. Perhaps when they heard the angel's message, they gained insight into the true identity of the newborn child—the Savior who would give his life as the <u>Lamb of God</u> and would forever remove the need for sacrificing sheep, for he would take away the sins of the world.

Today some followers of Jesus may be members of the world's "rich and famous," but the vast majority of his followers are ordinary people whose hearts are open to the truth of who Jesus is and how he has become their personal Savior. In other words, there are many modern-day shepherds. Maybe you're one of them!

> **Luke 2:15–20** When the angels had left them and gone into heaven, the shepherds said to one another, "Let's go to Bethlehem and see this thing that has happened, which the Lord has told us about."
>
> So they hurried off and found Mary and Joseph, and the baby, who was lying in the manger. When they had seen him, they spread the word concerning what had been told them about this child, and all who heard it were amazed at what the shepherds said to them. But Mary treasured up all these things and pondered them in her heart. The shepherds returned, glorifying and praising God for all the things they had heard and seen, which were just as they had been told.

☞ **GO TO:**

Luke 1:46–55 (Mary)

Luke 1:67–79 (Zechariah)

FAST FORWARD

☞ **GO TO:**

John 1:29 (Lamb of God)

KEY POINT

The babe who lay in a feeding trough was the Son of God himself!

Shepherds Are Not Sheepish

The shepherds made a quick decision to investigate what they had heard. There was no question in their minds that the God of Israel had given them the announcement. They hurried off to Bethlehem and found the baby with Mary and Joseph, exactly as the angel had said.

Immediately they spread the word, sharing with everyone who would listen what the angel had said. Townspeople were amazed at the news. But Mary was more than amazed. She *"treasured up"* what had happened and *"pondered them"* deeply *"in her heart."* She kept as a precious jewel the confirmation of what the angel Gabriel had told her: she was the mother of the Savior of the world.

The shepherds were filled with joy as they returned to their sheep. Their hearts overflowed and their voices proclaimed their praises to God.

FAST FORWARD

As God revealed his plan for saving the world, the reaction was consistent. People responded with praise. Take Zechariah in the Temple. First, he was fearful and full of doubt. But when John was born, he expressed wholehearted praise. Elizabeth received Mary with joyful praise to God. When Mary learned God was keeping his promise to send the Savior, she responded with a song of praise. After the birth of Jesus, the shepherds were unrestrained in their praise to God for all they had seen and heard.

What is your PQ (praise quotient) as you consider the birth of Jesus? Every reason we have for rejoicing is linked to God's love for us and for his **unfathomable** *mercy in sending his Son to be our Savior.*

unfathomable: beyond understanding

What Others are Saying:

William Barclay: In Palestine the birth of a boy was an occasion of great joy. When the time of the birth was near at hand, friends and local musicians gathered near the house. When the birth was announced and it was a boy, the musicians broke into music and song, and there was universal congratulation and rejoicing. If it was a girl the musicians went silently and regretfully away! There was a saying, "The birth of a male child causes universal joy, but the birth of a female child causes universal sorrow."[2]

INSIGHTFUL BLESSINGS

> **Luke 2:21–24** On the eighth day, when it was time to circumcise him, he was named Jesus, the name the angel had given him before he had been conceived.
>
> When the time of their purification according to the Law of Moses had been completed, Joseph and Mary took him to Jerusalem to present him to the Lord (as it is written in the Law of the Lord, "Every firstborn male is to be consecrated to the Lord"), and to offer a sacrifice in keeping with what is said in the Law of the Lord: "a pair of doves or two young pigeons."

By The Book

Mary and Joseph were careful to obey the laws that God had given and to follow the customs of Jews who were new parents. This involved three ceremonies.

First, on the eighth day of their baby's life, Mary and Joseph observed the ceremony of <u>circumcision</u> and <u>naming</u> the child. Naming a new child seems to have been the responsibility of the mother usually, but the responsibility could be assumed by the father. In this case Mary and Joseph named their baby Jesus, as <u>Gabriel</u> had directed.

Second, forty days after the birth of Jesus, Mary and Joseph took him from Bethlehem to the Temple in Jerusalem for the ceremony of <u>purification</u>. Women who gave birth were unclean, according to the law, until they participated in this ceremony. The mother was to make two offerings—a lamb and a dove. However, the law allowed those who could not afford a lamb to offer two doves or two young pigeons. Mary chose the alternate offering—a public indication that she could not afford a lamb.

The third ceremony was for the redemption of the <u>firstborn son</u>. The law said that every firstborn son should be "presented to God" or dedicated for service to him. Then the son would be **redeemed** for the "redemption price" of five shekels.

J. C. Ryle: The word *Jesus* means simply "Savior" . . . a name which speaks of mercy, grace, help, and deliverance for a lost world. It is as a deliverer and redeemer that he desires principally to be known.[3]

☞ **GO TO:**

Genesis 17:9–14 (circumcision)

1 Samuel 1:20 (naming)

Matthew 1:21; Luke 1:31 (Gabriel)

Leviticus 12:1–4, 22–24 (purification)

Numbers 18:15–16 (firstborn son)

redeemed: to "buy back"

What Others are Saying:

> **Luke 2:25–35** Now there was a man in Jerusalem called Simeon, who was righteous and devout. He was waiting for the consolation of Israel, and the Holy Spirit was upon him. It had been revealed to him by the Holy Spirit that he would not die before he had seen the Lord's Christ. Moved by the Spirit, he went into the temple courts. When the parents brought in the child Jesus to do for him what the custom of the Law required, Simeon took him in his arms and praised God, saying: "Sovereign Lord, as you have promised, you now dismiss your servant in peace. For my eyes have seen your salvation, which you have prepared in the sight of all people, a light for revelation to the Gentiles, and for glory to your people Israel."
>
> The child's father and mother marveled at what was said about him. Then Simeon blessed them and said to Mary, his mother: "The child is destined to cause the falling and rising of many in Israel, and to be a sign that will be spoken against, so that the thoughts of many hearts will be revealed. And a sword will pierce your own soul too."

Simeon's Dreams Come True

Simeon was old and ready to die—but not yet! He had been waiting for God to send the Messiah, and lived in such a close relationship with God that he knew from the Holy Spirit that he would not die before seeing that Promised One.

On the day Mary and Joseph brought Jesus to the Temple, Simeon was gently nudged by the Spirit to meet them there. Taking the baby in his arms, he praised God for sending the one who would be the light of the world—not only to the Jews for whom he was promised, but also to the **Gentiles** who needed a Savior just as badly.

Gentiles: non-Jews

Turning to the astonished parents, Simeon made predictions that were fulfilled both within their lifetimes and afterward. Mary's child would have a pivotal effect on people. Those who refused him would fall, while those who received him would rise and be blessed. Her son would also be *"a sign that would be spoken against,"* meaning his sinless life and his open relationship with God his Father would provoke hatred in the hearts of the unbelieving.

Simeon concluded his speech with a special word for Mary. The privilege of being the mother of Jesus came with a cost. Her soul would be pierced when she witnessed the **rejection** of her son and his eventual **crucifixion** as a common criminal.

rejection: refusal to accept

Frederick Buechner: What [Simeon] saw in [Mary's] face was a long way off, but it was there so plainly he couldn't pretend. "A <u>sword</u> will pierce through your soul," he said.

He would rather have bitten off his tongue than said it, but in that holy place he felt he had no choice. Then he handed her back the baby and departed in something less than the perfect peace he'd dreamed of all the long years of his waiting.[4]

What Others are Saying:

crucifixion: form of capital punishment whereby the victim was tied or nailed to a cross

 PHYSICIAN'S PERSPECTIVE—Dr. Luke includes words from Simeon's song that articulate a perspective on death that believers may enjoy. For Simeon, the pleasures of earthly life had lost their appeal and the fear of the grave had lost its terror. As a physician who had doubtless observed the agonizing passing of his patients, Luke must have marveled at the testimony of this righteous man who had complete confidence that he was in God's hands. He had a secure future beyond physical death and was ready to go whenever God called him.

☞ **GO TO:**

Luke 2:35 (sword)

> **Luke 2:36–38** There was also a prophetess, Anna, the daughter of Phanuel, of the tribe of Asher. She was very old; she had lived with her husband seven years after her marriage, and then was a widow until she was eighty-four. She never left the temple but worshiped night and day, fasting and praying. Coming up to them at that very moment, she gave thanks to God and spoke about the child to all who were looking forward to the redemption of Jerusalem.

Not Your Average Little Old Lady

Having been married for seven years and widowed for eighty-four, Anna must have been more than a hundred years old. She may have been frail, but her spirit was lively. Anna's devout heart kept her always at the Temple, worshiping, fasting, praying, seeking. A prophetess, Anna lived so close to God that he gave her revelations to share with others. We can easily imagine a youthful curiosity drawing Anna to the temple doors whenever they opened.

On the day Mary and Joseph presented Jesus at the Temple, she sensed instantly the longed-for Messiah! She lifted her heart in praise to God and spoke to all the faithful that God had kept his promise. The Savior had come.

 PHYSICIAN'S PERSPECTIVE—Medical professionals see them every day—the elderly and frail, the very old whose minds and bodies are wasting away. They often hole themselves up in their homes or apartments and rarely go out. Surely Dr. Luke had seen his fair share of such people. Their needs were great and their caregivers could do little to bring comfort or relief, for old age cannot be reversed.

Some elderly people are exceptional, however. Though bodies age and frailty creeps in, the inner spirit does not have to harden or become brittle with disillusionment or disappointment. Even in their advanced years, Simeon's and Anna's hopes were vibrant; their spirits sang with youthful praise to God. They did not consider cocooning an option. They were out and about. They were actively engaged in public worship and daily contact with people of faith.

Just to hear about the radiance that shone through the eyes of aged Simeon and Anna must have brightened Dr. Luke's heart so much that he included their visits in his Gospel.

What Others are Saying:

John Piper: I think Luke tells us about Simeon and Anna to illustrate the way holy and devout people feel about the promise of Christ's coming, and how God responds to their longings. They see more than others see. They may not understand fully all the details about how the Messiah is coming—Simeon and Anna surely didn't—but God mercifully gives them, before they die, a glimpse of what they so passionately wanted to see.[5]

> **Luke 2:39–40** When Joseph and Mary had done everything required by the Law of the Lord, they returned to Galilee to their own town of Nazareth. And the child grew and became strong; he was filled with wisdom, and the grace of God was upon him.

Boyhood Briefly

In one sentence Luke summarizes the next few years of Jesus' life. The child Jesus grew normally, becoming strong in body and spirit and filled with unusual wisdom. Clearly, God's grace was on this very special boy.

MORE INFORMATION—For more of the story we must turn to Matthew's account of Jesus' early years in Matthew 2. After Mary and Joseph presented Jesus at the Temple, Matthew says the young family returned to Bethlehem. After living there approximately two years, their circumstances suddenly changed.

Wise men, the Magi from the East, arrived unannounced in Jerusalem and inquired about a new "king of the Jews." Their query upset King Herod—an evil ruler who was paranoid of losing his position and brutally killed anyone he wished. God guided the wise men by a star to the house where they found Jesus. After they bowed down and worshiped him, they presented him with gifts of gold, incense, and myrrh. They returned to their country without reporting back to King Herod, disobeying his orders. Furious, Herod ordered his troops to go to Bethlehem and kill every male child two years old and younger.

But Jesus was not there. An angel had warned Joseph, urging him to take Mary and the young child to Egypt. They were to stay there until the threat had passed.

There were three wise men. Fact or fiction? The wise men worshiped the infant Jesus at the manger in Bethlehem. Fact or fiction? Both ideas are fiction. Nowhere does the Bible record how many wise men arrived. The idea that there were three wise men arose from the number of gifts the wise men presented. Furthermore, by the time the wise men arrived, Joseph had moved his family from the stable to a house. King Herod found it necessary to kill all boys two years old and younger, which means Herod knew it was possible Jesus was no longer a newborn. The wise men required months to travel from Babylon to Jerusalem, so it's likely Jesus was between six months and two years old when the wise men arrived to worship him.

TO THE TEMPLE AND BACK AGAIN

Luke 2:41–50 Every year his parents went to Jerusalem for the Feast of the Passover. When he was twelve years old, they went up to the Feast, according to the custom. After the Feast was over, while his parents were returning home, the boy Jesus stayed behind in Jerusalem, but they were unaware of it. Thinking he was in their company, they traveled on for a day. Then they

KEY POINT

Jesus already knew his father was God, not Joseph.

A Missing Messiah

son of the commandment: English for bar mitzvah

When Jesus reached age twelve, he became a "**son of the commandment**." He was a member of the synagogue and was accountable for obeying the law of Moses (see GWLC, page 41). He was also allowed to accompany Mary and Joseph on their annual trip to Jerusalem where they celebrated the **Feast of Passover**. When it was time to return to Nazareth, the celebrants left in groups. Mary enjoyed the companionship of other women, while Joseph traveled with men. Both assumed Jesus was with the other group. When evening came and it was time to set up camp for the night, they discovered Jesus was missing.

Feast of Passover: celebration of Israel's freedom from Egyptian slavery

Mary and Joseph set off for Jerusalem, anxiously looking for their son. On the third day they found him in the Temple. He was perfectly comfortable, seated with members of the Jewish **Sanhedrin**, listening and contributing to their theological discussions and raising such perceptive questions that the religious elders were amazed at his understanding and insights.

Sanhedrin: seventy leaders who served as the high council and supreme court in Hebrew law

Mary's frustration erupted as she announced to Jesus that she and Joseph had been frantically searching for him for three days. Jesus was surprised. He thought it was obvious that if he wasn't with Mary and Joseph, they would know he was in his *"Father's house."*

What happened in the Temple revealed how Jewish leaders trained young rabbis. Students not only listened to their teachers, but they also were encouraged to raise questions.

Today we encourage children and teens to search out information on their own. What they cannot find in books they can

FAST FORWARD

surely find on the internet. In our contact with young people we need to ask ourselves if we value an insightful question even more than a correct answer to a question. We need to listen thoughtfully to young people and never discourage them from raising valid questions. Their insights may stump us and cause us to seek out deeper wisdom.

What Others are Saying:

R. C. Sproul: How significant that the first recorded words of Jesus are ones that go to the heart of his own destiny, to his vocation and calling as the Messiah. Here Jesus is consciously identifying himself as the Son of God, because it was his Father's house. [6]

Leon Morris: Jesus had a relationship to God shared by no other. Joseph and Mary did not understand this. They learned what Jesus' Messiahship meant bit by bit.[7]

> **Luke 2:51–52** Then he went down to Nazareth with them and was obedient to them. But his mother treasured all these things in her heart. And Jesus grew in wisdom and stature, and in favor with God and men.

Home Sweet Home

We may wonder what the threesome talked about as they made the trip from Jerusalem back to Nazareth. Jesus quickly shifted gears from his intellectual discussions in the Temple to the more simple interests of his parents. Mary must have looked at Jesus with wonder, tucking away in her memory the insights she had gathered about her unusual son. She treasured these as evidence that Jesus was indeed who the angel had promised he would be.

For the next eighteen years, Jesus fit into the everyday life of Nazareth and was obedient to his parents in all ways. But he never forgot even for a moment who his real Father was, and he lived to <u>please him</u> in every way.

☞ **GO TO:**

John 5:30 (please him)

PHYSICIAN'S PERSPECTIVE—Dr. Luke made a special comment on Jesus' total fitness. As an adolescent growing into manhood, Jesus was perfectly balanced. He grew *"in wisdom"*—intellectually. He grew *"in stature"*—physically. He grew *"in favor with God"*—spiritually. And he grew in favor with the people of Nazareth—socially.

Jesus did not overemphasize any aspect of growth. While our culture may favor one aspect of healthy growth over another, we need to remember that what was important to the perfect Son of God should also be important to us: to strive for healthy growth intellectually, physically, spiritually, and socially.

What Others
are Saying:

Oswald Chambers: Jesus Christ developed in the way that God intended human beings to develop, and He exhibited the kind of life we ought to live when we have been born from above.[8]

Study Questions

1. What event led Jesus to be born in Bethlehem, as foretold in Micah?
2. In Bethlehem, where was Jesus born? Why was he born in such inhospitable surroundings?
3. What was the significance of the angel announcing to shepherds the birth of the Savior?
4. What did Simeon and Anna say and do that showed they recognized the true identity of the baby Mary and Joseph presented at the temple?
5. What did Jesus reveal about himself when he was twelve years old and visited Jerusalem for the Feast of the Passover?

CHAPTER WRAP-UP

- Caesar Augustus ordered a census that required Joseph to go to Bethlehem to register. While there, Mary gave birth to Jesus. Angels announced the birth of Jesus the Savior to shepherds who were watching their sheep in the fields near Bethlehem. After the shepherds went to see the baby lying in the manger, they rejoiced and spread the happy news of the Savior's birth. (Luke 2:1–20)

- Mary and Joseph fulfilled the requirements of the law at the temple and presented the sacrifice allowed for the poor. (Luke 2:21–24)

- Simeon, a devout man in Jerusalem, was eagerly looking for the coming of the promised Messiah. The Holy Spirit alerted him to go to the temple court, where he met the baby Jesus. Simeon, recognizing that he was the Messiah, gave glory to God. Anna, an elderly woman who worshiped frequently at the Temple, also recognized who Jesus was and shared the good news with others who were looking for God's promised Messiah. (Luke 2:25–38)

- Mary and Joseph took Jesus to live in Nazareth, where Jesus grew as a normal, healthy boy. (Luke 2:39–40).

- When Jesus was twelve years old, Mary and Joseph took him to Jerusalem for the Feast of Passover. As they returned, they discovered Jesus was missing. Hurrying back, they found Jesus in the Temple discussing important theological issues. He was surprised that they did not understand where he would be—in his Father's house. Jesus went back to Nazareth, where he lived in obedience to them and matured into perfect manhood. (Luke 2:41–52)

LUKE 3: A DESERT CALL

CHAPTER HIGHLIGHTS

- John's Message
- Jesus' Baptism
- Jesus' Genealogy

Let's Get Started

In the last chapter we found out about the amazing events that surrounded the birth of two babies, John and Jesus. Both births were miracles—John's because Zechariah and Elizabeth were too old to have children and Jesus' because Mary was a virgin.

John grew up and chose a rugged life in the desert. Luke accounts for Jesus' life up to when Jesus astonished teachers and religious leaders in the Temple at age twelve. Then Luke leaves Jesus in Joseph's carpenter shop in Nazareth where Jesus grew from boyhood to manhood. These have been called the "hidden years" of Jesus. Luke's third chapter turns to the public ministry of John.

JOHN'S MESSAGE

Luke 3:1–6 In the fifteenth year of the reign of Tiberius Caesar—when Pontius Pilate was governor of Judea, Herod tetrarch of Galilee, his brother Philip tetrarch of Iturea and Traconitis, and Lysanias tetrarch of Abilene—during the high priesthood of Annas and Caiaphas, the word of God came to John son of Zechariah in the desert. He went into all the country around the Jordan, preaching a baptism of repentance for the forgiveness of sins. As is written in the book of the words of Isaiah the prophet:

KEY POINT

Luke places events in their historical context.

> "A voice of one calling in the desert, 'Prepare the way for the Lord, make straight paths for him. Every valley shall be filled in, every mountain and hill made low. The crooked roads shall become straight, the rough ways smooth. And all mankind will see God's salvation.'"
>
> John's clothes were made of camel's hair, and he had a leather belt around his waist. His food was locusts and wild honey. People went out to him from Jerusalem and all Judea and the whole region of the Jordan. Confessing their sins, they were baptized by him in the Jordan River.

The Desert Preacher

☞ **GO TO:**

Luke 1:3
(orderly account)

Malachi 3:1 (prepare)

Malachi 4:5–6
(announce)

2 Kings 1:8 (Elijah)

In keeping with his promise to deliver an <u>orderly account</u>, Luke placed events in their historical context by telling the reader who was ruling and who the high priests were. Back then people didn't assign numbers to years the same way we do today, so people didn't go around saying so-and-so happened in 2002. Instead they referred to who was in power, as Luke did above, to let people know when in history an event occurred.

Years before, God told his people that he would send a special messenger to <u>prepare</u> the way for and <u>announce</u> the coming of the Messiah. He told them to look for Elijah, so it was not by chance that John bore a striking resemblance to <u>Elijah</u>.

John dressed like Elijah, went to the desert where Elijah had lived, and preached a message every bit as fiery as Elijah's had been. Like Elijah, John hated being politically correct. He did not preach in the courts of the Temple in Jerusalem, inviting the religious leaders to share the platform with him. He stayed in the desolate wilderness with the windswept rocks providing the backdrop for his stern words. He had no public relations staff to enhance his image, no promotional agents to whip up interest in his campaign. Still, people flocked to him, their attention riveted on his message. They were overcome with an awareness of how far they were from God.

baptism: a sacred rite involving water, symbolizing purification from sin

☞ **GO TO:**

Exodus 30:17–21
(purification)

As people confessed their sins, John baptized them in the Jordan River. This **baptism** was a public statement of their sincere repentance. Up to this point the Jews had followed the Old Testament directions for personal <u>purification</u>, but John used baptism as an outward sign of inward spiritual cleansing. John was doing something new.

> **Luke 3:7–9** John said to the crowds coming out to be baptized by him, "You brood of vipers! Who warned you to flee from the coming wrath? Produce fruit in keeping with **repentance**. And do not begin to say to yourselves, 'We have Abraham as our father.' For I tell you that out of these stones God can raise up children for Abraham. The ax is already at the root of the trees, and every tree that does not produce good fruit will be cut down and thrown into the fire."

An Unlikely Public Speaker

John broke every rule in the book for effective public speaking. He didn't start with a good joke. He made no promises to win votes. On the contrary, his razor-sharp words cut deep into the hearts of his listeners. As descendants of Abraham, the Jews who listened to John considered themselves so favored by God they would not face God's judgment, which was certain to come to other nations. They believed their status of being favored by God was guaranteed. John destroyed the foundation on which all their beliefs were built. He called for a complete change of heart!

What Others are Saying:

R. Kent Hughes: In characterizing his hearers as "vipers," he was saying they were like snakes fleeing a brush fire, trying to escape but having no intention of allowing their evil natures to be changed. John's language was also meant to convey the repulsive nature of their hypocritical smugness.[1]

Gilbert Bilezikian: If sin is telling God to move over because we're taking over, repentance is falling on our knees so he can take over.[2]

> **Luke 3:10–14** "What should we do then?" the crowd asked.
>
> John answered, "The man with two tunics should share with him who has none, and the one who has food should do the same."
>
> Tax collectors also came to be baptized. "Teacher," they asked, "what should we do?"
>
> "Don't collect any more than you are required to," he told them.
>
> Then some soldiers asked him, "And what should we do?"
>
> He replied, "Don't extort money and don't accuse people falsely—be content with your pay."

Something For Everyone!

John's fiery warnings got through to the people. Terror gripped their hearts. Knowing they needed to do something to avoid God's wrath, they asked what they should do. True repentance is a heart attitude, but it shows itself in one's behavior.

Tax collectors and soldiers were in positions of authority in the first-century world. Tax collectors routinely asked for more money than the law required because they were allowed to keep any extra money for themselves. The Roman government knew this happened and didn't do anything to stop it. Soldiers had the influence of military force. Today in the United States if police get carried away with their authority and unduly beat people up, often they are taken to court for excessive use of force. They can lose their jobs and get thrown into jail. The Roman "police" didn't worry about getting punished for excessive force. In fact, we can tell from what John said that at least some soldiers made a practice of taking people's money by force and falsely accusing people for their own selfish ends.

People from the crowd, tax collectors, and soldiers asked John what they should do. In each case John's response had to do with either their possessions or their money. John knew that the way people handled their material goods and wealth reflected the condition of their hearts.

FAST FORWARD

John was saying clearly that for everyone true inner repentance will be revealed in outer actions. We demonstrate our change of heart in the way we treat other people even if we live in a society filled with injustice and suffering. We are to hold our possessions in open hands and show compassion by making available what we have to those who have less. We should demonstrate our righteous attitudes in the workaday world. This involves being fair, even when being so is not required of us.

Something
to Ponder

Contrary to the standards of today's society, true success is not measured by how much we get but by how much we give. When the desire of our hearts is to follow God, we will give evidence of this desire in the way we treat people around us.

> **Luke 3:15–18** The people were waiting expectantly and were all wondering in their hearts if John might possibly be the Christ. John answered them all, "I baptize you with water. But one more powerful than I will come, the thongs of whose sandals I am not worthy to untie. He will baptize you with the Holy Spirit and with fire. His winnowing fork is in his hand to clear his threshing floor and to gather the wheat into his barn, but he will burn up the chaff with unquenchable fire." And with many other words John exhorted the people and preached the good news to them.

Stop Thinking What You're Thinking

The crowds came for Elijah, but they could see plainly John wasn't Elijah. Still, they could not account for the power of his words and the grip he had on their hearts. As they came to be baptized by him in the Jordan River, they began to wonder if he was more than a prophet. Could he possibly be the promised Messiah, the One whose coming they had anticipated for hundreds of years?

John addressed the speculation as forthrightly as he had dealt with their sins. Absolutely, without any shadow of doubt, he was *not* the Messiah. John told the people his role was only to prepare the way for the Promised One, and that he was not worthy to untie Jesus' sandals (see illustration below), let alone fulfill his mission.

John told people about the differences between the baptism he was offering and the baptism Jesus would offer. Getting baptized

Sandals of Commoners

Common people in first-century Israel wore sandals like the one pictured here. Sandals left people's feet exposed to the sand of the desert, so people often washed their feet or received a foot washing from slaves upon entering a home. Here you can see the "thongs" or straps to which John refers in Luke 3:16.

Only Christ can transform a person's life from the inside out.

by John was to participate in an outward water baptism of repentance. Getting baptized by Jesus was to participate in the inward life-transforming work of the Holy Spirit. Only the Messiah could bring the work of the Spirit. He would baptize with fire—judging and cleansing from sin. And he would remove the useless chaff—actions and attitudes displeasing to God—from the lives of all who turned to him.

Paul N. Benware: John's baptism could not forgive and remove sins, since the Scriptures clearly teach that the removal of sin is based on blood, not water. The removal of sin begins with repentance, and baptism is the outward declaration that the person has a new spiritual identity. John demanded that those who wished to be baptized give some evidence that they had indeed repented of their sins.[3]

MORE INFORMATION—Other Gospel writers tell "the rest of the story" of John's dynamic ministry.

- Matthew points out that John's sternest words were directed to many **Pharisees** and **Sadducees**, the religious elite of Jewish society (Matthew 3:1–12).

Pharisees: teachers of Jewish law and religious tradition

Sadducees: rich priestly leaders who ran the Temple

- Mark includes John's clear statement: *"After me will come one more powerful than I, the thongs of whose sandals I am not worthy to stoop down and untie"* (Mark 1:7).

- John, writer of the fourth Gospel, fills in some of the details about priests who were sent from Jerusalem to demand that John identify himself and present his credentials for baptizing people (John 1:15–28). John responded by referring to himself as *"a voice of one calling in the desert,"* publicly acknowledging that he was the messenger whose coming was <u>foretold</u> hundreds of years before.

☞ **GO TO:**

Isaiah 40:3 (foretold)

Robert C. Girard: Dissatisfied with John's answers, "some Pharisees" pressed the cross-examination, "Where then did you get your authority to baptize?" Baptism was normally administered by Temple priests to pagan proselytes converting to Judaism. John upset the applecart by baptizing people who were already (they thought) "God's people." Grassroots Jews readily admitted their spiritual poverty and came to him for baptism like brand new converts. None of this had been approved by the established authorities, nor was it likely to be![4]

> **Luke 3:19-20** But when John rebuked Herod the tetrarch because of Herodias, his brother's wife, and all the other evil things he had done, Herod added this to them all: He locked John up in prison.

Sin Accumulation

John's scathing indictments reached Herod's palace. John rebuked the tyrant for dismissing his wife and replacing her with his sister-in-law, an act forbidden by God (see GWLC, page 40, for a chart of Herod's family tree). He also addressed his many other evil deeds, spelling out what nobody else would dare to say. Herod was <u>furious</u> to be confronted in this way. He was also fearful that John would incite the masses into a political uprising.

Here Luke leaps ahead and records what happened later. Herod added one more transgression to his already large and ever-growing pile of sins when he arrested John and threw him into a dungeon. Later, because Herodias hated John for his stern rebuke, Herod had John beheaded (Luke 9:7–9).

☞ **GO TO:**

John 15:18–25 (furious)

The best way to handle wrongdoing in others is to ignore it, avoiding all confrontation. Fact or Fiction? Many are likely to assume this is a good idea. In our culture this seems to be a prime tenet of how to win friends and influence people. "Don't rock the boat. Mind your own business. Do what you're told," are the messages our culture sends us.

John knew better than to accept such erroneous thinking. He responded to a higher authority—the One who had given him his mission. He risked rejection from the people, denunciation from the religious authorities, and punitive action from Herod. But he spoke with unmistakable clarity about the specific sins and certain judgment of Governor Herod. He serves as a good example of someone who had the courage to confront wrongdoing in his zeal to take a stand for God.

Bible
Fairy Tales
FACT OR FICTION

JESUS' BAPTISM

> **Luke 3:21-22** When all the people were being baptized, Jesus was baptized too. And as he was praying, heaven was opened and the Holy Spirit descended on him in bodily form like a dove. And a voice came from heaven: "You are my Son, whom I love; with you I am well pleased."

Water And Wellness

Note Luke's introductory phrase: *"When all the people were being baptized . . ."* Luke seems to be emphasizing how Jesus identified himself with the common people—the sinners. Jesus didn't get a special mountaintop baptism. He was right there with the rest of them, wading into the grime of sin that was being washed down the Jordan with each immersion.

Don't be mistaken. We know from elsewhere in Scripture that Jesus *"was without sin"* (Hebrews 4:15), so he was not getting baptized for the same reason everyone else was, namely, to participate in the outward symbol of an inward spiritual cleansing. Jesus did not need a spiritual cleansing. In fact, he could have stayed on his throne in heaven, if he wanted to, but instead he lovingly came down and stood shoulder to shoulder with sinners. This wasn't the first time he'd done so, and it certainly would not be the last.

After Jesus' baptism the Holy Spirit descended upon him, affirming that he was God's Anointed, the Messiah. It was not until after this anointing—his baptism—that Jesus performed miracles. (Read a concise overview about miracles in the Bible in GWBI, page 86.)

MORE INFORMATION—We turn to other Gospel writers for more details of this incredible scene.

- Matthew records that when Jesus came to be baptized, John tried to deter him. John knew immediately Jesus was no sinner. Jesus should baptize him! Jesus responded that it was right for him to be baptized by John (Matthew 3:13–17).

- Mark makes the point that it was as Jesus was coming up out of the water that the heavens opened and the Spirit came down (Mark 1:9–11).

- From Gospel writer John we learn that at least one of the descending Spirit's purposes was to show John the Baptist who the <u>Promised One</u> was (John 1:29–34). When John the Baptist saw the dove rest on Jesus, he knew this was the Messiah. John recounted what he saw and heard at Jesus' baptism as evidence that Jesus was the Christ (see GWJN pages 14–15).

☞ **GO TO:**

John 15:26
(Promised One)

Robert C. Girard: By presenting himself for baptism, Jesus was not confessing that he was a sinner. He was saying,

1. "I am with John."
2. "I'm committed to live a righteous life."
3. "I want to live under God's reign."
4. "I'm one of you."[5]

JESUS' GENEALOGY

Luke 3:23–37 Now Jesus himself was about thirty years old when he began his ministry. He was the son, so it was thought, of Joseph, the son of Heli, the son of Matthat, the son of Levi, the son of Melki, the son of Jannai, the son of Joseph, the son of Mattathias, the son of Amos, the son of Nahum, the son of Esli, the son of Naggai, the son of Maath, the son of Mattathias, the son of Semein, the son of Josech, the son of Joda, the son of Joanan, the son of Rhesa, the son of Zerubbabel, the son of Shealtiel, the son of Neri, the son of Melki, the son of Addi, the son of Cosam, the son of Elmadam, the son of Er, the son of Joshua, the son of Eliezer, the son of Jorim, the son of Matthat, the son of Levi, the son of Simeon, the son of Judah, the son of Joseph, the son of Jonam, the son of Eliakim, the son of Melea, the son of Menna, the son of Mattatha, the son of Nathan, the son of David, the son of Jesse, the son of Obed, the son of Boaz, the son of Salmon, the son of Nahshon, the son of Amminadab, the son of Ram, the son of Hezron, the son of Perez, the son of Judah, the son of Jacob, the son of Isaac, the son of Abraham, the son of Terah, the son of Nahor, the son of Serug, the son of Reu, the son of Peleg, the son of Eber, the son of Shelah, the son of Cainan, the son of Arphaxad, the son of Shem, the son of Noah, the son of Lamech, the son of Methuselah, the son of Enoch, the son of Jared, the son of Mahalalel, the son of Kenan, the son of Enosh, the son of Seth, the son of Adam, the son of God.

Climbing The Family Tree

David: *Israel's greatest king*

Abraham: *father of the Jews*

Adam: *first man*

Luke traces Jesus' family tree from Joseph, the assumed father of Jesus, back to **David**, to **Abraham**, and to **Adam**, who was created by God. In doing so Luke confirms Jesus came from the same roots as Jews and Gentiles alike, the first man, Adam.

MORE INFORMATION—Matthew 1:1–17 is another genealogy of Jesus. Matthew's purpose was to establish for his Jewish readers that Jesus fulfilled the ancestral requirements of the Messiah as detailed in the Old Testament. Jesus was born into the lineage of Abraham and King David, both of whom had received prophecies that the Messiah would be one of their descendants (Genesis 12:1–3, 7; 2 Samuel 7:16).

FACT OR FICTION

It is obvious even to a casual reader that Luke's genealogy is not identical to Matthew's, so there must be inaccuracies. Fact or fiction? That's a good question. Let me explain the differences.

One difference between the genealogies is a matter of how far back the genealogies go. Luke's genealogy goes all the way back to Adam, presumably to emphasize the humanity of Jesus. Matthew goes back to Abraham and no further, presumably to emphasize the fact that Jesus fulfilled the ancestral requirements of Messiahhood. This makes sense because Luke was writing to Gentiles and Matthew to Jews. This difference can hardly be considered problematic. Jim may walk farther up a road than Sally, but that doesn't mean they're on different roads.

From Abraham to David the genealogies are the same.

From David to Jesus' earthly father, Joseph, the genealogies differ, but there are a number of explanations for this. The most common explanation is that "Luke traces the lineage through Mary, and Matthew through Joseph. Thus Joseph who is Jesus' father (*"so it was thought"*) is the son-in-law of Heli in Luke's genealogy rather than son. The word 'son' may indicate either."[6]

Bob Girard lists additional explanations in his book *Life of Christ, Volume 1—God's Word for the Biblically-Inept* as follows:

"Matthew gives the royal descent of Jesus, establishing his right to David's throne [Romans 1:3]. . . .

"The differences may be explained by the fact that many Jewish men were known by more than one name [John 1:42].

"The differences may be due to the fact that in Jewish culture it was common practice, when a man died, for his brother to marry the widow and raise children in his own name or in the name of the deceased [Deuteronomy 25:5–10]."[7]

KEY POINT

Don't panic when you notice apparent contradictions in Scripture. There are explanations.

Matthew Henry: [Luke's] genealogy concludes with this, *who was the son of Adam, the son of God.* He was both the *Son of Adam* and the *Son of God,* that he might be a proper Mediator between God and the sons of Adam, and might bring the sons of Adam to be, through him, the *sons of God.*[8]

Study Questions

1. What was John's God-given mission?
2. Suppose John were preaching today in our society. To whom, do you think, would he direct his most pointed warnings?
3. What specific "fruit of repentance" do you think John would call for? How can you and your circle of family and friends demonstrate this fruit?
4. According to John, in what ways was he inferior to the Messiah, whose coming he was announcing?
5. How did God confirm Jesus' identity when he was baptized by John?
6. How would you account for the differences between the genealogies given by Matthew and Luke?

CHAPTER WRAP-UP

- John suddenly appeared on the scene, coming from the desert rather than the religious elite of Jerusalem. He bore a striking resemblance to the Old Testament prophet Elijah. (Luke 3:1–3)

- John's mission was to prepare the hearts of the people to receive the Messiah. People who responded to John's message came to him at the Jordan River to be baptized. (Luke 3:4–14)

- For people who wondered if he were the Messiah, John had only one answer. He was not the Messiah, but a voice announcing his coming. John publicly rebuked Herod for his immoral personal life and for his many evil acts. (Luke 3:15–20)

- Jesus came to John and requested to be baptized by him. God confirmed the identity of Jesus when the Holy Spirit descended on Jesus in the form of a dove, and a voice spoke from heaven confirming that Jesus was God's Son. (Luke 3:21–22)

- Luke's genealogy traces Jesus' lineage to Adam. There are multiple valid explanations for the differences between Matthew's genealogy and Luke's. (Luke 3:23–37)

LUKE 4: TEMPTATION AND TRIUMPH

Let's Get Started

The curtains part and the scene is one of desolation. One figure, deep in thought, moves alone among the rocks and sandy soil. There's silence in this windswept desert of temptation. Who is he? What's going on? Draw closer and listen. Luke, our narrator, is about to tell us the story.

TEMPTATION

> **Luke 4:1–2** Jesus, full of the Holy Spirit, returned from the Jordan and was led by the Spirit in the desert, where for forty days he was tempted by the devil. He ate nothing during those days, and at the end of them he was hungry.

Jesus Gets Ready

Now that Jesus was *"full of the Holy Spirit,"* what would the Spirit tell him to do? Conquer some illnesses? Beat up some demons? Calm some storms? That's what we might expect, but instead Jesus had some preparation to do before he could begin his public ministry. And the preparation wasn't going to be easy. The Spirit led Jesus into a desert where he was **tempted** by the **devil** for over a month (see GWLC, pages 66–67).

devil: *evil being, also known as Satan*

tempted: *to be enticed to do wrong*

☞ **GO TO:**

Deuteronomy 9:9
(mountain)

Exodus 16:4;
Deuteronomy 8:2
(son)

Luke's first readers probably would have seen parallels between Jesus and Israel, for just as Jesus was in the desert for forty days, Israel was in the desert for forty years. Also, Moses went without food for forty days when he climbed up the <u>mountain</u> to receive God's law. The parallel becomes even more apparent when one remembers that Israel is considered God's "<u>son</u>" in several Old Testament passages.

Did you catch that it was the *Holy Spirit* who led Jesus into the desert? In other words, though God did not tempt Jesus, God led Jesus to a place where he would be tempted. If Jesus was tempted, Christians should not be surprised when they are tempted. Temptation is part of life. The question is why? Why does God allow Satan to tempt us? A little later we'll get an answer, but for now hang close to Jesus as he walks from temptation to temptation to temptation.

Other Names for Satan

Throughout Scripture Satan is described with various names that give word pictures of his evil character. Here are a few:

KEY POINT

God does not tempt us, but sometimes he leads us into tempting situations.

Accuser (Revelation 12:10)

Ancient serpent (Revelation 12:9)

Beelzebub or prince of demons (Matthew 12:24)

Devil, meaning "destroyer" (1 Peter 5:8)

Evil one (Matthew 13)

Father of lies (John 8:44)

God of this age (2 Corinthians 4:4)

Murderer (John 8:44)

One who leads the whole world astray (Revelation 12:9)

Prince of this world (John 12:31)

Spirit at work in those who are disobedient (Ephesians 2:2)

Tempter (Matthew 4:3)

FAST FORWARD

☞ **GO TO:**

Hebrews 2:14–18
(able to help)

We are tempted today, but we do not have to face it alone. Jesus stands with us, assuring us that he endured the same pressures we face. He knows from personal experience the pleasures that are offered, the glittering rewards that dance before our eyes, the subtle pull to step away from what God has for us. He withstood it all and is <u>able to help</u> us through our own temptations.

William MacDonald: The purpose of the temptation was not to see if He *would* sin but to prove that He could *not* sin. Only a holy, sinless Man could be our Redeemer.[1]

R. C. Sproul: Christ triumphed over Satan because he believed God. He trusted God, he put his life in the hands of God, and he was victorious.[2]

> **Luke 4:3–4** The devil said to him, "If you are the son of God, tell this stone to become bread."
> Jesus answered, "It is written: 'Man does not live on bread alone.'"

Spiritual Stomach

The last verse of the previous passage sets us up for Satan's first ploy. After forty days of not eating, Jesus was hungry. Now turning a stone to bread is not by itself a sinful thing to do. Most people know that Jesus had no problem with multiplying bread later in his life. Also, Jesus' need was legitimate. He was hungry. Who wouldn't be? And he had the power to perform the miracle. So what could possibly be wrong with turning this stone into bread?

The answer is in Christ's reply, which is a direct quote from Deuteronomy. Deuteronomy is largely comprised of a series of speeches Moses gave to the Israelites when they were waiting to enter the land God had promised them. Moses reminded Israel of God's faithfulness to them, saying *"He humbled you, causing you to hunger and then feeding you with manna, which neither you nor your fathers had known, to teach you that man does not live on bread alone but on every word that comes from the mouth of the LORD"* (Deuteronomy 8:2–3). Jesus knew his hunger was from God, and he had faith that God would eventually feed him, just as he fed the Israelites with manna. God the Father may have been teaching Jesus by experience (because experience is the best teacher) that life is about more than physical sustenance; it's about spiritual sustenance as well. In short, it would have been wrong for Jesus to turn the stone into bread because doing so would have required Jesus to reject his dependence on God.

Jesus had strength to resist temptation by relying on the authority of Scripture and submitting to God.

PHYSICIAN'S PERSPECTIVE—Jesus fasted for forty days. As a physician, Luke would know that after Jesus had gone without food for this long, his body would be depleted and he would be near collapse from exhaustion. Further, throughout this time Jesus had been exposed to the elements and had been deprived of human companionship. Satan tempted Jesus when he was physically and psychologically weak, but Jesus proved strong enough to resist temptation by relying on God's Word and submitting to his Father.

What Others are Saying:

John Piper: Fasting is God's testing ground—and healing ground. Will we murmur as the Israelites murmured in the absence of bread? For Jesus the question was: Would he leave the path of sacrificial obedience and turn stones into bread? Or would he "live by every word that proceeds out of the mouth of God"? Fasting is a way of revealing to ourselves and confessing to our God what is in our hearts. Where do we find our deepest satisfaction—in God or in his gifts?[3]

> **Luke 4:5–8** The devil led him up to a high place and showed him in an instant all the kingdoms of the world. And he said to him, "I will give you all their authority and splendor, for it has been given to me, and I can give it to anyone I want to. So if you worship me, it will all be yours."
>
> Jesus answered, "It is written: 'Worship the Lord your God and serve him only.'"

A Prickly Proposition

It is not wrong to have *"authority and splendor,"* but it is wrong to gain them by allegiance to Satan. Jesus recognized what Satan was offering and rejected it immediately. Again he quoted Old Testament Scripture that we are to worship the Lord our God and serve <u>him only</u>.

☞ **GO TO:**

Deuteronomy 6:13 (him only)

As with Jesus' previous quote, Moses gave this instruction to the Israelites as they prepared to enter the land God had promised to give them. For years they had labored as slaves in Egypt. And for forty years they had lived as sojourners in the desert. Suddenly, prosperity lay within their reach, and so did danger. As God made the land fruitful and surrounded the Israelites with comfort, the Israelites ran the risk of forgetting the Lord and giving credit for their good fortune to themselves.

Similarly, Satan was promising good things—authority and splendor—to Jesus, luring him away from worshiping and serving God alone. But Jesus resisted firmly and completely.

> **Luke 4:9–13** The devil led him to Jerusalem and had him stand on the highest point of the temple. "If you are the Son of God," he said, "throw yourself down from here. For it is written: "'He will command his angels concerning you to guard you carefully; they will lift you up in their hands, so that you will not strike your foot against a stone.'"
>
> Jesus answered, "It says: 'Do not put the Lord your God to the test.'"
>
> When the devil had finished all this tempting, he left him until an opportune time.

Satan As Proctor

Satan swept Jesus to the highest point of the Temple and dared him to make a spectacular leap over the side to the Kedron Valley some 450 feet below (see the map of Jesus' trial and crucifixion, appendix B). This time Satan quoted Scripture, assuring Jesus that God would <u>rescue</u> him.

Jesus retorted with yet another quote from Moses, saying we should never put God to the test. When <u>Moses said</u> this, he was referring to a time when the Israelites complained about not having anything to drink. They put God to the test in that they did not believe God would provide for them, or at least they were not content with God's timing, so they whined and blamed Moses for their thirst. Moses cried out to God, saying he didn't know what to do with the people, as they were about to stone him. God heard Moses' cry and gave him instructions to produce water from a stone. Despite God's willingness to bend to the Israelites' complaints, <u>throughout Scripture</u> this interaction between God and his people is cast in a dim light. The Israelites failed to trust God and so put him to the test. What Jesus says to Satan reminds us that we are to live in full dependence on God without trying to manipulate him to prove that he is with us.

Satan quoted Scripture to tempt Jesus, which teaches us that just because someone is quoting the Bible doesn't necessarily mean we should heed their teaching or buy their book or

☞ **GO TO:**

Psalm 91:11–12 (rescue)

Deuteronomy 6:16; Exodus 17:7 (Moses said)

Deuteronomy 33:8; Numbers 20:1–13, 24; Psalm 81:7; Hebrews 3:7–12 (throughout Scripture)

Remember This . . .

do what they tell us to do. Iain Provan, professor at Regent College in Canada, said in a lecture, "It is just as possible to be biblical and wrong as it is to be biblical and right." Discerning whether someone is using the Bible correctly takes thought, prayer, and often research.

 MORE INFORMATION—Gospel writers Matthew and Mark give their perspective of Jesus' temptation (Matthew 4:1–11; Mark 1:12–13). In Matthew's account, the second and third temptations are the reverse of Luke's. Some Bible students see this as an indication that Jesus endured these temptations simultaneously. Others point out that Matthew's account is chronological while Luke's is thematic. Both Matthew and Mark add that angels came and ministered to Jesus after Satan left him. Mark includes that wild animals were present in the desert.

What Others are Saying:

Raymond B. Dillard and Tremper Longman: Jesus' replies to Satan . . . are taken from Moses's speech recorded in Deuteronomy (8:3; 6:13; 6:16), in which he admonishes Israel not to behave as they did in the wilderness. Jesus thus demonstrates to his followers that he is obedient precisely where the Israelites were rebellious.[4]

Derek Prime: The timely encouragement of the angels at the end of Jesus' period of temptation gives a clue to the intensity of the testing through which he passed.

That was not the end of the conflict, for it continued throughout the next three years. Jesus was frequently tempted to shrink from full obedience to His Father's will. The people regularly asked him for a <u>spectacular sign</u> as a ground for believing in his identity as the Messiah. As the cross drew nearer, the devil made temptation all the greater. But at the beginning, Jesus showed the way he was determined to go.[5]

☞ **GO TO:**

Mark 8:11; John 2:18; 6:30
(spectacular sign)

REJECTION

> **Luke 4:14–15** Jesus returned to Galilee in the power of the Spirit, and news about him spread through the whole countryside. He taught in their synagogues, and everyone praised him.

Ministry Moxie

Luke 4:14 begins with gusto. Jesus returns to Galilee *"in the power of the Holy Spirit."* It sounds like Jesus has been energized by his victory in the desert. And look at the results! The news spread. Everyone praised him. In other words, Jesus was effective in his ministry. This is a clue into why God allows people to be tempted. He does so to prepare his people for work that he wants them to do in the future.

 MORE INFORMATION—John is the only Gospel writer to record the events that took place in Judea and Jerusalem before Jesus arrived in Galilee (John 1:19–4:45). During this period of time (about one year), Jesus called Andrew, John, Simon Peter, Philip, and Nathanael to be his disciples, turned water into wine at a wedding in Cana, talked with Nicodemus and the woman at the well, and healed a royal official's son. (See GWJN, chapters 1–4.)

> **Luke 4:16–19** He went to Nazareth, where he had been brought up, and on the Sabbath day he went into the synagogue, as was his custom. And he stood up to read. The scroll of the prophet Isaiah was handed to him. Unrolling it, he found the place where it is written:
> "The Spirit of the Lord is on me, because he has anointed me to preach good news to the poor. He has sent me to proclaim freedom for the prisoners and re-covery of sight for the blind, to release the oppressed, to proclaim the year of the Lord's favor."

Local Man Becomes Celebrity

Imagine the excitement in Nazareth when one of their own re-turned as a celebrity. We can be sure his family stood on eager tiptoes to see him, backed by enthusiastic neighbors and friends.

On the Sabbath, the townsfolk gathered, and Jesus was given an opportunity to participate in the service. As an act of courtesy, the ruler of the synagogue invited Jesus to read the Scripture (see illus-tration, page 58). When handed the sacred scroll, Jesus unrolled it to the writings of Isaiah and began to read the text he selected, Isaiah 61:1–2 (see illustration, page 59). Everyone in the synagogue un-derstood that the words Jesus read were a <u>description</u> of the Mes-siah, but as he read, did they know the reading referred to Jesus? Did they know Jesus was revealing the desires of his own heart?

☞ **GO TO:**

Isaiah 11:1–5 (description)

Synagogue Reader

It was common in Jesus' day
for synagogue officials to
invite qualified visitors to read
Scripture and make com-
ments, as this illustration
depicts.

☞ **GO TO:**

Deuteronomy 6:4–9;
   11:13–21
   (confession of faith)

A Synagogue Bulletin

Here's what a typical order of service was like back then, repeated
in synagogues every Sabbath throughout Israel.

1. Invocation
2. Recitation of <u>confession of faith</u>
3. Prayer
4. Readings from the law and the prophets
5. Brief message or sermon (given by a rabbi or one of the
   men of the congregation)
6. Closing prayer and dismissal

> **Luke 4:20–22** Then he rolled up the scroll, gave it back
> to the attendant and sat down. The eyes of everyone in
> the synagogue were fastened on him, and he began by
> saying to them, "Today this scripture is fulfilled in your
> hearing."
>
> All spoke well of him and were amazed at the gra-
> cious words that came from his lips. "Isn't this Joseph's
> son?" they asked.

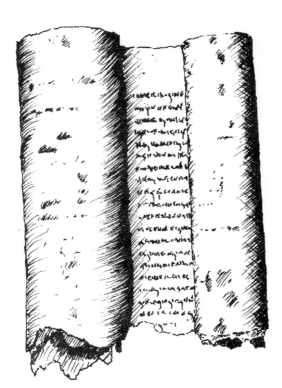

Scroll

Scrolls were made of leather sheets sewn together or river reeds pressed into papyrus paper as shown here. The Scriptures were carefully copied in columns.

Like My Bio?

Having read from the prophet Isaiah, Jesus rolled up the sacred scroll and gave it to an attendant to be returned to its honored place. He then sat down, which was the custom of someone who was about to deliver a sermon. That's why *"the eyes of everyone in the synagogue were fastened on him."* Jesus began with a message no one had heard before. He said the reading from Isaiah, which everyone associated with the promised Messiah, was about him.

Let's look at the Isaiah passage more closely to determine exactly what Jesus was claiming. Jesus was claiming that God's Spirit was on him, that he had been anointed to bring hope and healing and grace to all, especially to those who needed it most: the poor, the prisoners, the blind, and the oppressed.

And the reaction? At first people were won over by a sense of God's grace. The townspeople nodded at each other. You can almost hear them saying, "That's our boy! Amazing, isn't it?" But they were also skeptical. "Isn't he just Joseph the carpenter's son? Who does he think he is?"

> **Luke 4:23–27** Jesus said to them, "Surely you will quote this proverb to me: 'Physician, heal yourself! Do here in your hometown what we have heard that you did in Capernaum.'"
>
> "I tell you the truth," he continued, "no prophet is accepted in his hometown. I assure you that there were many widows in Israel in Elijah's time, when the sky was shut for three and a half years and there was a severe famine throughout the land. Yet Elijah was not sent to any of them, but to a widow in Zarephath in the region of Sidon. And there were many in Israel with leprosy in the time of Elisha the prophet, yet not one of them was cleansed—only Naaman the Syrian."

God Likes Gentiles Too

grace: favor, generosity, joy, mercy

Jesus knew their thoughts. He knew they wanted him to do miracles in Nazareth like he had done elsewhere. And he understood the problem. They saw him only as Joseph's carpenter-son. They didn't believe he was who he claimed to be.

Further, Jesus knew they were resolutely opposed to the idea of God showing **grace** to Gentiles. Their hearts turned to stone when Jesus reminded them that because of unbelief in Israel, the prophet Elijah had helped a <u>Gentile widow</u> in Sidon, ignoring widows in Israel. Then Elisha had healed a Gentile <u>leper</u> from Syria.

☞ **GO TO:**

1 Kings 17:8–16 (Gentile widow)

2 Kings 5:1–15 (leper)

What Others are Saying:

Warren W. Wiersbe: Our Lord's message of grace was a blow to the proud Jewish exclusivism of the congregation, and they would not repent. (Imagine this hometown boy saying that Jews had to be saved by grace just like the pagan Gentiles!)[6]

> **Luke 4:28–30** All the people in the synagogue were furious when they heard this. They got up, drove him out of the town, and took him to the brow of the hill on which the town was built, in order to throw him down the cliff. But he walked right through the crowd and went on his way.

GOD'S WORD FOR THE BIBLICALLY-INEPT

From Listening To Lynching

The Israelites were outraged. Note how quickly they went from being *"amazed at the gracious words that came from his lips"* to being *"furious when they heard this."* They wanted a Messiah who would rid them of Gentile oppression and pour out his mighty wrath upon them, and here Jesus was talking about how God showed them grace. Without discussion or a trial they were united in their impulse and determination to kill Jesus as if he were a <u>false prophet</u>! They didn't even wait for the Sabbath service to finish but removed him from the synagogue and marched him out of town to throw him over a cliff. But Jesus walked calmly through the crowd and left town.

Warren W. Wiersbe: The congregation was so angry, they took action to kill Jesus! St. Augustine said, "They love truth when it enlightens them, but hate truth when it accuses them." That applies well to many congregations today, people who want "gracious words" (verse 22) but who don't want to face <u>the truth</u>.[7]

> In Nazareth's synagogue Jesus defined his mission, and it was unlike anything people had anticipated of the Messiah. He would confront and heal the heartbreaking problems of the human race:
>
> Poverty: Jesus would preach the Gospel to the poor and give them hope.
> Bondage: Jesus would proclaim liberty to the captives.
> Disabilities: Jesus would give sight to the blind.
> Oppression: Jesus would free those who were oppressed.
> In other words, Jesus came to "proclaim the year of the Lord's favor." But as Jesus read from the scroll of Isaiah, he stopped short. He did not include the familiar words that followed in Isaiah 61:2, "and the day of vengeance of our God," which may be why the grace of his words is emphasized in Luke 4:22.
> Today we are living "in the year of the Lord's favor." The "day of vengeance of our God" will come. But for now it is for us to identify with Jesus' mission and do all we can to heal the problems in our world.

☞ **GO TO:**

Deuteronomy 13:1–11 (false prophet)

What Others are Saying:

☞ **GO TO:**

John 1:17 (the truth)

FAST FORWARD

POWER OVER AN EVIL SPIRIT

> **Luke 4:31–37** Then he went down to Capernaum, a town in Galilee, and on the Sabbath began to teach the people. They were amazed at his teaching, because his message had authority.
>
> In the synagogue there was a man possessed by a demon, an evil spirit. He cried out at the top of his voice, "Ha! What do you want with us, Jesus of Nazareth? Have you come to destroy us? I know who you are—the Holy One of God!"
>
> "Be quiet!" Jesus said sternly. "Come out of him!" Then the demon threw the man down before them all and came out without injuring him.
>
> All the people were amazed and said to each other, "What is this teaching? With authority and power he gives orders to evil spirits and they come out!" And the news about him spread throughout the surrounding area.

Demon Demolition

When Jesus left Nazareth, he went to Capernaum, which became his headquarters. There he taught the people with amazing authority. What did he teach? We'll find out a little later, but for now let's look at something he did in the synagogue.

An evil spirit interrupted a Sabbath service by speaking through the voice of a man, calling Jesus *"the Holy One of God."* Jesus rebuked the evil spirit and commanded it to come out of the man.

Imagine the immediate effect this had on the congregation. God had enabled Old Testament prophets to perform miracles, but no one knew anything about demon exorcism. Jesus had come to destroy the devil's work, so Luke appropriately records this account as Jesus' first work of healing.

It is no surprise that Jesus' fame spread throughout the area. Jesus taught with authority and proved that his authority extended over and against demonic forces.

Jesus could not have healed people who were possessed by demons, because there is no such thing as demons. Fact or fiction? Luke has no hint of embarrassment in stating as fact that demons truly exist and that Jesus clearly has authority over them. This truth is clearly supported throughout the New Testament (see GWLC, pages 149–151).

☞ **GO TO:**

1 John 3:8 (destroy)

COMPASSION FOR ALL

> **Luke 4:38–39** Jesus left the synagogue and went to the home of Simon. Now Simon's mother-in-law was suffering from a high fever, and they asked Jesus to help her. So he bent over her and rebuked the fever, and it left her. She got up at once and began to wait on them.

Fever Be Gone

The text says "they" asked Jesus to help Simon's mother-in-law. This is probably a reference to a group of family members who requested Jesus' presence. They must have heard of Jesus' ability to heal, or perhaps one or more of them was in the synagogue during the exorcism.

Luke the physician records the woman's condition—a high fever—which indicates this probably wasn't a twenty-four-hour bug or a slight case of indigestion. Jesus went to her place, which probably means the poor woman wasn't able to go to him. Back then there was no such thing as antibiotics or vaccinations or even aspirin! People routinely died of such fevers as the one mentioned here.

The text gives us no room to think Jesus was a showboat when he healed the woman—a word of rebuke, and the fever was gone. Fast. Quiet. Effective. And note the woman's response. Immediately, she got up and served the people in her home.

See what a difference people can make? The people who asked Jesus to heal Simon's mother-in-law were at least partially responsible for her recovery. If they hadn't asked, who knows if she would have recovered? This should encourage us to pray on the behalf of those who are sick, especially for our relatives and close friends, because it is often by the prayers and requests of people that God dispenses his blessings.

FAST FORWARD

Simon's mother-in-law could have done any number of things upon being healed. She could have run out of the house and shouted to the neighborhood what Jesus had done for her. She could have thanked Jesus and sat around talking about it with her family. She could have taken a nap. What she did instead was serve those around her. She's a good role model. The proper way to show gratitude to God and to people is through service.

Remember
This . . .

John Piper: There is a rebuke from Jesus that cannot be resisted. It carries in it, not just the will to stop a thing, but the force to stop it. A fever is a chemical reaction in the cells of the body, producing excessive heat in response to infection. It has to do with molecules and electrons and the laws of physics and chemistry. In his divinity Jesus designed those laws ages ago (Colossians 1:16), and in his divinity he sustains them so that they work for us daily (Colossians 1:17; Hebrews 1:3). In his humanity he entered into those laws and became subject to them so that he could die by their **ineluctable constancy**. But from inside he revealed that his word is also about these laws of physics and chemistry. He spoke, and the force of his word reversed the fever-flaming effect of infection.[8]

ineluctable: inescapable, cannot be evaded

constancy: steadfastness, loyalty

> **Luke 4:40–41** When the sun was setting, the people brought to Jesus all who had various kinds of sickness, and laying his hands on each one, he healed them. Moreover, demons came out of many people, shouting, "You are the Son of God!" But he rebuked them and would not allow them to speak, because they knew he was the Christ.

Jesus, M.D.

In Luke's Gospel, Jesus' healings began with the expulsion of a demon and continued with the healing of Simon's mother-in-law. In this passage we learn that Jesus healed many more people— people with *"various kinds of sicknesses."*

Jesus continued his demon casting, but here Luke includes a curious detail about Jesus' interaction with the demons. Upon being exorcised, many of the demons shouted that Jesus was the Son of God. Luke goes on to say they knew he was *"the Christ."* You might expect Jesus to be pleased the demons were telling the truth for once, but instead he slapped some spiritual duct tape over their mouths. He *"would not allow them to speak."* Why? Answers vary, but one possible reason is that he didn't want to draw too much attention to himself this early in his ministry. If word got to the Roman establishment that this teacher, Jesus, had a bunch of followers and that these followers were calling him Christ or "Messiah," the Romans probably wouldn't have been too happy. But to understand why, you need to understand a little more about the Jewish concept of Messiah.

The Messiah Concept

The Jews believed many different things about the Messiah, but one of the most important things they believed was that he would be an unstoppable political ruler from King David's <u>lineage</u>. The Romans knew this, so whenever they heard there was a "messiah" or "Christ" around, they took it as a direct threat to their own power. In addition to crucifying Jesus, the Romans crucified many supposed "messiahs" before and after Jesus' life.

Where did the Jews get this idea of Messiah? From a combination of Scripture and their own misguided hopes. We learn from passages like Zechariah 9:9 that the Messiah was to be a king, but God's idea of kingship was different from the Jews' idea. The Jews wanted God to raise up a king who would stomp on their enemies. God raised up a king on the wooden beams of a cross—a king who cleansed both Jews and their enemies of sin and now sits on a celestial, eternal throne.

☞ **GO TO:**

1 Kings 2:1–4 (lineage)

> **Luke 4:42–44** At daybreak Jesus went out to a solitary place. The people were looking for him and when they came to where he was, they tried to keep him from leaving them. But he said, "I must preach the good news of the kingdom of God to the other towns also, because that is why I was sent." And he kept on preaching in the synagogues of Judea.

So Long, Farewell, Auf Wiedersehen, Adieu

Luke moves quickly from dusk to dawn. We can't know for sure why Jesus sought out a solitary place, but given all that happened the day before, it seems reasonable to think he had grown weary of the attention he was getting. He may have been pondering whether people were as enamored of God as they were of God's gifts. He may have been praising God for all the healing he had done.

Jesus' response to the people who found him that morning must have saddened, humbled, and perhaps shocked them. Suddenly they realized they were not Jesus' only concern. He felt an urgent need to *"preach the good news of the kingdom of God to the other towns also."* In addition to telling us about Jesus' target audience, this brief quote gives us some insight into what Jesus was teaching up in verses 4:31–32. To learn all the details of his teaching, you'll have to wait until chapter 6.

Jesus mentioned that he had been sent, and the question that naturally arises from this statement is, Who sent him? The answer: God himself, the ruler of the kingdom about which Jesus was to spread the good news.

Study Questions

1. Why was it necessary for Jesus to be tempted?
2. Jesus' forty days in the desert run parallel to what in the Old Testament?
3. In what general areas was Jesus tempted?
4. Why did the people of Nazareth reject Jesus?
5. How did Jesus prove his authority over evil spirits?
6. How did Jesus show compassion on people with physical needs?

CHAPTER WRAP-UP

- Jesus was led by the Holy Spirit into the desert to be tempted by the devil. The three temptations Jesus faced were in the areas of (1) not relying on God's promised provision and care, (2) seeking success apart from God's plan, and (3) testing God. (Luke 4:1–13)

- The people of Nazareth rejected Jesus because they refused to believe he was the promised Messiah unless he performed miracles for them. Also they bitterly resented his point that God's grace extends to Gentiles. (Luke 4:14–30)

- Jesus demonstrated his authority over evil spirits by commanding them to keep silent and by commanding that they leave their victims. (Luke 4:31–37)

- As Jesus' popularity grew, he kept his focus on his mission: to demonstrate his power to heal physical illness and to proclaim the good news of the kingdom of God. (Luke 4:38–44)

Part Two

MIRACLES, TEACHINGS, AND ACTIONS

REVEREND FUN

Silicone, huh? I might run away to see if my father will give me a fatted calf when I get back.

LUKE 5: BREAKING THE RULES

CHAPTER HIGHLIGHTS

- No Debt
- No Discrimination
- No Boundaries
- No Restrictions

Let's Get Started

By this point in Luke's record, Jesus' public ministry was in full swing. In this chapter Jesus goes about building a team of followers—followers who become the first Christian missionaries after Jesus leaves the earth. Jesus breaks away from convention as he does more healing and more teaching. As you read through this chapter, remember that Jesus was the ideal human. From him we can learn what it means to be human.

NO DEBT

> **Luke 5:1–3** One day as Jesus was standing by the **Lake of Gennesaret**, with the people crowding around him and listening to the word of God, he saw at the water's edge two boats, left there by the fishermen, who were washing their nets. He got into one of the boats, the one belonging to Simon, and asked him to put out a little from shore. Then he sat down and taught the people from the boat.

Lake of Gennesaret: known as Sea of Galilee, Sea of Tiberias, or Sea of Gennesaret

Floatable Pulpit

Why did Jesus choose to teach from a lakeshore? There are at least two possible reasons. One is that the acoustics may have been good there, especially if the ground sloped toward the lake creating an amphitheater effect. Also, he might have anticipated the people would crowd him—the water made an ideal natural boundary between him and them. Note that Peter was either in or near the boat, so he would have had a front row seat for the sermon.

Jesus taught the *"word of God."* This phrase or its cousin *"the word of the Lord"* appears throughout both Old and New Testaments and refers to a message that is divinely inspired by God. Sometimes the phrases mean "the commandment of the Lord"— something to be obeyed or disobeyed. Often the Bible speaks of the word of the Lord as coming to people. Here, Jesus speaks *"the word of God"* and everyone listens.

> **Luke 5:4–7** When he had finished speaking, he said to Simon, "Put out into deep water, and let down the nets for a catch."
>
> Simon answered, "**Master**, we've worked hard all night and haven't caught anything. But because you say so, I will let down the nets."
>
> When they had done so, they caught such a large number of fish that their nets began to break. So they signaled their partners in the other boat to come and help them, and they came and filled both boats so full that they began to sink.

Master: a term of respect

Fish Finding

When Jesus had finished his teaching, he told Simon to move the boat into deeper water and let down the freshly cleaned nets. This request was ridiculous to a veteran fisherman, for Jesus' instruction violated common knowledge that the time to fish was at night and the place to fish was in shallow water. But Simon obeyed, and to his amazement, the nets filled with so many fish they began to break. Another team of fishermen quickly came to help, but both boats began to sink as the men filled them with the miraculous catch.

Something to Ponder

If you were Simon, what would you have learned from this experience? Perhaps you would have learned that where previously there was death and nothingness, Jesus could bring life and good fortune. You might have learned that Jesus did not need to operate by conventional means; he had power from beyond this world. Maybe you would have learned that Jesus is trustworthy; when he asks you to do something, you can be confident he has a reason for it.

> **Luke 5:8–11** When Simon Peter saw this, he fell at Jesus' knees and said, "Go away from me, Lord; I am a sinful man!" For he and all his companions were astonished at the catch of fish they had taken, and so were James and John, the sons of Zebedee, Simon's partners.
>
> Then Jesus said to Simon, "Don't be afraid; from now on you will catch men." So they pulled their boats up on shore, left everything and followed him.

Peter's Blues

Here Luke refers to Simon as Simon Peter. We learn from the other Gospels that Jesus was the one who assigned Simon the new name of Peter. If Luke's readers knew of this fisherman-turned-disciple, they probably would have known him as Peter or Simon Peter, so Luke may be consciously making the connection between Simon and Peter for the sake of his readers.

As the fish came in, Peter was overwhelmed. Something about listening to the teacher speak the *"word of God"* and watching him bring in two boatloads of fish brought Peter to new realizations—about Jesus and about himself. Suddenly it didn't matter whether they were able to haul all the fish on board. In the face of Jesus' grace and power, all Peter could do was hit the deck and beg Jesus to leave, proclaiming himself *"a sinful man."*

But Jesus responded quickly to replace Peter's fear with hope. Jesus knew about Peter's sin, of course, but that didn't matter—at least, it didn't prohibit Peter from being a vital part of Jesus' ministry. With Jesus' power Peter had caught fish. Soon with the same power he would capture people to follow Jesus.

The fishermen were so impressed by Jesus' miracle that they made a commitment to him. They left their huge haul of fish, their boats, and their nets to follow him.

Luke records events that took place in the first century. What do these events have to do with us today? They are relevant in several ways. First, God notices whatever we make available to him (Peter made his boat available) and whatever we do for

KEY POINT

Jesus rewards our obedience by giving us a deeper understanding of who he is.

FAST FORWARD

☞ **GO TO:**

Luke 18:29–30 (reward)

him (Peter pushed the boat from the shore as Jesus requested). He promises to <u>reward</u> us—in this life or when we see him face-to-face. Also, we learn from the fishermen that obedience opens the gate to Christ's power in our lives.

Whenever we become personally aware of who Jesus is, we cannot keep from feeling what Peter expressed to Jesus. Suddenly aware of our sinfulness, we shrink from being in the presence of the Son of God. But, as with Peter, Jesus reaches out to us with grace and promises to help us become what we could never become on our own—effective ambassadors for him.

When we truly believe that Jesus is calling us to follow him, we are willing to make a genuine commitment. This is true despite the fear of commitment that has become an epidemic in our generation.

What Others are Saying:

R. Kent Hughes: Jesus' word comes, and it is demanding. We have some initial reticence. But we are sure he is the one who is speaking, and there is no doubt.[1]

NO DISCRIMINATION

Luke 5:12–16 While Jesus was in one of the towns, a man came along who was covered with leprosy. When he saw Jesus, he fell with his face to the ground and begged him, "Lord, if you are willing, you can make me clean."

Jesus reached out his hand and touched the man. "I am willing," he said. "Be clean!" And immediately the leprosy left him.

Then Jesus ordered him, "Don't tell anyone, but go, show yourself to the priest and offer the sacrifices that Moses commanded for your cleansing, as a testimony to them."

Yet the news about him spread all the more, so that crowds of people came to hear him and to be healed of their sicknesses. But Jesus often withdrew to lonely places and prayed.

Touch Of Compassion

He ventured out of isolation—this man with leprosy who had been consigned to live outside his hometown. When he saw Jesus, he begged to be made clean of his disease.

Jesus responded with compassion. He defied the laws rigidly followed for generations and reached out to touch the man. Jesus healed him, cautioning him not to share his good news, but to go to the priest and fulfill the obligations of the law. Jesus may have been guarding himself against attention that would distract people from his teaching.

Still the news of Jesus' miracle spread so that people flocked to him. They begged to have Jesus touch them as he had touched the man with leprosy. They clamored to hear what he had to say and they wanted him to heal their sicknesses. But it was all for themselves. They were not acknowledging God, either in praise to him for Jesus' miracles or in hunger for God and his righteousness. Although the multitudes listened to Jesus' teaching, they kept God, the center of Jesus' life, on the outside. So Jesus often slipped away from the crowds to draw close to his Father in hours of prayer.

Larry Richards: In Judaism a person with an infectious skin disease was <u>ritually unclean</u> and could not participate in the community's religious life. He or she was also forced to live in isolation from others. When cured, the leper visited a priest, who certified his or her recovery, and pronounced him clean. Thus in asking Jesus to make him clean, the leper expressed his faith that Jesus could cure him of the disease and restore him to fellowship within the faith community.[2]

Being a leper was a designation that consigned a person to the worst discrimination and hopelessness. Fact or fiction? Judge for yourself. In Bible times the only way to deal with the disease of leprosy was quarantine because it was highly contagious. God gave laws that required a person with leprosy to live alone or in a separate colony with other lepers (see GWLC, page 161). It's hard to imagine the inner pain of a person with leprosy. It would be bad enough to have a disease for which there was no cure. But it must have been a living death to be cut off from any gesture of compassion, any interaction with friends or family.

God's quarantine laws were given for the protection of others, but today discrimination against people with leprosy, which

What Others are Saying:

☞ **GO TO:**

Leviticus 13:1–14:32 (ritually unclean)

FACT OR *FICTION*

is now called Hanson's Disease, is not warranted. Most forms of the disease are not contagious, and medication is available to greatly relieve the effects of the disease.

What Others are Saying:

Philip Yancey: Mother Teresa, whose sisters in Calcutta run both a hospice and a clinic for leprosy patients, once said, "We have drugs for people with diseases like leprosy. But these drugs do not treat the main problem, the disease of being unwanted. That's what my sisters hope to provide." The sick and the poor, she said, suffer even more from rejection than material want.[3]

Michael Card: When Jesus felt alone, it was because His Father was so visibly absent in the world. Jesus sought his presence in lonely places.[4]

FAST FORWARD

Jesus reached out to touch a man who was covered with leprosy. In doing so, Jesus violated a law and followed the rule of love and compassion, which superceded it. Today Jesus calls us to reach out with compassion to people whom society has given up on. Because Jesus is not here in physical form, we are to be the hands of Jesus.

NO BOUNDARIES

KEY POINT

No human condition is beyond Jesus' compassion and power to heal.

Luke 5:17–26 One day as he was teaching, Pharisees and teachers of the law, who had come from every village of Galilee and from Judea and Jerusalem, were sitting there. And the power of the Lord was present for him to heal the sick. Some men came carrying a paralytic on a mat and tried to take him into the house to lay him before Jesus. When they could not find a way to do this because of the crowd, they went up on the roof and lowered him on his mat through the tiles into the middle of the crowd, right in front of Jesus.

When Jesus saw their faith, he said, "Friend, your sins are forgiven."

The Pharisees and the teachers of the law began thinking to themselves, "Who is this fellow who speaks blasphemy? Who can forgive sins but God alone?"

Jesus knew what they were thinking and asked, "Why are you thinking these things in your hearts? Which is

> easier: to say, 'Your sins are forgiven,' or to say, 'Get up and walk'? But that you may know that the Son of Man has authority on earth to forgive sins. . . ." He said to the paralyzed man, "I tell you, get up, take your mat and go home." Immediately he stood up in front of them, took what he had been lying on and went home praising God. Everyone was amazed and gave praise to God. They were filled with awe and said, "We have seen remarkable things today."

Forgiven First

Word spread that Jesus was not only a miracle worker, but also an amazing teacher. Instead of relying on the authority of ancient teachers, as was the custom of teachers, Jesus spoke with the assurance of one who was the authority. This drew the intellectuals from surrounding areas who came to hear him.

One day Jesus' teaching session was suddenly interrupted. Men who had tried to get their paralytic friend in to see Jesus had been refused admittance. Showing great ingenuity and determination, they removed some tiles in the roof and lowered their friend to Jesus. This must have amazed the people. Even more stunning was Jesus' response. When he saw their faith, he looked at the paralytic and said, *"Friend, your sins are forgiven."*

The audience was shocked to the point of outrage. How could Jesus dare to forgive sin, something only God can do? This was **blasphemy**!

Then, to demonstrate his authority, Jesus told the man to get up, pick up his mat, and go home. In healing the man's paralysis, Jesus proved that he also had power to heal the man's deepest need: forgiveness of sin.

blasphemy: *slanderous speech directed toward God, punishable by death*

☞ **GO TO:**

Leviticus 24:10–16, 23 (blasphemy)

What Others are Saying:

KEY POINT

Jesus' act of healing was proof that he had the authority to forgive sins.

William Barclay: We must remember that sin and suffering were in Palestine inextricably connected. It was implicitly believed that if a man was suffering he had sinned. . . . [The scribes and Pharisees] objected to Jesus claiming to extend forgiveness to the man. But on their own arguments and assumptions the man was ill because he had sinned; and if he was cured that was proof that his sins were forgiven. The complaint of the Pharisees recoiled on them and left them speechless.[5]

Philip Yancey: Jesus never met a disease he could not cure, a birth defect he could not reverse, a demon he could not exorcise.

But he did meet skeptics he could not convince and sinners he could not convert. Forgiveness of sins requires an act of will on the receiver's part, and some who heard Jesus' strongest words about grace and forgiveness turned away unrepentant.[6]

> **Luke 5:27–30** After this, Jesus went out and saw a tax collector by the name of Levi sitting at his tax booth. "Follow me," Jesus said to him, and Levi got up, left everything and followed him.
>
> Then Levi held a great banquet for Jesus at his house, and a large crowd of tax collectors and others were eating with them. But the Pharisees and the teachers of the law who belonged to their sect complained to his disciples, "Why do you eat and drink with tax collectors and 'sinners'?"

Partying With Sinners

As Levi collected duty on merchandise at his tollbooth, he was constantly aware that he belonged to a group that was despised by the Jews—on a par with robbers and murderers. He was a Jew who had signed up for employment by the hated Roman government. One day Jesus approached him, saying, *"Follow me."* Immediately this hard-headed tax officer left everything and went with Jesus.

It may be that at this time Jesus changed his name from Levi to Matthew, which means "the gift of God."

To make public the decision he had made and to honor Jesus, Matthew invited his friends and colleagues to a banquet at his house. Tax collectors and **sinners** were among the many guests.

sinners: irreligious Jews, synagogue dropouts

scribes: scholars, experts in the law of Moses

The **scribes** and Pharisees who were hostile to all at the gala affair were also extremely critical of Jesus. How could he enjoy eating with these outcasts? He was compromising the standards they followed of keeping separate from sinners. Instead, he was seeking them out—and enjoying himself!

> **Luke 5:31–32** Jesus answered them, "It is not the healthy who need a doctor, but the sick. I have not come to call the righteous, but sinners to repentance."

The Doctor's Clientele: A Primer

Jesus pointed out that the doctor's office is not full of healthy people but the sick whose ailments have driven them to seek help. Similarly, Jesus had not come to call the righteous, those who considered themselves so healthy that they did not need him, but to bring healing to sinners through repentance and turning to him in faith.

KEY POINT

Jesus came to save those who were willing to admit their need of him.

Max Anders: The Pharisees prided themselves in the fact that they never came in contact with sinners: They viewed it as evidence of their purity. Jesus, however, readily associated with sinners. This was a direct affront to religious leaders, and, by implication, exposed the bleakness of their lives.[7]

What Others are Saying:

The Personal Growth Study Bible: Tax collectors and sinners were welcomed by Jesus. They knew they needed Jesus' help. The Pharisees, however, carried the terrible self-imposed burden of having to appear righteous.

The person who feels he must appear righteous fears the very thing that can heal him. He is unable to acknowledge the fact that he is imperfect and to seek Christ's mercy. Jesus spread the good news of forgiveness to the sinners in his society who acknowledged their sickness. But he would do nothing for the self-proclaimed righteous who pretended to be unaffected by the disease of sin.[8]

NO RESTRICTIONS

> **Luke 5:33–35** They said to him, "John's disciples often fast and pray, and so do the disciples of the Pharisees, but yours go on eating and drinking."
>
> Jesus answered, "Can you make the guests of the bridegroom fast while he is with them? But the time will come when the bridegroom will be taken from them; in those days they will fast."

Everybody's Doing It!

On another occasion Jesus' critics pointed out how he and his disciples were different from John's disciples and those of the Pharisees.

While John's and the Pharisees' followers fasted and prayed, Jesus' disciples did not fast but enjoyed regular meals. The Pharisees and teachers of the law thought this proved they were not spiritual!

Jesus observed that it would be entirely inappropriate for a party of wedding guests to fast, as if the bridegroom were dead. Jesus went on to say that a time would come when the bridegroom (Jesus) would be *"taken from them."* Then it would make sense for his followers to fast. Jesus seems to be referring to his own future death here. The idea behind Jesus' words may have been, "Don't worry, Pharisees. My followers will fast soon enough—when you kill me. But then they will not be doing ceremonial fasting, which you hold so precious; they will be doing the fasting that naturally follows the death of a loved one."

What Others are Saying:

Warren W. Wiersbe: Jewish weddings lasted a week and were times of great joy and celebration. By using this image, Jesus was saying to his critics, "I came to make life a wedding feast, not a funeral. If you know the bridegroom, then you can share his joy." He said that one day he would be "taken away," which suggested rejection and death; but meanwhile, there was good reason for joy, for sinners were coming to repentance.[9]

Jesus was a man who bore the burdens and sorrows of the world on his shoulders. Fact or fiction? It is true that Jesus was a "man of sorrows" who wept over the sins and unbelief of Jerusalem. It is also true that a spirit of joy pervaded his ministry. His first miracle was performed at a wedding, and he spoke of himself as a groom. Anyone who's been to a wedding knows how the groom's happiness permeates the occasion. Misinterpreting this spirit of joy, his accusers thought Jesus was a drunkard!

FAST FORWARD

☞ **GO TO:**

Isaiah 53:3 (man of sorrows)

Luke 19:41 (wept)

Luke 10:21; John 15:11; 17:13 (joy)

Luke 7:34 (drunkard)

Luke 5:36–39 He told them this parable: "No one tears a patch from a new garment and sews it on an old one. If he does, he will have torn the new garment, and the patch from the new will not match the old. And no one pours new wine into old wineskins. If he does, the new wine will burst the skins, the wine will run out and the wineskins will be ruined. No, new wine must be poured into new wineskins. And no one after drinking old wine wants the new, for he says, 'The old is better.'"

Garments And Goatskins

In a **parable** Jesus used everyday items—garments and wine-skins—to announce that he had come to bring something new.

Nobody would take a piece from a new garment to patch a hole in an old garment—both would be ruined. Similarly, Jesus had not come to patch up the old religious forms of the law but to create something fresh and totally new.

Problems would come if new wine were poured into old wine-skins, because as the wine fermented, it would burst the old wine-skin (see illustration below). Not only would the new wine spill out, but the old wineskin would be ruined. People who are famil-iar with old things are content to stick with what they know and are unwilling to try the new. Similarly, the people in Jesus' day were familiar with the laws of Moses and the traditions that had grown through the years. Jesus came to bring something new. Like wine that would burst out of old containers, his salvation could not be delivered in Judaism. Further, his listeners were unwilling to try the new because they preferred to stick with what was fa-miliar.

Jesus came as a teacher, but one who reached far beyond the expected norms. No one was outside his circle of influence. In this chapter alone Luke shows Jesus teaching crowds of common people, calling fishermen to be his close associ-ates, and healing an outcast leper. He taught the Pharisees and teachers of the law—students whose view of him regis-tered anywhere from critical to hostile. And he called Levi (Matthew)—a wealthy, influential tax collector regarded as a "sinner" by the law-abiding establishment—to be his dis-ciple. What should we learn from this? That nobody is be-yond the reach of Jesus!

KEY POINT

Jesus came not to reform the old legalis-tic system but to replace it.

Something
to Ponder

Wineskin

Wine was kept in a goatskin bottle as shown here. New skin was supple but in time became dried, hard, and cracked.

Study Questions

1. Why did Jesus' instructions to Simon to cast for fish seem ridiculous? What were two results of Simon's obedience?
2. What did Jesus reveal of himself when he healed the leper?
3. What did Jesus prove to the religious leaders when he healed the paralyzed man?
4. How did Jesus upset common practice when he called Matthew to follow him?
5. What did Jesus want his critics to understand when he replied to their question about fasting?

CHAPTER WRAP-UP

- Jesus instructed Simon to go into deep water and cast his net. The huge catch that resulted was clearly a miracle. Recognizing Jesus' power, Peter fell at his feet and acknowledged that he was a sinner. Jesus reassured Peter not to be afraid but to be prepared to catch men. (Luke 5:1–11)

- Jesus touched a leper and healed him instantly. He told the man to show himself to the priest so he could be pronounced clean. (Luke 5:12–16)

- One day when Jesus was teaching the religious elite, four men opened the roof of the house and let the man down in front of Jesus. Noting their faith, Jesus told the man his sins were forgiven. The religious leaders silently accused Jesus of speaking blasphemy, since only God can forgive sins. Jesus healed the man, proving he had power both to heal and to forgive sins. (Luke 5:17–26)

- Jesus called Levi to follow him, though he was a tax collector on the payroll of the hated Roman government. When the religious leaders complained that Jesus socialized with outcasts, Jesus said he had come to call sinners who recognized their need of him. (Luke 5:27–32)

- Jesus' critics asked why his followers did not practice regular fasting and prayers, as they did and as John the Baptist's followers did. Jesus claimed that he had come to replace the old legalistic system with something new and better. (Luke 5:33–39)

LUKE 6: JESUS, PH.D.

CHAPTER HIGHLIGHTS

- Jesus and His Critics
- Twelve World Changers
- Jesus' Keynote Speech

Let's Get Started

Jesus had launched a mission that touched the lives of people from all over the land, but his outreach lacked the trappings of modern ministries. He had no assistants organizing his schedule, sending out press releases, or setting up photo opportunities. There were no direct mail campaigns to solicit gifts or offer tickets to special healing events.

Jesus concentrated on people—individuals who needed to know about his Father's love and care. Jesus helped them understand that God's ways were so different from their ways that he had come to turn their way of doing things upside down!

In this chapter we'll discover Jesus' concept of the Sabbath. We'll also be introduced to all twelve of Jesus' disciples. Most importantly, we'll learn about one of Jesus' most important sermons. Up until now we've heard *that* Jesus taught; in this chapter we'll learn *what* Jesus taught. So settle in behind your desk. Professor Jesus is about to enter the classroom.

☞ **GO TO:**

Isaiah 55:8–9
(God's ways)

JESUS AND HIS CRITICS

> **Luke 6:1–5** One Sabbath Jesus was going through the grainfields, and his disciples began to pick some heads of grain, rub them in their hands and eat the kernels. Some of the Pharisees asked, "Why are you doing what is unlawful on the Sabbath?"

> Jesus answered them, "Have you never read what David did when he and his companions were hungry? He entered the house of God, and taking the consecrated bread, he ate what is lawful only for priests to eat. And he also gave some to his companions." Then Jesus said to them, "The Son of Man is Lord of the Sabbath."

Pharisees Go To Sunday School

☞ **GO TO:**

Leviticus 19:9–10;
  Deuteronomy 23:4–
  25 (grain)

1 Samuel 21:1–6
  (David)

Taking grain was not stealing. God had told farmers to leave some of their <u>grain</u> to provide for the needs of people who could not afford to buy it. The problem for the Pharisees was not in eating the grain but in the day on which the disciples did it. Rubbing heads of grain to release the kernels was considered threshing, and threshing was not allowed on the Sabbath according to Jewish tradition.

Jesus' reply set them back on their heels. He pointed out that King <u>David</u>, whom the Pharisees held in the highest esteem, had gone into the tabernacle and taken consecrated bread to eat. This was food that only priests could eat. Further, he gave some of the bread to his companions! This was a blatant disregard of the law. Jesus ended his argument with an exclamation point by telling the Pharisees that he himself was Lord of the Sabbath—the author of the whole idea of Sabbath and the person in charge of how it should be kept.

FAST FORWARD

☞ **GO TO:**

Isaiah 58:13–14
  (delight)

God set apart the Sabbath, the seventh day of the week (Saturday), as a reminder of his completion of Creation and as a day of rest for people. The Sabbath was designed to remind the Jews that they were God's people and that they had a special commitment to him. He specified that his people, their servants, and even their animals were to refrain from ordinary work so they could delight in this day set apart for him.

In time the people began to focus more on the no-work clause of God's commandment than on the rest- and <u>delight</u>-in-the-Lord clauses. The religious leaders drew up long, detailed statements about what was "work" and what wasn't. One list gave thirty-nine activities that were prohibited on the Sabbath (see GWLC, page 171).

What are we to make of all this? Are we responsible for obeying the Sabbath laws, as the Pharisees demanded in Jesus' day? Obviously not, as Jesus didn't even follow the Pharisees' laws.

But are we to keep the Sabbath at all? Christians have different ideas about how to view the Sabbath, but this much we know: Jesus' first-century followers did not observe the Jewish Sabbath. They did, however, meet for worship on the first day of the week, which was Sunday (see GWAC, pages 233–234). On this day they remembered that Jesus rose from the dead.

What Others are Saying:

Joy Davidman: To keep the Sabbath holy, ultimately, meant obeying 1,521 different blue laws—for example, you had to remove your false teeth. To keep the name of God holy, you had to give up using it altogether; eventually its very syllables were forgotten. The frightened men of Christ's day, groaning under the intolerable social security of the Roman peace, turned to their law and found only a tangle of gobbledy-gook. Like us, they could obey it blindly or reject it blindly; but they could not possibly make sense of it.[1]

Richard J. Foster: Before we dismiss this Old Testament Sabbath rule out of hand, it is important to see that there is a lot more behind it than the desire for a periodic breather. For instance, it has a way of tempering our gnawing need always to get ahead. If we ever want to know the degree to which we are enslaved by the passion to possess, all we have to do is observe the difficulty we have maintaining a Sabbath rhythm.[2]

> **Luke 6:6–11** On another Sabbath he went into the synagogue and was teaching, and a man was there whose right hand was shriveled. The Pharisees and the teachers of the law were looking for a reason to accuse Jesus, so they watched him closely to see if he would heal on the Sabbath. But Jesus knew what they were thinking and said to the man with the shriveled hand, "Get up and stand in front of everyone." So he got up and stood there.
>
> Then Jesus said to them, "I ask you, which is lawful on the Sabbath: to do good or to do evil, to save life or to destroy it?"
>
> He looked around at them all, and then said to the man, "Stretch out your hand." He did so, and his hand was completely restored. But they were furious and began to discuss with one another what they might do to Jesus.

Rotten Nasty Filthy Healing

Jesus' critics were aching to make an accusation against him. Would he dare to break the Sabbath law and perform a miracle of healing? Jesus knew how eager his critics were to accuse him, so he posed a question. Which is obeying the Sabbath law: doing good or doing evil? Saving life or destroying it? The only reply was silence as Jesus looked around the room. Then he told a man to stretch out his atrophied hand, and right before their eyes, Jesus healed the hand. Without question, Jesus reflected his Father's heart when he put loving, caring human relationships over slavish adherence to man-made laws. The critics were almost crazy with anger at Jesus.

 MORE INFORMATION—Matthew and Mark fill in the incident by recording that as the Pharisees made their exit from the synagogue that day, they plotted with the **Herodians** how they could have Jesus killed (Matthew 12:14; Mark 3:6).

Herodians: political group, supporting Herod Antipas, who joined the Pharisees to oppose Jesus

TWELVE WORLD CHANGERS

> **Luke 6:12–16** One of those days Jesus went out to a mountainside to pray, and spent the night praying to God. When morning came, he called his disciples to him and chose twelve of them, whom he also designated apostles: Simon (whom he named Peter), his brother Andrew, James, John, Philip, Bartholomew, Matthew, Thomas, James son of Alphaeus, Simon who was called a Zealot, Judas son of James, and Judas Iscariot, who became a traitor.

Team Building Jesus-Style

KEY POINT

Jesus prayed because he depended on his Father for guidance.

One day Jesus left the crowds and went to spend the night alone in conversation with his Father. He sought guidance. The next morning Jesus called his followers together and selected from them twelve men to be in his inner circle, both as disciples to follow him on earth and as apostles to continue his work after he returned to his Father.

Jesus the Son of God had laid aside his divine ability to know all, so he acknowledged his dependence on his Father for the wisdom he needed in choosing the twelve who would become his disciples. If Jesus needed to spend time with his Father seeking guidance, how much more do we need that time alone with God?

FAST FORWARD

The Jesus Team

Name	Nickname or Family Affiliation	Distinguishing Characteristics
Peter	Also called Simon, Cephas (Rock)	▪ Fisherman; became one of three disciples closest to Jesus; wrote two New Testament books
Andrew	Peter's brother	▪ Brought Peter to Jesus
James	Son of Zebedee and Salome	▪ One of the three disciples closest to Jesus
John	Brother of James	▪ Known with James as Son of Thunder; one of the three disciples closest to Jesus; probably *"the disciple Jesus loved"*; wrote five New Testament books
Philip		▪ Brought Nathanael to Jesus
Bartholomew	May be Nathanael, Philip's friend or brother	
Matthew	Also called Levi	▪ Tax officer; hosted a banquet for Jesus; wrote one New Testament book
Thomas	Also called Didymus (The Twin)	▪ Because of his hesitancy to believe that Jesus rose from the dead, became known as Doubting Thomas
James	Also called James the Younger	
Simon	Also called The Zealot	▪ May have been active in the movement committed to overthrow Roman rule
Judas	Also called Thaddaeus Son of James, also one of the Twelve	
Judas Iscariot		▪ Treasurer of the group; betrayed Jesus

R. Kent Hughes: All except Judas Iscariot were Galileans, "country boys." Four were fishermen. One was a hated tax-gatherer. Not one of them was famous or rich or noble or well-connected. Not one of them was a scribe of a priest or an elder or a ruler of the people. They were, as their detractors labeled them, "<u>unschooled, ordinary</u>" men." All were poor.[3]

What Others are Saying:

☞ **GO TO:**

Acts 4:13
(unschooled, ordinary)

The men who made up the Twelve were a diverse group. They seemed to have little in common, yet they became a tightly knit group that changed the world. What bound them together was their relationship to Jesus.

JESUS' KEYNOTE SPEECH

> **Luke 6:17–19** He went down with them and stood on a level place. A large crowd of his disciples was there and a great number of people from all over Judea, from Jerusalem, and from the coast of Tyre and Sidon, who had come to hear him and to be healed of their diseases. Those troubled by evil spirits were cured, and the people all tried to touch him, because power was coming from him and healing them all.

Wanted: Crowd Control

Was there no escape? Crowds surrounded Jesus: the newly chosen Twelve, his friends, and a great number of hopefuls who had come from a wide radius. They all wanted to hear him teach what would later become known as the Sermon on the Plain, so called because of his location—*"a level place."* Many in the crowd had come because they were desperate for healing. Among them were some who were in bondage to evil spirits, and others with various diseases. The people pressed against Jesus, because they were healed if they only touched him.

> **Luke 6:20–26** Looking at his disciples, he said: "Blessed are you who are poor, for yours is the kingdom of God. Blessed are you who hunger now, for you will be satisfied. Blessed are you who weep now, for you will laugh. Blessed are you when men hate you, when they exclude you and insult you and reject your name as evil, because of the Son of Man.
> "Rejoice in that day and leap for joy, because great is your reward in heaven. For that is how their fathers treated the prophets.
> "But woe to you who are rich, for you have already received your comfort. Woe to you who are well fed

> now, for you will go hungry. Woe to you who laugh now, for you will mourn and weep. Woe to you when all men speak well of you, for that is how their fathers treated the false prophets."

The World According To Jesus

Jesus began to teach his disciples, but the setting was not an enclosed classroom. Though Jesus was clearly showing his chosen disciples that they would be a people set apart from others, the crowd listened in.

Jesus gave a series of contrasts: blessings for some and woes for others. What he said went against conventional wisdom—it simply didn't make sense. The table below summarizes what Jesus said. As you read it, remember that the disciples were about to experience the conditions that Jesus talked about—poverty, hunger, mourning, and persecution—because of their loyalty to Jesus.

Jesus' Sermon Summarized

Blessing	Woe
Blessed are you if you're poor. You have the kingdom of God.	Woe to you if you're rich. You have all the benefits you're going to get.
Blessed are you if you're hungry. You'll be satisfied.	Woe to you if you are greedily filling your stomach now. You'll go hungry.
Blessed are you if you're crying. You will laugh again.	Woe to you who are laughing as if sorrow can't touch you. Some day you will mourn and weep.
Blessed are you when others hate you because of me. They will exclude you and reject you because of your loyalty to me.	Woe to you when everyone speaks well of you. Even the false prophets could win in a popularity contest.

Peter Kreeft: The point of our lives in this world is not comfort, security, or even happiness, but training; not fulfillment but preparation. It's a lousy home, but it's a fine gymnasium. . . . Jesus didn't make it into a rose garden when he came, though he could have. Rather, he wore the thorns from this world's gardens.[4]

John Piper: One way of rejoicing in suffering comes from fixing our minds firmly on the greatness of the reward that will come to us in the resurrection. The effect of this kind of focus is to make our present pain seem small by comparison to what is coming.[5]

Jesus showed deep compassion for the poor, the hungry, those who mourned, and those who were rejected. He offered them hope. In contrast, he did not offer hope to the wealthy, the well-fed, the merrymakers, and those who compromised in order to win the admiration of others. They had it all now!

With which group of people do we identify today? Are we among those Jesus labeled "blessed" or those to whom he said, "Woe to you"? Do we acknowledge the dignity and value of people whom the world ignores? Do we show compassion for people in need and seek to give relief in practical, self-sacrificing ways?

> **Luke 6:27–36** "But I tell you who hear me: Love your enemies, do good to those who hate you, bless those who curse you, pray for those who mistreat you. If someone strikes you on one cheek, turn to him the other also. If someone takes your cloak, do not stop him from taking your tunic. Give to everyone who asks you, and if anyone takes what belongs to you, do not demand it back. Do to others as you would have them do to you.
>
> "If you love those who love you, what credit is that to you? Even 'sinners' do that. And if you lend to those from whom you expect repayment, what credit is that to you? Even 'sinners' lend to 'sinners,' expecting to be repaid in full. But love your enemies, do good to them, and lend to them without expecting to get anything back. Then your reward will be great, and you will be sons of the Most High, because he is kind to the ungrateful and wicked. Be merciful, just as your Father is merciful."

Habits Worth Having

Jesus went on to say his disciples should view other people in a radically different way than they were used to. They were to love their enemies, show acts of kindness to those who hated them, and share generously with those who made demands. They were to deal with others with the quality of love and generosity that Jesus' Father showed to people who were ungrateful and wicked.

And the reward? Jesus promised that his disciples would be greatly rewarded—the more they loved with his supernatural love, the more they would become like his Father.

KEY POINT

We will become like God as we show his love to the undeserving.

Tit for tat is the only way to get along with people. Fact or fiction? We walk around carrying an invisible scorecard on which we track how we have been treated. One favor done to us requires a favor back in return. One act of discourtesy or unkindness done to us requires a payback of equal discourtesy or unkindness. That's how it works. Well, that's how it *seems* to work, but Jesus showed a better way—a way straight from his Father's heart. Jesus calls us to toss out the scorecard entirely and to orient ourselves to others with a love and generosity that gives to those who do not deserve it.

FACT OR FICTION

What Others are Saying:

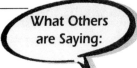

Marcus Borg: [Matthew 5:39] specifies that the person has been struck on the *right* cheek. . . . In that world, people did not use the left hand to strike people. It was reserved for "unseemly" uses. Thus, being struck on the right cheek meant that one had been backhanded with the right hand. Given the social customs of the day, a backhand blow was the way a superior hit an inferior, whereas one fought social equals with fists.

This means the saying presupposes a setting in which a superior is beating a peasant. What should the peasant do? "Turn the other cheek." What would be the effect? The only way the superior could continue the beating would be with an overhand blow with the fist—which would have meant treating the peasant as an equal.[6]

Darrell L. Bock: Jesus' disciples should love with an exceptional love, a love so different that the world can see it. Such love is rewarded because it marks out the presence of the children of God, who reflect the character of God. God himself is kind to the ungrateful and selfish. To be his child is to reveal the <u>Father's character</u>.[7]

☞ **GO TO:**

Psalm 112:4–5
(Father's character)

Paul N. Benware: Disciples are to respond to evil with good and with love. Patience and not retaliation is to be the response of the follower of Christ. These are radical words, and they are also impossible to obey. They drive the serious disciple to his knees as he realizes that without the enablement and the grace of God such commands cannot be kept.[8]

> **Luke 6:37–38** "Do not judge, and you will not be judged. Do not condemn, and you will not be condemned. Forgive, and you will be forgiven. Give, and it will be given to you. A good measure, pressed down, shaken together and running over, will be poured into your lap. For with the measure you use, it will be measured to you."

The Boomerang Effect

Jesus does not tell his disciples to be gracious to others because it's the right thing to do, though of course it is. Instead, Jesus tells his disciples to be gracious to others because there are perks for doing so! What's in it for you if you avoid condemning others? You'll get the rich benefits of not being condemned. What will you get if you give things to people and forgive people? You'll be given things! You'll be forgiven!

What Others are Saying:

John Piper: Jesus made it very clear that the key to our joy and our love in the midst of hard times is the deep, unshakable confidence that every loss on this earth in the service of love for the sake of the kingdom will be abundantly restored, "pressed down, shaken together, running over." The mandate is clear: let us devote ourselves to cultivating stronger faith in the "great reward" of future grace. This is the power to love.[9]

> **Luke 6:39–40** He also told them this parable: "Can a blind man lead a blind man? Will they not both fall into a pit? A student is not above his teacher, but everyone who is fully trained will be like his teacher."

A Teaching About Teaching

In this passage Jesus gave basic truth about how education works, but it's unclear how he meant for his listeners to take it. Maybe Jesus was encouraging his disciples to know their place and keep it. Or perhaps he was informing any aspiring teachers in the crowd (including those among the disciples) that the title of "teacher" came with a big responsibility, that of being sure not to misguide people. Maybe he was letting the disciples know they could expect to see the same bad attitudes in the Pharisees' disciples as they were used to seeing in the Pharisees. It's possible Jesus meant all of these things and more.

Regardless of what Jesus wanted people to do with the information, the information he gave was clear: a student is not better than but rather becomes like his teacher.

FAST FORWARD

Many of Jesus' teachings were uniquely relevant to his time and place, and certainly this "teaching about teaching" had implications that were peculiar to his listeners. But this teaching also has a universal quality about it, which invites us of the twenty-first century to explore its implications for our world. One point we can glean from the idea that students become like their teachers is that it is important for us to choose our teachers wisely. People often assume that the responsibility of a student is merely to do the work that a teacher sets before him or her, but this isn't true. It's also the student's responsibility to make sure he or she is being taught by a worthy teacher.

Also, Jesus' teaching reminds us that when we witness people doing bad things or making bad decisions, we ought to be slow to judge them. Too often we call people names in our minds and quickly dismiss them. We ought to remember that every person has had influences in his or her life, and these influences are at least partly to blame for the wrongs people commit.

> **Luke 6:41–42** "Why do you look at the speck of sawdust in your brother's eye and pay no attention to the plank in your own eye? How can you say to your brother, 'Brother, let me take the speck out of your eye,' when you yourself fail to see the plank in your own eye? You hypocrite, first take the plank out of your eye, and then you will see clearly to remove the speck from your brother's eye."

Jesus, The Stand-Up Comic

Most people have heard this passage so often that it's lost its humor, but Jesus seems to be painting a word picture of hilarity here. Think of a librarian who yells at someone to keep his voice down, thus creating even more noise in the process, and hopefully you'll catch some of the humor Jesus intended. Don't increase sin by committing the sin of ignoring your own sin.

> **Luke 6:43–45** "No good tree bears bad fruit, nor does a bad tree bear good fruit. Each tree is recognized by its own fruit. People do not pick figs from thorn bushes, or grapes from briers. The good man brings good things out of the good stored up in his heart, and the evil man brings evil things out of the evil stored up in his heart. For out of the overflow of his heart his mouth speaks."

Filling And Filtering

This passage is instructive in two ways. One is that it helps people to determine the extent to which they should trust people. Don't trust people whose lives are characterized by bad things—corruption, gossip, unnecessary complaining, dissension, and so on. Instead, trust people whose lives are full of *"good fruit"*—kindness, generosity, joy, and peace.

☞ **GO TO:**

Galatians 5:22 (fruit)

But this passage promotes more than filtering one's outside influences. It also calls for internal maintenance. Jesus is calling his listeners to be sure that they cultivate hearts that please God. An effort to do so, Jesus says, will result in *"good things."* Jesus seems to be likening people to sponges. People, like sponges, can release only that which has already been absorbed.

Jesus places special emphasis on what people say, linking what is in one's heart with that which proceeds from one's mouth. This link between the heart and mouth runs throughout Scripture. Just look:

- *"No, the word* [of God's commandment] *is very near to you; it is in your mouth and in your heart for you to observe"* (Deuteronomy 30:14).

- *"Agree with God, and be at peace; in this way good will come to you. Receive instruction from his mouth, and lay up his words in your heart"* (Job 22:21–22).

- *"My mouth shall speak wisdom; the meditation of my heart shall be understanding"* (Psalm 49:3).

- *"For one believes with the heart and so is justified, and one confesses with the mouth and so is saved"* (Romans 10:10).

One thing we can conclude, therefore, is that what we say is a fairly reliable indicator of who we are, of what lives in our hearts. If we find ourselves saying things that routinely have an ill effect on those around us, it's time for us to do some heart work—praying, reading Scripture, and seeking God.

> **Luke 6:46–49** "Why do you call me, 'Lord, Lord,' and do not do what I say? I will show you what he is like who comes to me and hears my words and puts them into practice. He is like a man building a house, who dug down deep and laid the foundation on rock. When a flood came, the torrent struck that house but could not shake it, because it was well built. But the one who hears my words and does not put them into practice is like a man who built a house on the ground without a foundation. The moment the torrent struck that house, it collapsed and its destruction was complete."

Practice What I Preach

In this parable it's important to notice that both men have heard Jesus' words. The only thing different is that one man puts Christ's words into action and the other doesn't.

The message? Putting Jesus' words into practice makes them a part of you. This enables you to resist evil influences and say no to temptations that foreshadow destruction. If, however, you fail to apply Jesus' words to your everyday life, evil will have its way with you. You won't be able to stand up to temptation, and you'll experience the usual consequences of sin—pain, confusion, and devastation.

KEY POINT

Knowing God's Word is not enough; we need to obey it.

Oswald Chambers: If a man has built himself up in private by listening to the words of Jesus and obeying them, when the crisis comes it is not his strength of will that keeps him, but the tremendous power of God—"kept by the power of God." Go on building up yourself in the Word of God when no one is watching you, and when the crisis comes you will find you stand like a rock; but if you have not been building yourself up on the Word of God, you will go down no matter what your will is like.[10]

What Others are Saying:

Dallas Willard: In actually doing what Jesus knows to be best for us, we build a life that is absolutely indestructible, "on the Rock." "And that Rock was Christ."[11]

☞ **GO TO:**

1 Corinthians 10:1–4 (Rock)

Study Questions

1. How did Jesus differ from the religious leaders when it came to the Sabbath? What did this reveal about who Jesus was?
2. How many men did Jesus choose to be in his inner circle of disciples? What is the difference between a disciple and an apostle?
3. How would you characterize the differences between people Jesus pronounced as blessed and those he pronounced as under judgment?
4. What result comes to disciples who show God's love and generosity to the undeserving?
5. What is the key to having strength to stand firm in times of temptation?

CHAPTER WRAP-UP

- In contrast to following the Pharisees' long list of prohibitions to keep the Sabbath holy, Jesus demonstrated that the Sabbath was to be a day of rest, delighting in God, and doing good to others. (Luke 6:1–11)

- Jesus chose twelve men to be in his inner circle of disciples and taught them and others with his Sermon on the Plain. (Luke 6:12–19)

- Jesus gave good news to his disciples, who were going to experience poverty, hunger, pain, and persecution because of their allegiance to him. He promised that they would be blessed. In contrast, people who enjoyed prosperity and popularity now, with no regard of heavenly values, would not be blessed. (Luke 6:20–26)

- Jesus taught that his disciples should reflect his Father's love and mercy, not just to their friends, but to the most undeserving. Though they would pay a price for doing so, they would be rewarded by becoming more like his Father in heaven. (Luke 6:27–38)

- Jesus warned that the heart attitudes his disciples held would certainly be reflected in their actions—for the benefit of others or for their ill. Jesus taught that the only way to stand firm in a time of temptation is to build on the firm foundation of obeying his words. (Luke 6:39–49)

LUKE 7: JESUS, M.D.

CHAPTER HIGHLIGHTS

- A Gentile's Faith
- Death Overturned
- John as Investigative Reporter
- Soul Doctor

Let's Get Started

This chapter has a lot to teach us about the relationship between people's faith and God's power. Jesus proved he is the Great Physician who is able to heal the diseased and raise the dead. He also proved he is the Great Physician of the soul, who knows people's hearts and forgives sins.

Read about a Roman soldier who went above and beyond the call of duty. Find out how to impress Jesus. Watch Jesus perform his first resurrection. Listen in on John the Baptist's interview with Jesus. And witness the extraordinary love of a "sinful" woman for her Lord.

A GENTILE'S FAITH

Luke 7:1–6a When Jesus had finished saying all this in the hearing of the people, he entered Capernaum. There a centurion's servant, whom his master valued highly, was sick and about to die. The centurion heard of Jesus and sent some elders of the Jews to him, asking him to come and heal his servant. When they came to Jesus, they pleaded earnestly with him, "This man deserves to have you do this, because he loves our nation and has built our synagogue." So Jesus went with them.

Centurion Goodness

The man spotlighted in this passage is a Gentile, a Roman centurion (see illustration below). While centurions were trained to be take-charge representatives of Rome, this one was a man with a warm and caring heart. When one of his slaves became deathly ill, the centurion sent for the community leaders. He asked them to contact Jesus and request that he come to heal this slave whom the centurion *"valued highly."* The centurion must have heard of or seen previous healings performed by Jesus.

Luke highlights the centurion's fondness for Jews, saying he built their synagogue. Remember that Luke was writing to Theo, a Greek Gentile. With this account of the centurion, Luke may be promoting kind interaction between Gentiles and Jews. He might also be giving his Gentile readers a model of faith that they can look up to without reservation. Luke may also be demonstrating that Christ's love was not limited to Jews, nor is God's power reserved for only one group of people.

 PHYSICIAN'S PERSPECTIVE—Luke identified with the centurion. While a doctor's concern is for his patient, he cannot be indifferent to the pleas of the patient's loved ones who wring their hands and say, "Doctor, do something!" Families want desperately to see everything made right, but are helpless to do anything about it.

Centurion

Centurions, such as the one shown here, were Roman officers in command of a hundred soldiers. They are spoken highly of in a number of places in the New Testament. See Mark 15:39; Acts 10:2; and Acts 27:43.

> **Luke 7:6b–8** He was not far from the house when the centurion sent friends to say to him: "Lord, don't trouble yourself, for I do not deserve to have you come under my roof. That is why I did not even consider myself worthy to come to you. But say the word, and my servant will be healed. For I myself am a man under authority, with soldiers under me. I tell this one, 'Go,' and he goes; and that one, 'Come,' and he comes. I say to my servant, 'Do this,' and he does it."

The Wisdom Of A Military Man

The elders carried out the centurion's request faithfully, and Jesus responded by making his way to the centurion's house. Before Jesus got there, the centurion sent friends to stop him from entering his house, saying, *"Don't trouble yourself. . . ."* This may be a reference to how long it would take Jesus to walk to the centurion's house, but it's more likely to be a reference to the ridicule Jesus would bring upon himself for entering a Gentile's home. The centurion obviously had a lot of respect for Jesus because he said he didn't deserve to have Jesus enter his house.

The soldier then made a fascinating analogy. In the same way that people beneath the centurion did what he said because he had the power of the Roman Empire backing him, so Jesus could issue orders that would be carried out because Jesus had the power of God behind him. The centurion demonstrated an outstanding comprehension of who Jesus was, who he represented, and what he could do.

G. Campbell Morgan: [The centurion] had a remarkable apprehension of the truth concerning all that Jesus was doing. He recognized that [Jesus] was in authority, and that all forces would obey him, because he recognized also the nature of the authority to which our Lord was himself submitted. Somehow this man had seen to the very heart of the truth concerning Jesus.[1]

What Others are Saying:

> **Luke 7:9–10** When Jesus heard this, he was amazed at him, and turning to the crowd following him, he said, "I tell you, I have not found such great faith even in Israel." Then the men who had been sent returned to the house and found the servant well.

What Impresses Jesus

Jesus was taken aback. This centurion, who was not one of God's covenant people, demonstrated more faith than Jesus had ever seen from anyone in Israel. In fact, Jesus yearned for his fellow Jews to have as much faith as this Gentile man. Needless to say, his servant was healed instantly.

Have you ever wanted to know how to impress Jesus? Here's the answer according to Luke. Practice a faith in God that goes beyond the accepted norm.

 MORE INFORMATION—Matthew, in recording this same miracle, points out that Jesus marveled at the centurion's amazing faith because this was the kind of response he longed to see in Israel (Matthew 8:5–13). While the Jews of Jesus' day thought they were guaranteed entrance into Christ's kingdom because they were Jews, Jesus demonstrated that one's ethnicity didn't matter. What mattered was faith.

☞ **GO TO:**

Mark 6:6 (unbelief)

Warren W. Wiersbe: Twice in the Gospel record we are told that Jesus marveled. Here in Capernaum, he marveled at the faith of a Gentile; and in Nazareth, he marveled at the <u>unbelief</u> of the Jews.[2]

DEATH OVERTURNED

> **Luke 7:11–17** Soon afterward, Jesus went to a town called Nain, and his disciples and a large crowd went along with him. As he approached the town gate, a dead person was being carried out—the only son of his mother, and she was a widow. And a large crowd from the town was with her. When the Lord saw her, his heart went out to her and he said, "Don't cry."
>
> Then he went up and touched the coffin, and those carrying it stood still. He said, "Young man, I say to you, get up!" The dead man sat up and began to talk, and Jesus gave him back to his mother.
>
> They were all filled with awe and praised God. "A great prophet has appeared among us," they said. "God has come to help his people." This news about Jesus spread throughout Judea and the surrounding country.

A Powerful Love

One day as Jesus traveled to Nain, a town about twenty-five miles from Capernaum (see map in appendix A), he saw a funeral procession—men carrying a stretcher with a cloth-covered body and a grieving widow whose only son had died just that day. Following her was a large crowd of sympathizers, including professional mourners whose wails and doleful flute playing added to the misery.

Jesus felt great compassion for the grieving woman. In the death of her son she had lost not only the one person who could support and protect her, but the one who could carry on her family name. Jesus approached her and said, "Don't cry." Though many have said those words in tragic circumstances, only Jesus had the power to give this woman reason to stop crying.

He went to the bier, touched it, and told the young man to get up! To the amazement of all, the dead man sat up and spoke. We can picture Jesus taking the young man to his mother and clasping their hands together. Everyone was filled with worshipful awe. They praised God and quickly spread the word about Jesus. He was the greatest physician they had ever encountered. No human doctor could raise patients from the dead!

In Jesus' day it was customary on the day of the death to wrap a dead body in cloth and carry it on a stretcher for immediate burial. A procession was formed, usually including musicians and professional wailers. Even the poorest family was expected to hire two flute players and one female mourner.

Funeral customs have changed since then, but Jesus has <u>not changed</u>. His heart is still filled with compassion. He has sympathy for those who are bereaved. Therefore, it is still appropriate to stand with those who grieve the loss of a loved one. Even when we have <u>hope</u> that we will be reunited with those who have placed their faith in Jesus Christ, we should still offer sympathy and practical help.

FAST FORWARD

☞ **GO TO:**

Hebrews 13:8 (not changed)

1 Thessalonians 5:13–18 (hope)

 PHYSICIAN'S PERSPECTIVE—A doctor takes on a patient who is in critical condition, marshals all his skills in treating him, and finally when the patient is recovered, he dismisses him. Luke must have known some of the satisfaction a doctor experiences when he returns a patient to his family. He receives their expressions of joy and gratitude. As he recorded this incident of Jesus raising the son from death, he must have pictured the response of the grieving widow. Luke makes mention of three "only children" whom Jesus restored: the son of the widow of Nain, the <u>daughter</u> of Jairus, and the <u>boy</u> possessed by an evil spirit.

What Others are Saying:

☞ **GO TO:**

Luke 8:40–56
(daughter)

Luke 9:37–43 (boy)

KEY POINT

Jesus feels our pain and grief and offers his comfort.

Darrell L. Bock: Death is not the end for those who know him. It involves a transfer into a level of life not known on this earth. While this miracle reminds us of our frailty and mortality, it also shouts out to us about God's power to raise and transform. No wonder the crowd who saw this miracle was filled with awe. We should be too, as we contemplate his creative power and compassion.[3]

JOHN AS INVESTIGATIVE REPORTER

Luke 7:18–23 John's disciples told him about all these things. Calling two of them, he sent them to the Lord to ask, "Are you the one who was to come, or should we expect someone else?"

When the men came to Jesus, they said, "John the Baptist sent us to you to ask, 'Are you the one who was to come, or should we expect someone else?'"

At that very time Jesus cured many who had diseases, sicknesses and evil spirits, and gave sight to many who were blind. So he replied to the messengers, "Go back and report to John what you have seen and heard: The blind receive sight, the lame walk, those who have leprosy are cured, the deaf hear, the dead are raised, and the good news is preached to the poor. Blessed is the man who does not fall away on account of me."

Are You Who I Think You Are?

☞ **GO TO:**

Matthew 11:2 (prison)

John paid a great price for being faithful. He was thrown in <u>prison</u> for confronting Herod about his sinful lifestyle. While in prison, John heard regularly from his disciples about the activities of Jesus. But events were not coming together as John thought they would. Perhaps he was expecting that by now Jesus would have taken action to overthrow the Roman occupation of their land.

Deeply troubled and acting like an investigative journalist, John sent two of his followers to ask Jesus a subtly accusing question: "Are you the Messiah, or should we be looking for someone else?"

Jesus dealt with the question, not behind closed doors, but out in the open where people watched him perform healings. He then told John's followers to go back and report what they had seen. They had watched the Great Physician in action.

Jesus was fulfilling the mission he had announced in Nazareth when he read and interpreted the passage from <u>Isaiah</u>. In other words, he counted on John to understand that he was fulfilling prophecy about the Messiah. Then Jesus added that there's a special blessing for John—and for all—who keep their trust in him in spite of difficulties that raise doubts in their minds.

☞ **GO TO:**

Luke 4:16–19; Isaiah 61:1–2 (Isaiah)

Darrell L. Bock: We sometimes think that the great saints never doubted. In doing so, we deny that they were normal human beings. The Scripture is honest and open about such struggles and doubts, just as the Christian community today should be.[4]

What Others are Saying:

Charles R. Swindoll: Two words will help you cope when you run low on hope: *accept* and *trust*. *Accept* the mystery of hardship, suffering, misfortune, or mistreatment. Don't try to understand it or explain it. Accept it. Then, deliberately *trust* God to protect you by his power from this very moment to the dawning of eternity.[5]

KEY POINT

Jesus asks us to trust, even when we do not understand.

God never abandons his suffering follower. He promises that when we pass through the <u>waters</u> of doubt, discouragement, pain, and suffering, he will be with us. He is a doctor not only of our bodies but also of our emotions and souls.

Remember This . . .

Luke 7:24–28 After John's messengers left, Jesus began to speak to the crowd about John: "What did you go out into the desert to see? A reed swayed by the wind? If not, what did you go out to see? A man dressed in fine clothes? No, those who wear expensive clothes and indulge in luxury are in palaces. But what did you go out to see? A prophet? Yes, I tell you, and more than a prophet. This is the one about whom it is written:

"'I will send my messenger ahead of you, who will prepare your way before you.'

"I tell you, among those born of women there is no one greater than John; yet the one who is least in the kingdom of God is greater than he."

☞ **GO TO:**

Isaiah 43:1–3 (waters)

A Recipe For True Success

After John's disciples left, Jesus talked about him to the crowd. Was John a wimp that could be bent by the wind of opinion? Was he a sham dressed in the latest designer wear? No, he was a prophet who had fulfilled his mission. And, Jesus added, there was no greater prophet than John, for he had been privileged to announce the coming of the Messiah! However, anyone who enlisted for service in the kingdom of God, which Jesus was bringing, would enjoy blessings that John had only announced.

Leon Morris: Jesus' coming marked a watershed. He came to inaugurate the kingdom. And the least in that kingdom is greater than the greatest of men. This is a statement of historical fact. John belonged to the time of promise. The least in the kingdom is greater, not because of any personal qualities he may have, but because he belongs to the time of fulfilment.[6]

> **Luke 7:29–35** (All the people, even the tax collectors, when they heard Jesus' words, acknowledged that God's way was right, because they had been baptized by John. But the Pharisees and experts in the law rejected God's purpose for themselves, because they had not been baptized by John.)
>
> "To what, then, can I compare the people of this generation? What are they like? They are like children sitting in the marketplace and calling out to each other:
>
> "'We played the flute for you, and you did not dance; we sang a dirge, and you did not cry.'
>
> "For John the Baptist came neither eating bread nor drinking wine, and you say, 'He has a demon.' The Son of Man came eating and drinking, and you say, 'Here is a glutton and a drunkard, a friend of tax collectors and "sinners."' But wisdom is proved right by all her children."

Rejection Analysis

Jesus, having defended John, addressed the crowd and accused the unbelieving Pharisees and experts in the law. They would never be satisfied with the messenger of God because they did not want to believe the message of God. They had falsely accused John of being demon-possessed because they didn't like his **austere** lifestyle. On the other hand, they falsely accused Jesus of being

austere: rigorously self-disciplined

too unrestrained—a glutton, a drunkard, and a friend of outcast sinners! Jesus said people could tell both his message and John's were valid because of the changes in their followers' lives.

Jesus pointed out that many people could not be pleased. They didn't like the way John preached the truth and they didn't like the way Jesus related to people on the "outside."

Today some people excuse their lack of response to the truth because they don't care for the mode in which it comes. They may be bored with traditional worship, for example, or turned off by contemporary worship. Jesus turns our focus away from the channels through which his message travels and toward the message itself. In many ways, Jesus is the message. The question is, Will you accept him or not?

FAST FORWARD

KEY POINT

Jesus warns us not to mix the style of the messenger with the substance of his message.

SOUL DOCTOR

> **Luke 7:36–38** Now one of the Pharisees invited Jesus to have dinner with him, so he went to the Pharisee's house and reclined at the table. When a woman who had lived a sinful life in that town learned that Jesus was eating at the Pharisee's house, she brought an alabaster jar of perfume, and as she stood behind him at his feet weeping, she began to wet his feet with her tears. Then she wiped them with her hair, kissed them and poured perfume on them.

A Special Party Favor

Simon, a Pharisee, invited Jesus to dinner. All the diners were reclining on couches and enjoying a leisurely meal when a woman with a bad reputation entered through the open doorway, carrying an expensive jar of perfume (see illustration, page 104). She approached Jesus and stood with her tears falling on his feet. She wiped them away with her hair, kissed his feet, and poured her perfume on them.

When we see Jesus for who he really is, we have to respond, either by turning and going our own way or by acknowledging him with humility and love. The woman had seen Jesus and believed that he could forgive her and turn her life

Something to Ponder

around. She understood that Jesus had healed her soul. So great was her gratitude that she went to incredible lengths to express her love. Have we seen Jesus for who he really is? What is our response?

> **Luke 7:39–43** When the Pharisee who had invited him saw this, he said to himself, "If this man were a prophet, he would know who is touching him and what kind of woman she is—that she is a sinner."
>
> Jesus answered him, "Simon, I have something to tell you."
>
> "Tell me, teacher," he said.
>
> "Two men owed money to a certain moneylender. One owed him five hundred denarii, and the other fifty. Neither of them had the money to pay him back, so he canceled the debts of both. Now which of them will love him more?"
>
> Simon replied, "I suppose the one who had the bigger debt canceled."
>
> "You have judged correctly," Jesus said.

Jesus Teaches Accounting

Simon was far more critical of Jesus than he was of the woman. He thought that if Jesus were truly a prophet he would have known what an outcast this woman was and would refuse her gestures.

Jesus, of course, knew Simon's thoughts and posed a situation to his host. Suppose two men owed money: one a small amount of fifty **denarii** and the other a greater amount of five hundred

denarii: plural for denarius, Roman coins representing a day's wage for a workman denarii. Since neither man could repay the debt, we can only imagine their relief and joy when the moneylender canceled their obligations. Which man, Jesus asked, would love the moneylender more? Simon gave the logical answer somewhat reluctantly. *"I suppose,"* he answered, *"the one who had the bigger debt canceled."* Jesus was pointing out that this "sinful" woman obviously loved God more than Simon did.

> **Luke 7:44–50** Then he turned toward the woman and said to Simon, "Do you see this woman? I came into your house. You did not give me any water for my feet, but she wet my feet with her tears and wiped them with her hair. You did not give me a kiss, but this woman, from the time I entered, has not stopped kissing my feet. You did not put oil on my head, but she has poured perfume on my feet. Therefore, I tell you, her many sins have been forgiven—for she loved much. But he who has been forgiven little loves little."
>
> Then Jesus said to her, "Your sins are forgiven."
>
> The other guests began to say among themselves, "Who is this who even forgives sins?"
>
> Jesus said to the woman, "Your faith has saved you; go in peace."

Love's Expression

Jesus then pointed out to Simon that he had disregarded the common courtesies of a host. The woman had fulfilled these out of love for him. Jesus turned to the woman and pronounced her forgiven not on the basis of what she had done but on the basis of her faith. There's no mention of Simon piping up after this (perhaps he'd been put in his place), but other guests did. They wondered about Jesus' identity. "Who is this?" was their question. *"Who is this who even forgives sins?"*

This is an interesting question because in New Testament times Jews did not necessarily expect their Messiah to be divine. They believed he would be a mighty king, but not God necessarily. The question that the guests ask in the above passage might indicate that they were willing to accept that Jesus was Messiah but wondered if they should go even further. Could it be that Jesus was a divine doctor of the soul? Was he God? All circumstances pointed toward that conclusion, but they struggled to believe.

KEY POINT

Great love wells up in the heart when a great debt is forgiven.

What Others are Saying:

Sue and Larry Richards: The Pharisee was admired and respected and even held in awe for his apparent piety, while the sinful woman was despised and rejected. However, it is one's attitude toward Jesus that opens the door to God's kingdom. Simon's attitude toward Jesus was dismissive and unbelieving. The sinful woman's attitude toward Jesus was shaped by awareness of her need and trust in Christ's willingness to forgive. She had found forgiveness in Christ, and as a result, she loved him deeply. In turn Jesus accepted her love, commended her faith, and confirmed her forgiveness.[7]

Study Questions

1. What caused Jesus to comment on the Roman centurion's faith?
2. In raising the widow's son from the dead, what did Jesus reveal about himself?
3. Suppose you were John the Baptist in prison. Would Jesus' answer satisfy your question? Why, or why not?
4. How would you explain that John was the greatest prophet, yet the "least" in the kingdom of God is greater?
5. Why would Jesus say that his unbelieving religious critics were behaving as spoiled children?

CHAPTER WRAP-UP

- Even Jews who had been taught God's ways from their early years had not shown such understanding and faith as the Roman centurion. (Luke 7:1–10)

- Jesus feels compassion for the poor and for those who suffer and grieve. He still has compassion for all who are in need of his touch. (Luke 7:11–17)

- John wrestled with doubt that Jesus was the Messiah whose coming he had announced. Jesus' reply was proof that he was fulfilling Isaiah's prophecy of the Messiah. He had a special blessing for John if he kept trusting, in spite of his disappointment that Jesus had not yet established his kingdom. (Luke 7:18–35)

- The sinful woman lavishly expressed her love for Jesus and her longing for forgiveness. In contrast, Simon the Pharisee expressed no love because he had no longing to be forgiven. Jesus forgave the woman's sins on the basis of her faith. (Luke 7:36–50)

LUKE 8: THE WAY OF JESUS

Let's Get Started

To prepare the disciples to go out and minister, Jesus demonstrated his power both in the truth he taught and in the miracles he performed. Not everyone understood his message, and some refused what he said because, though they understood what he was saying, they did not want to accept it. Jesus' words were backed by deeds of love and compassion, and his demonstrations of power drew people from all over the surrounding area. They couldn't leave him alone!

JESUS' SUPPORT TEAM

Luke 8:1–3 After this, Jesus traveled about from one town and village to another, proclaiming the good news of the kingdom of God. The Twelve were with him, and also some women who had been cured of evil spirits and diseases: Mary (called Magdalene) from whom seven demons had come out; Joanna the wife of Cuza, the manager of Herod's household; Susanna; and many others. These women were helping to support them out of their own means.

Jesus Groupies

As Jesus traveled from place to place, he was accompanied by his twelve disciples. In addition, Luke alone records, certain women followed him, quietly supporting him and his band. Much as the disciples had little in the way of education or position, these women had few credentials that would impress the religious leaders in Jerusalem. But Jesus had touched them and given them healing. Now they expressed their devotion to him by serving him and giving of their means.

Luke gives us the names of three of these women:

- Mary (called Magdalene) served from a heart that overflowed with gratitude. Jesus had cast seven demons out of her.
- Joanna, wife of Cuza, Herod's **steward**. Her presence on the team indicates that Jesus' influence had penetrated the palace.
- Susanna, of whom we know nothing beyond her name.

These women who came from very different backgrounds had one thing in common: their devotion to Jesus and their willingness to support him by using their money to provide food and other necessities. The depth of their <u>devotion</u> was proven when they stayed by Jesus during his crucifixion—even after his disciples had deserted him.

Jesus rescued Mary Magdalene from a life of prostitution. Fact or fiction? Through the years Mary has been portrayed as a former prostitute. Nowhere in Scripture is this supported. She was troubled by evil spirits, which Jesus cast out of her. This prompted her to follow Jesus so wholeheartedly that she helped support him and his band of twelve disciples.

Sue and Larry Richards: [Mary] was healed of demon possession, and from that point on she never wavered in her commitment to Christ. Mary loved her Lord, not with a passion that would burn out, but with unceasing intensity.[1]

Jesus the Son of God was <u>rich</u> beyond our comprehension. He left the glories of heaven, stepping down and taking the role of a <u>servant</u>. As an itinerant teacher, Jesus led the Twelve from town to town and village to village with no visible income. Women willingly gave from their personal finances to fund Jesus' ministry. These women set an example for us, showing that it is our <u>duty to share</u> with those who feed us spiritually and enrich our lives.

steward: finance minister

☞ **GO TO:**

Matthew 27:55–56; Mark 15:40–41; Luke 23:49 (devotion)

2 Corinthians 8:9 (rich)

Philippians 2:6–8 (servant)

Galatians 6:6 (duty to share)

FACT OR FICTION

What Others are Saying:

Something to Ponder

DURABLE PARABLES

Luke 8:4–8 While a large crowd was gathering and people were coming to Jesus from town after town, he told this parable: "A farmer went out to sow his seed. As he was scattering the seed, some fell along the path; it was trampled on, and the birds of the air ate it up. Some fell on rock, and when it came up, the plants withered because they had no moisture. Other seed fell among thorns, which grew up with it and choked the plants. Still other seed fell on good soil. It came up and yielded a crop, a hundred times more than was sown."

When he said this, he called out, "He who has ears to hear, let him hear."

A Tale Of The Exceptionally Ordinary

Many people followed Jesus, swarming around him from all nearby towns. They heard him teach—but did they really listen? On the surface, there was nothing too special about his story. He spoke of what the people had seen again and again in the fields that lay outside their villages.

A farmer went out to sow (see illustration, page 110). As he tossed out the seed, some fell on the hardened path, where it made a meal for the birds. Some seeds fell on a thin layer of soil that covered stone. Because these seeds could not take root or find moisture, they sprouted, but soon withered and died. Some seed fell among thorns. Before long the weeds crowded them out. Finally, some seed was scattered on the good, tilled soil and yielded a bumper crop.

So what? The people must have wondered why Jesus told them the story. That's why he called out to them, asking if they *really* heard what he was saying.

James tells us that exposure to the Scriptures is like looking in a <u>mirror</u> that shows us what we look like. If we merely glance at it and go on our way, we lose out. Spiritual growth comes as we hear the Word with <u>spiritual understanding</u> and respond with active obedience.

KEY POINT

Jesus uses the gifts offered from hearts that are devoted to him.

☞ **GO TO:**

James 1:22–25 (mirror)

Romans 10:17 (spiritual understanding)

Remember
This . . .

Sowing

A farmer would carry seed in heavy cloth and scatter it by flinging it a handful at a time as shown here.

> **Luke 8:9–15** His disciples asked him what this parable meant. He said, "The knowledge of the secrets of the kingdom of God has been given to you, but to others I speak in parables, so that, "'though seeing, they may not see; though hearing, they may not understand.'"
>
> "This is the meaning of the parable: The seed is the word of God. Those along the path are the ones who hear, and then the devil comes and takes away the word from their hearts, so that they may not believe and be saved. Those on the rock are the ones who receive the word with joy when they hear it, but they have no root. They believe for a while, but in the time of testing they fall away. The seed that fell among thorns stands for those who hear, but as they go on their way they are choked by life's worries, riches and pleasures, and they do not mature. But the seed on good soil stands for those with a noble and good heart, who hear the word, retain it, and by persevering produce a crop."

Jesus Does Some Unpacking

When Jesus' disciples asked him what his story meant, he answered first by explaining why he had spoken in a parable form. He wanted everyone to know the truth, but he knew many were not really open to hearing it. Those who were hungry for the truth would understand, while those who were only looking for a way to trip him up would be <u>confused</u> by the parable.

☞ **GO TO:**

Isaiah 6:9–10 (confused)

Then Jesus explained the story:

- The seed being scattered by the farmer is the *"word of God."* The Contemporary English Version of the Bible translates this as "God's message," which might make the meaning a little more clear. Today, when Christians hear the phrase "Word of God" or "God's Word," they immediately think of the Bible. But we need to remember that in Jesus' day, the New Testament did not exist, and back then there was some debate about what in our Old Testament was Scripture and what wasn't. Some scholars think Jesus used *"word of God"* to refer to himself.

- The packed-down path represents people with hard hearts who are not open to the truth. They listen with superficial interest. What they hear doesn't stick but is snatched away by the **enemy**.

  enemy: Satan

- The rocky soil represents people who accept the truth, but when they are tested, they easily reject what they claimed to have believed.

- The thorny soil represents people who put the affairs of this life ahead of spiritual growth. Their concerns and their many interests in comfort, career, and family crowd out what the Word of God is saying to them so that they do not bear spiritual fruit.

- The good soil represents people who receive the word with open, teachable hearts that put into practice what they hear, and thus bear fruit for God.

Helmut Thielicke: [Jesus] says: Weed out the thorns; see to it that the seed does not fall on the path; be careful lest you be people so shallow that the Word cannot take root. Jesus says: Be good soil. And that means: Hold on to the Word in stillness, get rid of the hardness and callousness; don't squeeze God into a few cracks and crevices of your day's business, but give him a space of daily quiet.[2]

What Others are Saying:

The four kinds of soil were represented in the listeners whenever Jesus taught—and they still are whenever God's Word is taught today. The preacher of the Word has a responsibility, and so do we, the hearers. The preacher needs to scatter the seed faithfully. We need to have prepared hearts that will receive the seed and allow it to take root and grow through our daily obedience to it.

FAST FORWARD

Remember This . . .

KEY POINT

We bear spiritual fruit when we hear and heed God's Word.

KEY POINT

When we hear God's Word, we become responsible to obey.

Max Lucado: If the ratio in the story is significant, three-fourths of the world isn't listening to God's voice. Whether the cause be hard hearts, shallow lives, or anxious minds, 75 percent of us are missing the message.

It's not that we don't have ears; it's that we don't use them.[3]

The fruitfulness that resulted from the sowing of God's Word depended largely on the receptivity of the soil. We may make excuses when we do not grow spiritually, but the blame belongs to us. Are our hearts open to receive God's Word? Are we ready to allow God's Word to bear fruit in our lives?

> **Luke 8:16–18** "No one lights a lamp and hides it in a jar or puts it under a bed. Instead, he puts it on a stand, so that those who come in can see the light. For there is nothing hidden that will not be disclosed, and nothing concealed that will not be known or brought out into the open. Therefore consider carefully how you listen. Whoever has will be given more; whoever does not have, even what he thinks he has will be taken from him."

A Light's Place

When darkness falls we turn on a lamp so that we can see to move around. It would be ineffective, not to mention downright silly, to turn on a lamp and then cover it. Jesus used this parable to help people understand that he is the light of the world. When we receive his truth, we become lights to shine in a dark world. We are not to hide that light, but to place it on a stand so that others can be helped.

Further, the day is coming when God's light will shine on everything—even the secret thoughts and deeds that we have tried to hide. Our responsibility is to act in response to God's Word as we hear it. Then we do not need to fear exposure.

God will give more understanding to those who receive his initial message. Those who do not accept his initial message will forfeit their chance to hear more instruction.

JESUS' FAMILY

> **Luke 8:19–21** Now Jesus' mother and brothers came to see him, but they were not able to get near him because of the crowd. Someone told him, "Your mother and brothers are standing outside, wanting to see you."
>
> He replied, "My mother and brothers are those who hear God's word and put it into practice."

Family Redefined

In this passage Jesus seems to dismiss his birth family as if they're of little concern to him. But just because Luke doesn't record anything Jesus said or did that would have shown more concern, this does not necessarily mean Jesus refrained from doing such things. Also, we should notice that Jesus certainly doesn't insult or belittle his birth family. Rather, he applauds those who hear and obey God's Word. Here are just a few Scriptures that address how we should treat other people, including our families:

KEY POINT

Those who seek to obey God enjoy a close relationship with him.

- *"Honor your father and your mother, so that you may live long in the land the LORD your God is giving you"* (Exodus 20:12).

- *"Be devoted to one another in brotherly love. Honor one another above yourselves"* (Romans 12:10).

- *"So in everything, do to others what you would have them do to you, for this sums up the Law and the Prophets"* (Matthew 7:12).

Note Jesus' emphasis on putting God's Word into practice. More than once we've read that according to Jesus, it's not enough merely to hear God's Word. Doing no more than hearing God's Word is like building your house on sand, remember? The *NIV Bible Commentary* puts it this way: "Most Christians would probably say that we come closest to Jesus through prayer and reading the Bible. . . . Hours of praying and reading the Bible will not bring disobedient Christians as close to the Lord as doing his truth brings even the simplest believer."[4]

 MORE INFORMATION—It seems clear from other Gospel accounts that Jesus' relatives had not arrived to enjoy a family visit with him (see Matthew 12:24, 46–50; Mark 3:20–35). The Pharisees were accusing him of being empowered by **Beelzebub**. Opposition against him

Beelzebub: meaning "lord of flies" or "lord of filth"; Satan

was growing. Jesus and his disciples were so busy ministering they did not have time to eat. So Jesus' family was fearful that he was wearing himself out or losing his mind (see GWLC, page 217); that's why they came to see him.

A TEMPESTUOUS TRIP

> **Luke 8:22–25** One day Jesus said to his disciples, "Let's go over to the other side of the lake." So they got into a boat and set out. As they sailed, he fell asleep. A squall came down on the lake, so that the boat was being swamped, and they were in great danger.
>
> The disciples went and woke him, saying, "Master, Master, we're going to drown!"
>
> He got up and rebuked the wind and the raging waters; the storm subsided, and all was calm. "Where is your faith?" he asked his disciples.
>
> In fear and amazement they asked one another, "Who is this? He commands even the winds and the water, and they obey him."

Quashing The Squall

Real seamen don't get scared in a storm, right? Well, maybe they don't panic in a normal storm, but when a violent squall swooped down, whipping up waves that threatened to swamp the boat, Jesus' disciples were terrified. They woke Jesus, crying, *"We're going to drown!"*

Jesus rebuked the wind and water and immediately the waters were calm. In the Old Testament God is the one who controls the sea, first in the creation story (Genesis 1:2) and then in the flood story (Genesis 7), so imagine what the disciples were thinking when they watched this man put a stop to the thrashing waves. Did this guy have the power of God? Luke characterizes their reaction with the words *"fear and amazement."*

What Others are Saying:

William Barclay: He trusted his men; they were the fishermen of the lake and he was content to leave things to their skill and seamanship, and to relax. He trusted God; he knew that he was as near to God by sea as ever he was by land.[5]

Warren W. Wiersbe: The disciples failed this test of faith because they did not lay hold of his word that he was going to the other side. It has well been said that faith is not believing in spite of circumstances; it is obeying in spite of feelings and consequences. The disciples looked around and saw danger, and looked within and saw fear; but they failed to look up by faith and see God. Faith and Fear cannot dwell together in the same heart.[6]

DEMONS BEGONE

Luke 8:26–31 They sailed to the region of the Gerasenes, which is across the lake on the eastern shore of Galilee. When Jesus stepped ashore, he was met by a demon-possessed man from the town. For a long time this man had not worn clothes or lived in a house, but had lived in the tombs. When he saw Jesus, he cried out and fell at his feet, shouting at the top of his voice, "What do you want with me, Jesus, Son of the Most High God? I beg you, don't torture me!" For Jesus had commanded the evil spirit to come out of the man. Many times it had seized him, and though he was chained hand and foot and kept under guard, he had broken his chains and had been driven by the demon into solitary places.

Jesus asked him, "What is your name?"

"Legion," he replied, because many demons had gone into him. And they begged him repeatedly not to order them to go into the Abyss.

Troubles Worse Than Death

Jesus arrived at the eastern shore of the Sea of Galilee, a Gentile area, which shows Jesus' ministry extended beyond the Jews. Some scholars think the storm in the previous passage was a demonic attempt to prevent Jesus from liberating this man of the tombs.

As soon as Jesus stepped ashore, he was met with spine-chilling howls and shouts. They came from a man who was inhabited by demons. The demons gave him violent, superhuman strength. He was a danger to himself and the nearby community.

Jesus spoke with authority, commanding the demons to come

Legion: *unit in the Roman army of three thousand to six thousand men*

Abyss: *place where God will send all evil spirits*

☞ **GO TO:**

Revelation 20:1–3
(Abyss)

out of the man. Amazingly, the demons recognized who Jesus was and begged not to be tortured.

Jesus asked, *"What is your name?"* to which the answer was **Legion**. The many demons begged Jesus again and again not to order them to go into the **Abyss**.

MORE INFORMATION—Matthew's account tells of two demon-possessed men, but Mark and Luke single out the one who spoke. According to Matthew 8:28–34 the men were so violent that the locals did not dare come near them. Mark 5:1–20 explains that day and night the man cried out and cut himself with stones (see GWMK, pages 94–100).

> **Luke 8:32–33** A large herd of pigs was feeding there on the hillside. The demons begged Jesus to let them go into them, and he gave them permission. When the demons came out of the man, they went into the pigs, and the herd rushed down the steep bank into the lake and was drowned.

Jesus Grants Demons' Request

It seems strange that Jesus would do the demons a favor, but in this passage he does just that. It's difficult to say why, but we can be sure Jesus didn't allow the demons to reenter this man. At long last he was free.

Note the symmetry between the storm and the pigs running off a cliff into the sea. The waves were not able to swallow up Jesus and his disciples, but they were able to swallow up this legion of demons. How large was this herd of pigs? We learn from Mark there were some <u>two thousand</u> of them.

☞ **GO TO:**

Mark 5:13
(two thousand)

FACT OR FICTION

It was unfair to send evil spirits into the pigs because it resulted in their deaths. Fact or fiction? The destruction of the pigs seems unwarranted until we stop to consider the value of the man who had been inhabited by the evil spirits. This man had been made in the image of God but had been robbed of this image by the evil spirits. In healing the tortured, demented man, Jesus restored him to the level of dignity that God had planned for humanity. While all of creation is important to God, the Bible consistently places the needs of humans above those of animals.

R. C. Sproul: Man is the crowning act of God's creation, he is given dominion over the world. The pig is the servant of the man, not the man the servant of the pig. If these demons must inhabit some place . . . it is nothing less than a totally redemptive act on Christ's part to release the man from this infestation of the demonic world, even at the cost of a herd of swine.[7]

What Others are Saying:

Lawrence O. Richards: The New Testament portrays demons as living, malignant, conscious individual beings, subordinate to Satan and active in their allegiance to his kingdom. They will also share the fate of Satan, which is an eternity in what the Bible calls the "lake of fire."[8]

☞ **GO TO:**

Revelation 20:14–15;
Matthew 25:41
(lake of fire)

FAST FORWARD

Demons were real in Jesus' day. People were painfully aware of their destructive influence on men and women. When Jesus proved his authority over them, he proved that he was indeed the Son of God.

Demons are still active in our world today. Many people make light of them, as if they are imaginary creatures from fairy tales. Others seek them out in the occult. Still others fear them. What should be our attitude? First, we should not make light of demons, because they do exist, but we ought not be fearful of them or consumed with figuring out how they work. After all, Satan himself is only a fallen angel and under the complete control of our Father God. In other words, Jesus has as much authority over demons today as he demonstrated in the New Testament. In Deuteronomy 18:9–12 God told his people to stay away from occult practices, so we certainly should not seek out demons through involvement in occult practices.

KEY POINT

Jesus elevated the demon-tortured man as made in God's image when he commanded the demons to leave him.

Luke 8:34–37 When those tending the pigs saw what had happened, they ran off and reported this in the town and countryside, and the people went out to see what had happened. When they came to Jesus, they found the man from whom the demons had gone out, sitting at Jesus' feet, dressed and in his right mind; and they were afraid. Those who had seen it told the people how the demon-possessed man had been cured. Then all the people of the region of the Gerasenes asked Jesus to leave them, because they were overcome with fear. So he got into the boat and left.

The Ungrateful Crowd

Word spread fast about what Jesus had done. Naturally, a crowd gathered to investigate the fuss. What they found was this man, whom everyone knew was a dangerous lunatic, sitting at Jesus' feet, *"dressed and in his right mind."* Luke tells us their response was that of <u>fear</u>—not joy, not astonishment, but fear. This doesn't mean joy and astonishment were entirely absent, but it does mean Luke wanted his readers to understand the people were fearful.

☞ **GO TO:**

1 John 4:18 (fear)

Why were they afraid? Maybe they were scared Jesus would ruin more of their livestock, even though it wasn't really Jesus who did the ruining. All Jesus did was give the demons permission to enter the pigs. The demons were the ones who entered the pigs and then caused them to be drowned. Maybe the people were afraid of Jesus' power. If Jesus could make short order of the demons, what might he do to them?

Whereas the demons asked Jesus to let them enter the pigs so they could leave, the people asked Jesus to leave. And just as Jesus granted the demons' request, he granted the people theirs as well. *"He got into the boat and left."*

> **Luke 8:38–39** The man from whom the demons had gone out begged to go with him, but Jesus sent him away, saying, "Return home and tell how much God has done for you." So the man went away and told all over town how much Jesus had done for him.

Homework

As Jesus returned to the boat, the healed man begged to go with him. But Jesus sent him back home to tell everyone how much God had done for him. This is a reminder to us that God has different missions for different people. One mission is no less or more important than another.

CAN JESUS HELP JAIRUS?

> **Luke 8:40–44** Now when Jesus returned, a crowd welcomed him, for they were all expecting him. Then a man named Jairus, a ruler of the synagogue, came and fell at Jesus' feet, pleading with him to come to his house

> because his only daughter, a girl of about twelve, was dying.
>
> As Jesus was on his way, the crowds almost crushed him. And a woman was there who had been subject to bleeding for twelve years, but no one could heal her. She came up behind him and touched the edge of his cloak, and immediately her bleeding stopped.

A Miraculous Moment

The man who fell at Jesus' feet, Jairus, was a ruler of the synagogue. A prominent citizen, he was in charge of the synagogue building and all the services held there. Note that Jesus did not favor one group over another when it came to helping people. He ministered with equal compassion to both the community leaders and the riffraff, the rich and the poor, the sick and the healthy, the Jews and the Gentiles, the so-called sinners and the so-called righteous, men and women, adults and children.

Luke would not have said, *"the crowds almost crushed"* Jesus, unless he wanted to emphasize just how much attention Jesus was getting. People literally threw themselves at Jesus, begging him to heal them. They really believed that this carpenter from the north country had the power to make all their problems go away. And it's no wonder. One touch of his cloak and a woman's bleeding problem was completely and instantly healed.

According to levitical law, this woman's condition would have made her and anything she sat or lay upon <u>unclean</u>. She would not have been allowed to participate in community worship. People would have kept their distance from her. She wouldn't have been invited to parties, family gatherings, or public feasts. She must have been desperate to be in this crowd looking for Jesus, because Jewish law and custom said she should not have been there.

☞ **GO TO:**

Leviticus 15:25–33 (unclean)

> **Luke 8:45–48** "Who touched me?" Jesus asked.
>
> When they all denied it, Peter said, "Master, the people are crowding and pressing against you."
>
> But Jesus said, "Someone touched me; I know that power has gone out from me."
>
> Then the woman, seeing that she could not go unnoticed, came trembling and fell at his feet. In the presence of all the people, she told why she had touched him and how she had been instantly healed. Then he said to her, "Daughter, your faith has healed you. Go in peace."

The Human Healing Dispenser

Jesus stopped and asked, *"Who touched me?"*

The woman probably wanted to disappear into the crowd.

The disciples, not knowing what had happened, thought Jesus' question was the most ridiculous thing they had ever heard. Peter said, "Look, Jesus, I hate to point this out to you, but *lots* of people are touching you. In fact, if you don't keep moving, they're about to crush you!"

Not to be deterred, Jesus said he knew power had left him, and that's when the woman fell, trembling at his feet. Out came her sad history and her glad testimony that she had been healed the instant she touched his robe. Jesus knew power had gone out of him, but he may not have known *where* it went! In most of Jesus' healings, he first decided who to heal and then did it. In this case, God the Father may have given his healing power to someone without the Son knowing who the recipient was.

Everyone expected the unclean woman to contaminate Jesus because that was how things had worked for as long as anyone could remember. This time something different happened. Jesus purified the woman. And thus Jesus did a lot more than physically heal this woman. He gave her a new life; the hugs of friends and family, a dignified place in society, and community worship were just a few of the blessings that followed.

William Barclay: Almost everybody would have regarded the woman in the crowd as totally unimportant. For Jesus she was someone in need, and therefore he, as it were, withdrew from the crowd and gave himself to her. "God loves each one of us as if there was only one of us to love."[9]

> **Luke 8:49–50** While Jesus was still speaking, someone came from the house of Jairus, the synagogue ruler. "Your daughter is dead," he said. "Don't bother the teacher any more."
>
> Hearing this, Jesus said to Jairus, "Don't be afraid; just believe, and she will be healed."

No-Cost Healing

It looked as though healing the bleeding woman came with a cost. Because Jesus stopped to address her, he was delayed in seeing Jairus's daughter, who died in Jesus' absence. From the people's perspective, all was hopeless. Once death slammed the door on a human life, there was no opening it. They couldn't see the sense in asking Jesus to do something about it. Obviously, Jesus saw things differently.

It's interesting to step back and notice how different people responded to Jesus and his power in different ways. The centurion in Luke 7 believed Jesus could do a long-distance healing. The messenger from Jairus's house believed no such thing. Of course, the centurion's servant was only sick, while Jairus's daughter was dead, but the responses of these two men were fundamentally different. One was born of faith and hope; the other, of fear and despair.

Jairus must have been horrified to hear about his daughter's death, but Jesus immediately consoled him, saying, *"Don't be afraid; just believe. . . ."* People may have expected Jesus to tell Jairus to increase the speed with which they were going to his home. Instead Jesus told him to increase his faith.

KEY POINT

No situation is beyond the reach of Jesus' compassion and power.

> **Luke 8:51–52** When he arrived at the house of Jairus, he did not let anyone go in with him except Peter, John and James, and the child's father and mother. Meanwhile all the people were wailing and mourning for her. "Stop wailing," Jesus said. "She is not dead but asleep."

Jesus' View Of Death

At various points in Jesus' ministry he separated Peter, John, and James from the rest of the disciples, like when he led them up a mountain and was **transfigured**. Perhaps these three disciples were closer to Jesus than the other disciples, but if so, we know from other passages that these men were far from perfect. In other words, it was not because of their merit that Jesus was closer to them; it was because of Jesus' grace.

Why did Jesus choose to do this healing in relative privacy? No one is absolutely sure, but scholars have made a number of educated guesses. One is that Jesus was not interested in showboating. His concern was for the girl, not for becoming famous. Also, Jesus knew he had more work to do, so he may have been trying to avoid the extra attention that would have resulted from people calling him the Messiah.

Jesus and the three disciples entered the home to find friends and neighbors following the usual custom of loud mourning that

☞ **GO TO:**

Mark 9:2 (transfigured)

Mark 10:35–40; John 18:10–11 (far from perfect)

transfigured: *outwardly transformed with a spiritual brilliance*

preceded burial on the day of death. Jesus told the people who were present that the girl was not dead but asleep. As we shall see, only someone with the power of God would refer to this girl as asleep, because only God can raise the dead.

> **Luke 8:53–56** They laughed at him, knowing that she was dead. But he took her by the hand and said, "My child, get up!" Her spirit returned, and at once she stood up. Then Jesus told them to give her something to eat. Her parents were astonished, but he ordered them not to tell anyone what had happened.

The Day The Laughing Stopped

If you or I had been one of the bystanders, we may have laughed too. But imagine how quickly the laughing ceased when the little girl's *"spirit returned"* and she stood up.

The phrase, "spirit returned," means the girl was definitely dead before Jesus told her to get up. And this wasn't the only time Jesus brought a person back to life. You'll recall he did the same for the widow's son at Nain (Luke 7:11–15), and in John you can read about when he raised his dead friend, Lazarus, to life (see John 11:1–44 and GWJN, pages 145–156).

FAST FORWARD

Jesus instructed those present to give the revived girl something to eat. Scott Pinzon, author of Mark—God's Word for the Biblically-Inept, *points out that in so doing Jesus demonstrated that supernatural power and common sense go together. Sometimes we Christians use faith in God's power as an excuse for irresponsibility. We figure it's all in God's hands, so why should we try our best. But plain old common sense says otherwise. Of course we should ask God to bless the endeavors we undertake. But it's equally important for us to work hard at whatever task the Lord has set before us. To do less is to fail to use God's gifts— our minds and bodies—to his glory.*

PHYSICIAN'S PERSPECTIVE—Dr. Luke must have listened with interest as he gathered the information for this chapter. He shines the spotlight on Jesus' power to do what was beyond the knowledge and skills of the medical profession of his day—and is still beyond modern science. Jesus had power

- to command forces of nature,
- to dismiss the powers of demons,
- to heal "hopeless" physical conditions, and
- to raise the dead.

Larry Richards: There are no "hopeless cases" with the Lord. And there are no "hopeless people" either. The power of Jesus Christ is great enough to meet every need, and to transform any sinner as well.[10]

What Others are Saying:

Study Questions

1. What motivated women to assume a special role in Jesus' ministry?
2. In the parable of the farmer sowing seeds, what did the seed represent? The packed-down path? The rocky soil? The thorny soil? The good soil?
3. In what ways should Jesus' use of the image of a lamp impact you?
4. How can you be a member of Jesus' family?
5. What did the disciples learn when Jesus calmed the storm?
6. Suppose you are a reporter writing about the event of the woman being healed from twelve years of hemorrhaging. What do you say about the woman? What about Jesus?
7. Though Jesus seemed to do too little too late for Jairus's daughter, how did Jesus prove his power?

CHAPTER WRAP-UP

- Women who had received Jesus' healing were especially devoted to him. They traveled with his group, sharing their personal finances to provide practical assistance to him. (Luke 18:1–3)

- Jesus told a parable in which the seed was the Word of God. The packed-down path represented people with hard hearts who are not open to the truth. The rocky soil represented those who accept God's message but reject it when they are tested. The thorny soil represented hearers who give more attention to this life than to eternal values. The good soil represented people who receive and obey God's Word. (Luke 8:4–15)

- Jesus is the light of the world. As believers we are like lamps, shining in a dark world. Jesus' light also shines within us, exposing our secret thoughts and actions. If we try to conceal them instead of confessing and forsaking them, He will expose them. We are responsible to act on the light we receive. (Luke 8:16–18)

- We become a close member of Jesus' family when we hear and heed God's Word. (Luke 8:19–21)

- Jesus wanted his disciples to trust him even when everything was in such chaos that death seemed certain. When Jesus demonstrated his authority to calm a tempest, they realized that Jesus was Lord of creation. (Luke 8:22–31)

- Jesus had authority to command demons to leave the man they had controlled. Though they could empower the man to break chains intended to restrain him, they had no power to resist Jesus. (Luke 8:26–39)

- A woman who had a twelve-year hemorrhage had faith that if she only touched Jesus' garment, she would be healed. Jairus, a ruler of the synagogue, appealed to Jesus for the healing of his dying daughter. Though she died before Jesus arrived at the home, Jesus raised her to life again. (Luke 8:43–56)

LUKE 9: WHO JESUS IS

Let's Get Started

In this chapter Luke combines significant events. First, he relates how Jesus sent out the Twelve to do the work they would be commissioned to do after Jesus left the earth. The twelve disciples would become the world's first Christian missionaries. Their mission would be to move throughout the land and preach the Gospel. Luke then gives his account of Jesus feeding the five thousand, followed by Peter's amazing confession of Christ, the Transfiguration, and Jesus' teaching on God's kingdom. Want to find out how God's views on greatness, tolerance, and priorities are unique? Keep reading.

ON THE FRONT LINE

> **Luke 9:1–6** When Jesus had called the Twelve together, he gave them power and authority to drive out all demons and to cure diseases, and he sent them out to preach the kingdom of God and to heal the sick. He told them: "Take nothing for the journey—no staff, no bag, no bread, no money, no extra tunic. Whatever house you enter, stay there until you leave that town. If people do not welcome you, shake the dust off your feet when you leave their town, as a testimony against them." So they set out and went from village to village, preaching the gospel and healing people everywhere.

On Assignment

Up until the above passage the disciples watched and learned from Jesus. Now Jesus sent them out to do some ministering of their own. He gave them both power and **authority**, perhaps to distinguish them from <u>other people</u> at the time who had power to do supernatural acts but were without God-given authority. Also note that the disciples were not given titles; they were given tasks.

Jesus' instructions would have forced the disciples to trust God for food and lodging. They did not have the option of relying on their own protection or comfort. They were to stay in one home in each village, even if another home afforded better accommodations. This, many scholars argue, was a way of being polite. Hosts would have felt snubbed if the disciples moved from one house to another.

If a particular place rejected the disciples, they were to knock the dirt off their feet as they left and move on. Why? This act of knocking dirt off the feet was something Jews did as they left Gentile territory and entered Jewish territory. By knocking dirt off their feet the disciples made an outward declaration that the house they left was **heathen**.

Matthew Henry: The communicating of Christ's power to those who were sent forth in his name was an *amazing* and *convincing* proof of his being the Messiah. That he could not only work miracles *himself,* but empower others to work miracles too, spread his fame more than anything.[1]

R. Kent Hughes: The reason Jesus ordered them to travel light was to avoid looking like other false missionaries in the ancient world who made personal profit from their preaching.[2]

> **Luke 9:7–9** Now Herod the tetrarch heard about all that was going on. And he was perplexed, because some were saying that John had been raised from the dead, others that Elijah had appeared, and still others that one of the prophets of long ago had come back to life. But Herod said, "I beheaded John. Who, then, is this I hear such things about?" And he tried to see him.

---

authority: the right to perform a task

☞ **GO TO:**

Acts 13:6–10; 19:13 (other people)

KEY POINT

When following Christ's orders, we'll have what we need to meet the challenges that face us.

heathen: not of God

What Others are Saying:

No Peace In The Palace

Jesus was so popular that Jerusalem became a hotbed of speculation. News of his activities even reached **Herod Antipas** in the palace. Excitement mounted as rumors spread that Jesus was actually John the Baptist raised from the dead. Other rumors were that Jesus was the prophet Elijah or another resurrected Old Testament prophet.

Herod's question, "Who is this?" is one the disciples asked after Jesus calmed the storm in 8:25 and one that Jesus will pick up in 9:18–20. Luke spotlights the question because he knows how important its answer is.

Herod Antipas: Herod the Great's son; ruler of Galilee during Jesus' ministry

 MORE INFORMATION—Luke does not include information about the execution of John the Baptist—facts that Matthew (14:3–12) and Mark (6:17–29) provide (see also GWLC, pages 253–254). Herod had arrested John and put him in prison because John had sternly rebuked him for marrying Herodias, his brother's wife. Herod would have killed him immediately, but did not dare because of John's popularity with the people. However, a year and a half later, Herod celebrated his birthday with a lavish party for the elite. As part of the entertainment, the daughter of Herodias danced and so pleased Herod that he rashly promised to give her anything she wanted. After she consulted with her mother, she presented her request: the head of John the Baptist.

Herod was in a bind. He had sworn by oath to give her what she asked and did not want to be made a fool in front of his guests. So he gave the order for John's execution.

JESUS FEEDS FIVE THOUSAND

Luke 9:10–17 When the apostles returned, they reported to Jesus what they had done. Then he took them with him and they withdrew by themselves to a town called Bethsaida, but the crowds learned about it and followed him. He welcomed them and spoke to them about the kingdom of God, and healed those who needed healing.

Late in the afternoon the Twelve came to him and said, "Send the crowd away so they can go to the surrounding villages and countryside and find food and lodging, because we are in a remote place here."

> He replied, "You give them something to eat."
>
> They answered, "We have only five loaves of bread and two fish—unless we go and buy food for all this crowd." (About five thousand men were there.)
>
> But he said to his disciples, "Have them sit down in groups of about fifty each." The disciples did so, and everybody sat down. Taking the five loaves and the two fish and looking up to heaven, he gave thanks and broke them. Then he gave them to the disciples to set before the people. They all ate and were satisfied, and the disciples picked up twelve basketfuls of broken pieces that were left over.

Soul Food

The Twelve must have been aglow as they reported on their tour. Although they had a great time, they were exhausted. They hoped to get away from the crowds to rest and reflect. When the crowds came, Jesus did not hang up a "Do not disturb" sign. He welcomed them, teaching them *"about the kingdom of God"* and healing those who needed his touch.

In the late afternoon the Twelve suggested that it was time to send the people away to find food and lodging. They were astonished when Jesus challenged *them* to feed their uninvited guests. How could they? There were five thousand men there, plus women and children. And food? They had only five loaves of bread and two fish.

Jesus instructed the Twelve to seat the people in orderly groups. He took the little bit of available food, gave thanks for it, and began to hand it to the disciples to serve the hungry people. Again and again the food was multiplied, so that all the people ate until they were satisfied. Luke is careful to say that when the disciples picked up the leftovers, they filled twelve baskets.

 MORE INFORMATION—This is the only miracle recorded in all four Gospels, which testifies to its importance. John (6:4–13) points out that the five loaves and two fish came from a boy. The loaves were not loaves of bread as we think of them, but more like buns or flat pitas. Once their stomachs were filled, the crowd wanted to take Jesus by force and make him king. The hope of more free meals would get their vote any day! (You can read the other accounts in Matthew 14:15–21 and Mark 6:35–44.)

The main point of the feeding of five thousand is the importance of sharing our resources with others. Fact or fiction? While God does want us to <u>share</u> our resources, the point of Jesus' miracle was to help his disciples recognize who Jesus was and to learn that he was able to take care of everyone's needs.

PETER'S WORDS OF WISDOM

☞ **GO TO:**

Romans 12:13; James 2:14–19 (share)

> **Luke 9:18–20** Jesus moved on to the area of Caesarea Philippi. Once when he was praying in private and his disciples were with him, he asked them, "Who do the crowds say I am?"
>
> They replied, "Some say John the Baptist; others say Elijah; and still others, that one of the prophets of long ago has come back to life."
>
> "But what about you?" he asked. "Who do you say I am?"
>
> Peter answered, "The Christ of God."

Peter's Confession

Jesus and the disciples moved north from Bethsaida to Caesarea Philippi (see map in appendix A), named after Augustus Caesar and the tetrarch, Herod Philip 1. Here we have the privilege of "listening in" on one of Jesus' private discussions with his disciples. Earlier in this chapter we heard Herod ask, *"Who is this?"* in reference to Jesus. Now we hear Jesus ask, *"Who do the crowds say I am?"*

The disciples related to Jesus some of the rumors that were going around—the same rumors Herod heard. Some believed he was John the Baptist, others thought he was Elijah, and still others thought he was an Old Testament prophet.

Jesus is purposefully making a distinction between the crowds and the disciples, because his question to the latter begins with "But." It's as if Jesus is anticipating a different response from the disciples than he would expect from the crowds. This makes sense when you consider that the disciples were closer to Jesus than the crowds. The disciples spent private time with Jesus. He explained at least some of his parables to them, and they obeyed orders from Jesus.

Jesus' question to the disciples is one of the most profound in all of Scripture. *"But what about you?"* he asked. *"Who do you say I am?"* As if on cue, Peter answers by saying, *"The Christ of God."*

"Christ" comes from the Greek word that referred to the Messiah; "of God" emphasizes Jesus' divinity.

 MORE INFORMATION—Matthew 16:13–20 and Mark 8:27–30 provide additional information to Peter's identification of Jesus as the Christ. Jesus confirmed that Peter's response was not just off the top of his head, but was an insight that had been revealed by Jesus' Father in heaven. Jesus also added that he would build his church on Peter's correct understanding of who Jesus was.

> **Luke 9:21–22** Jesus strictly warned them not to tell this to anyone. And he said, "The Son of Man must suffer many things and be rejected by the elders, chief priests and teachers of the law, and he must be killed and on the third day be raised to life."

Mum's The Word

Jesus told the disciples to button up about his being the Messiah. This is probably because he didn't want to start an uprising. The Jews expected the Messiah to start a revolution and lead them into power, but Jesus had no such agenda. Also, the people didn't think the Messiah should declare himself the Messiah. They believed the real Messiah would first *do the acts* of Messiah, and then others would proclaim him such. Incidentally, this is why Jesus lists in his message to John the Baptist what he has done instead of flatly declaring himself the Messiah.

Jesus then makes his first prediction within Luke's Gospel that he will be persecuted and killed and raised to life on the third day.

> **Luke 9:23–27** Then he said to them all: "If anyone would come after me, he must deny himself and take up his cross daily and follow me. For whoever wants to save his life will lose it, but whoever loses his life for me will save it. What good is it for a man to gain the whole world, and yet lose or forfeit his very self? If anyone is ashamed of me and my words, the Son of Man will be ashamed of him when he comes in his glory and in the glory of the Father and of the holy angels. I tell you the truth, some who are standing here will not taste death before they see the kingdom of God."

Count The Cost

This passage begins with *"then he said to them all."* It is unclear whether "all" refers to all the disciples or the disciples plus a crowd of observers. In any case, if anybody had ideas of being swept into Camelot with Jesus as reigning king, he or she needed a wake-up call. Jesus spelled out clearly the cost of committing to him. What he said might be restated in this way: "Do you want to follow me? Don't look for recognition and praise. Instead, choose to deny yourself. Expect self-sacrifice and pain. Do you want to hang on to your life? You'll lose it! But if you lose your life for me, you'll save it. Do you want to gain the whole world? Aim for that and you'll lose your very self. Are you ashamed of me and my word? I'll be ashamed of you when I come in glory."

Jesus ended his teaching by saying that some of the people listening to him would *"see the kingdom of God"* before dying. Scholars and theologians aren't exactly sure what Jesus meant by this, but he may have been referring to the **Transfiguration**, which is what Luke recounts next.

Transfiguration: supernatural change of appearance in which Jesus was glorified

---

Jack Hayford: Jesus explains the paradox of discipleship. To lose life is to find it; to die is to live. To deny oneself is not to assume some false, external asceticism, but to put the interests of the kingdom first and foremost in one's life. To take up the cross does not mean to endure some irritating burden, but to renounce self-centered ambitions. Such sacrifice results in eternal life and the fullest experience of kingdom life now.[3]

> **What Others are Saying:**

Jesus did not promise to award his disciples with the trappings of success that our society values today. Christ has special rewards for those who deny themselves, are willing to lose their lives in humble service for others, and set aside selfish ambition for the sake of Christ. The rewards? A clearer revelation of himself, a quiet undercurrent of joy even in times of struggles and difficulties, and a keen sense of his nearness.

Something to Ponder

THE TRANSFIGURATION

> **Luke 9:28–33** About eight days after Jesus said this, he took Peter, John and James with him and went up onto a mountain to pray. As he was praying, the appearance of his face changed, and his clothes became as bright as a flash of lightning. Two men, Moses and

> Elijah, appeared in glorious splendor, talking with Jesus. They spoke about his departure, which he was about to bring to fulfillment at Jerusalem. Peter and his companions were very sleepy, but when they became fully awake, they saw his glory and the two men standing with him. As the men were leaving Jesus, Peter said to him, "Master, it is good for us to be here. Let us put up three shelters—one for you, one for Moses and one for Elijah." (He did not know what he was saying.)

The Ultimate In Mountaintop Experiences

Jesus took Peter, James, and John up onto a mountain, but which mountain? Bible scholars are not in agreement. Some think it was Mt. Hermon (see GWLC2, pages 10–11), but others think it was Mount Tabor or Mount Meron.

After their long climb Jesus' friends grew drowsy in the cool night air while he talked with his Father. Suddenly they were aroused by a spectacular sight. In a simultaneous flash they saw the past and the future fused in one scene. They saw Jesus' face changed with an out-of-this-world glow and his clothes became dazzling bright. This was a preview of how Jesus will look in heaven's <u>glory</u>. Standing with Jesus were men from the past— Moses, who had been dead nearly 1,500 years (see GWMB, pages 71–90), and Elijah, who had been swept from earth in a whirlwind some eight centuries before (see GWMB, pages 130–140). They were talking with Jesus about his coming death.

The disciples were witnesses to what is called the Transfiguration and were in awe when they realized what they had seen. As Moses and Elijah left, Peter came up with what he considered a bright idea. In his excitement and enthusiasm he didn't sense how far off base he was. As Peter saw it, this was a majestic moment that should be honored. Why not build three memorials—one for Jesus, one for Moses, and one for Elijah?

☞ **GO TO:**

Revelation 1:12–18 (glory)

KEY POINT

We cannot please God apart from listening to his Son and obeying him.

> **Luke 9:34–36** While he was speaking, a cloud appeared and enveloped them, and they were afraid as they entered the cloud. A voice came from the cloud, saying, "This is my Son, whom I have chosen; listen to him." When the voice had spoken, they found that Jesus was alone. The disciples kept this to themselves, and told no one at that time what they had seen.

A Voice From The Cloud

The God of heaven and earth had spoken from the cloud. What would be the appropriate response? Silence. What the disciples had seen and heard was so amazing it was beyond words. They didn't know what to make of what happened until much later.

What made the Transfiguration an unforgettable experience?

- The three disciples were <u>eyewitnesses</u> to Jesus' glory as the Son of God.
- They recognized intuitively that <u>Moses</u> and <u>Elijah</u> came to talk about Jesus' <u>departure</u> (his death, resurrection, and return to heaven).
- They saw that glory lay ahead of suffering and death.
- They heard God's voice saying they should heed Jesus' teaching and follow him as disciples.

A Jew's View of Clouds

Clouds stirred up a number of thoughts and memories in the minds of Jews back then. Here is a list of what clouds meant to first-century Jews:

- After the exodus from Egypt God led the Jews through the desert with a "pillar of cloud" (Exodus 13:21–22; 16:10; 24:16; 40:34–38).
- Clouds were linked with the future coming of the "**Son of Man**" (Daniel 7:13 and GWDN, page 192).
- Clouds were associated with the Second Coming of the Messiah (Isaiah 4:5).
- Most importantly, clouds represented the presence of God (Exodus 19:16).[4]

☞ **GO TO:**

John 1:14; 2 Peter 1:16–19 (eyewitnesses)

Deuteronomy 18:15 (Moses)

Malachi 4:5 (Elijah)

John 16:28 (departure)

Son of Man: how Daniel described the person he saw coming from heaven with divine power at the end of the world

JESUS HEALS A BOY

Luke 9:37–43a The next day, when they came down from the mountain, a large crowd met him. A man in the crowd called out, "Teacher, I beg you to look at my son, for he is my only child. A spirit seizes him and he suddenly screams; it throws him into convulsions so that he foams at the mouth. It scarcely ever leaves him and is destroying him. I begged your disciples to drive it out, but they could not."

> "O unbelieving and perverse generation," Jesus replied, "how long shall I stay with you and put up with you? Bring your son here."
>
> Even while the boy was coming, the demon threw him to the ground in a convulsion. But Jesus rebuked the evil spirit, healed the boy and gave him back to his father. And they were all amazed at the greatness of God.

Downhill . . . In More Ways Than One

consternation: dismay and confusion

☞ **GO TO:**

Luke 9:1, 6
   (power and authority)

Matthew 17:19–20
   (faith)

Jesus and his three disciples came down from the mountain of transfiguration and found a scene of **consternation**. A father was wringing his hands in despair. He asked the disciples to heal his son, who was being tormented by an evil spirit. But they couldn't.

Jesus was disappointed. He had given them power and authority to heal, and they had some success. Their failure was not because they lacked power but because they lacked faith. When Jesus healed the boy and gave him back to his father, all the people were amazed at God's greatness.

 PHYSICIAN'S PERSPECTIVE—Dr. Luke's heart must have been tugged as he heard the report of the distressed father and his son who was suffering from an evil spirit. The boy's seizures often caused him to fall into the fire or into the water (Matthew 17:15). The boy would foam at the mouth, gnash his teeth, and become rigid (Mark 9:18). According to the father, the spirit was destroying his son by its persistent activity.

Even as the father brought his son to Jesus, the demon caused another violent convulsion. Jesus rebuked the evil spirit and handed the boy back to his father completely healed. Certainly if Luke had been on the scene he would have joined all who were amazed at the greatness of God!

> **Luke 9:43b–45** While everyone was marveling at all that Jesus did, he said to his disciples, "Listen carefully to what I am about to tell you: The Son of Man is going to be betrayed into the hands of men." But they did not understand what this meant. It was hidden from them, so that they did not grasp it, and they were afraid to ask him about it.

Tough Times Are Coming

As usual, Jesus' attitude was very different from that of everyone around him. While everyone else was celebrating, Jesus warned his disciples that he would soon be betrayed into the hands of his enemies. They did not understand what he was saying partly because it was kept from them and partly because they were afraid to ask Jesus what he meant.

Luke emphasized their fear. Why were they afraid? Maybe they were afraid because they had just seen Jesus use the power of God to cast out yet another demon (this is Jesus' third demon exorcism in Luke). Maybe they were afraid because they couldn't bear the thought of people doing harm to him. Whatever the reason, they were too afraid to ask. So, Luke implied, they missed an opportunity to find out more about what was in store for Jesus and what was in store for them.

PUZZLING PARADOXES

Luke 9:46–50 An argument started among the disciples as to which of them would be the greatest. Jesus, knowing their thoughts, took a little child and had him stand beside him. Then he said to them, "Whoever welcomes this little child in my name welcomes me; and whoever welcomes me welcomes the one who sent me. For he who is least among you all—he is the greatest."

"Master," said John, "we saw a man driving out demons in your name and we tried to stop him, because he is not one of us."

"Do not stop him," Jesus said, "for whoever is not against you is for you."

Diverting Agendas

By this point in Luke's account the disciples believed Jesus was the Messiah, so they assumed he would do what the Messiah was supposed to do—defeat the Jews' oppressors and lead God's people into power. But which individuals would be at the helm, the disciples wondered. Who would be the greatest, the highest in rank? This was the subject of the disciples' argument—an argument hardly worth having when moments earlier Jesus predicted his own betrayal. Obviously the disciples' focus was very different from Jesus' focus.

KEY POINT

Pride and envy lead to a breakdown in relationships with others and with Christ.

Earlier in Luke's Gospel the disciples dropped their nets to follow Jesus, asked him questions, and marveled at his miracles. But as Luke progresses we read about the disciples being afraid of Jesus, lacking the faith necessary to heal people, and getting into foolish arguments born of pride and ambition. As the climax of Jesus' ministry grew closer and closer, the disciples seemed to divert farther and farther from his agenda.

While the disciples bickered about who would be Jesus' right-hand man, Jesus quietly brought a child to his side. Jesus was saying, "You want to know who my right-hand man will be? I pick this child."

What a shock! In that culture children had no social status whatsoever, yet here one was, standing right beside the Messiah. Jesus' profound action was followed by profound words. "Stop worrying so much about yourselves and your precious positions," he might be paraphrased as saying. "Follow my example. Concern yourselves with the neglected and the rejected. This is how to have God within you."

John reported that when they had seen a man driving out demons in Jesus' name, they tried to stop him, thinking that they were earning Jesus' favor. But Jesus counseled him that if a person was not an enemy, they should treat him as a friend.

What Others are Saying:

☞ **GO TO:**

Matthew 17:24–27
(temple tax)

FACT OR FICTION

Warren W. Wiersbe: Perhaps this debate started because of envy (three of the disciples had been with Jesus on the mount), or because of pride (the other nine had failed to cast out the demon). Also, just before this, Jesus had paid Peter's temple tax for him; and this may have aroused some envy.[5]

If you want to be great, build your credentials in education, achievements, popularity, and personal finance. Fact or fiction? Since the early chapters of Genesis, Scripture records human competition and a drive to come out on top and to be recognized as the greatest. Jesus used a child to teach that how we relate to children—and others who need our care and protection—will reveal how we relate to him. Do we want to be great by his measurement? Then we need to stoop to help those for whom Jesus has compassion.

> **Luke 9:51–56** As the time approached for him to be taken up to heaven, Jesus resolutely set out for Jerusalem. And he sent messengers on ahead, who went into a Samaritan village to get things ready for him; but the people there did not welcome him, because he was heading for Jerusalem. When the disciples James and John saw this, they asked, "Lord, do you want us to call fire down from heaven to destroy them?" But Jesus turned and rebuked them, and they went to another village.

How To Handle Rejection

There was no Red Roof Inn down the road, so Jesus sent messengers ahead to a Samaritan village to announce his arrival. This was an amazing move, for Jews and Samaritans avoided one another. Jesus was offering to break down the prejudice and accept their offer of hospitality. But the Samaritans refused to welcome him. They knew he was going to Jerusalem, "which they refused to acknowledge as a valid center of worship."[6] James and John were furious and wanted to pray for fire to descend from heaven and destroy the whole village. But Jesus corrected their attitude and moved on to another village.

Darrell L. Bock: The journey starts with Jesus' expanding his ministry into Samaritan territory. To Jews, this ethnic group was traitors, a collection of half-breeds. The name came from the capital of the separatist northern kingdom of Israel, Samaria, in a rule founded by Omri. The Samaritans intermarried with the pagan nations and were thus seen as unfaithful to the nation of Israel.[7]

What Others are Saying:

☞ **GO TO:**

1 Kings 16:21–24
(Omri)

> **Luke 9:57–62** As they were walking along the road, a man said to him, "I will follow you wherever you go."
>
> Jesus replied, "Foxes have holes and birds of the air have nests, but the Son of Man has no place to lay his head."
>
> He said to another man, "Follow me."
>
> But the man replied, "Lord, first let me go and bury my father."
>
> Jesus said to him, "Let the dead bury their own dead, but you go and proclaim the kingdom of God."

> Still another said, "I will follow you, Lord; but first let me go back and say good-by to my family."
>
> Jesus replied, "No one who puts his hand to the plow and looks back is fit for service in the kingdom of God."

The Cost Of Discipleship

Three men could have followed Jesus but did not. One wanted the security of a home. Another wanted to bury his father, and the third man had a divided heart and put his family ahead of Jesus.

At first glance Jesus appears to be harsh and unfeeling. Caring for and loving our families is not wrong. But Jesus wanted to emphasize the radical requirements involved in following him. Those who say they will follow Jesus wherever he leads rarely understand the cost of doing so. They must be fully committed to him, not trying to live with one foot in both worlds as the third man was asking to do.

Some scholars disagree about whether the second man's father was dead. If the father was dead, scholars believe the man would not have been talking with Jesus. The man would have been home, consumed with duties and details of the funeral and the estate. These scholars believe the man was asking to stay home and care for his aged father until he died. This could have taken years, and Jesus was saying that working for him required immediate service.

Other scholars believe the man's father was literally dead. If so, Jesus' response was radical. To Jews the duties involved in a burial had a greater urgency than studying the law, going to the Temple, killing a Passover sacrifice, or having a child circumcised. Jesus was saying that the spiritual duties of his servants were more important than all these things—even burying the dead.

As a final illustration Jesus spoke of a farmer. Looking back is clearly not the way to plow a field. The rows get crooked if a farmer doesn't watch where he's going. Discipleship demands immediate and wholehearted commitment to Jesus Christ.

Jesus calls us to love him so deeply that we put responding to him ahead of everything else. There's no excuse for procrastination when Jesus calls us to follow him.

KEY POINT

Jesus wants our wholehearted commitment to him—with no turning back.

Remember This . . .

Jerry White: Ordinary people who make simple, spiritual commitments under the lordship of Jesus Christ make an extraordinary impact on their world. Education, gifts, and abilities do not make the difference. Commitment does.[8]

What Others are Saying:

Study Questions

1. What did the Twelve learn from their preaching tour?
2. Peter identified Jesus as the Christ of God. How did he come to this insight? Why did Jesus tell his disciples not to talk about it?
3. Why did Jesus spell out the standards of being his disciple? In terms of living today, how do his four points apply?
4. What did the Transfiguration reveal about Jesus?
5. What did Jesus say is the way to greatness?

CHAPTER WRAP-UP

- Jesus gave the Twelve power and authority to go out preaching and healing. News of Jesus' ministry spread even to Herod's palace. (Luke 9:1–9)

- Jesus fed five thousand by multiplying a boy's lunch, showing the disciples firsthand that he was able to supply resources for them to serve others. (Luke 9:10–17)

- Jesus asked his disciples who they thought he was. Peter answered that Jesus was the Christ of God. Jesus warned his disciples not to share this truth, because he had yet to suffer rejection, death, and resurrection. He warned his disciples that they too would face rejection and persecution. (Luke 9:18–27)

- Jesus took Peter, James, and John with him to a mountain. As Jesus prayed he was changed so that his true glory shone brightly. Moses and Elijah appeared with him. (Luke 9:28–36)

- A distressed father brought his son to Jesus' disciples for healing, but they couldn't cast out the evil spirit. Jesus expressed his disappointment with the unbelieving disciples, and then healed the boy. (Luke 9:37–45)

- Jesus explained several paradoxes of his kingdom to his disciples. He who wants to be the greatest should be the servant of all. Christ's followers reach out to everyone and don't take revenge on those who don't welcome them. He who wants to save his life must first be willing to lose it. (Luke 9:46–62)

LUKE 10: SIGNIFICANT DECISIONS

CHAPTER HIGHLIGHTS

- The Seventy-Two
- Expert Lawyer Quiz
- Best Buds

Let's Get Started

Jesus had been ministering in Galilee and had sent the Twelve out to represent him in surrounding areas. Now he turned his attention to Judea and sent seventy-two disciples ahead to prepare the area for his coming. He grieved over the cities that heard the good news but rejected it. The seventy-two were elated over the success of their mission, but Jesus expressed joy at the salvation of individuals who truly believed in him.

An expert in the Old Testament tested Jesus by asking what he needed to do to inherit eternal life. Jesus answered by telling a story that illustrated the deepest and fullest meaning of the law—loving as our neighbor anyone who is in need.

Later, in the home of Mary and Martha, Jesus lovingly told Martha that listening to him pleased him more than laboring for him to the point of exasperation.

THE SEVENTY-TWO

Luke 10:1–4 After this the Lord appointed seventy-two others and sent them two by two ahead of him to every town and place where he was about to go. He told them, "The harvest is plentiful, but the workers are few. Ask the Lord of the harvest, therefore, to send out workers into his harvest field. Go! I am sending you out like lambs among wolves. Do not take a purse or bag or sandals; and do not greet anyone on the road."

On A Mission

Jesus' ministry in Galilee was complete. He now prepared to go to Judea to the south and eventually to Jerusalem where he would offer himself as sacrifice for the sins of the world. In the meantime, there was much to do, and time was short.

He selected seventy-two of his followers (not the Twelve) and sent them out in pairs to prepare the people for his coming. They were to go with a clear sense of mission, not only to preach but also to pray earnestly that those who listened to them would join them as workers in the spiritual harvest. They were to go with a sense of urgency, knowing they would not be welcomed by everyone.

What Others are Saying:

Leon Morris: *Lambs in the midst of wolves* are in no enviable situation. The simile points both to danger and to helplessness. God's servants are always in some sense at the mercy of the world, and in their own strength they cannot cope with the situation in which they find themselves. They must look to God.[1]

> **Luke 10:5–12** "When you enter a house, first say, 'Peace to this house.' If a man of peace is there, your peace will rest on him; if not, it will return to you. Stay in that house, eating and drinking whatever they give you, for the worker deserves his wages. Do not move around from house to house.
>
> "When you enter a town and are welcomed, eat what is set before you. Heal the sick who are there and tell them, 'The kingdom of God is near you.' But when you enter a town and are not welcomed, go into its streets and say, 'Even the dust of your town that sticks to our feet we wipe off against you. Yet be sure of this: The kingdom of God is near.' I tell you, it will be more bearable on that day for Sodom than for that town."

Keep The Focus

Jesus gave specific instructions to the seventy-two. Their to-do list was similar to the instructions Jesus gave the Twelve when he sent them out. This was no pleasure excursion. There must be no **lollygagging**! They were to enter a town, find a house that would welcome them, and then get down to the business of announcing the **kingdom of God** and healing the sick. No theatrics, no

lollygagging: wasting time in idle socializing

kingdom of God: place where God reigns as King

fundraising, no making themselves into stars. If a town would not welcome them and their message, they were to leave with a solemn warning that by refusing their message they were inviting severe judgment.

> **Luke 10:13–16** "Woe to you, Korazin! Woe to you, Bethsaida! For if the miracles that were performed in you had been performed in Tyre and Sidon, they would have repented long ago, sitting in sackcloth and ashes. But it will be more bearable for Tyre and Sidon at the judgment than for you. And you, Capernaum, will you be lifted up to the skies? No, you will go down to the depths.
>
> "He who listens to you listens to me; he who rejects you rejects me; but he who rejects me rejects him who sent me."

Nothing To Joke About

Jesus spoke of Korazin and Bethsaida, towns on the north side of the Sea of Galilee where he had ministered earlier (see map in appendix A). He also mentioned Capernaum, his adopted home-town. People in those towns who refused his message were facing severe judgment—even more severe than the judgment awaiting those in the pagan cities of Tyre, Sidon, and <u>Sodom</u>, who had never heard the message of God's kingdom nor seen his miracles of compassion.

☞ **GO TO:**

Genesis 19:24–29 (Sodom)

Sackcloth was a coarse material that was worn as a sign of sorrow. Ashes were a symbol of repentance. Jesus said even the residents of pagan towns would have had enough sense to repent and be sorry for their sins if they had heard Jesus' message. Things didn't look good for these Jewish towns.

The seventy-two were authorized representatives so that those who listened to their message were in reality listening to Jesus, and those who rejected their message were in reality rejecting Jesus and the Father who had sent him.

 MORE INFORMATION—Matthew includes Jesus' condemnation of the three towns in Galilee that had refused his message (Matthew 11:20–30). Then Matthew adds Jesus' comforting invitation to all who are hesitant to respond to his message. "Come," he said to the weary and burdened. "Don't be afraid to identify with and obey me. If you learn my ways, I will give rest to your soul."

> **Luke 10:17–20** The seventy-two returned with joy and said, "Lord, even the demons submit to us in your name."
>
> He replied, "I saw Satan fall like lightning from heaven. I have given you authority to trample on snakes and scorpions and to overcome all the power of the enemy; nothing will harm you. However, do not rejoice that the spirits submit to you, but rejoice that your names are written in heaven."

Satan's Bungee Jump Without A Cord

The seventy-two were elated as they returned from their short-term mission. They were excited to report that even demons were subject to their authoritative commands! By simply speaking they were able to do things that stumped the medical profession.

Jesus acknowledged that Satan's power had been broken at his command and that Satan had already been defeated. He had taken a giant bungee jump without a cord. But Jesus cautioned the seventy-two to rejoice more in their personal relationship with God than in their power and authority. We should be most joyful about our salvation.

We may measure our success as Christ's followers by the good things we can achieve. Jesus, however, reminds us that our joy should not lie in what we do but in what He has done for us in providing the way for our names to be recorded in heaven in the Lamb's Book of Life (see GWRV, page 48).

Remember This . . .

☞ **GO TO:**

Revelation 3:5; 21:27 (Lamb's Book of Life)

KEY POINT

Our personal relationship with God should be the source of our joy.

> **Luke 10:21–24** At that time Jesus, full of joy through the Holy Spirit, said, "I praise you, Father, Lord of heaven and earth, because you have hidden these things from the wise and learned, and revealed them to little children. Yes, Father, for this was your good pleasure.
>
> "All things have been committed to me by my Father. No one knows who the Son is except the Father, and no one knows who the Father is except the Son and those to whom the Son chooses to reveal him."
>
> Then he turned to his disciples and said privately, "Blessed are the eyes that see what you see. For I tell you that many prophets and kings wanted to see what you see but did not see it, and to hear what you hear but did not hear it."

Time Out For Praise

Jesus was so thrilled he lifted his heart in spontaneous praise to his Father. His gang was getting it! Though the intellectual elite refused his message and rejected him, the ordinary, unschooled "nobodies" who made up his disciples were accepting the truth as innocently as little children. They were receiving the truth as God revealed it to them, while that truth was hidden from the hearts and minds of the "wise."

Turning to his disciples, he said that what they were seeing first-hand was what believing Old Testament people had longed to see.

The Bible Knowledge Commentary: The three Persons of the Godhead are clearly seen: Jesus the Son was doing the Father's will in the power of the Holy Spirit. Each had a specific function.[2]

John Piper: What is being hidden and revealed is not just the presence of the kingdom, but the true personal identity and divine glory of the messianic King and his Father.[3]

God has truths in the Bible that he hides from certain people. Fact or fiction? It's a fact! People who boast of being wise and having it all together without the slightest need for God will not discover the truths of Scripture. They may have the facts but will miss the experience of knowing God. Jesus said that God reveals himself to those who come to the Scripture with childlike dependence on him.

FACT OR FICTION

EXPERT LAWYER QUIZ

Luke 10:25–29 On one occasion an expert in the law stood up to test Jesus. "Teacher," he asked, "what must I do to inherit eternal life?"

"What is written in the Law?" he replied. "How do you read it?"

He answered: "'Love the Lord your God with all your heart and with all your soul and with all your strength and with all your mind'; and, 'Love your neighbor as yourself.'"

"You have answered correctly," Jesus replied. "Do this and you will live."

But he wanted to justify himself, so he asked Jesus, "And who is my neighbor?"

Who's Testing Whom?

Students sometimes ask tricky questions in an attempt to stump their teacher. An expert in Jewish law asked Jesus a question with a different motive. He wanted to get Jesus into trouble by tricking him into giving an answer that would be **heresy**! The question: *"What must I do to inherit eternal life?"* His question indicates that he thought eternal life could be earned.

Knowing that the man was insincere, Jesus answered with a question that any expert in the law would know. *"What is written in the Law? How do you read it?"*

The expert answered smoothly, *"'Love the Lord your God with all your heart and with all your soul and with all your strength and with all your mind'; and, 'Love your neighbor as yourself.'"*

Jesus replied that he had answered the question correctly. His job was to put into practice what he already knew he should be doing. Knowing and doing are two different things.

The man squirmed, knowing he could not perfectly obey the law and that he was not willing to admit his shortcomings, especially in front of everyone. This test was not going the way he planned.

To raise his failing grade, the lawyer tried to limit his responsibilities by bringing up another question: *"And who is my neighbor?"*

> **Luke 10:30–32** In reply Jesus said: "A man was going down from Jerusalem to Jericho, when he fell into the hands of robbers. They stripped him of his clothes, beat him and went away, leaving him half dead. A priest happened to be going down the same road, and when he saw the man, he passed by on the other side. So too, a Levite, when he came to the place and saw him, passed by on the other side."

Passing On

Jesus answered the lawyer with a dramatic story. In his cast of characters he chose a Jew who was assaulted by robbers and left half dead on the side of the road. Next, he chose a **priest** who came along and avoided the injured man because he was fearful of becoming ceremonially unclean by any slight contact with him. Jesus also included a respected **Levite** who also avoided the man.

heresy: false interpretation of the Old Testament

☞ **GO TO:**

Deuteronomy 6:5
(Love the Lord)

Leviticus 19:18
(Love your neighbor)

priest: middleman between God and the Jews, charged to offer sacrifices

Levite: responsible to oversee temple services

☞ **GO TO:**

Leviticus 21:1
(ceremonially unclean)

> **Luke 10:33–37** But a Samaritan, as he traveled, came where the man was; and when he saw him, he took pity on him. He went to him and bandaged his wounds, pouring on oil and wine. Then he put the man on his own donkey, took him to an inn and took care of him. The next day he took out two silver coins and gave them to the innkeeper. 'Look after him,' he said, 'and when I return, I will reimburse you for any extra expense you may have.'
>
> "Which of these three do you think was a neighbor to the man who fell into the hands of robbers?"
>
> The expert in the law replied, "The one who had mercy on him."
>
> Jesus told him, "Go and do likewise."

Will The Real Neighbor Please Stand Up!

Jesus rounded out his cast of characters with a despised **Samaritan** who helped the hurt man. To Jewish minds there was no such thing as a good Samaritan—until Jesus invented this story. The Samaritan's heart was filled with concern and sympathy that moved him to take immediate action. He stopped and applied first aid, probably using his own wine as disinfectant and his own clothing as bandages. Then he placed the man on his donkey and took him to an inn where he personally cared for the man. The next day he gave the innkeeper two silver coins—enough to feed the patient for three weeks—and promised to reimburse the innkeeper for any additional expenses.

Jesus cut the story off with a penetrating question. *"Which of these three do you think was a neighbor?"*

The answer was obvious, though it must have stuck in the throat of the self-righteous expert. He answered, *"The one who had mercy on him."*

By answering this way, the expert had just given himself a final exam grade of *F*. Love is shown by doing loving deeds, not by a strict following of law, as the Jews were fond of thinking. Love is costly. It requires great sacrifices of us. It calls us out of our comfort zone. Loving like God loves makes us dependent on Christ for strength.

Samaritan: despised mixed-race descendant of Israel following a corrupt form of Moses' laws

John Piper: Another way of asking the lawyer's question would be, "Teacher, whom do I not have to love? Which groups in our society are exceptions to this commandment? Surely the Romans,

What Others are Saying:

lackeys: *menial servants*

oppressors of God's chosen people; and their despicable **lackeys**, the tax collectors; and those half-breed Samaritans—surely all these are not included in the term 'neighbor.' Tell me just who my neighbor is, Teacher, that as I examine various candidates for my love, I will be sure to choose him alone."[4]

Something to Ponder

☞ **GO TO:**

Matthew 25:31–46 (love God)

Loving others sounds so simple until we are confronted by the needs of someone we hate. When Jesus said, *"Go and do likewise,"* he set a high standard that he knew could be only reached when his followers used his power and love. The lawyer did not love God totally and therefore he could not possibly love others whose only claim to his acts of pity and mercy was their desperate need. Those who do not <u>love God</u> will not fully be able to love their fellow humans and vice versa.

 PHYSICIAN'S PERSPECTIVE—When Dr. Luke heard about the Samaritan, he could have said, "That's my man!" The Samaritan acted as any caring physician would. He couldn't call 911, so he treated the victim immediately without asking, "Who is he? What's his race? What's his economic status? Will his HMO reimburse me? Can I possibly be sued for giving medical treatment to this stranger?"

What Others are Saying:

Dallas Willard: Of course the words good Samaritan do not occur in the story. For those listening to Jesus, that phrase would have been what we call an "oxymoron": a combination of words that makes no sense. For the Jews generally, at that time, we could say that "the only *good* Samaritan was a dead Samaritan."[5]

KEY POINT

How we relate to hurting people who are not like us demonstrates how we relate to Christ.

Gary A. Haugen: Christians of mature faith know that love is both a deeply mystical and a profoundly practical calling. In some mysterious way, when we feed the hungry, visit the sick and clothe the naked, we do it for him also (Matthew 25). Jesus' model for love, a nameless Samaritan, messed up his clothes and his schedule by picking up a stranger who lay wounded and naked in the ditch (Luke 10). Acts of love like this are so important to God that when the Israelites couldn't be bothered with the workaday practicalities of what it takes "to loose the chains of injustice" and "to set the oppressed free," God stopped listening to their prayers (Isaiah 58:1–6).[6]

BEST BUDS

> **Luke 10:38–42** As Jesus and his disciples were on their way, he came to a village where a woman named Martha opened her home to him. She had a sister called Mary, who sat at the Lord's feet listening to what he said. But Martha was distracted by all the preparations that had to be made. She came to him and asked, "Lord, don't you care that my sister has left me to do the work by myself? Tell her to help me!"
>
> "Martha, Martha," the Lord answered, "you are worried and upset about many things, but only one thing is needed. Mary has chosen what is better, and it will not be taken away from her."

Is This Martha Stewart?

One day Jesus stopped by the home of Martha. She and her sister, Mary, and brother, Lazarus, lived in Bethany and were some of Jesus' best buddies. Both Martha and Mary loved Jesus and welcomed him whenever he visited them (see GWWB, pages 257–259).

Martha began preparations for a meal that was appropriate for honoring their special guest and his disciples. She wanted to dish up a good spread that would make Martha Stewart proud. If all twelve disciples were there, she was preparing to serve a meal to at least sixteen people. She whipped up her favorite dishes and didn't dream of "cheating" on the old family recipes. Without the conveniences of four burners, a family-size oven, a microwave, a refrigerator and freezer, she had taken on a large task.

Nearby Mary sat at Jesus' feet, hanging on his every word. She should have known how hard Martha was working, but if she did, she made no indication. She had committed herself to the role of a disciple, a learner. This role had been reserved by the religious leaders for men alone, so Mary was something of a feminist.

Martha was feeling overloaded. So she walked up to Jesus and scolded him. Didn't he notice or care that Mary had abandoned her duties and left Martha to slave away in the kitchen? He should tell Mary to get to work!

But Jesus responded differently. He understood that Martha was stressed out about the many details she was handling. A lavish meal was not needed, especially when doing so took Martha away from spending time with him. With all that Jesus was facing as he proceeded to Jerusalem, he needed a peaceful environment and the support of loving, understanding friends. There was only one essential and Mary had chosen it—listening to him. Food and lodging were temporary. What Mary had chosen would last forever and never be taken away from her.

☞ **GO TO:**

Romans 12:13; 1 Peter 4:10 (serving)

Luke 8:15 (listening)

PHYSICIAN'S PERSPECTIVE—As a doctor, even without meeting Martha personally, Luke could immediately detect that she was a Type A personality. She was competitive, perfectionistic, and verbal. She pushed herself with a distinct sense of urgency.

Something to Ponder

Both Martha and Mary made choices—one to work her fingers to the bone <u>serving</u> Jesus as a gracious hostess, while inwardly fuming, and the other to sit at his feet <u>listening</u> to him. Do we have to choose one or the other? It's possible to be Mary and Martha in one: doing much service and enjoying close fellowship with Jesus at the same time. But if a choice is required, then we need to set priorities and remember that Jesus said Mary made the better choice.

What Others are Saying:

Lawrence O. Richards: Jesus' rebuke might be paraphrased, "Just a casserole, Martha, not a smorgasbord." Love for God is expressed best in listening and responding to Jesus' words, not in busily doing "for" him.[7]

FAST FORWARD

contemplative: *capable of considering thoroughly and thinking deeply*

Some people see Martha and Mary as having very different temperaments. Martha was the zealous put-faith-in-action type and Mary was the easygoing, docile, **contemplative** type. But consider this: Martha accused Mary of having left her. This would indicate that Mary had served acceptably in the kitchen. Her work was missed! Consider also that Jesus said that Mary had chosen to spend time with him. Martha could have made the same choice.

Today we too make choices. We can choose to carve out time to read the Bible and reflect on it prayerfully. Do we excuse ourselves by saying, "I'm just not the type" or "I'm too busy"?

Study Questions

1. Why did Jesus send out seventy-two followers to Judea, and what happened?

2. To whom does God choose to reveal the truths of Scripture? Why?

3. What purpose did the expert in the law have in asking Jesus what he must do in order to inherit eternal life? What did he learn from Jesus' response?

4. If the Samaritan was neighbor to the half-dead Jew, to whom should the expert in the law be a neighbor? To whom should you be a neighbor?

5. In what different ways did Martha and Mary show their love for Jesus? Which way is better? In what ways are you like Martha and Mary?

CHAPTER WRAP-UP

- Jesus appointed seventy-two followers to go ahead of him into the towns of Judea. They returned from their mission rejoicing that even the demons had submitted to them. (Luke 10:1–20)

- Jesus rejoiced that God had chosen to reveal the truths of Scripture not to the wise but to the childlike—those who were humble and dependent on God. The disciples received the truth and acted on it with childlike trust. (Luke 10:21–24)

- An expert in the law posed a question to Jesus, hoping to trap him. Jesus, in turn, asked the expert to quote from Old Testament Scripture what God had said—to love him supremely and to love one's neighbor. (Luke 10:25–29)

- Jesus told a story in which a despised Samaritan was neighborly to a wounded Jew who had been bypassed by a priest and a Levite. The point was that love is shown by actions, not by a strict following of law. (Luke 10:30–37)

- While visiting the home of Martha and Mary, Jesus explained that loving, personal devotion to him was better than acts of service. (Luke 10:38–42)

LUKE 11: CANDID CONVERSATIONS

CHAPTER HIGHLIGHTS

- Prayer Powwow
- Power Questioned
- Painful Pronouncements

Let's Get Started

It became increasingly impossible for people to be neutral as they heard Jesus teach and watched him perform miracles. The disciples, observing his close relationship with his Father in heaven, asked Jesus to teach them to pray. Then when Jesus cast out a demon, the crowd recognized his power. Some were amazed, some accused him of being in league with Satan, and others demanded an even greater miracle—a sign from heaven.

In his candid conversations Jesus stressed that our heart attitudes enable us to receive the truth or prevent us from recognizing the truth when it is presented to us. The Pharisees and experts in the law were highly respected for their adherence to the Scripture but were missing the point of that Scripture because they had closed hearts.

PRAYER POWWOW

> **Luke 11:1–4** One day Jesus was praying in a certain place. When he finished, one of his disciples said to him, "Lord, teach us to pray, just as John taught his disciples."
>
> He said to them, "When you pray, say:
> "'Father,
> hallowed be your name,

> your kingdom come.
> Give us each day our daily bread.
> Forgive us our sins,
>   for we also forgive everyone who sins against us.
> And lead us not into temptation.'"

Prayer Pattern

Again and again the disciples had seen Jesus step aside from them to spend time talking to his Father in prayer, but sometimes he prayed in their presence. Remembering that John the Baptist had given his followers instruction in prayer, the disciples asked Jesus to give them lessons on prayer.

In response, Jesus gave a prayer pattern that can be followed by every culture and every person from a child to an **octogenarian** and beyond. First, approach God as your Father. God loves you as a perfect <u>Father</u>, who cares for you and wants to give you what is best for you.

Then, make these requests:

- *May your name be honored.* By your words and actions demonstrate your desire that the name and character of God your Father will be lovingly reverenced.

- *May your kingdom come.* Live each day under Christ's kingdom rule—doing his will, obeying him, and working to extend his kingdom throughout the earth.

- *Provide us daily food.* Depend on your Father to provide for your everyday needs.

- *Forgive our sins.* Trust God to forgive your sins even as you keep an open heart to forgive others.

- *Keep us from being tempted.* Aware of your weakness, ask God to keep you from yielding to temptation.

octogenarian: a person in his or her eighties

☞ **GO TO:**

Romans 8:15–17 (Father)

KEY POINT

Jesus did not give a prayer to be recited mindlessly, but a pattern to be adapted in the words of our hearts.

What Others are Saying:

Richard J. Foster: Jesus' relationship with God the Father is, of course, absolutely unique, but experientially we are invited into the same intimacy with Father God that he knew while here in the flesh. We are encouraged to crawl into the Father's lap and receive his love and comfort and healing and strength. We can laugh, and we can weep, freely and openly. We can be hugged and find comfort in his arms. And we can worship deep within our spirit.[1]

Dallas Willard: I believe the most adequate description of prayer is simply, "Talking to God about what we are doing together."[2]

Jesus gives us permission to do what no Old Testament saint would have dared to do. We can approach God as a child comes to his or her earthly father—trustfully, lovingly, respectfully—and address him as **Abba**—Daddy!

 MORE INFORMATION—Matthew gives us what is called The Lord's Prayer, which is slightly longer than Luke's version, but is essentially the same.

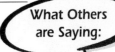

Matthew 6:9–13	Luke 11:1–4
Our Father in heaven,	Father,
Hallowed be your name,	hallowed be your name,
Your kingdom come,	your kingdom come.
Your will be done on earth as it is in heaven.	
Give us today our daily bread.	Give us each day our daily bread.
Forgive us our debts, as we also have forgiven our debtors.	Forgive us our sins, for we also forgive everyone who sins against us.
And lead us not into temptation, but deliver us from evil.	And lead us not into temptation.

> **Luke 11:5–8** Then he said to them, "Suppose one of you has a friend, and he goes to him at midnight and says, 'Friend, lend me three loaves of bread, because a friend of mine on a journey has come to me, and I have nothing to set before him.'
>
> "Then the one inside answers, 'Don't bother me. The door is already locked, and my children are with me in bed. I can't get up and give you anything.' I tell you, though he will not get up and give him the bread because he is his friend, yet because of the man's boldness he will get up and give him what he needs."

Power In Persistence

Jesus told a story to encourage his disciples to bring their needs to God in prayer. Luke is the only Gospel writer to share it.

In Bible times homes often had only one room. People slept on mats spread out on the floor. To get up in the middle of the night to answer the door meant that the father would have to step over (and probably fall on) his sleeping children to reach the door. Then he'd have to slide back the heavy bolt that kept the door shut. By this time everyone in the family would be awake—and not too happy! You can understand why he told his friend to go away and not bother him.

But his friend was desperate. Hosts in the first century were expected to welcome their guests regardless of when they arrived. Guests couldn't go to the local motel or sleep in their cars until morning. There were no coffee shops open all night long. This host was in a bind and he knew his friend could help. The host persisted without embarrassment. Finally, the friend gave in and handed over the bread—not because the host was his friend but because he was so boldly persistent!

What Others are Saying:

Darryl DelHousaye: Isn't prayer simply talking to your heavenly Father? Why is something appearing to be so simple so difficult?

The theology of prayer continues to be a mystery. How does praying effect the sovereign hand of God? Isn't He going to do what He's going to do anyway?

Jesus doesn't talk about the mystery of the theology of prayer here. He takes a pragmatic approach.

Do it![3]

FACT OR FICTION

badger: harass, pester, nag

The point of Jesus' story seems to be that God doesn't want to be bothered with our prayers, and he reluctantly grants our requests because we **badger** him. Fact or fiction? Fiction! Jesus is contrasting the reluctant friend with our loving Father. Even a good friend might not want to be disturbed, but God our Father would never say, "Don't bother me." We are to come boldly with our requests as this host did, knowing that our heavenly Father will respond much more graciously.

Remember This . . .

Prayer isn't something we impose on God, like the uninvited telephone solicitors who annoy us. God welcomes us, even encouraging us to pray without interruption.

☞ **GO TO:**

1 Thessalonians 5:17 (pray)

> **Luke 11:9–13** "So I say to you: Ask and it will be given to you; seek and you will find; knock and the door will be opened to you. For everyone who asks receives; he who seeks finds; and to him who knocks, the door will be opened.

> "Which of you fathers, if your son asks for a fish, will give him a snake instead? Or if he asks for an egg, will give him a scorpion? If you then, thou you are evil, know how to give good gifts to your children, how much more will your Father in heaven give the Holy Spirit to those who ask him!"

No Side Orders Of Scorpions Or Snakes

To reinforce the point of his story, Jesus gave more examples. An earthly father would never respond to his son's request for food with something hurtful. Jesus encourages us to count on our Father's kindness and willingness to meet our needs. Keep two points in mind. First, God is our heavenly Father and will do nothing less than what an earthly father would do for his children. Second, God is perfect. He will do much more than what earthly, sinful fathers would do. God never loses his patience with us. And he will give us only <u>good gifts</u>—even fulfilling our request for the Holy Spirit.

KEY POINT

We can come to God as our loving heavenly Father, trusting him to give us only what he knows is best for us.

☞ **GO TO:**

Romans 8:32 (good gifts)

POWER QUESTIONED

> **Luke 11:14–16** Jesus was driving out a demon that was mute. When the demon left, the man who had been mute spoke, and the crowd was amazed. But some of them said, "By Beelzebub, the prince of demons, he is driving out demons." Others tested him by asking for a sign from heaven.

Demon Power?

A hush came over the crowd. They pressed forward to watch as Jesus performed yet another miracle. He healed a man who had never been able to speak because he had been under the control of a demon. Suddenly, to the astonishment of the crowd, the man was released from both his disability and the demon that had oppressed him.

Mixed with the amazement of the onlookers, though, were other reactions. Some made a wicked accusation that Jesus could drive out demons only because he was in league with **Beelzebub**. Others taunted, "This miracle was good, but show us something better. Let's have a sign from heaven."

Beelzebub: *meaning "lord of flies" or "lord of filth"; Satan*

> **Luke 11:17–20** Jesus knew their thoughts and said to them: "Any kingdom divided against itself will be ruined, and a house divided against itself will fall. If Satan is divided against himself, how can his kingdom stand? I say this because you claim that I drive out demons by Beelzebub. Now if I drive out demons by Beelzebub, by whom do your followers drive them out? So then, they will be your judges. But if I drive out demons by the finger of God, then the kingdom of God has come to you.

Right Reason

Jesus had every right to flare out in anger. Their accusation was outrageous; their unbelief, inexcusable. Instead, Jesus chose to reason with them, to give them yet another opportunity to believe in him and the One who sent him.

It would be self-defeating, he argued, for Satan to weaken his kingdom by driving out his demons. Further, their followers credited God's power when they drove out demons. Therefore, if the **finger of God** was Jesus' power, then it must indicate that the kingdom of God had come.

☞ **GO TO:**

Exodus 8:19
(finger of God)

finger of God: the Holy Spirit

> **Luke 11:21–26** "When a strong man, fully armed, guards his own house, his possessions are safe. But when someone stronger attacks and overpowers him, he takes away the armor in which the man trusted and divides up the spoils.
>
> "He who is not with me is against me, and he who does not gather with me, scatters.
>
> "When an evil spirit comes out of a man, it goes through arid places seeking rest and does not find it. Then it says, 'I will return to the house I left.' When it arrives, it finds the house swept clean and put in order. Then it goes and takes seven other spirits more wicked than itself, and they go in and live there. And the final condition of that man is worse than the first."

Let Me Illustrate My Point

Jesus told a brief parable to illustrate his point. A strong man (Satan) keeps his house secure until a stronger man (Jesus) overpowers him and takes all. Some of what he takes, obviously, would include those formerly possessed by demons whom Jesus had released from Satan's oppression.

Obviously, no one can be neutral in the contest between God and Satan. Each in the crowd listening to Jesus that day had to make a choice. Those who believed that Jesus was empowered by Beelzebub to cast out demons were actively against him.

And this was serious business. If the man who had been healed joined Jesus' accusers in crediting Satan for his healing, his condition would become far worse than it was before Jesus healed him.

What Others are Saying:

Jack Hayford: The immediate application of [Jesus'] teaching is to those who lack the spiritual discernment to recognize Jesus as the Savior. In rejecting him they have nothing left but empty rites and ceremonies, making them even more susceptible to Satan's deception.[4]

> **Luke 11:27–28** As Jesus was saying these things, a woman in the crowd called out, "Blessed is the mother who gave you birth and nursed you."
>
> He replied, "Blessed rather are those who hear the word of God and obey it."

Tense Moment

The atmosphere was so tense it was seconds away from exploding. Suddenly a woman spoke out clearly from the crowd. She blessed Jesus' mother for bringing him into the world.

Jesus didn't disagree, but he expanded her blessing to include all who hear God's Word and obey it. His words were an encouragement to the woman—and to all who are on his side.

Jesus' words were a real encouragement to this nameless woman. She risked derision and censure for standing by him. Maybe she spoke out of a surge of emotion as a member of his fan club, or maybe she spoke out of deep conviction. Whatever, he gave her a blessing, and his blessing extends to us today. Yes, Mary had a special privilege in being chosen to be the mother of Jesus. Truly she was blessed, but he said, "Blessed rather . . ." and that includes us. We are blessed rather when we hear God's Word and follow through with practical obedience in our everyday lives.

FAST FORWARD

The key to God's blessing is listening to his Word and doing what he says.

> **Luke 11:29–32** As the crowds increased, Jesus said, "This is a wicked generation. It asks for a miraculous sign, but none will be given it except the sign of Jonah. For as Jonah was a sign to the Ninevites, so also will the Son of Man be to this generation. This Queen of the South will rise at the judgment with the men of this generation and condemn them; for she came from the ends of the earth to listen to Solomon's wisdom, and now one greater than Solomon is here. The men of Nineveh will stand up at the judgment with this generation and condemn it; for they repented at the preaching of Jonah, and now one greater than Jonah is here.

One Down, One To Go

Jesus' attackers had accused him of healing the demon-possessed man by Satan's power. He had just answered that. Now he spoke to those who wanted a sign from heaven to prove the source of his power.

☞ GO TO:

Jonah 3 (Jonah)

1 Kings 10 (Queen of Sheba)

Jesus would give them the same sign <u>Jonah</u> gave the people of Nineveh—his presence and his message. Jonah was a prophet of old who was called to preach to the people of Nineveh. Instead of obeying, Jonah ran away. But his flight was cut short when he was the cause of a terrible storm at sea, was thrown overboard, and was swallowed by a large fish. Inside the fish for three days, Jonah repented. God gave him a second chance by having the fish deposit him on land remarkably close to Nineveh. This time Jonah obeyed and preached to the Ninevites.

Both Jesus and Jonah preached repentance. Jesus, like Jonah, would be buried for three days and then be made alive again. The people of Nineveh responded in droves and God withheld his judgment. Too bad the same couldn't be said of Jesus' attackers.

Jesus also spoke of the <u>Queen of Sheba</u> who traveled from a great distance to hear the wisdom of Solomon. Now, in the person of the Son of God, the people hearing Jesus had the opportunity to hear someone infinitely greater than Solomon. Would they open their hearts to listen, as she did?

FAST FORWARD

Jesus was grieved by the crowds who followed him because they hoped to see a great miracle performed. Their hearts were not hungry for the truth that would have brought a greater miracle— change of their hearts toward God.

Today we may be tempted to search for unusual signs of God's blessing on a ministry and get on board because it is exciting. While we do that, however, we may miss what God wants to do in our hearts if we would just listen and obey!

Luke 11:33–36 "No one lights a lamp and puts it in a place where it will be hidden, or under a bowl. Instead he puts it on its stand, so that those who come in may see the light. Your eye is the lamp of your body. When your eyes are good, your whole body also is full of light. But when they are bad, your body also is full of darkness. See to it, then, that the light within you is not darkness. Therefore, if your whole body is full of light, and no part of it dark, it will be completely lighted, as when the light of a lamp shines on you."

Burning Light

Jesus pictured his preaching of the truth as a lamp that was lit and placed where all could see its bright light. If the people could not see the light it was because their eyes were bad. Those who had good eyes could receive the light and their whole bodies would be flooded with it.

The bad eye Jesus referred to was not a physical disability. It was a heart attitude that was closed to the truth, not wanting its sin to be exposed by the light. In contrast, the good eye was a sincere openness to truth, a desire to have sin exposed and removed, and a willingness to allow the truth of Jesus to transform a person's life.

We are not condemned because of doing wrong. We are condemned because God has provided <u>light</u> and we refuse to come to it in order to have our wrongdoings exposed and removed.

PAINFUL PRONOUNCEMENTS

Luke 11:37–41 When Jesus had finished speaking, a Pharisee invited him to eat with him; so he went in and reclined at the table. But the Pharisee, noticing that Jesus did not first wash before the meal, was surprised.

Something to Ponder

☞ **GO TO:**

John 3:19 (light)

> Then the Lord said to him, "Now then, you Pharisees clean the outside of the cup and dish, but inside you are full of greed and wickedness. You foolish people! Did not the one who made the outside make the inside also? But give what is inside the dish to the poor, and everything will be clean for you.

Dinner Roast

As soon as Jesus finished speaking, a Pharisee invited him to his home for dinner. This was a dinner with a purpose. The host hoped to roast Jesus as the main course. Jesus, however, turned out to be the one doing the roasting.

Before the meal, the Pharisee completed an elaborate ritual of washing his hands, as was his custom. Just as pointedly, Jesus declined to observe the ritual. When the Pharisee expressed his surprise, Jesus made his point. Pharisees were like dishes that were clean on the outside, but inside, where cleanliness really mattered, the dishes were dirty. Pharisees followed all the rules on the outside, but inside they were full of greed and evil. To become clean, they needed to get rid of their greed and give generously to the poor.

KEY POINT

It's what is inside that counts.

What Others are Saying:

Max Anders: While Jesus was very patient, understanding, and compassionate with those with weaknesses, he was very direct with those who were stubbornly unbelieving. Many times the Bible says that the religious leaders did not believe in Jesus because they were jealous of him. He challenged their pride of position and prestige over the people. Jesus was not patient with these leaders and was very forthright in his responses to them.[5]

> **Luke 11:42–44** "Woe to you Pharisees, because you give God a tenth of your mint, rue and all other kinds of garden herbs, but you neglect justice and love of God. You should have practiced the latter without leaving the former undone.
>
> "Woe to you Pharisees, because you love the most important seats in the synagogues and greetings in the marketplaces.
>
> "Woe to you, because you are like unmarked graves, which men walk over without knowing it."

GOD'S WORD FOR THE BIBLICALLY-INEPT

Triple Whammy Of Woes, Round One

Jesus pronounced the Pharisees guilty on three counts.

First, they were meticulous in giving their **tithes** while they neglected the poor. There's nothing wrong with donating to good causes, but these Pharisees took it too far. They counted the herbs picked from their gardens and gave one-tenth to God. They were so busy being spiritual they didn't have time to help the poor. The Old Testament Scriptures said God's people were to show <u>justice and mercy</u> for their fellows, giving <u>generously</u> out of <u>love</u> for God.

Second, far from being humble, the Pharisees paraded their self-righteousness. Dressed in their religious costumes as they attended the synagogue, they sought to sit in the seats reserved for the honored. In the marketplace they loved to be greeted as persons of great importance.

Third, Jesus said that the Pharisees were like unmarked graves. God's law declared that a person who stepped on a grave had been <u>defiled</u>. For this reason graves were always marked in some way. For example, <u>whitewashing</u> was common. The meaning here was clear. By their influence, these Pharisees defiled people by actually spreading false teaching and unbelief and keeping others from the truth.

tithes: one tenth of one's income

☞ **GO TO:**

Micah 6:8 (justice and mercy)

Deuteronomy 15:10–11 (generously)

Deuteronomy 6:5 (love)

Numbers 19:11 (defiled)

Matthew 23:27 (whitewashing)

What Others are Saying:

Max Anders: Today, it would be considered impolite and going overboard to speak in this way to any religious leader, and perhaps so. But Jesus being God saw the true nature of their hearts and had the moral authority to speak so directly. He was not one to trifle with if you were deliberately cooperating with sin.[6]

> **Luke 11:45–52** One of the experts in the law answered him, "Teacher, when you say these things, you insult us also."
>
> Jesus replied, "And you experts in the law, woe to you, because you load people down with burdens they can hardly carry, and you yourselves will not lift one finger to help them.
>
> "Woe to you, because you build tombs for the prophets, and it was your forefathers who killed them. So you testify that you approve of what your forefathers did; they killed the prophets, and you build their tombs. Because of this, God in his wisdom said, 'I will send them prophets and apostles, some of whom they will kill and others they will persecute.' Therefore this

generation will be held responsible for the blood of all the prophets that has been shed since the beginning of the world, from the blood of Abel to the blood of Zechariah, who was killed between the altar and the sanctuary. Yes, I tell you, this generation will be held responsible for it all.

"Woe to you experts in the law, because you have taken away the key to knowledge. You yourselves have not entered, and you have hindered those who were entering."

Triple Whammy Of Woes, Round Two

A lawyer in the audience was becoming increasingly uncomfortable. Finally, he spoke up protesting that when Jesus condemned the Pharisees he was also insulting the experts in the law. Right on! Jesus responded with three jabs especially suited to the lawyers.

First, they had made it their business to formulate excessive laws—some six thousand of them—which they piled on top of the laws God had given through Moses. It was not enough that they kept the laws themselves, but they burdened the people with them. Jesus faulted them not for making the laws but for making life miserable for the people they should have been helping.

Second, with brilliant discernment Jesus took aim at their project of building beautiful tombs to honor the prophets who had delivered God's Word to his people—while at the same time they were demonstrating the very attitude of those who had killed the prophets.

Third, Jesus accused the experts in the law of removing the key to knowledge—the truth of the Scriptures. Not only did they not want the truth for themselves but, with their preoccupation with rule keeping, they were preventing the common people from having the truth of Scripture.

FAST FORWARD

The men Jesus addressed at the dinner were among the most respected in the land. They majored on being righteous. They followed religious rules with zeal. But Jesus pointed out that they had completely missed the point. They were majoring on minors. We would never be guilty of that—or would we? Take this test to see how you measure up.

- *I am more concerned about my inner attitude of compassion for people in need than I am about an outward show of my faith.*

- *I am more concerned about justice for others and love for God than I am about letting people know how much I give to worthy causes.*

- *I am content to know I have God's praise and I don't seek the applause of others.*

- *Instead of being judgmental of others, I seek to encourage them.*

- *I listen to God's messengers with a humble, teachable attitude.*

- *I portray God as lovingly beckoning sinners rather than imposing a view of God as a hard-hearted judge.*

When we focus all our attention on our behavior with the view of impressing others, we neglect what Christ says is most important. When we let Christ transform our hearts, however, our actions will become those that please him and others.

Something to Ponder

> **Luke 11:53–54** When Jesus left there, the Pharisees and the teachers of the law began to oppose him fiercely and to besiege him with questions, waiting to catch him in something he might say.

The Darkening Cloud

The meal in the Pharisee's house ended with the Pharisees and experts in the law in a state of rage. The air was tense as they rolled out their heavy artillery of accusations and questions designed to catch Jesus in a false statement. The ominous cloud of hateful opposition gained strength.

Study Questions

1. What elements did Jesus include in the pattern for prayer he gave the disciples?
2. How did Jesus answer those who accused him of being empowered by Satan?
3. How did Jesus answer the woman who said Mary was blessed for being the mother of Jesus?
4. How did Jesus answer those who demanded a sign from heaven?
5. What three traits did Jesus condemn in the Pharisees?
6. What three traits did Jesus condemn in the experts in the law?

CHAPTER WRAP-UP

- Jesus gave his disciples a pattern for prayer that showed God as a loving heavenly Father. (Luke 11:1–13)

- When Jesus cast out the demon from the man who was mute, some in the crowd accused him of getting his power from Satan and others asked for a sign from heaven. Jesus answered his critics by pointing out that Satan would not weaken his kingdom by working against himself. Jesus said his presence was the sign they sought. (Luke 11:14–33)

- Jesus said those who were open to his message would be able to see the light of his truth. (Luke 11:33–36)

- At a dinner Jesus condemned the Pharisees and experts in the law for their lack of interest in righteous attitudes. He said their meticulous adherence to man-made laws was worthless if they overlooked their inner heart attitudes toward God and man. (Luke 11:37–52)

- After Jesus pronounced three woes on the Pharisees and experts in the law, they became furious and sought ways to trap him. (Luke 11:53–54)

LUKE 12: WISE WORDS

Let's Get Started

Luke 12 is a series of warnings and promises that Jesus gave. Some were for his disciples. Others were for the crowds who followed him, some who were seeking truth, perhaps, but more who were hoping to see a spectacular miracle.

Throughout his warnings to those who crowded around him, Jesus gave words that we would do well to heed today. We need to pay special attention, because what he had to say is contrary to all that society offers as answers to our needs. We, as well as Jesus' listeners, have to make a choice.

 MORE INFORMATION—The contents of Luke 12 are scattered in parts of the Gospels of Matthew and Mark. This leads many Bible experts to believe that here Luke is compiling some of Jesus' teachings given on a number of different occasions. Compare Matthew 6:5–6 and Mark 8:14–15 with Luke 12:1–2. Compare Matthew 10:26–33 with Luke 12:3–9. Compare Matthew 12:31–32 and Mark 3:28–30 with Luke 12:10. And compare Matthew 10:19–20; Mark 13:11; and Luke 21:14–15 with Luke 12:11–12.

A WORD FOR THE INNER CIRCLE

> **Luke 12:1–3** Meanwhile, when a crowd of many thousands had gathered, so that they were trampling on one another, Jesus began to speak first to his disciples, saying: "Be on your guard against the yeast of the Pharisees, which is hypocrisy. There is nothing concealed that will not be disclosed, or hidden that will not be made known. What you have said in the dark will be heard in the daylight, and what you have whispered in the ear in the inner rooms will be proclaimed from the roofs."

On Guard, Men!

Jesus was like a reporter on *60 Minutes* exposing a scam. He warned his disciples about the **yeast** of the Pharisees—something he labeled **hypocrisy**. The Pharisees made rules, talked about following those rules, and then made a charade of keeping the rules while their hearts remained in opposition to God.

The word "hypocrite" was used originally by the Greeks to mean an actor, a person who used a mask and acted and spoke behind that facade. Jesus warned against hypocrisy and called for **transparency**. Though his disciples might be tempted to follow the ways of the Pharisees and even seem to succeed with spiritual role-playing, the truth would be exposed some day. You can fool people, but you can't fool God.

R. Kent Hughes: Full disclosure will come on Judgment Day. Everything will be revealed, and the disclosure will be ruthless. The things whispered invisibly in the dark will be shouted in full light from the rooftops. The limitless capacities of divine **omniscience** assure perfect exposure of hypocrisy.[1]

> **Luke 12:4–7** "I tell you, my friends, do not be afraid of those who kill the body and after that can do no more. But I will show you whom you should fear: Fear him who, after the killing of the body, has power to throw you into hell. Yes, I tell you, fear him. Are not five sparrows sold for two pennies? Yet not one of them is forgotten by God. Indeed, the very hairs of your head are all numbered. Don't be afraid; you are worth more than many sparrows."

---

yeast: *fermenting agent allowing dough to rise, symbol of evil*

hypocrisy: *acting a part, masking one's true self*

charade: *pretense, deception*

transparency: *being open, concealing nothing in order to create a good impression*

What Others are Saying:

omniscience: *ability to know all*

KEY POINT

Christ does not expect perfection but transparency.

Bad Fear, Good Fear

As the disciples saw the growing hostility of the religious leaders against Jesus, they were probably afraid that they too would become the targets of wrath. But Jesus pointed out that whatever these leaders did, they could hurt the disciples only temporarily here on earth. If they were going to be afraid, the disciples should fear God, who has power over them on earth and in eternity!

But God is not a big meanie in the sky. Jesus hastened to remind them that God, who cares for the throwaway sparrows, cares for his own so intimately that he keeps count of the hairs on their heads. (And for some of us, that's a shrinking job.) Surely, they can rely on his love and care for them now—and for eternity.

R. C. Sproul: A healthy fear and respect for God should always be balanced by our confidence that in God's sight we are of exceedingly great value. Yes, God knows us intimately, knows the secrets that we harbor in our hearts, yet we should not allow our fear of divine disclosure to drive us to despair. Rather it should drive us to embrace the redemption that is ours in Christ.[2]

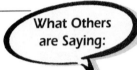

What Others are Saying:

KEY POINT

If we fear God, we need not fear men.

> **Luke 12:8–10** "I tell you, whoever acknowledges me before men, the Son of Man will also acknowledge him before the angels of God. But he who disowns me before men will be disowned before the angels of God. And everyone who speaks a word against the Son of Man will be forgiven, but anyone who blasphemes against the Holy Spirit will not be forgiven."

I'll Stand By You

When faced with opposition, Jesus' followers might be tempted to deny their allegiance to him. For this, Jesus had strong words: If people are faithful to me, I will stand by them and in heaven will acknowledge them as my own. But heavenly hosts will note it if they are ashamed of me and deny their association with me.

MORE INFORMATION—From Luke's account it is hard to understand the meaning of "blaspheme," sometimes called the "unpardonable sin." Matthew 12:25–36 and Mark 3:23–30 show that blaspheming the Holy Spirit is giving Satan credit for God's works. We may sin against

God in attitudes and actions and be forgiven. We may even reject Christ at one point in life and, by God's grace, change our minds later in life. But total, complete, sustained denial of God the Father, Jesus the Son, and the Holy Spirit results in eternal damnation. That sin is unforgivable.

Jesus' warning points out the importance of making good choices on earth because those choices determine where we spend eternity. Most of us today are not in a position in which our lives are at risk because we acknowledge Jesus. We can deny Jesus as the Son of God, however, when we fail to obey all that the Bible teaches. If we pick and choose only what is convenient or easy to believe and obey, we deny Christ. Jesus says that some day we will stand in God's presence and our sinful attitudes will be exposed.

> **Luke 12:11–12** "When you are brought before synagogues, rulers and authorities, do not worry about how you will defend yourselves or what you will say, for the Holy Spirit will teach you at that time what you should say."

Don't Worry About This Test

Some form of persecution would be unavoidable if the disciples remained loyal to Jesus, and Jesus assured them not to worry. True believers don't speak against the Holy Spirit. And better yet, when they are persecuted, they will discover that the Holy Spirit gives them words to say. When under pressure of his enemies, God would guide their speech.

God will not leave his faithful follower to deal with persecution alone. He promises that he will <u>never leave</u> his own. That's why the disciple can face even cruel and unjust mistreatment without fear.

A WORD FOR THE GREEDY

> **Luke 12:13–15** Someone in the crowd said to him, "Teacher, tell my brother to divide the inheritance with me."

FAST FORWARD

KEY POINT

The choice is ours: Will we acknowledge Jesus Christ as the Son of God?

Remember This . . .

☞ **GO TO:**

Hebrews 13:5–6 (never leave)

> Jesus replied, "Man, who appointed me a judge or an arbiter between you?" Then he said to them, "Watch out! Be on your guard against all kinds of greed; a man's life does not consist in the abundance of his possessions."

Mind Reader

Because it was common for rabbis to offer judgment on matters of dispute, a man felt free to bring up a personal concern to Jesus. Jesus did not take part in the dispute but not because he didn't have advice or because he didn't care. Rather, he spoke to something over which no one else had authority—attitudes or motives. Jesus could read minds and hearts. Everyone in the audience faced a loss caused by greed. Jesus said that getting wrapped up in material things blinds us to the only significant values.

Jesus made a statement that would rock today's society back on its heels when he said that what makes us persons of significance does not depend on what we have, even when we have an abundance of possessions. Tell that to business corporations, their marketing departments and their advertising agencies. Commercials seek to persuade us that we are the toothpaste we use, the vehicle we drive, the vacation spots we visit, and the size of our investments.

FAST FORWARD

Luke 12:16–21 And he told them this parable: "The ground of a certain rich man produced a good crop. He thought to himself, 'What shall I do? I have no place to store my crops.'

"Then he said, 'This is what I'll do. I will tear down my barns and build bigger ones, and there I will store all my grain and my goods. And I'll say to myself, "You have plenty of good things laid up for many years. Take life easy; eat, drink and be merry."'

"But God said to him, 'You fool! This very night your life will be demanded from you. Then who will get what you have prepared for yourself?'

"This is how it will be with anyone who stores up things for himself but is not rich toward God."

Boss Man

To make his point, Jesus told a parable that probed the heart of each listener. A rich farmer hauled in bumper crops and patted himself on the back not only for having a great harvest but also for what he thought was wise storage and estate planning. He thought he had it made.

Notice how selfish he was. In a few short sentences the farmer used the words "I" or "my" ten times. He wasn't concerned about the needs of the poor or even about passing on an inheritance to his relatives. He wanted to indulge in a life of luxury and ease.

God showed him who was boss. Possessions stored away cannot predict the future or save a person from death and eternal judgment. When a person who is rich in this world dies, he or she can suddenly discover he or she is poor in God's eyes.

PHYSICIAN'S PERSPECTIVE—We may wonder what crossed Dr. Luke's mind as he heard about the story Jesus told. Any doctor knows there is a price to be paid for luxury living—laziness and indulgence with no concern for anything beyond eating, drinking, and partying. Since the body pays a price, what about the soul?

Life begins when you win the lottery. Security is having a fat, guaranteed-to-grow retirement account. Fact or fiction? Jesus' parable about the rich farmer points out the fiction in any promise that wealth brings contentment or security.

What Others are Saying:

Warren W. Wiersbe: Wealth cannot keep us alive when our time comes to die, nor can it buy back the opportunities we missed while we were thinking of ourselves and ignoring God and others.[3]

Darrell L. Bock: Richness towards God means responding to life and blessing in a way that he desires, in a way that honors him—through <u>service and compassion</u>. The conclusion condemns greed as the attitude that piles up stuff simply for one's own use.[4]

☞ **GO TO:**

Ephesians 4:28 (service and compassion)

A WORD FOR THE WORRIED

> **Luke 12:22–26** Then Jesus said to his disciples: "Therefore I tell you, do not worry about your life, what you will wear. Life is more than food, and the body more than clothes. Consider the ravens: They do not sow or reap, they have no storeroom or barn; yet God feeds them. And how much more valuable you are than birds! Who of you by worrying can add a single hour to his life? Since you cannot do this very little thing, why do you worry about the rest?"

KEY POINT

Worry doesn't work. Let God supply your needs.

Perspective Is Everything

Jesus' disciples did not share the rich farmer's problem of overabundance. They had given up everything to follow him, and most of them didn't have many material things to give up. They had no guaranteed provision for the next day, let alone their future. Jesus quickly put their concerns to rest. God provides even for ugly <u>ravens</u> or crows. How much more lovingly he would provide them with the food they needed!

As for worry—what good does it do? Since worrying can't add a single hour to life or an inch to height, why indulge in something so useless when they could trust their loving Father?

☞ **GO TO:**

Leviticus 11:13–15; Deuteronomy 14:11–14 (ravens)

Leon Morris: From the sins of greed and selfishness Jesus turns to that of worry, which in a way is connected with the other two. 'Greed can never *get* enough, worry is afraid it may not *have* enough' (Arndt).[5]

What Others are Saying:

> **Luke 12:27–31** "Consider how the lilies grow. They do not labor or spin. Yet I tell you, not even Solomon in all his splendor was dressed like one of these. If that is how God clothes the grass of the field, which is here today, and tomorrow is thrown into the fire, how much more will he clothe you, O you of little faith! And do not set your heart on what you will eat or drink; do not worry about it. For the pagan world runs after all such things, and your Father knows that you need them. But seek his kingdom, and all these things will be given to you as well."

Proper Priorities

lilies: scarlet poppies and anemones, which bloom for a day then die

Solomon: Israel's richest, wisest king

☞ **GO TO:**

2 Chronicles 9:13–21 (Solomon)

In assuring his disciples that God would provide for them, Jesus gave them a visual reminder of his care—the **lilies** that grew wild in the fields. King **Solomon** in all his royal robes was not dressed as elegantly as these common flowers. Knowing this, Jesus' disciples did not need to focus on their need for food and clothing. God had already promised to care for these. Instead, they should put their hearts and minds on one thing—seeking God's kingdom on earth. As they did, God would provide all that they needed.

> **Luke 12:32–34** "Do not be afraid, little flock, for your Father has been pleased to give you the kingdom. Sell your possessions and give to the poor. Provide purses for yourselves that will not wear out, a treasure in heaven that will not be exhausted, where no thief comes near and no moth destroys. For where your treasure is, there your heart will be also."

Treasures Guaranteed

Jesus promised his disciples that if they trusted all to him, they would enjoy a prosperity that the world could never provide. Their heavenly Father would give them the kingdom—plus, as they shared their earthly provisions with the poor, they would be storing treasure away in heaven. This meant not only guaranteed praise and reward from God in the future but also abundance now in terms of proper perspectives, knowing that nothing could destroy their treasures because they were secure in God.

KEY POINT

Keep first things first. Seek God's kingdom.

 PHYSICIAN'S PERSPECTIVE—Doctors are concerned with the needs of their patients. How appropriate that Luke includes Jesus' calling his disciples *"little flock."* This is the only use of this form of address in the New Testament. It implies that the disciples and all believers are to expect God to care for them just as a shepherd cares for his helpless sheep.

What Others are Saying:

Bob Benson: What was it that drew men to Jesus? Yes, he spoke with authority and he did deeds of miracle and wonder, but I really think the one thing that men could not ignore was the compassion and love that drained out of his heart and on to his face and into his words and deeds.

If we abide in him as he abides in us, we begin to see things differently. We begin to look at things with his eyes.[6]

Do we sometimes think that our gifts to care for the physical needs of the poor are less spiritual than gifts for building churches and publishing Bibles? Jesus made no such distinction. He consistently showed his heart of compassion for those in humble circumstances.

Something to Ponder

A WORD FOR THE WATCHFUL

> **Luke 12:35–40** "Be dressed ready for service and keep your lamps burning, like men waiting for their master to return from a wedding banquet, so that when he comes and knocks they can immediately open the door for him. It will be good for those servants whose master finds them watching when he comes. I tell you the truth, he will dress himself to serve, will have them recline at the table and will come and wait on them. It will be good for those servants whose master finds them ready, even if he comes in the second or third watch of the night. But understand this: If the owner of the house had known at what hour the thief was coming, he would not have let his house be broken into. You also must be ready, because the Son of Man will come at an hour when you do not expect him."

Living On Alert

Worry-free living does not mean careless living. To be *"dressed ready for service"* in the first century meant that the person tucked his outer robe up into his belt to get it out of the way, allowing free movement. He was then ready for hard work, vigorous travel, or dangerous battle. Likewise, Jesus' followers have strenuous duties. Jesus told his disciples that they were to live on alert—watching and waiting for his return.

For awhile they would not see him, but when he returned he expected them to be ready, as servants would be ready for their master to return from a wedding ceremony bringing his bride with him. Much as a thief breaks in when a homeowner least expects him, Jesus will return at an unexpected hour. Disciples need to be looking for him in an attitude of tiptoed expectancy.

Jesus may return at any time—when we least expect him. Fact or fiction? If we believe what Jesus says, we will say fact. But the proof of what we believe is in how we live. Do we say it is a fact but make our choices as if it were fiction?

> **Luke 12:41–46** Peter asked, "Lord, are you telling this parable to us, or to everyone?"
>
> The Lord answered, "Who then is the faithful and wise manager, whom the master puts in charge of his servants to give them their food allowance at the proper time? It will be good for that servant whom the master finds doing so when he returns. I tell you the truth, he will put him in charge of all his possessions. But suppose the servant says to himself, 'My master is taking a long time in coming,' and he then begins to beat the menservants and maidservants and to eat and drink and get drunk. The master of that servant will come on a day when he does not expect him and at an hour he is not aware of. He will cut him to pieces and assign him a place with the unbelievers."

Employees On Trial

Peter, spokesman for the group, asked about responsibility. Jesus answered with a question and a parable that showed the disciples had a special responsibility.

A boss needed to leave for an extended time. He put a manager in charge, gave specific work assignments, provided for the needs of all workers, and promised to return. What should he find when he returned? If the workers had been negligent, they would be punished in proportion to the responsibilities and resources they had been given.

> **Luke 12:47–48** "That servant who knows his master's will and does not get ready or does not do what his master wants will be beaten with many blows. But the one who does not know and does things deserving punishment will be beaten with few blows. From everyone who has been given much, much will be demanded; and from the one who has been entrusted with much, more will be asked."

KEY POINT

Serve with faithfulness, knowing that someday you will be evaluated.

Earned Degrees

This parable illustrated the idea of degrees of punishment. The ignorant workers were judged because they should have made it their responsibility to find out what the boss wanted. While everyone was responsible for his or her actions, the workers who knew what the boss wanted but did not obey were told to expect harsher treatment than those who were ignorant of the boss's instructions. Both groups were punished according to their level of responsibility.

In Bible times business travelers did not enjoy the convenience of instant contact with the home office. An executive would prepare his staff as best he could before leaving, but once he was gone he would have to trust the faithfulness of his staff to carry on until he returned.

Though we have technology for communication that was undreamed of in Bible days, we have the kind of responsibility Jesus spoke of in this parable. He, like the business executive, is gone for an extended time. We are to be faithful in conducting his business. When he returns, there will be an accounting.

First, he will <u>expose</u> actions and motives that we have concealed from others. Then, if we have been faithful even in the hidden things, he will praise us for fulfilling the duties he assigned us.

FAST FORWARD

☞ **GO TO:**

1 Corinthians 4:5 (expose)

A WORD FOR THE UNCOMMITTED

Luke 12:49–53 "I have come to bring fire on the earth, and how I wish it were already kindled! But I have a baptism to undergo, and how distressed I am until it is completed! Do you think I came to bring peace on earth? No, I tell you, but division. From now on there will be five in one family divided against each other, three against two and two against three. They will be divided, father against son and son against father, mother against daughter and daughter against mother, mother-in-law against daughter-in-law and daughter-in-law against mother-in-law."

Family Feud

Jesus had a warning for the uncommitted. If they were expecting a smooth ride into his kingdom, they needed to stop and count the cost. Commitment to him carries a price. Much as people were split in their acceptance of him, so people would be split in their acceptance of his followers. Families would be divided, often bitterly, between those who followed Jesus and those who rejected him.

FACT OR FICTION

☞ **GO TO:**

Luke 2:14 (on earth)

Romans 5:1 (who trust)

John 7:12, 43; 9:16; 10:19 (division)

Luke 19:38 (in heaven)

When Jesus was born, God sent angelic messengers to announce peace, but now we have Jesus declaring that he was bringing division, not peace. So is peace on earth fact or fiction?

The angel announced peace <u>on earth</u> at Jesus' birth. Jesus gives inner peace to those <u>who trust</u> him, but sometimes their loyalty to Jesus causes <u>division</u> and opposition with family and friends. But even if we do not find peace on earth among earth-dwellers, we have Jesus' promise of peace <u>in heaven</u> throughout eternity.

A WORD FOR THE UNPREPARED

Luke 12:54–59 He said to the crowd: "When you see a cloud rising in the west, immediately you say, 'It's going to rain,' and it does. And when the south wind blows, you say 'It's going to be hot,' and it is. Hypocrites! You know how to interpret the appearance of the earth and the sky. How is it that you don't know how to interpret this present time.

"Why don't you judge for yourselves what is right? As you are going with your adversary to the magistrate, try hard to be reconciled to him on the way, or he may drag you off to the judge, and the judge turn you over to the officer, and the officer throw you into prison. I tell you, you will not get out until you have paid the last penny."

Weather Watch Blindness

Jesus had stern words for those who could use clues from the sky and wind to predict weather, but who were blind to the overwhelming evidence that he was the promised Messiah. They could prepare for changes in the weather but were not prepared to heed his warnings for repentance. He could warn, but he could not spare them the judgment that lay ahead if they continued to reject him.

FAST FORWARD

Jesus was saying that people in his day were interested in weather reports that would influence their activities for the next few hours. In contrast, they were paying no attention to his words, which would influence them for the rest of their lives—and for all eternity!

Today we listen to our televisions for weather and stock market reports. We listen to political pundits for what's ahead for our country, to sound bites for what's coming in medical advances. Where are we turning for authoritative information for our spiritual lives? We need to ask ourselves how much time we are spending in the Word of God.

Study Questions

1. What spiritual danger did Jesus identify as yeast of the Pharisees? How could this be a danger for his disciples?
2. What antidote did Jesus offer to his disciples for their natural fear of Jesus' enemies?
3. According to Jesus, why is greed such a destructive sin?
4. What did Jesus say should be our attitude toward "things"?
5. What was the point of Jesus' parable about the servants who awaited their master's return from his wedding? How does this impact us today?
6. In what way does Jesus disrupt family relationships?
7. What did Jesus say is more important than keeping alert to such current events as weather?

CHAPTER WRAP-UP

- Jesus warned against the yeast of Pharisees, which he identified as hypocrisy. (Luke 12:1–3)

- Jesus taught that his followers should not fear those who can hurt the body but fear God who has power over this life and the next. (Luke 12:4–12)

- Jesus warned against greed, which blinds us to God's desire for us to share with others who have needs and keeps us from building treasure in heaven. (Luke 12:13–21)

- Jesus gave clear guidelines about our attitude toward "things." Since God will provide for our needs we should not worry.

Rather we should focus on doing his will. (Luke 12:22–34)

- Jesus challenged his disciples to be faithful to the assignments he gave them—even when he would be absent from them. (Luke 12:35–48)

- Jesus warned that belief in him would disrupt family relationships because allegiance to him must come before allegiance to family members. (Luke 12:49–53)

- We are alert enough to pay attention to signs of weather change, but need to be even more alert and responsive to what Jesus teaches that impacts our lives now—and forever. (Luke 12:54–59)

LUKE 13: GOING AGAINST THE GRAIN

CHAPTER HIGHLIGHTS

- Repentance Required
- Hypocrisy Exposed
- Human Standards Challenged
- Sincerity Sought
- Heart Murmurs Wanted

Let's Get Started

Sometimes love has to be tough. Sometimes the truth has to be spoken even if it offends. A warning has to hurt before it can be heeded.

Jesus moved toward Jerusalem where his ministry would climax in his death. While he didn't step back from his compassionate work of healing and teaching the common people, he stepped up his confrontation with the religious leaders, calling on them to turn from their pride and hypocrisy and to believe his teaching. His mission had consistently disturbed and angered the unbelieving leaders, and the time had come for him to openly state his claim as Messiah.

REPENTANCE REQUIRED

Luke 13:1–5 Now there were some present at that time who told Jesus about the Galileans whose blood Pilate had mixed with their sacrifices. Jesus answered, "Do you think that these Galileans were worse sinners than all the other Galileans because they suffered this way? I tell you, no! But unless you repent, you too will all perish. Or those eighteen who died when the tower in Siloam fell on them—do you think they were more guilty than all the others living in Jerusalem? I tell you, no! But unless you repent, you too will all perish."

Accident Or Punishment?

Jesus spoke of two events with which his audience was familiar. First, he responded to a horrible report that some Galileans had been killed by Pilate's soldiers while they were at the Temple to offer sacrifices. In another unfortunate event, eighteen people died when a tower fell on them. In Bible times people generally accepted the idea that anyone who died tragically had been punished by God. Jesus differed. He said that those who died were not *"worse sinners"* than others. In fact, unless all those listening to him **repented**, they would also perish. This meant changing their hearts and minds about Jesus.

repent: to be sorry for sin and be willing to change

FACT OR FICTION

A person going through a series of misfortunes asks, "What did I do to deserve this?" Compounding the problem, onlookers conclude, "He must have done something bad because this happened." Bad things happen to people because they have done something wrong. Fact or fiction? Jesus clearly says that troubles and death are common to all. Calamities happen without regard to individual guilt. Every person is sinful. What is truly individual is each person's attitude about Jesus and the need to repent.

KEY POINT

The need for individual repentance brings everyone down to the same level.

> **Luke 13:6–9** Then he told this parable: "A man had a fig tree, planted in his vineyard, and he went to look for fruit on it, but did not find any. So he said to the man who took care of the vineyard, 'For three years now I've been coming to look for fruit on this fig tree and haven't found any. Cut it down! Why should it use up the soil?'
> "'Sir,' the man replied, 'Leave it alone for one more year, and I'll dig around it and fertilize it. If it bears fruit next year, fine! If not, then cut it down.'"

Upsetting The Fruit Basket

Jesus told a parable to help his listeners apply his point. He had told them that they needed to repent (verses 3 and 5). Now he said that if their lives did not show spiritual vitality, then repentance was not present and judgment would surely come for them.

The parable dealt with planting a fig tree. For three years the owner looked in vain for the tree to bear fruit. Disgusted, he directed that it should be cut down to make room for another planting. The caretaker pleaded for the unproductive tree, asking for one more year. He would give it every possible advantage and if it still did not bear fruit, he would cut it down.

The point? For three years Jesus had been proclaiming the truth about himself. Would the people believe him? If so, their lives would have indications of spiritual fruit. If there was no fruit, then judgment was sure to come.

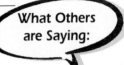

KEY POINT

God patiently waits for fruit.

Charles C. Ryrie: Every Christian will bear spiritual fruit. Somewhere, sometime, somehow. Otherwise that person is not a believer. Every born-again individual will be fruitful. Not to be fruitful is to be faithless, without faith, and therefore without salvation.[1]

HYPOCRISY EXPOSED

> **Luke 13:10–13** On a Sabbath Jesus was teaching in one of the synagogues, and a woman was there who had been crippled by a spirit for eighteen years. She was bent over and could not straighten up at all. When Jesus saw her, he called her forward and said to her, "Woman, you are set free from your infirmity." Then he put his hands on her, and immediately she straightened up and praised God.

Praise Reaction

In a synagogue one Sabbath Jesus used an opportunity to make his claims even more clear. Seeing a woman who had been crippled for eighteen years, he called her to step forward and said words she must have yearned to hear: *"Woman, you are set free from your infirmity."* He reached out to put his hands on her, and immediately she was relieved of her problem and able to stand up straight and move about. Her instant response was praise to God.

 PHYSICIAN'S PERSPECTIVE—Even doctors can be taken by surprise. Luke the physician reports the details of this miracle. The woman was bent over so severely that she could not even look upward. For eighteen years she had been unable to straighten her back. That she made it to the synagogue was no small undertaking! When Jesus spoke to her, freeing her of the restraints that prevented her movement, she was able to stand up and move uninhibited. No medication was prescribed, no surgery, no physical therapy—just instant healing!

What Others are Saying:

☞ **GO TO:**

Job 2:7 (Job's boils)

2 Corinthians 12:7–9 (Paul's thorn)

William MacDonald: The curvature of the spine was caused by Satan. We know from other parts of the Bible that some sicknesses are the result of Satanic activity. <u>Job's boils</u> were inflicted by Satan. <u>Paul's thorn</u> in the flesh was a messenger of Satan to buffet him. The devil is not allowed to do this on a believer, however, without the Lord's permission. And God overrules any such sickness or suffering for His own glory.[2]

> **Luke 13:14–17** Indignant because Jesus had healed on the Sabbath, the synagogue ruler said to the people, "There are six days for work. So come and be healed on those days, not on the Sabbath."
>
> The Lord answered him, "You hypocrites! Doesn't each of you on the Sabbath untie his ox or donkey from the stall and lead it out to give it water? Then should not this woman, a daughter of Abraham, whom Satan has kept bound for eighteen long years, be set free on the Sabbath day from what bound her?"
>
> When he said this, all his opponents were humiliated, but the people were delighted with all the wonderful things he was doing.

Critical Response

In contrast to the woman's reaction of praise, the instant response of the synagogue ruler was indignation. Rather than speaking to Jesus directly, he lashed out at the innocent people, saying they had no business seeking miracles on the Sabbath. He insisted that Jesus' healing clinic be closed on the Sabbath.

Jesus spoke up, pointing out the hypocrisy of having Sabbath rules that allowed care for animals but not for humans.

He made his point. His opponents were humiliated.

KEY POINT

Jesus ignored man-made rules to bring healing.

HUMAN STANDARDS CHALLENGED

> **Luke 13:18–21** Then Jesus asked, "What is the kingdom of God like? What shall I compare it to? It is like a mustard seed, which a man took and planted in his

garden. It grew and became a tree, and the birds of the air perched in its branches."

Again he asked, "What shall I compare the kingdom of God to? It is like yeast that a woman took and mixed into a large amount of flour until it worked all through the dough."

Small Quiet Power

Luke placed two illustrations here to teach more about the kingdom of God. The Jewish religious system had added thousands of rules to God's laws; yet it was powerless to bring about heart changes. Jesus contrasted that massive system with the seemingly insignificant kingdom of God. His kingdom was like a tiny **mustard** seed, which grows gradually so that it takes over the garden, providing a lush environment for birds to enjoy. His kingdom could bring about true change and it would do so gradually.

His kingdom was also like a little yeast that slowly changes flour so that it rises to make bread. The power of both the seed and the yeast is inherent or built-in. Both work quietly from the inside out. Likewise, the power of the kingdom of God is built-in, and it works quietly from the inside out to change people's hearts and lives.

Lawrence O. Richards: The rabbis of Jesus' day used the mustard seed as a symbol of anything tiny or insignificant. In each of the five references to the mustard seed in the New Testament, Jesus mentions this seed in the familiar rabbinical way. . . . Thus, the Kingdom of God looks insignificant to the world but holds within it the power of transforming growth.[3]

> *The Jews were looking for a kingdom that would burst onto the world political scene with power and majesty. Instead, the kingdom Jesus proclaimed seemed insignificant. Beyond the miracles he performed, there was almost no evidence of what the Old Testament prophets had promised.*
>
> *But quietly throughout the centuries the kingdom has spread to cover the whole earth. Much as a mustard seed grows to cover a garden or a pinch of yeast moves throughout a large quantity of dough, Jesus' kingdom is advancing through the church now and in his reign to come.*

☞ **GO TO:**

Matthew 13:31; 17:20; Mark 4:31; Luke 17:6 (mustard)

mustard: *plant grown for its aromatic, oily seeds; could get ten to fifteen feet high; its seeds attracted birds*

What Others are Saying:

FAST FORWARD

KEY POINT

God chooses to do a great work through what appears tiny and insignificant.

Tom Sine: It is still God's policy to work through the embarrassingly insignificant to change his world and create his future. He has chosen to work through the foolishness of human instrumentality. And he wants to use your life and mine to make a difference in his world. Just as Jesus invited that first unlikely bunch of fishermen, he invites us to drop our nets and abandon our boats and join him in the adventure of changing the world.[4]

SINCERITY SOUGHT

> **Luke 13:22–27** Then Jesus went through the towns and villages, teaching as he made his way to Jerusalem. Someone asked him, "Lord, are only a few people going to be saved?"
>
> He said to them, "Make every effort to enter through the narrow door, because many, I tell you, will try to enter and will not be able to. Once the owner of the house gets up and closes the door, you will stand outside knocking and pleading, 'Sir, open the door for us.'
>
> "But he will answer, 'I don't know you or where you come from.'
>
> "Then you will say, 'We ate and drank with you, and you taught in our streets.'
>
> "But he will reply, 'I don't know you or where you come from. Away from me, all you evildoers!'"

Head Scratching

Jesus' teaching was so revolutionary that listeners scratched their heads. If the religious leaders were not on the right track, what hope was there for the common people to be saved? Jesus must be saying heaven will be sparsely populated. So someone asked, *"Lord, are only a few people going to be saved?"*

Jesus did not answer the question numerically, but dealt rather with *who* would be saved. Only those who make the personal choice to enter through the narrow door would be in heaven.

This was a shock to his listeners. As descendants of Abraham, Isaac, and Jacob, the listeners assumed they would have automatic entrance into the kingdom. But Jesus said, "Not so!"

The invitation is for everyone, but only those who make the personal choice to enter will be included in God's kingdom. Those who do not make that decision will someday find that it is too late.

The words *"make every effort"* can also be translated "strive." It means whole-hearted action like an athlete training for the Olympics. Half-hearted attempts to gain access to God's kingdom will not work, but any genuine efforts will be rewarded. No matter how people have outwardly identified with God's followers, only those who have made the inner choice to follow him will be included in the kingdom.

We enter this world alone. We leave it alone. And somewhere in between we make our decision about Jesus alone. No one can make it for us.

Remember This . . .

> **Luke 13:28–30** "There will be weeping there, and gnashing of teeth, when you see Abraham, Isaac and Jacob and all prophets in the kingdom of God, but you yourselves thrown out. People will come from east and west and north and south, and will take their places at the feast in the kingdom of God. Indeed there are those who are last who will be first, and first who will be last."

Outside Looking In

Some people we expect to see in heaven will not be there. Others we expect *not* to see will be there. Jesus told the Jews that if they weren't careful to accept his teachings they would find themselves on the wrong side of the door of heaven. They thought they were God's privileged people, guaranteed a spot at the banquet with the Messiah. Jesus said the Gentiles would be sitting at places of honor around the table, while the Jews would be on the outside looking in.

HEART MURMURS WANTED

> **Luke 13:31–33** At that time some Pharisees came to Jesus and said to him, "Leave this place and go somewhere else. Herod wants to kill you."
>
> He replied, "Go tell that fox, 'I will drive out demons and heal people today and tomorrow, and on the third day I will reach my goal.' In any case, I must keep going today and tomorrow and the next day—for surely no prophet can die outside Jerusalem!"

Duty Calls

Some Pharisees came to Jesus with a warning—"Get out of here because Herod is after you!"

Jesus' reply must have mystified the messengers. He would continue his ministry until he reached Jerusalem, and he would do this with a deep sense of his mission. Luke emphasizes Jesus' strong sense of duty by using the words "must," "today," and "goal." Jesus' goal was to die on the cross.

FACT OR FICTION

God forbids speaking evil of one's ruler. Therefore Jesus was wrong to call Herod a fox. Fact or fiction? Fiction! Jesus was speaking the truth. His reference to a fox was to a destroyer, someone who was out to get him. It was not Jesus' time to die.

> **Luke 13:34–35** "O Jerusalem, Jerusalem, you who kill the prophets and stone those sent to you, how often I have longed to gather your children together, as a hen gathers her chicks under her wings, but you were not willing! Look, your house is left to you desolate. I tell you, you will not see me again until you say, 'Blessed is he who comes in the name of the Lord.'"

Sorry City

Jesus turned then to express his deep sorrow for Jerusalem and for the whole Jewish nation who had not believed him and was about to reject him by killing him. Jesus was deeply concerned about the city and the Jewish people. Although they had a history of rejecting God's messengers, Jesus had not rejected them. He still cared about them.

☞ **GO TO:**

2 Kings 21:16; Jeremiah 26:20–23 (rejecting)

MORE INFORMATION—In a different context Matthew includes Jesus' prayer for Jerusalem with its poignant reference to a hen caring for her chicks (Matthew 23:37–39). This tender image came from God to his people during their long journey from slavery in Egypt to the land of promise and was picked up in other Old Testament books (see Deuteronomy 32:11; Ruth 2:12; Psalms 17:8; 91:4). His care and protection came as the overflow of his love, and Jesus longed to spare them the consequences of their wrongdoing.

Philip Yancey: I sense in that spasm of emotional pain something akin to what a parent feels when a son or daughter goes astray, flaunting freedom, rejecting everything he or she was brought up to believe. Or the pain of a man or woman who has just learned a spouse has left—the pain of a jilted lover. It is a helpless, crushing pain of futility, and it staggers me to realize that the Son of God himself emitted a cry of helplessness in the face of human freedom. Not even God, with all his power, can force a human being to love.[5]

Study Questions

1. How did Jesus turn the generally accepted interpretation of two news events into something that had personal implications?
2. After Jesus healed the woman, how did Jesus expose the hypocrisy of the synagogue ruler?
3. In what way is the kingdom of God like a tiny mustard seed and a pinch of yeast?
4. What was the point of Jesus' warning about the narrow door? What application does it have for us today?
5. What prompted Jesus' expression of deep sorrow over Jerusalem?

CHAPTER WRAP-UP

- People assumed that tragedy was punishment from God. Jesus said that wasn't true and that each person was responsible to repent and avoid eternal judgment. (Luke 13:1–5)

- In the parable of the fig tree, Jesus taught that genuine repentance leads to spiritual life and fruit. (Luke 13:6–9)

- On a Sabbath Jesus healed a woman who had been severely disabled for eighteen years. In responding to the synagogue ruler's indignation over his violation of Sabbath laws, Jesus pointed out that the rules showed more compassion for an animal than for a human. (Luke 13:10–17)

- Jesus said his kingdom was like a tiny mustard seed and like a small amount of yeast. Both seem insignificant but in time grow and provide nourishment for many. (Luke 13:18–21)

- Jews assumed they would be in God's kingdom simply because they were descendants of Abraham. Jesus pointed out that unless they had personal faith in him, they would be left outside looking in. (Luke 13:22–30)

- Jesus sorrowed over Jerusalem because the Jews had rejected him and would bear terrible consequences for their rejection. (Luke 13:31–35)

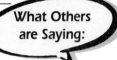

What Others are Saying:

KEY POINT

Christ never stops loving and caring, but he cannot spare us the consequences of our decision to reject him.

LUKE 14: RELATING TO PEOPLE

Let's Get Started

Luke gives a series of Jesus' teachings that involve relating to others. First, Jesus was tested one Sabbath in the home of a prominent Pharisee. Would Jesus heal a man suffering from dropsy? Jesus healed him and said that his accusers valued an ox more than a suffering human.

Then Jesus pointed out the Pharisees' habit of self-seeking as they tried to outdo each other in taking places of honor at the dinner. Jesus advised his host to stop inviting only those guests who could pay him back with similar meals and to include those who could not do so. In showing generosity to them he would be sure of God's reward.

To illustrate, Jesus told a parable that exposed self-centeredness. The Jews claimed exclusive rights to God's kingdom, but when Jesus came to invite them to his banquet they were too occupied with their own interests to respond.

Finally, Jesus clearly outlined the cost of discipleship. Of all relationships people sought, their relationship with him was costly but paramount.

VALUING PEOPLE

> **Luke 14:1–6** One Sabbath, when Jesus went to eat in the house of a prominent Pharisee, he was being carefully watched. There in front of him was a man suffering from dropsy. Jesus asked the Pharisees and experts in the law, "Is it lawful to heal on the Sabbath or not?"

> But they remained silent. So taking hold of the man, he healed him and sent him away.
> Then he asked them, "If one of you has a son or an ox that falls into a well on the Sabbath day, will you not immediately pull him out?" And they had nothing to say.

All The Trappings

On a Sabbath day Jesus accepted an invitation for dinner in the home of a well-known Pharisee. Rather than being a gracious gesture on the part of the host, it was a trap. The seating around the table was not haphazard, for the Pharisee had placed in front of Jesus a man who was obviously afflicted with **dropsy**.

dropsy: edema, an abnormal accumulation of fluid in the body cavities or limbs, causing swelling

The trap was set. While everyone in the room watched to see what Jesus would do, Jesus turned the trap on the Pharisees by asking if it was lawful to heal on the Sabbath.

The Pharisees and experts in the law chose not to answer. If they said it was lawful, they would be violating one of their man-made Sabbath laws and could not complain if Jesus healed him. If they said it was unlawful, they would be showing callous indifference to the afflicted man. Their silence spoke volumes.

Jesus reached out and touched the man, healed him, and sent him home. Then he turned to his accusers and asked if any of them would rescue a son or an ox that fell into a well on the Sabbath day. Again they were trapped, so had to remain silent.

 PHYSICIAN'S PERSPECTIVE—Luke the physician probably took great interest in the report of Jesus' healing. The man with dropsy was obviously retaining fluid, caused by kidney, heart, or liver trouble. He was very ill and the medical profession could offer little to relieve his discomfort.

Jesus showed compassion in sending the healed man away so that he would not have to hear the question he would raise with those who were eager to accuse him for performing the miracle of healing on the Sabbath.

What Others are Saying:

Lawrence O. Richards: It must have been frustrating, to be an opponent of Jesus. Whenever they attempted to act against him, they simply injured themselves!

As long as we live in the spirit of Jesus, maintaining his compassion for others, any who criticize us will also expose only their own hardness of heart.[1]

> **Luke 14:7–11** When he noticed how the guests picked the places of honor at the table, he told them this parable: "When someone invites you to a wedding feast, do not take the place of honor, for a person more distinguished than you may have been invited. If so, the host who invited both of you will come and say to you, 'Give this man your seat.' Then, humiliated, you will have to take the least important place. But when you are invited, take the lowest place, so that when your host comes, he will say to you, 'Friend, move up to a better place.' Then you will be honored in the presence of all your fellow guests. For everyone who exalts himself will be humbled, and he who humbles himself will be exalted."

KEY POINT

Jesus had compassion for all, but the proud and self-righteous remained untouched by his love.

Humble Etiquette

Jesus noted that the guests at the Pharisee's home scrambled for places of honor next to the host. He pointed out their self-seeking in a parable about a wedding feast. He warned, "Don't assume you are the most important guest and assign yourself a place of honor at the table. Imagine your humiliation when the host asks you to move down in order to make room for someone who has been invited to take that place next to the host. Instead, come with a humble attitude. Take a low place. Then the host will invite you to move up to a place of honor."

Jesus then gave a principle that has implications for all our interactions with others. If we puff up ourselves as important, we will be <u>knocked down</u>. But if we sincerely humble ourselves following Jesus' <u>example</u>, God will see that we are exalted.

☞ **GO TO:**

Proverbs 18:12 (knocked down)

Philippians 2:5–11 (example)

C. Samuel Storms: I'm often amused, as well as saddened, when people go to great lengths to have their names publicly displayed or preserved. Those who can afford it bequeath huge sums of money to universities or charitable foundations, hoping to see their name in the cornerstone of a building or in some other way enshrined in the memory of future generations.[2]

What Others are Saying:

Jesus has a special word for people who are humble and are not self-seeking. They value God's approval more than the admiration of their peers. God, who sees the heart, will reveal himself to those who are humble.

Remember This . . .

> **Luke 14:12–14** Then Jesus said to his host, "When you give a luncheon or dinner, do not invite your friends, your brothers or relatives, or your rich neighbors; if you do, they may invite you back and so you will be repaid. But when you give a banquet, invite the poor, the crippled, the lame, the blind, and you will be blessed. Although they cannot repay you, you will be repaid at the resurrection of the righteous."

Dinner Round Robin

The host at the dinner had followed the prevailing custom of the day. He invited friends and relatives who could repay him with an invitation to their homes. It was a social game of ping pong. This was no problem for the "in" group. In fact, it was a self-serving system. They could count on a steady flow of return invitations. Jesus' concern was for the "out" group—the poor and people with disabilities—who were never included on the guest list.

Granted these people could not reciprocate, but Jesus promised that such acts of kindness and generosity would be rewarded, not with notes in the social columns of the newspaper, but with God himself in the resurrection.

What Others are Saying:

Dallas Willard: [Jesus] . . . is . . . telling us to provide for more than our little circle of mutual appreciation, and thus to place ourselves in the larger context of heaven's rule where we have a different kind of mind and heart regardless of who we do or do not have over for dinner.[3]

FACT OR FICTION

☞ **GO TO:**

John 12:42–43
(from men)

A man is known by the company he keeps. Fact or fiction? The Pharisees certainly thought that was true. How hard some people in Jesus' day worked to build a reputation for being at the top—or at least having the favor of the few who had made it to that level! Jesus pointed the prominent Pharisee in a different direction when he told him to invite society's outcasts. Reaching out to these people would not enhance his reputation on earth, but would win God's favor. It's a fact that a man *is* known by the company he keeps. The question is, whose opinion matters more: man's or God's?

Human nature has not changed through the centuries. Some leaders actually believed in Jesus, but, because they valued their reputations, did not dare to let that be known. They yearned for praise <u>from men</u> more than praise from God. Today many people

FAST FORWARD

place great emphasis on networking and name-dropping, all in an effort to impress others with their status.

Jesus cuts through all that kind of motivation as he points out that we should value all people, not just the individuals who help elevate our status.

INVITING PEOPLE

Luke 14:15–20 When one of those at the table with him heard this, he said to Jesus, "Blessed is the man who will eat at the feast in the kingdom of God."

Jesus replied: "A certain man was preparing a great banquet and invited many guests. At the time of the banquet he sent his servant to tell those who had been invited, 'Come, for everything is now ready.'

"But they all alike began to make excuses. The first said, 'I have just bought a field, and I must go and see it. Please excuse me.'

"Another said, 'I have just bought five yoke of oxen, and I'm on my way to try them out. Please excuse me.'

"Still another said, 'I just got married, so I can't come.'

Excuses, Excuses

Someone broke into the conversation to express his anticipation of eating at the feast in God's kingdom. It was a self-righteous statement and possibly implied that while he and the other law-abiding Jews at the Pharisee's Sabbath dinner would be blessed in God's kingdom, Jesus would not!

Jesus answered with a parable about a man who planned a banquet and whose invited guests did not come. The guests had accepted the advance invitations, but now they insulted their gracious host by giving flimsy excuses for not coming.

The Pharisees could not miss the point of Jesus' parable. They assumed that as law-abiding Jews they would have a secure place in God's kingdom. However, when Jesus came to invite them to commit themselves to him, they made excuses.

Helmut Thielicke: It is easy enough to understand why someone may reject an excessive demand. Many of us have burdensome demands made upon us. How many there are who are always wanting something from us; wanting us to give money, wanting

What Others are Saying:

us to support this cause or that, wanting us to provide dwellings and jobs and so forth . . . But here the situation is different. Here an invitation is being refused.[4]

Something to Ponder

In Jesus' parable people had accepted the invitation to the banquet, but at the last minute they made excuses for not attending. Their desire for pleasure and financial security was too important to them. What kinds of things keep us from being committed to God's kingdom?

> **Luke 14:21–24** "The servant came back and reported this to his master. Then the owner of the house became angry and ordered his servant, 'Go out quickly into the streets and alleys of the town and bring in the poor, the crippled, the blind, and the lame.'
>
> "'Sir,' the servant said, 'what you ordered has been done, but there is still room.'
>
> "Then the master told his servant, 'Go out to the roads and country lanes and make them come in, so that my house will be full. I tell you, not one of those men who were invited will get a taste of my banquet.'"

Invitations For Outcasts

The host sent his servant to comb the streets and back alleys and urge the riffraff and outcasts to come to the party. When this was accomplished and there was still room in the banquet hall, the host sent the servant to go outside the town and persuade even more such people to come.

And the men who had been invited in the first place? They would not be allowed even one bite of the sumptuous food! Since they rejected him, God welcomed those whom the Pharisees considered inferior and unworthy: the man with dropsy, the poor, crippled, lame, and blind. Further, God welcomed the Gentiles into his kingdom.

DISCIPLESHIP DILEMMAS

> **Luke 14:25–27** Large crowds were traveling with Jesus, and turning to them, he said: "If anyone comes to me and does not hate his father and mother, his wife and

> children, his brothers and sisters—yes, even his own life—he cannot be my disciple. And anyone who does not carry his cross and follow me cannot be my disciple."

Words That Thinned Out The Crowd

Crowds gathered around Jesus wherever he went. As he moved toward <u>Jerusalem</u> where he would give his life, he gave his would-be followers a sudden eye-opener. Anyone who wanted to follow him as a disciple must be so committed to Jesus that he would put Jesus first in everything. Every other relationship—good and worthy as it may be—must take second place. Further, the would-be follower must be willing to pay the price of loyalty to Jesus. This would mean suffering and even death.

R. Kent Hughes: What Jesus was saying paradoxically was that our love for him must be so great and so pervasive that our natural love of self and family pales in comparison. We are to subordinate everything, even our own being, to our love and commitment to Christ. He is to be our first loyalty.[5]

Jesus was not saying that his followers must harbor ill will toward family and friends. The reality is that the closer a disciple is to Jesus the more loving he or she becomes to others. In fact, Jesus commanded his disciples to <u>love</u> one another and said that the badge that identified his true disciples would be their love. But if a follower of Christ ever had to choose between Christ or family, he must choose Christ.

> **Luke 14:28–30** "Suppose one of you wants to build a tower. Will he not first sit down and estimate the cost to see if he has enough money to complete it? For if he lays the foundation and is not able to finish it, everyone who sees it will ridicule him, saying, 'This fellow began to build and was not able to finish.'"

A Commitment To Completion

Many a town has an incomplete building or road, and the townspeople don't fail to mock the city "planners." Before even marking out the place for the foundation, the builder needs to work on

☞ **GO TO:**

Luke 13:33 (Jerusalem)

What Others are Saying:

Something to Ponder

☞ **GO TO:**

John 13:34–35 (love)

his budget. Does he have enough money to complete the tower? If not, he will become the butt of many a joke.

> **Luke 14:31–33** "Or suppose a king is about to go to war against another king. Will he not first sit down and consider whether he is able with ten thousand men to oppose the one coming against him with twenty thousand? If he is not able, he will send a delegation while the other is still a long way off and will ask for terms of peace. In the same way, any of you who does not give up everything he has cannot be my disciple."

A Commitment To Confrontation

Jesus then spoke of a king who is suddenly threatened by an enemy. He needs to weigh his options. He has an army of ten thousand. His enemy is approaching with an army of twenty thousand. If he is not willing to risk confronting the enemy, he would do well to send a delegation to negotiate a peaceful settlement to their dispute. But if he decides to risk the confrontation, he must be willing to give it his all.

What Others are Saying:

Oswald Chambers: Discipleship means personal, passionate devotion to a Person, our Lord Jesus Christ. There is a difference between devotion to a person and devotion to principles or to a cause. Our Lord never proclaimed a cause; he proclaimed personal devotion to himself.[6]

> **Luke 14:34–35** "Salt is good, but if it loses its saltiness, how can it be made salty again? It is fit neither for the soil nor for the manure pile; it is thrown out.
> "He who has ears to hear, let him hear."

A Disciple Worth His Salt

Salt was essential to everyday living. It was used to add zest to food. It was also needed to preserve food and to be a cleansing agent. But if it became mixed with impurities, it would lose its value. Similarly, a disciple is unworthy if he or she comes with mixed motives and less-than-a-sober renunciation of everything other than Christ.

Paul N. Benware: Salt that has lost its seasoning has no value and has lost its purpose for existence. And so, the believer who chooses not to fulfill these requirements and follow Christ as a disciple will have a life with little value and purpose.[7]

Study Questions

1. What attitude did Jesus expose in the Pharisees when he healed the man with dropsy?
2. What false attitudes did Jesus expose in the way (a) men chose seats at the dinner and (b) the host had chosen his guests?
3. In Jesus' parable of the great banquet, what was the significance to the Jewish people of the banquet? Who did the host invite in place of the guests who refused to come?
4. What standards did Jesus give for his disciples?

CHAPTER WRAP-UP

- The Pharisees set a trap for Jesus at a Sabbath meal by putting a man with dropsy in front of him. Jesus healed the man and silenced the Pharisees. (Luke 14:1–6)

- Guests of the Pharisee elbowed their way to the seats of honor next to the host. Jesus said they should be humble and generous toward others. (Luke 14:7–14)

- The Pharisees understood that the reference to the feast related to their standing in God's kingdom. Jesus told a parable about a host whose guests made flimsy excuses not to come to his banquet. The host invited the poor and outcasts and they came. (Luke 14:15–24)

- Jesus told his followers that if they wanted to be his disciples they needed to count the cost and be totally committed to him. (Luke 14:25–35)

LUKE 15: LOST AND FOUND

CHAPTER HIGHLIGHTS

- Saved Sheep
- Coined Celebration
- Homecomings

Let's Get Started

Luke gives us a chapter that glows like a ring set with precious stones, for here Jesus tells three parables that give a sparkling revelation of his Father's heart of love. In each story something highly valued is lost, and the joy when it is recovered becomes a picture of the rejoicing in heaven when a lost person is found by the loving Father.

Jesus told his stories to a mixed audience. A large group of social outcasts gathered around him. On the outer edge stood Pharisees and experts in religion who not only despised the outcasts as sinners but also considered themselves superior to Jesus. Jesus' parables had a strong message to each listener—and to each of us today.

SAVED SHEEP

Luke 15:1–2 Now the tax collectors and "sinners" were all gathering around to hear him. But the Pharisees and the teachers of the law muttered, "This man welcomes sinners and eats with them."

Sin By Association

Pharisees and teachers of the law looked on with extreme distaste as they observed tax collectors and "sinners" flocking to Jesus and listening intently to his teaching. The Pharisees and teachers of the law had spent their lives observing every law and keeping separate from anything designated as unclean. They were horrified that Jesus mingled with the very people they considered to be both social and religious outcasts. They fumed as they watched him mingling with them and actually eating with them as if he enjoyed their company.

Jesus knew the complaints of his critics. Instead of judging them as they were judging him, Jesus told three parables that revealed his love and compassion for those who were despised—and for those who did the despising. How he longed for them to see that they too were lost and in need of being found by the Savior!

Nobody has the right to try to win another person over to his or her religion. It is wrong to **proselytize**. Fact or fiction? If that is a fact, then by today's standards, Jesus violated human rights! He made it his priority to go out of his way to seek out those who had been discarded by the religious leaders. He made them his friends and taught them of his Father's love for them.

FACT OR FICTION

What Others are Saying:

proselytize: *attempt to convert someone from one religious belief to another*

☞ **GO TO:**

1 Corinthians 13:7 (love)

Fall: *Adam and Eve's first disobedience to God that plunged all humankind into sin*

Gilbert Bilezikian: Because God is love, he created human life out of love. <u>Love</u> bears all things, endures all things, and never ends. Therefore, as horrible as it was, the **Fall** could not make God stop loving the beings he had created in his image.[1]

Luke 15:3–7 Then Jesus told them this parable: "Suppose one of you has a hundred sheep and loses one of them. Does he not leave the ninety-nine in the open country and go after the lost sheep until he finds it? And when he finds it, he joyfully puts it on his shoulders and goes home. Then he calls his friends and neighbors together and says, 'Rejoice with me; I have found my lost sheep.' I tell you that in the same way there will be more rejoicing in heaven over one sinner who repents than over ninety-nine righteous persons who do not need to repent."

Searching For Blacky

Jesus used a common scenario to illustrate truth about God. A shepherd led his flock to the sheepfold where they were protected as they rested for the night (see illustration below). One hundred was a common-sized flock. When the shepherd noticed he was missing one sheep, he didn't say, "Oh well, ninety-nine is close enough." He set out to find the lost sheep, leaving the ninety-nine secure in the sheepfold, perhaps under the watch of a neighbor (see GWJN, pages 132–134).

In case his listeners missed the point, Jesus made it clear. All who heard the story were <u>sheep</u>. The <u>lost</u> sheep pictured a sinner who repented because he knew he was lost. The <u>shepherd</u> was the Savior who searched for him, gently lifted him on his strong shoulders, and <u>carried</u> him to safety.

Notice that in this analogy Jesus initiated the search for the lost. The idea is that God actively seeks sinners and wants to bring them into relationship with him. And when he does, he throws a party to celebrate. God is jubilant when the lost are saved. In heaven there is more celebration over one sinner who repents than over ninety-nine law-abiding "righteous" people who feel no need to be rescued by the Savior.

☞ **GO TO:**

Psalm 95:7; 100:3 (sheep)

Isaiah 53:6 (lost)

Ezekiel 34:31 (shepherd)

Isaiah 46:3–4 (carried)

Sheepfold

Towns often had community sheepfolds such as the one depicted here where shepherds could place their sheep for a safe night's rest. Shepherds took turns guarding the entrance as not all sheepfolds had doors.

Lost people are as helpless as sheep, but God can rescue them.

PHYSICIAN'S PERSPECTIVE—Dr. Luke understood the shepherd's unhesitating decision to search for the one missing sheep. What physician has not extended himself to relieve someone who was suffering, no matter what personal cost was involved? Luke identified with Jesus' compassion for the missing, who may not even be aware that he or she was missing, and the joy when that one was found and brought home.

MORE INFORMATION—Matthew 18:1–14 includes Jesus' parable in a different context. Jesus speaks of the loving concern his followers should have for young children. Children are significant to God—so much so that their angelic beings are constantly in his presence in heaven. The trust that children have, their unhesitating response to Jesus' love, is a quality that Jesus looks for in adult hearts. He warns of the consequences of leading children to sin. Then he tells the parable of the lost sheep to show that all his followers should be tireless in their efforts to seek and restore any little one who strays.

What Others are Saying:

Phyllis Kilbourn: Our heavenly Father fully understands the pain and fear of the world's suffering children, whatever difficult circumstances engulf them. I am convinced that his deepest heart-longing is to stir us, his people, to reach out with God-given compassion toward them—the youngest members of our worldwide family. We have the responsibility to bring them the message of God's redeeming love, holistic healing and hope.[2]

COINED CELEBRATION

> **Luke 15:8–10** "Or suppose a woman has ten silver coins and loses one. Does she not light a lamp, sweep the house and search carefully until she finds it? And when she finds it, she calls her friends and neighbors together and says, 'Rejoice with me; I have found my lost coin.' In the same way, I tell you, there is rejoicing in the presence of the angels of God over one sinner who repents."

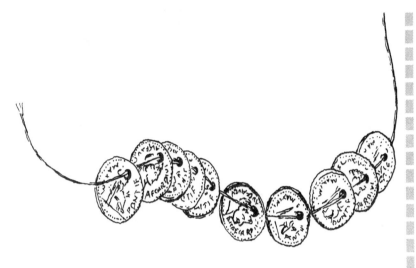

Dowry Coins

The woman in Jesus' parable may have worn a headband of silver coins with holes drilled in them and placed on a string, signifying that she was a wife. The headband was regarded as we today regard a wedding ring.

Capital Recovery

In Jesus' second parable, a woman had ten silver coins, each worth far more than their monetary value of a day's wage. These coins probably were her **dowry**, worn on her headdress (see illustration above). How much the woman valued her lost coin is reflected in her aggressive search.

Her house was dark with only a small window to allow light, so she lit a lamp, seized her broom, and carefully swept her house. She didn't stop for a coffee break or for a friendly chat with her neighbors. She swept and swept, turning over furniture and shaking out every cloth covering. She dropped to her knees and felt around the floor with her hands, all the time looking for a glint of light reflecting from the coin or listening for a whisper of its movement across the dirt floor. She did not give up until she found it!

She had not recruited her friends to help her find it, but kept the loss to herself. Now her joy simply had to be expressed. A celebration was in order. She called her friends and neighbors to join her in marking the occasion of her great find.

No Giving Up

Jesus' parable made two points that must have astonished his listeners. First, God doesn't merely tolerate sinners and let them go their own way. He seeks to rescue them. Then, he doesn't give up when they do not respond to him. He keeps pursuing them. This was contrary to the Israelites' view of Jehovah the Lawgiver.

dowry: gift given to the bride's father by the groom or, in this case, gift given to a bride by her father

KEY POINT

Lost people are precious to God.

What Others are Saying:

FAST FORWARD

Lawrence O. Richards: *To God, people are a prize! We are important and valued, and the transformation of a single sinner brings joy, not only to God, but also to all who share his heart of love.*[3]

Jesus calls his followers to be like the shepherd who went out to search for the lost sheep and to be like the woman who searched until she found her lost coin. Today he still asks his followers to care for all who need the Father's love and are willing to come to the Savior.

HOMECOMING

> **Luke 15:11–16** Jesus continued: "There was a man who had two sons. The younger one said to his father, 'Father, give me my share of the estate.' So he divided his property between them.
>
> "Not long after that, the younger son got together all he had, set off for a distant country and there squandered his wealth in wild living. After he had spent everything, there was a severe famine in that whole country, and he began to be in need. So he went and hired himself out to a citizen of that country, who sent him to his fields to feed pigs. He longed to fill his stomach with the pods that the pigs were eating, but no one gave him anything."

From Riches To Rags

In Jesus' third parable, what was lost was not an animal or a valued coin but a son who deliberately chose to be lost. He made a callous decision to ask his father to give him the part of the estate that he would receive when his father died. The father divided his <u>estate</u> in the way custom demanded. As soon as the younger son got his hands on the money, he took off, probably for the bright lights of the city.

Once there, he lived it up, and before long he had wasted all his money and was in need. Food was hard to find because the country was in the grip of a famine, and jobs were so scarce he had to feed pigs. Evidently a food allowance was not part of his employment contract. He was so hungry that he wished he could eat the **pods** that made up the pigs' diet.

☞ **GO TO:**

Deuteronomy 21:15–17 (estate)

pods: *from a carob tree which, when ripe, are filled with a sweet syrup*

Without question, the younger son had gone from riches to rags. As a Jew, having any contact with <u>pigs</u> was detestable. He had hit bottom.

☞ **GO TO:**

Leviticus 11:7; Deuteronomy 14:8 (pigs)

What Others are Saying:

The Bible Knowledge Commentary: The hearers immediately would have understood the point of the story. Jesus had been criticized for associating with sinners. The sinners were considered people who were far away from God, squandering their lives in riotous living. In contrast with the younger son, the older son continued to remain with the father and did not engage in such practices.[4]

> **Luke 15:17–20a** "When he came to his senses, he said, 'How many of my father's hired men have food to spare, and here I am starving to death! I will set out and go back to my father and say to him: Father, I have sinned against heaven and against you. I am no longer worthy to be called your son; make me like one of your hired men.' So he got up and went to his father."

Is McDad Hiring?

The younger son was at the end of his rope and in despair. *"He came to his senses"* implies repentance. He knew he had no right to be treated as a son, but he reasoned that being a servant in his father's household would be better than living where he was. The servants in his father's house had more than enough to eat.

As the son traveled toward home, he rehearsed the words he would say to his father. He was courageous enough to admit that he had sinned and to request a chance to come home and be treated like a hired man. The son assumed he could not be forgiven, but hoped to be tolerated.

What Others are Saying:

Henri J. M. Nouwen: The prodigal's return is full of ambiguities. He is traveling in the right direction, but what confusion! He admits that he was unable to make it on his own and confesses that he would get better treatment as a slave in his father's home than as an outcast in a foreign land, but he is still far from trusting his father's love. . . . There is repentance, but not a repentance in the light of the immense love of a forgiving God. It is a self-serving repentance that offers the possibility of survival.[5]

> **Luke 15:20b** "But while he was still a long way off, his father saw him and was filled with compassion for him; he ran to his son, threw his arms around him and kissed him."

Race For Love

What a beautiful picture! The father was waiting, looking for his son, and recognized him while he was still at a distance. According to the Old Testament law, the son should have been <u>stoned</u> to death because of the disgrace he had brought on the family and the community. However, with a heart overflowing with compassion for his boy, the father ran up to his son, embraced him and kissed him.

☞ **GO TO:**

Deuteronomy 21:18–21 (stoned)

What Others are Saying:

John Piper: Well-to-do, dignified, aristocratic, aging men don't run, they walk. They keep their composure. They show that they are on top of their emotions. But not in Jesus' story about God's joy over his people.[6]

> **Luke 15:21–24** "The son said to him, 'Father, I have sinned against heaven and against you. I am no longer worthy to be called your son.'
>
> "But the father said to his servants, 'Quick! Bring the best robe and put it on him. Put a ring on his finger and sandals on his feet. Bring the fattened calf and kill it. Let's have a feast and celebrate. For this son of mine was dead and is alive again; he was lost and is found.' So they began to celebrate."

Party Hearty!

Before the son could spill his whole speech, the father interrupted. He could not contain himself. He called to his servants to make preparations for a grand celebration. First, he called for the robe, the ring, and sandals for his son—all designed to confirm his status as son. The robe was a ceremonial garment reserved for honored guests. The ring may have been a signet ring, which meant the wearer had authority. Since only slaves went barefoot, the shoes marked the son as a freeman.

Then, the father called for the fattened calf to be killed. Such a calf was kept for special occasions, and the father showed by this action that he felt his lost son's return was worthy of its use.

His son had been as good as dead and now was alive. He was lost, and now was found. The father's joy spread throughout the household as the celebration began.

Max Lucado: <u>Grace</u> is created by God and given to man. . . . On the basis of this point alone, Christianity is set apart from any other religion in the world. [John Stott says,] "No other system, ideology or religion proclaims a free forgiveness and a new life to those who have done nothing to deserve it but deserve judgment instead."[7]

What Others are Saying:

grace: God's action taken to meet human need

Remember This . . .

☞ **GO TO:**

Ephesians 2:1–10 (grace)

God, the loving heavenly Father, never gives up waiting for lost ones to come home. He waits to welcome each repentant sinner with open arms.

> **Luke 15:25–27** "Meanwhile, the older son was in the field. When he came near the house, he heard music and dancing. So he called one of the servants and asked him what was going on. 'Your brother has come,' he replied, 'and your father has killed the fattened calf because he has him back safe and sound.'"

Mysterious Music

The older brother had been out working in the field and was unaware of what had happened. As he approached the house, he heard music and dancing performed by entertainers hired for the party. He asked a servant, "What's up with the music?"

The servant relayed the news in a straightforward style, saying the younger brother was safe and sound.

> **Luke 15:28–30** "The older brother became angry and refused to go in. So his father went out and pleaded with him. But he answered his father, 'Look! All these years I've been slaving for you and never disobeyed your orders. Yet you never gave me even a young goat so I could celebrate with my friends. But when this son of yours who has squandered your property with prostitutes comes home, you kill the fattened calf for him!'"

Count Me Out!

The older brother was so angry he refused to join the merrymakers. His father left the party to reason with him. But all the father heard in response were scathing complaints against both himself and his son.

"It's not fair!" the older son said. "For all these years I have done the backbreaking work and have never once disobeyed you. Yet you never once gave even a little party for me and my friends. Yet now this deadbeat brother comes home having squandered all your money and disgraced our family, and you have the nerve to put on this big celebration. You should be ashamed of yourself. It isn't fair to me, and I won't go in."

The older brother's remarks show a slew of bad attitudes—self-righteousness, pride, disrespect toward his father, discontent, and unforgiveness.

What Others are Saying:

Henri J. M. Nouwen: Outwardly, the elder son was faultless. But when confronted by his father's joy at the return of his younger brother, a dark power erupts in him and boils to the surface. Suddenly, there becomes glaringly visible a resentful, proud, unkind, selfish person, one that had remained deeply hidden, even though it had been growing stronger and more powerful over the years.[8]

> **Luke 15:31–32** "'My son,' the father said, 'you are always with me, and everything I have is yours. But we had to celebrate and be glad, because this brother of yours was dead and is alive again; he was lost and is found.'"

Don't Worry, Be Happy

The father tried to point out that the issue wasn't how hard his older son had worked nor how wrong his younger son had been to waste the money—the issue was love and belonging. The older son had his father's love. He had the security of knowing that his father's resources were available to him. In other words, he had it all. Unfortunately, he did not value it for himself and did not want his wayward younger brother to have it either.

The Pharisees couldn't miss that the wayward son was like the publicans and sinners they so despised. They must have been astonished at the father's joy when the son returned even to the point of welcoming him into the family as an honored member.

But that was not the end of the story. Jesus went on to tell about the older brother, giving an amazingly accurate picture of those Pharisees. They worked hard to please God, obeying most of his laws and many others that they had added. They were critical of Jesus for associating with the lost and did not want to have anything to do with those who became converted.

The Pharisees had great pride in their strict adherence to the laws that governed every part of their lives. They abhorred sinners and wanted to stay as far away from them as they could. Through his parables Jesus showed that God's heart overflows with joy when anyone comes to him, and all heaven joins him in celebration.

The implications are clear for us today. As individuals we may share the attitude of the Pharisees as we discount certain people and discriminate against them in subtle or even overt ways. If we take Jesus' parables to heart, we cannot be indifferent to people whose lifestyles offend us, who are locked into poverty and hopelessness, who are chained by addictions, and who are labeled as dropouts or criminals. Nor can we look down on the self-righteous who sense no need of a Savior. Jesus seeks and welcomes each person—and so should we.

God tells us that when we truly <u>love</u> him, we will love and welcome each sinner who repents. In fact, we can measure our love for God by the love we have for the "least" in his kingdom and by the commitment in our hearts to obey his Word.

Study Questions

1. What prompted Jesus to give his three parables about the sheep, coin, and son?
2. What do we learn about God from Jesus' portrayal of the shepherd?
3. What does the woman's feeling about the lost coin tell us about God's attitude toward lost people?
4. In what ways are we like the younger son?
5. In what ways may we be like the older brother?
6. What do we learn about God from Jesus' portrayal of the father?

FAST FORWARD

Something to Ponder

☞ **GO TO:**

1 John 5:1–2 (love)

- The Pharisees were critical of Jesus for associating with "sinners," whom they despised. (Luke 15:1–2)
- Jesus told parables about a shepherd who searched for one lost sheep and about a woman who searched for a lost coin. Both stories showed how God rejoiced when sinners entered his kingdom. (Luke 15:3–10)
- Jesus' parable about a son who wasted his inheritance, repented, and returned home illustrated how God welcomed sinners who came to him. (Luke 15:11–27)
- The older brother's anger at his father's celebration upon the younger brother's return paralleled the Pharisees' contempt for sinners and Jesus' love for them. (Luke 15:28–32)

LUKE 16: MONEY MATTERS

CHAPTER HIGHLIGHTS

- Get Forever Friends
- Put God First
- Wealth Does Not Equal Favor

Let's Get Started

Money—or the lack of it—seems to influence every aspect of the world—whether at the gas pump or on the stock market. Jesus gives another perspective. Money—how we view it and how we use it—has direct bearing on what we will face in eternity. After death we cannot come back and make amends for bad choices. Therefore, Jesus said, we should use our money today to make deposits in our heavenly bank account. (Read more about proper handling of money in WBFW, chapter 5.)

Jesus addressed the disciples in the first part of chapter 16. They had left secure jobs and a stable future to follow him. Still, their attitude toward money needed some tweaking. In the second part of the chapter, Jesus included the Pharisees, who sneered at his no-spin warnings about their love of money.

GET FOREVER FRIENDS

Luke 16:1–4 Jesus told his disciples: "There was a rich man whose manager was accused of wasting his possessions. So he called him in and asked him, 'What is this I hear about you? Give an account of your management, because you cannot be manager any longer.'

"The manager said to himself, 'What shall I do now? My master is taking away my job. I'm not strong enough

> to dig, and I'm ashamed to beg—I know what I'll do so that, when I lose my job here, people will welcome me into their houses.'"

Crisis Management

Jesus told of a manager who had been entrusted with the affairs of a rich man. His duty was to watch over the accounts so that they would make a profit. Instead, he carelessly wasted the money.

When the rich man learned of his manager's mismanagement, he called for an audit and gave him a pink slip. Knowing he was in trouble, the manager decided on a crisis scheme that would provide him with friends who could help him out when he was unemployed.

> **Luke 16:5–7** "So he called in each one of his master's debtors. He asked the first, 'How much do you owe my master?'
>
> "'Eight hundred gallons of olive oil,' he replied.
>
> "The manager told him, 'Take your bill, sit down quickly, and make it four hundred.'
>
> "Then he asked the second, 'And how much do you owe?'
>
> "'A thousand bushels of wheat,' he replied.
>
> "He told him, 'Take your bill and make it eight hundred.'"

How To Win Friends

The manager had to work quickly and secretly while he still had his job. Employer loyalty, ethics, and honesty were thrown out the window. One by one he called in each person who owed his master and authorized a significant reduction in each one's debt. In a matter of hours he gained friends who would remember him long after he was relieved of his responsibilities as manager.

What Others are Saying:

William Barclay: [The steward] falsified the entries in the books so that the debtors were debited with far less than they owed. This would have two effects. First, the debtors would be grateful to him; and second, and much more effective, he had involved the debtors in his own misdemeanors, and, if the worst came to the worst, he was now in a strong position to exercise a little judicious blackmail![1]

> **Luke 16:8–9** "The master commended the dishonest manager because he had acted shrewdly. For the people of this world are more shrewd in dealing with their own kind than are the people of the light. I tell you, use worldly wealth to gain friends for yourselves, so that when it is gone, you will be welcomed into eternal dwellings."

You Got Me

The manager had probably mismanaged the rich man's wealth in other ways before he reduced people's debts. Nowhere in the passage does it say that the manager was dishonest by reducing the debts. It's possible that the debts may have been questionable in the first place. Jews were not supposed to charge interest to fellow Jews. But "smart" businessmen on the street reasoned their way around this by saying the law's intent was to protect the poor. If a borrower had a little wheat or oil, he was not destitute and therefore could be charged interest, payable in wheat and oil.

When the manager cancelled the debts, he put the owner in a tough spot. If the owner protested the loss of income from interest, he would appear to be acting unlawfully. The best thing the owner could do was put on a fake smile and congratulate the manager who had outsmarted him. The manager had made a quick decision in a time of crisis and used money to help himself and others!

Jesus commended the manager for being dishonest. Fact or fiction? Fiction. The owner commended the manager for being shrewd or savvy—not for being dishonest. Although this is one of the most puzzling passages in the Gospels, Jesus was not urging us to cheat. He was saying that we should use money wisely and generously to help others spiritually.

The people of the light could learn a lesson from the people of this world. The dishonest manager worked cleverly to gain friends for his own benefit. People of the light, who have all eternity ahead, should use their gifts and resources to gain friends who will enjoy eternity with them.

How tirelessly do we work to ensure that a host of friends will be in heaven because we have thoughtfully and generously invested our resources in relieving the distress of poverty and disease and in spreading the Gospel message around the world?

KEY POINT

Jesus used a bad example to make a good point.

FACT OR FICTION

Something to Ponder

☞ **GO TO:**

Ephesians 5:8–10 (of the light)

Charles R. Swindoll: Examine your heart. Nobody but you can do this. Open that private vault and ask several hard questions, like:

- Is my giving proportionate to my income?
- Am I motivated by guilt . . . or by contagious joy?
- If someone else knew the level of my giving to God's work, would I be a model to follow?
- Have I prayed about giving . . . or am I just an impulsive responder?[2]

PUT GOD FIRST

> **Luke 16:10–12** "Whoever can be trusted with very little can also be trusted with much, and whoever is dishonest with very little will also be dishonest with much. So if you have not been trustworthy in handling worldly wealth, who will trust you with true riches? And if you have not been trustworthy with someone else's property, who will give you property of your own?"

Rise To Responsibility

KEY POINT

Never forget we are accountable to the one we serve.

Jesus has a word for us all. Whatever we have, whether it is little or much, must be handled with faithfulness. If we are not faithful in handling matters of this life, who will trust us with spiritual wealth? And if we are not faithful in handling the affairs of another, who will trust us with our own wealth?

FACT OR **FICTION**

Money is a trap. In fact, craving money lies at the bottom of all kinds of temptation and wrong actions. Fact or fiction? This is a fact! God gives us a warning, but that's not all he has to say about money. Here's more:

Hebrews 13:5–6: We should be careful not to love money but to be content with what we have. God's presence in our lives is of far greater value than a big bank account.

1 Timothy 6:17–19: Money is a gift from God for our enjoyment and generous sharing, which lays up treasure in the life to come.

1 Corinthians 4:2: We should handle money as a trust for which we will need to give an account.

Galatians 6:9–10: Having money allows us to do good to all people, especially to believers.

1 John 3:15–18: God's love and generosity to us is a model for us to express self-sacrificing generosity to people who have needs.

2 Corinthians 9:6–15: God loves us when we give cheerfully and enables us to be generous so that he receives praise.

> **Luke 16:13–15** "No servant can serve two masters. Either he will hate the one and love the other, or he will be devoted to the one and despise the other. You cannot serve both God and Money."
>
> The Pharisees, who loved money, heard all this and were sneering at Jesus. He said to them, "You are the ones who justify yourselves in the eyes of men, but God knows your hearts. What is highly valued among men is detestable in God's sight."

One Boss Is Enough

Jesus pointed out to the Pharisees that they were attempting something impossible. They were trying to serve both God and money—which was pulling them in opposite directions. They hated to hear this. They had a reputation to keep up. They had convinced themselves and the common people that their wealth proved they had God's stamp of approval. They worked hard for the admiration of people, but in their hearts they loved the power and prestige of money. Jesus saw through them and said plainly that God detested their attitudes.

God will never reject anyone who works hard to please him. Fact or fiction? The Pharisees would claim this to be a fact. But Jesus did not agree. Humans cannot set up the standard for what pleases God. Only he can do so, and Jesus spelled this out clearly.

FACT OR FICTION

> **Luke 16:16–18** "The Law and the Prophets were proclaimed until John. Since that time, the good news of the kingdom of God is being preached, and everyone is forcing his way into it. It is easier for heaven and earth to disappear than for the least stroke of a pen to drop out of the Law.
>
> "Anyone who divorces his wife and marries another woman commits adultery, and the man who marries a divorced woman commits adultery."

No Divorce Over Dinner

Although the Pharisees sneered at Jesus, he went right on with his verbal attack. Jesus said the Law and the Prophets (longhand for the Old Testament) were faithfully proclaimed until John the Baptist came to announce the good news of the kingdom of God. However, Jesus consistently claimed that the Old Testament would be <u>fulfilled</u> and that the Gospel of the kingdom of God did not **negate** the Old Testament. Jesus said his coming did not do away with the Old Testament.

While the Pharisees claimed to stand firmly on the Old Testament law, they broke it regularly. Jesus gave an example of laws they broke that carried over into the new kingdom of God. They were lax about applying the Old Testament laws about divorce because they wanted the approval of the people. Some rabbis taught that a man could divorce his wife for something so minor as burning his dinner.

☞ **GO TO:**

Matthew 5:17–18
(fulfilled)

negate: *cancel, cause to be ineffective*

MORE INFORMATION—Jesus used divorce to illustrate a law that transcended the Old Testament law and his Gospel of the kingdom of God. Matthew and Mark provide more of Jesus' teaching about divorce. See Matthew 5:32; 19:1–12 and Mark 10:11–12.

WEALTH DOES NOT EQUAL FAVOR

Luke 16:19–21 "There was a rich man who was dressed in purple and fine linen and lived in luxury every day. At his gate was laid a beggar named Lazarus, covered with sores and longing to eat what fell from the rich man's table. Even the dogs came and licked his sores."

A Have And A Have-Not

Jesus drew a picture of stark contrast: a rich man living at the height of luxury and a beggar existing in the depth of misery. The two were in daily eyesight of one another. The rich man's purple robes identified him as having high rank and much money. The purple dye, actually a deep crimson color with shades from red to blue, came from shellfish gathered from the floor of the eastern Mediterranean.

PHYSICIAN'S PERSPECTIVE—This parable is unique to Luke. As a physician Luke was interested in the plight of the poor and disabled. The poor were stripped of their dignity and were dependent on the compassion of others. Lazarus had to be carried to his place at the rich man's gate. There he lay, unable to help himself. People who passed by him ignored his helplessness, offering neither food nor medication for his open sores. His requests for leftovers from the rich man's table were ignored. His only companions were unclean dogs who repulsively licked his sores.

Accumulating wealth, whether by hard work, good investments, or "chance" is always a sign of God's blessing. Fact or fiction? The Pharisees regarded their resources as an indication that God had blessed them because of their strict adherence to the laws—many of which did not come from God but had been formulated by men. Jesus' parable proves that wealth is not necessarily proof of God's favor.

FACT OR FICTION

> **Luke 16:22–24** "The time came when the beggar died and the angels carried him to Abraham's side. The rich man also died and was buried. In hell, where he was in torment, he looked up and saw Abraham far away, with Lazarus by his side. So he called to him, 'Father Abraham, have pity on me and send Lazarus to dip the tip of his finger in water and cool my tongue, because I am in agony in this fire.'"

Role Reversal

Death changed everything. The beggar was carried by angels to lie in **paradise** by **Abraham's side**, whereas the rich man woke up in torment in **hell**. The rich man looked up, recognizing Lazarus as the beggar who used to lie outside his gate. It is interesting that the two men are again within eyesight of one another—or at least the rich man could see the former beggar. The rich man called to Father Abraham to have pity on him. The rich man thought he could order people around as he had in life, so he asked to have Lazarus run an errand for him.

paradise: location of the righteous dead awaiting resurrection

Abraham's side: metaphor for an honored place in paradise

hell: Greek: Hades, the place where the dead await final judgment

No Second Chances

Abraham reminded the rich man that he had enjoyed good things in life while Lazarus had endured poverty and affliction. Now Lazarus was in comfort while the rich man was in misery. The rich man had chosen material wealth and a life of ease instead of spending time in the things of God and caring for others. But there was no way to reverse things. There are no second chances after death.

Remember This . . .

We may think we have lived a good life, believing we have not done evil deeds. But at our final judgment, we may discover that we have not done a host of good things we ought to have done. Like the rich man, we may have ignored some of the good we should have done right at our doors—our spouses, our kids, our in-laws, our neighbors.

Ghostly Request

The rich man accepted that Abraham could do nothing to relieve his misery in hell. Then he thought of his five brothers and asked Abraham to send Lazarus to warn them so they could avoid his plight. Notice the rich man is still thinking like a rich earthling who has errand boys!

Abraham reminded him that they already had the warnings of Moses and the Prophets. The rich man thought something more spectacular would arrest their attention—a ghost or a talking dead person. But Abraham said that if they did not listen to the messengers God had already sent, they would not be persuaded even if someone spoke from the dead.

The words were sadly prophetic. Only a short while later Jesus died and rose from the dead and the Jews still rejected him. Those who reject the teachings of the Bible also reject the display of miracles done by Christ.

Both men in Jesus' parable faced eternity, but from opposite points of view.

Lazarus's name means "God, the Helper." Though this seemed a cruel mockery, Lazarus hung on in silent trust, and his faith was rewarded when he died. The rich man used his money selfishly. He focused only on his comforts, ignoring God's command to love his neighbor Lazarus.

The implications are clear for us today. Whether we have little or much, we are responsible to God for the money we have. How we use it has implications that will affect us after death.

Lawrence O. Richards: The choices we make during this life do fix our destiny. Those who wish can scoff at Jesus' warnings of the corrupting influence of wealth. But many have pushed heaven away while grabbing greedily for this world's worthless gold.[3]

Study Questions

1. What can we learn from Jesus' parable of the dishonest manager?
2. In what way can money—whether we have little or much—be an acid test of our character?
3. Why were the Pharisees blind to Jesus' teaching about the kingdom of God?
4. What can we learn from Jesus' parable of the rich man and Lazarus?

KEY POINT

Money matters—it exposes our values.

FAST FORWARD

☞ **GO TO:**

Leviticus 19:18 (God's command)

What Others are Saying:

CHAPTER WRAP-UP

- Jesus told a parable of a dishonest manager who reduced some debts before he was fired. These people would be inclined to help him once he was out of work. The owner commended him for his shrewdness in looking out for his future. (Luke 16:1–9)

- Jesus taught that we cannot serve both God and money. Our faithfulness in using money wisely, especially with eternal rewards in view, reveals our character. (Luke 16:10–15)

- The Pharisees sneered at Jesus' teaching. They could not receive it because of their slavish love of money and their desire to impress others. (Luke 16:16–18)

- Jesus told the parable of the rich man and Lazarus to point out the importance of listening to God's Word now and acting on it, because there will be no opportunity after death to make things right. (Luke 16:19–31)

LUKE 17: HEART ATTITUDES

CHAPTER HIGHLIGHTS

- Not Duty-Free
- Attitude of Gratitude
- Ready and Waiting

Let's Get Started

We value our independence. Beginning in the <u>Garden of Eden</u> when Adam and Eve chose to <u>disobey God</u> (see GWGN, pages 25–48), people have clung to the idea that they can make it on their own. We do not want to be accountable to anyone or responsible for anyone else.

Jesus says this is a false perspective. We are not islands. We are interconnected links in a chain. What we do impacts others, and we bear responsibility for that. Our standing with God has an impact on how we treat others. Jesus brings us back to where it all started in the Garden of Eden—we were created to live in a loving, dependent relationship with God that influences all our interactions with him and with others.

☞ **GO TO:**

Genesis 2
(Garden of Eden)

Genesis 3:1–13
(disobey God)

NOT DUTY-FREE

> **Luke 17:1–3a** Jesus said to his disciples: "Things that cause people to sin are bound to come, but woe to that person through whom they come. It would be better for him to be thrown into the sea with a millstone tied around his neck than for him to cause one of these little ones to sin. So watch yourselves.

Blame Game

Jesus pinpointed a problem most people want to overlook. A person may act in such a way that he or she leads others into sin. Of course that person wants to avoid any blame, but Jesus says that cannot be avoided. Punishment is certain. Who wants to be weighted down in the sea with a heavy stone used for grinding grain? Jesus said that the punishment awaiting such an offender is worse than that—worse than physical death!

Jesus has special concern for *"little ones."* These are children and believers who are immature in their faith. Older believers, especially teachers and leaders, need to be careful that their actions and attitudes do not cause little ones to fall into sin.

What we choose to do is our own business. Fact or fiction? Don't be fooled by this idea! We do not live in isolation. Jesus gave freedom from the cumbersome load of laws that the Pharisees imposed, but freedom carries responsibility. Jesus said we have to answer to him if we cause someone to sin.

> **Luke 17:3b–4** "If your brother sins, rebuke him, and if he repents, forgive him. If he sins against you seven times in a day, and seven times comes back to you and says, 'I repent,' forgive him."

Something to Ponder

Bible
Fairy Tales

FACT OR FICTION

Multiple Forgiveness

Jesus then told his disciples how to handle people who wrong them. Confront them! Compassionately rebuke them. If they repent, then forgive them. If they repeat the wrongdoing again and again and come back to request forgiveness, forgive them again and again. In other words, forgiveness is to be done so often it becomes a habit. It is not up to the believer to decide to forgive based on the genuineness of the offender's repentance.

J. C. Ryle: There are few Christian duties which the New Testament dwells on so frequently as forgiving other people. It has a prominent place in the Lord's Prayer. The only thing we do in the whole prayer is to forgive those who have sinned against us. This is a test for being forgiven ourselves. The person who cannot for-

☞ **GO TO:**

Luke 11:2–4; Matthew 6:9–15 (Lord's Prayer)

Matthew 18:35 (test)

What Others are Saying:

give his neighbor the few trifling offenses he may have committed against him can know nothing about the free and full <u>pardon</u> which Christ offers us.[1]

☞ **GO TO:**

Ephesians 4:32 (pardon)

> **Luke 17:5–6** The apostles said to the Lord, "Increase our faith!"
>
> He replied, "If you have faith as small as a mustard seed, you can say to this mulberry tree, 'Be uprooted and planted in the sea,' and it will obey you."

Pumping Faith Instead Of Iron

Which is more difficult: to rebuke an erring person or to forgive that person who has wronged you? The standard Jesus set was so staggering that the disciples could only ask that he would increase their faith so they could fulfill his demands. They wanted a heaping bushel basket of faith, but Jesus said it need not be larger than a tiny mustard seed.

How should we deal with a standard Jesus set that is far beyond our capacity to fulfill? Some may complain while others choose to ignore that standard, explaining that Jesus probably didn't mean his words to be taken literally. The disciples did not take that route. They wisely asked Jesus to increase their faith! And that's the only way to receive the strength to obey what Jesus asks us to do. The size of our faith is not the point. Rather it is the power of the One in whom we place our faith.

Something to Ponder

KEY POINT

Faith is the key to obeying Jesus' commands.

> **Luke 17:7–10** "Suppose one of you had a servant plowing or looking after the sheep. Would he say to the servant when he comes in from the field, 'Come along now and sit down to eat'? Would he not rather say, 'Prepare my supper, get yourself ready and wait on me while I eat and drink; after that you may eat and drink'? Would he thank the servant because he did what he was told to do? So you also, when you have done everything you were told to do, should say, 'We are unworthy servants; we have only done our duty.'"

☞ **GO TO:**

2 Timothy 4:7–8
   (of righteousness)

1 Peter 5:4 (of glory)

Revelation 22:12
   (reward)

Remember
This . . .

No Bragging Rights

Jesus outlined his high standards for disciples. They were to exercise caution not to cause anyone to sin. They were to confront and rebuke those who chose to sin. They were to exercise unwavering forgiveness. They were to apply faith, not as a *cognitive* virtue but as a trust that could be employed in fulfilling Jesus' requirements.

Then, before they could feel smug or self-righteous about measuring up to Jesus' standards, he told them that even when they have fulfilled his requirements they will have done only their duty.

There are two sides to the coin of following Jesus. Here he shows one side—no matter how faithfully we serve him, we will always be unworthy disciples who at best are only doing what he asks of us.

The other side of the coin is the reward he gives—eternal blessings for all who serve him faithfully. Paul wrote of a crown of righteousness, which would be awarded to him. Peter wrote of a crown of glory. And John recorded Jesus' promise that he will bring his reward with him when he comes.

What Others
are Saying:

Dallas Willard: An obsession merely with doing all God commands may be the very thing that rules out being the kind of person that he calls us to be. . . . The watchword of the worthy servant is not mere obedience but love, from which appropriate obedience naturally flows.[2]

ATTITUDE OF GRATITUDE

> **Luke 17:11–13** Now on his way to Jerusalem, Jesus traveled along the border between Samaria and Galilee. As he was going into a village, ten men who had leprosy met him. They stood at a distance and called out in a loud voice, "Jesus, Master, have pity on us!"

☞ **GO TO:**

Leviticus 13:45–46;
   Numbers 5:2
   (distance)

outcasts: *people rejected from living at home or in society*

Arresting Lepers

As Jesus made his way to Jesualem, he traveled along the border between Samaria and Galilee. On the outskirts of a village ten men tried to arrest his attention. They stood at a distance from him, required of **outcasts** because they had leprosy. In unison they called out, *"Jesus, Master, have pity on us!"*

> **Luke 17:14–19** When he saw them, he said, "Go, show yourselves to the priests." And as they went, they were cleansed.
>
> One of them, when he saw he was healed, came back, praising God in a loud voice. He threw himself at Jesus' feet and thanked him—and he was a Samaritan.
>
> Jesus asked, "Were not all ten cleansed? Where are the other nine? Was no one found to return and give praise to God except this foreigner?" Then he said to him, "Rise and go; your faith has made you well."

KEY POINT

A disciple's duty is to do whatever he is asked to do, but God looks for deeds that are prompted by a heart of love.

Lone Thanksgiving

Jesus did not respond by telling the lepers they were healed. Instead, he told them to go and show themselves to the priest as the law <u>commanded</u> those who had been healed of the disease. As the men obeyed in faith, they were healed.

Suddenly one man broke from the little procession. This man hurried back toward Jesus, calling out his thanksgiving to God. He fell at Jesus' feet to express his thanks—and he was a Samaritan, one viewed by Jews as least deserving of Jesus' miracle. Jesus expressed amazement that since all ten men had been healed, only one returned to praise God. Jesus commended him.

While all ten men had received physical healing, only this Samaritan had faith for spiritual healing as well. We know this because Jesus used an all-encompassing word for spiritual and physical healing when he said the thankful leper was "made well." The other lepers were merely "cleansed" or healed of the filth of leprosy.

☞ **GO TO:**

Leviticus 13:19; 14:1– 11 (commanded)

Darryl DelHousaye: Thanksgiving in everything is the key to joy. The experience of joy is all about well-being, a sense of security, a deep rest, the absence of fear. It's enjoyment! The absence of thanksgiving is what makes joy fade. It's God's design for us to give thanks lest any of our joy slip away.[4]

What Others are Saying:

Thankfulness for
blessings brings
additional blessings.

FAST FORWARD

☞ **GO TO:**

1 Thessalonians 5:18;
Hebrews 13:15–16
(thanks)

glorifies: *exalting God
through praise and
thanksgiving*

PHYSICIAN'S PERSPECTIVE—Luke had the practiced eye of a physician who could spot the patient most likely to regain good health. An attitude of appreciation and thankfulness goes far to ensure a full recovery. Sincere thankfulness to God banishes lethargy and depression that so frequently lingers even after a doctor has pronounced a patient well enough to resume a healthy lifestyle.

*Is a thankful heart an endangered species? Only one man in ten expressed thanks to Jesus for healing. What would be the ratio today? Giving <u>thanks</u> to God isn't just a polite ritual—it delights God's heart and **glorifies** him. (To read more about hope and humor when life seems depressing, see WBFW, pages 41–52.)*

READY AND WAITING

> **Luke 17:20–21** Once, having been asked by the Pharisees when the kingdom of God would come, Jesus replied, "The kingdom of God does not come with your careful observation, nor will people say, 'Here it is,' or 'There it is,' because the kingdom of God is within you."

If It Had Teeth, It Could Bite You!

The nation of Israel had long looked for God to establish his kingdom on earth. Jesus had spoken of the kingdom, but the Pharisees were not seeing the signs they were expecting. They asked him, as <u>John the Baptist</u> had asked earlier, when the kingdom would come.

Jesus knew the Pharisees were looking for a political leader who would rescue them from the domination of Rome. He told them that they should not look for signs because the kingdom of God was already in their presence! The words "within you" could be better translated "among you." The unbelief that they harbored in their hearts blinded them from recognizing that their King had come.

☞ **GO TO:**

Luke 7:18–23
(John the Baptist)

MORE INFORMATION—Some of the concepts Jesus introduces in this passage are also found in Matthew 24 and Mark 13. However, the contexts in which Jesus spoke are different. In Luke he answers the question raised by the Pharisees, whereas in Matthew and Mark he is speaking only to his disciples. What Jesus had to say about his coming kingdom was so important that he no doubt taught about it on more than one occasion.

> **Luke 17:22–25** Then he said to his disciples, "The time is coming when you will long to see one of the days of the Son of Man, but you will not see it. Men will tell you 'There he is!' or 'Here he is!' Do not go running off after them. For the Son of Man in his day will be like the lightning, which flashes and lights up the sky from one end to the other. But first he must suffer many things and be rejected by this generation."

KEY POINT

The power and glory of Jesus' kingdom must be preceded by rejection and death.

Suddenly Jesus

Jesus then directed his teaching to the disciples. *"One of the days of the Son of Man"* probably refers to the <u>day of the Lord</u>. That event will not be secret. No one will need to peer into corners to find it. One day Jesus will come with a sudden, majestic display of lightning that will flash across the globe. But before that happens, he must suffer rejection and death on the cross at the hands of those he came to save.

☞ **GO TO:**

2 Peter 3:10 (day of the Lord)

R. C. Sproul: As we look about [God's] world and see the play not yet through, we must focus on the ending. Paul tells us we are even now seated in the <u>heavenlies</u> with Christ Jesus and our <u>citizenship</u> is in heaven. We should, then, even here, <u>sing</u> with choirs of angels, "Holy, holy, holy, Lord God Almighty, who was and is and is to come!"

How strong is he? Stronger than all we could ever imagine. How strong was he? Stronger than all that ever was. How strong will he be? Strong enough to bring all things to pass, to conquer every enemy, and to stoop to us who are his children and wipe away every tear.

He is coming. And he will come in all his strength and in all his glory. Even so, come Lord Jesus.[5]

What Others are Saying:

☞ **GO TO:**

Ephesians 2:6 (heavenlies)

Philippians 3:20 (citizenship)

Revelation 4:8 (sing)

> **Luke 17:26–27** "Just as it was in the days of Noah, so also will it be in the days of the Son of Man. People were eating, drinking, marrying and being given in marriage up to the day Noah entered the ark. Then the flood came and destroyed them all."

Alert Or Inert?

KEY POINT

Live in a state of readiness for Jesus' return.

Christ will come again to set up his kingdom. That is certain. *When* he will come has not been revealed to us. The faithful will live "on alert," ready for his arrival, but the unbelieving will be living "business as usual," assuming that life, as they know it, will go on forever.

To illustrate his point Jesus gave his hearers a history lesson. For 120 years as Noah built the ark, he warned people that God's judgment would come (see GWGN, pages 71–90). But up until the <u>Flood</u> came, they refused to believe him and occupied themselves with the pleasures of life. Their actions showed their complete indifference to God, and when the Flood came suddenly, it caught them by surprise.

☞ **GO TO:**

Genesis 6–8 (Flood)

 MORE INFORMATION—Matthew 24:37–39 also includes Jesus' reference to the days of Noah, tying the attitudes of the unbelieving to those of people before Jesus returns. Much as the people in Noah's day were preoccupied with their daily affairs and deaf to Noah's warnings of coming judgment, so people will be so busy with the here and now that they will not heed the warning to be ready for Jesus' return.

> **Luke 17:28–37** "It was the same in the days of Lot. People were eating and drinking, buying and selling, planting and building. But the day Lot left Sodom, fire and sulfur rained down from heaven and destroyed them all.
>
> "It will be just like this on the day the Son of Man is revealed. On that day no one who is on the roof of his house, with his goods inside, should go down to get them. Likewise, no one in the field should go back for anything. Remember Lot's wife! Whoever tries to keep his life will lose it, and whoever loses his life will preserve it. I tell you, on that night two people will be in one bed; one will be taken and the other left. Two

> women will be grinding grain together; one will be taken and the other left."
>
> "Where, Lord?" they asked.
>
> He replied, "Where there is a dead body, there the vultures will gather."

Stop, Drop, And Run

Jesus pointed out that his coming will reveal what distinguishes people who seem to be very much alike. They are all occupied with everyday affairs, but those who live for the present will be preoccupied with the things of this world. Those who live for eternity will be ready to drop everything to welcome his coming.

When <u>Lot's wife</u> ran away from the <u>destruction of Sodom</u>, she looked back with longing for the possessions that had made life precious to her. She became a pillar of salt. Jesus said, "Don't make the same mistake. Run toward my kingdom, not away from it."

☞ **GO TO:**

Genesis 19:26
(Lot's wife)

Genesis 19:12–26
(destruction of Sodom)

Study Questions

1. Why should we be concerned about the impact of our lives on "little ones"?
2. How should we deal with someone who sins against us?
3. Why should a faithful disciple view himself as an unworthy servant?
4. What happened to the ten lepers?
5. As we wait for Jesus' return, what do we need to be aware of?

CHAPTER WRAP-UP

- Jesus warned that occasions to sin would certainly come, but that we should be careful not to cause anyone—especially children or new believers—to sin. (Luke 17:1–3a)

- When someone sins against us, we should rebuke him and forgive him—even if he offends again and again and comes back in repentance again and again. (Luke 17:3b–4)

- Living the Christian life involves duties to God and others. (Luke 17:5–10)

- Faith and obedience bring spiritual as well as physical healing. (Luke 17:11–19)

- Jesus said he would return, but before he could do so, he needed to suffer rejection and death. His followers need to be always prepared for his coming. (Luke 17:20–37)

LUKE 18: PEOPLE MAGAZINE

Let's Get Started

How do we measure people? We look at their ethnic background, physical appearance, education, economic status, accomplishments, associations—the list goes on and on. In Luke 18 we see a cross section of people—a defenseless widow; a crusty, unfair judge; a strutting Pharisee; breast-beating tax collector; eager, accepting children; a serious-minded, rich, young man; disciples with questions and uncertainty; and a blind beggar determined to see.

On the surface they don't have anything in common. But take a closer look at their hearts. One essential factor that distinguishes them is their heart attitude. That's how God measures people. They are the stars in his *People Magazine*.

PHYSICIAN'S PERSPECTIVE—Luke the physician shows that he has a heart for everyone, especially those neglected by the religious hierarchy in Jerusalem—widows, publicans, little children, and beggars. Jesus the Great Physician excludes no one who comes to him.

A PERSISTENT WIDOW

> **Luke 18:1–5** Then Jesus told his disciples a parable to show them that they should always pray and not give up. He said: "In a certain town there was a judge who neither feared God nor cared about men. And there was

> a widow in that town who kept coming to him with the plea, 'Grant me justice against my adversary.'
>
> "For some time he refused. But finally he said to himself, 'Even though I don't fear God or care about men, yet because this widow keeps bothering me, I will see that she gets justice, so that she won't eventually wear me out with her coming!'"

Not Her Again!

Jesus told a parable about a widow who desperately needed justice. She had several counts against her. First, she was a woman. In her culture women did not appear in court. Second, she was a widow and had no man to appear before the judge on her behalf. Third, she was poor and had nothing to use as a bribe to gain the ear of the judge.

Still she persisted with her plea for justice. Finally, the judge did what he should have done in the first place—he gave her a fair decision—not because he was just but because he wanted to get rid of her.

What Others are Saying:

Warren W. Wiersbe: As you study this parable, try to see it in its Eastern setting. The "courtroom" was not a fine building but a tent that was moved from place to place as the judge covered his circuit. The judge, not the law, set the agenda; and he sat regally in the tent, surrounded by his assistants. Anybody would watch the proceedings from the outside, but only those who were approved and accepted could have their cases tried. This usually meant bribing one of the assistants so that he would call the judge's attention to the case.[1]

> **Luke 18:6–8** And the Lord said, "Listen to what the unjust judge says. And will not God bring about justice for his chosen ones, who cry out to him day and night? Will he keep putting them off? I tell you, he will see that they get justice, and quickly. However, when the Son of Man comes, will he find faith on the earth?"

And Your Point?

Jesus' parable had a point that he did not want his disciples to miss. First, during waiting time before he would set up his kingdom, his disciples would have to endure injustice and persecution. He encouraged them to pray and not to give up. If this neglected widow finally got what she deserved from an insensitive judge, how much more would Jesus' disciples receive mercy from their loving Father in heaven.

> *Jesus' encouragement to his disciples to pray and not give up is relevant for us today. Unlike the widow who had to plead for justice, Jesus' followers are God's children who have his ear at all times. God cares for his own as a loving Father. He <u>hears</u> their prayers. Unlike the widow who had no one to plead her cause, Jesus' followers have an **<u>advocate</u>** in heaven. God hears and answers prayer, not because we harass him but because he is just. He may not answer according to our timetable, but he is at work behind the scenes.*
>
> *Jesus' warning is for us today. When we do not see our prayers answered we should not give up praying. Believers must persevere in faith until Jesus returns to earth.*

Sue and Larry Richards: The parable is intended to contrast the unjust judge with the Lord, who does have compassion on people and cares deeply for the plight of widows and orphans. While God cares and will avenge his own, we need to be as persistent in prayer as the widow was in pursuing her case.[2]

Randall D. Roth: Getting to prayer is half the battle. Staying there is the other half. Either we fall asleep, or our mind wanders, or we get disenchanted. We don't see ready answers to our petitions, so we give up. But like any other wise investment, prayer requires the discipline of delayed gratification.[3]

THE PURELY PROUD AND THE HUMBLE PURE

> **Luke 18:9–14** To some who were confident of their own righteousness and looked down on everybody else, Jesus told this parable: "Two men went up to the temple to pray, one a Pharisee and the other a tax collector.

FAST FORWARD

☞ **GO TO:**

Ephesians 2:18; 3:12; Hebrews 4:14–16 (hears)

Hebrews 2:17–18; 1 John 2:1 (advocate)

What Others are Saying:

advocate: *someone who pleads in behalf of another*

A proud, boastful heart makes communication with God one way.

> The Pharisee stood up and prayed about himself: 'God, I thank you that I am not like other men—robbers, evildoers, adulterers—or even like this tax collector. I fast twice a week and give a tenth of all I get.'
>
> "But the tax collector stood at a distance. He would not even look up to heaven, but beat his breast and said, 'God, have mercy on me, a sinner.'
>
> "I tell you that this man, rather than the other, went home justified before God. For everyone who exalts himself will be humbled, and he who humbles himself will be exalted."

Great Pride Not Justified

Jesus told another parable. This time he exposed the false illusions of the Pharisees who boasted of being favored by God. Two men went to the Temple to pray. The first, a Pharisee, stood up and bragged to God that he didn't do bad things. In addition, he went the second mile in earning brownie points. Though he was required to fast only one day a year, he fasted twice a week! Further, he didn't just donate a tenth of the required crops; he **tithed** his garden herbs. Surely God was pleased to hear his prayer!

tithed: gave one-tenth of one's goods to God

Standing at a distance from the Pharisee was a publican who was so aware of his shortcomings that he did not dare to lift his head. He prayed, pleading with God to have mercy on him, an unworthy sinner. He knew he deserved death for his sins, but he begged for God's mercy and forgiveness.

justified: declared innocent—"just as if" I'd never sinned

Jesus said that the publican's prayer was answered. He went home **justified** by God, whereas the Pharisee received no word from God.

What Others are Saying:

Matthew Henry: [The publican] confesses himself *a sinner* by nature, by practice, guilty before God. The Pharisee denies that he is a *sinner*. But the tax collector gives himself no other character than that of a *sinner*.[4]

Bible
Fairy Tales
FACT OR *FICTION*

We can figure how we stack up with God by comparing ourselves with other people. Fact or fiction? Pure fiction, Jesus says in this parable. The Pharisee commended himself because he condemned the sins of others. He thought he was better than others. The publican, on the other hand, could have felt he was an unworthy sinner because he did not measure up to the virtues of the Pharisee. Jesus' point is that both men were sinners equally in need of God's salvation.

WANTED: CHILDREN

> **Luke 18:15–17** People were also bringing babies to Jesus to have him touch them. When the disciples saw this, they rebuked them. But Jesus called the children to him and said, "Let the little children come to me, and do not hinder them, for the kingdom of God belongs to such as these. I tell you the truth, anyone who will not receive the kingdom of God like a little child will never enter it."

Let Them Come

Jesus was so approachable that parents had no hesitation in bringing their babies to him, as they would bring them to receive a blessing from a rabbi. Jesus overrode the rebukes of the disciples and encouraged the little ones to come to him. He went on to say that the kingdom of God could be received only by people who had open, trusting hearts like little children. Unlike the boastful Pharisee, children are humble and dependent on God, as was the repentant publican in Jesus' parable.

MORE INFORMATION—Both Matthew and Mark include this touching incident of Jesus and the little children. Matthew 19:13–15 adds that the parents wanted Jesus to pray for their children. Mark 10:13–16 says that Jesus took the little ones in his arms, placed his hands on them, and blessed them. Imagine how they snuggled close to him as he placed his hands on their heads and pronounced his Father's blessing on them.

In another context, Mark 9:36–37 tells of Jesus pulling a little child close to him and saying to his disciples that whoever welcomes a little child in Jesus' name is actually welcoming him, and in welcoming Jesus is welcoming the one who sent him—God himself!

Make room for children! Jesus says that we enter his kingdom by becoming as little children and by receiving children in his name. He wants us to cultivate traits of childlikeness and he wants us to welcome children into our lives so that we can guide them to him.

Remember This . . .

A RICH RULER

> **Luke 18:18–21** A certain ruler asked him, "Good teacher, what must I do to inherit eternal life?"
>
> "Why do you call me good?" Jesus answered. "No one is good—except God alone. You know the commandments: 'Do not commit adultery, do not murder, do not steal, do not give false testimony, honor your father and mother.'"
>
> "All these I have kept since I was a boy," he said.

Such A Fine Young Man

One day a fine young man approached Jesus. He was wealthy, already a leader in his community, and motivated to have it all. He wanted to receive a warm welcome, so he began with some basic flattery. *"Good teacher,"* he said. No one addressed a rabbi this way because the greeting gave to a man qualities only God could have. (Little did he know he was being prophetic!) He continued his spiritual **faux pas** by asking what he needed to do to work his way to heaven.

faux pas: mistake

Jesus' response indicates that he wanted the man to think about what he had just said. The young man had no idea the person to whom he was speaking was the true Messiah. When Jesus reminded him of the commandments given by God, the young man said, "Been there. Done that." But this guy wasn't even on first base! He did not understand that keeping the commandments was a matter of the heart, not mere outward actions. It is impossible for a human to keep all the laws perfectly.

What Others are Saying:

R. C. Sproul: For a deed to be ultimately good in the biblical sense, not only must it do what the law requires, but it must be motivated by a heart that loves God completely. No human being is good in that ultimate sense, and Jesus is reminding this young man of a deeper understanding of the nature of goodness, lest his superficial understanding of goodness be the very thing that keeps him out of the kingdom of God.[5]

> **Luke 18:22** When Jesus heard this, he said to him, "You still lack one thing. Sell everything you have and give to the poor, and you will have treasure in heaven. Then come, follow me."

One Thing More

Jesus looked deep into the heart of the young man. Jesus put his finger on the key issue and told the young man to sell everything and distribute his wealth among the poor. Jesus' request was designed to help the young man realize that he had not kept all the commands. He had not even kept the first commandment—*"You shall have no other gods before me"* (Exodus 20:3). His stuff had become his god. The man never considered his wealth as an opportunity to share with the needy around him and thus demonstrate that he truly loved his neighbor, as God commanded (Leviticus 19:18).

> **Luke 18:23–25** When he heard this, he became very sad, because he was a man of great wealth. Jesus looked at him and said, "How hard it is for the rich to enter the kingdom of God! Indeed, it is easier for a camel to go through the eye of a needle than for a rich man to enter the kingdom of God."

A Sad Walk Into The Sunset

The young man's short sprint to success skidded to a stop. He turned on his heel and left with a heavy heart. He could not part with any of the trappings of his lifestyle, let alone all of it. His very action proved that his wealth was his god.

As Jesus watched his departure he made no move to call him back. Instead, he commented sorrowfully that it is hard for the wealthy to enter the kingdom of God because they are tempted to rely on their own resources rather than God. Actually it would be easier for a camel to go through the eye of a needle than for a rich man to enter God's kingdom.

 PHYSICIAN'S PERSPECTIVE—A camel and the eye of a needle? What is one to make of this **hyperbole**? Some Bible experts speak of a small gate in the wall of a city, called a needle's eye, that a camel could enter only by kneeling down and creeping through. However, other experts note that Dr. Luke used a word that referred to a surgeon's needle. Thus, he expected readers to understand the silly word picture he painted.

hyperbole: intentional exaggeration not meant literally

Lawrence O. Richards: The rich ruler really did want to follow Jesus. This was not an easy choice for him. He was not like Esau, who quickly traded his birthright for a bowl of stew.

Yet never mistake spiritual yearnings for true spirituality. Our spirituality is seen not in what we want to do, but in what we choose to do![6]

MORE INFORMATION—Both Matthew and Mark include accounts of the rich young ruler coming to Jesus. Mark 10:17–31 records that when the young man approached Jesus he ran up to him and fell on his knees before him, showing his respect. Mark also includes the insight that when Jesus challenged the young man to go sell everything he had and give to the poor, he looked at him and loved him. (See also Matthew 19:16–30.)

> **Luke 18:26–27** Those who heard this asked, "Who then can be saved?"
>
> Jesus replied, "What is impossible with men is possible with God."

You Can't Make It On Your Own

"If the rich can't make it in, how are we ever gonna get there?" the hearers asked. They thought the rich were at least five rungs above the common people on the ladder to heaven.

The young man could boast a flawless record of keeping the external demands of God's laws. He could also preen himself before others, considering his wealth an indication of God's blessing. But Jesus made it clear that the rich young ruler could not make it to heaven on his own. No person can be made ready for heaven apart from God performing in the heart what that person could not manufacture on his own. Salvation is a gift of God.

William MacDonald: God could do what man cannot do. In other words, God can take a greedy, grasping, ruthless materialist, remove his love for gold, and substitute for it a true love for the Lord. It is a miracle of divine grace.[7]

> **Luke 18:28–30** Peter said to him, "We have left all we had to follow you!"
>
> "I tell you the truth," Jesus said to them, "no one who has left home or wife or brothers or parents or children for the sake of the kingdom of God will fail to receive many times as much in this age and, in the age to come, eternal life."

What About Us?

The disciples were far from rich. In fact, they had left everything, even their families and jobs, to follow Jesus. Were they wasting their time? Jesus quickly assured them that God had not overlooked them. They would be rewarded in this life and in eternity. Jesus was grafting them into a spiritual community where they would be <u>supported</u> by fellow believers. This was fulfilled in the early church. And when they died they would receive a heavenly reward.

☞ **GO TO:**

Acts 2:44–47; 4:32–37 (supported)

CONFUSED DISCIPLES

> **Luke 18:31–34** Jesus took the Twelve aside and told them, "We are going up to Jerusalem, and everything that is written by the prophets about the Son of Man will be fulfilled. He will be handed over to the Gentiles. They will mock him, insult him, spit on him, flog him and kill him. On the third day he will rise again."
>
> The disciples did not understand any of this. Its meaning was hidden from them, and they did not know what he was talking about.

I Have Bad News And Good News

Luke emphasized Jesus' determination to go to Jerusalem. He didn't want readers to misunderstand and think the events there were a terrible mistake. Jesus knew exactly what he was doing.

Jesus gave the disciples a prophecy lesson from the Old Testament. The bad news was he would be handed over to Gentiles for terrible mistreatment, which would end in his death. The good news was he would rise from the dead on the third day.

The disciples were completely mystified by his words. They

had no idea what he was telling them because it was so different from their expectations. They still thought he would soon set up an earthly kingdom. In addition, Luke said, some kind of supernatural blinding kept them from understanding.

What Others are Saying:

KEY POINT

The gate to glory opens through suffering.

William Barclay: Jesus never foretold the cross without foretelling the resurrection. He knew that shame lay before him, but he was equally certain that glory lay before him, too. He knew what the malice of men could do, but he knew also what the power of God could do. It was in the certainty of ultimate victory that he faced the apparent defeat of the cross. He knew that without a cross there can never be any crown.[8]

A BLIND BEGGAR

> **Luke 18:35–43** As Jesus approached Jericho, a blind man was sitting by the roadside begging. When he heard the crowd going by, he asked what was happening. They told him, "Jesus of Nazareth is passing by."
>
> He called out, "Jesus, Son of David, have mercy on me!"
>
> Those who led the way rebuked him and told him to be quiet, but he shouted all the more, "Son of David, have mercy on me!"
>
> Jesus stopped and ordered the man to be brought to him. When he came near, Jesus asked him, "What do you want me to do for you?"
>
> "Lord, I want to see," he replied.
>
> Jesus said to him, "Receive your sight; your faith has healed you." Immediately he received his sight and followed Jesus, praising God. When all the people saw it, they also praised God.

Sight For Sore Eyes

By this time in Jesus' life his reputation preceded him. Everywhere he went crowds followed, hanging on his words. As Jesus approached Jericho (see map in appendix A), a blind beggar heard the commotion and discovered that Jesus of Nazareth was passing by.

The blind man called out above the noise of the crowd, *"Jesus, Son of David, have mercy on me!"* Though without sight, he had discernment to recognize that Jesus was not merely a teacher from

Nazareth. He was the Son of David, the Promised One who had power to heal and overcome evil.

People close to the beggar told him to shut up. But the more they rebuked him and tried to keep him quiet, the more loudly he shouted.

Jesus took control of the situation. He had the man brought to him and asked, *"What do you want me to do for you?"*

Seems like a silly question, doesn't it? What blind person wouldn't want to see? But the blind man had only asked for mercy, and in light of his view of Jesus as the Messiah a gift of mercy from Jesus could have taken many forms.

Jesus told him, *"Receive your sight; your faith has healed you."* Jesus didn't mean the beggar's faith had created the cure. He meant that the beggar's faith had been the pipeline through which the healing had come.

Immediately the man could see. He followed Jesus, praising God with all his heart. When the crowd realized what had happened, they joined in the praises.

Luke opened this chapter with Jesus' parable of the persistent widow and closed it with the account of a blind beggar who persisted in calling out to Jesus, even though he was told to be quiet. Both the widow and the beggar received what they needed.

James, usually thought of as Jesus' brother, wrote that when we struggle with selfish desires, we are never satisfied. We do not have what we need because we do not <u>ask God</u> with the right attitude. Jesus encourages us to come to him with childlike trust and request what we need. And when we receive it, we <u>honor</u> him with our praise and thanksgiving.

Study Questions

1. What was the point of Jesus' parable of the persistent widow?
2. Contrast the attitudes of the Pharisee and the tax collector who prayed in the Temple. Which man went home justified?
3. What attitude should we have toward children? In what way should we be childlike?
4. What did the rich young ruler want? Why did he turn away from Jesus?
5. Why did Jesus' disciples not understand what he was telling them about his approaching death and resurrection?
6. What do we learn from the blind beggar's repeated pleas for Jesus' help?

KEY POINT

Prayer is the vehicle through which God gives us gifts and we give him the glory.

Something to Ponder

☞ **GO TO:**

James 4:2 (ask God)

Psalm 50:15 (honor)

CHAPTER WRAP-UP

- Jesus told a parable about an insensitive judge and a widow who persisted in her request to show how we should pray. (Luke 18:1–8)

- Jesus told another parable about a proud Pharisee and a humble tax collector to show how we should approach God. (Luke 18:9–14)

- Jesus received children with love to highlight the childlike attitudes his followers should have. (Luke 18:15–17)

- A rich young ruler sought eternal life and turned away from Jesus because the ruler loved his money more than God. (Luke 18:18–30)

- Jesus told his disciples about the Old Testament prophecies of his death and resurrection but they didn't understand. (Luke 18:31–34)

- Jesus healed a blind beggar who called out to him for help and persisted in doing so even though he was told to be quiet. (Luke 18:35–43)

GOD'S WORD FOR THE BIBLICALLY-INEPT

LUKE 19: LOVED LITTLE PEOPLE

CHAPTER HIGHLIGHTS

- Short Climb to Success
- Give and Take
- Praise Parade
- Temple Business

Let's Get Started

The media places great attention on the rich and famous, the movers and shakers in business and government. But the vast majority of the world's population is made up of individuals who will never attract attention outside their little spheres of influence. The world does not notice them—but God does. In his view, there are no little people.

In this last chapter before starting his account of Jesus' final week, Luke gives us insights into Jesus' heart of love for all people, the depth of his caring, and his desire to have them enjoy the salvation he came to provide.

SHORT CLIMB TO SUCCESS

> **Luke 19:1–6** Jesus entered Jericho and was passing through. A man was there by the name of Zacchaeus; he was a chief tax collector and was wealthy. He wanted to see who Jesus was, but being a short man he could not, because of the crowd. So he ran ahead and climbed a sycamore-fig tree to see him, since Jesus was coming that way.
>
> When Jesus reached the spot, he looked up and said to him, "Zacchaeus, come down immediately. I must stay at your house today." So he came down at once and welcomed him gladly.

Don't Tell Miss Manners

As Jesus approached Jericho, its citizens lined the roadway, eager to see him. The prominent members of the city demanded and got the spots that gave the best views. Zacchaeus was snubbed, for he was a supervisor of tax collectors who had become rich by skimming off more taxes than were required by the despised Roman Gentiles who levied the fees. People hated him.

Being creative and not afraid of ruining his dignity, Zacchaeus climbed a tree. He just planned to watch Jesus.

Throwing etiquette to the wind, Jesus singled out Zacchaeus by inviting himself to his home. He didn't *ask* to visit; he said he *must* visit. Jesus had a divine appointment.

Zacchaeus responded by rolling out the red carpet. Jesus showed <u>mercy</u> to the least likely person in Jericho. He did this because he cared. He discerned Zacchaeus's deep hunger and desperate need, and reached out, knowing as he did so that he would receive criticism from Jericho's most respected citizens.

☞ **GO TO:**

Matthew 5:7 (mercy)

What Others are Saying:

C. Samuel Storms: No one would come right out and say it, but a lot think it: "*Cursed* are the merciful, for they shall be bothered!" A Roman philosopher once called mercy "the disease of the soul"; mercy, like meekness, was considered a sign of cowardice in the ancient world.

Things haven't changed much. People still envy the carefree soul who is a world unto himself, far removed from the entangling complications that others' problems often bring. Many say, "Blessed is he who hasn't a care in the world." "On the contrary," says Jesus, "blessed is he who has a world of cares!" Of course he means the cares of *others*.[1]

> **Luke 19:7–10** All the people saw this and began to mutter, "He has gone to be the guest of a 'sinner.'"
>
> But Zacchaeus stood up and said to the Lord, "Look, Lord! Here and now I give half of my possessions to the poor, and if I have cheated anybody out of anything, I will pay back four times the amount."
>
> Jesus said to him, "Today salvation has come to this house, because this man, too, is a son of Abraham. For the Son of Man came to seek and to save what was lost."

Zach's Heart Transplant

While the citizens of Jericho criticized Jesus for choosing to dine with a "sinner," Jesus performed a heart transplant. Zacchaeus announced that he was giving back the excess tax money he had taken. The law required no more than the original amount <u>plus one-fifth</u>, but Zacchaeus was doing much more.

Jesus called Zacchaeus a son of Abraham, not only because he was biologically descended from Abraham but also because he was a true Jew who had the same saving faith as Abraham. Jesus had come to rescue those who were lost, to <u>call sinners</u> to repentance, and Zacchaeus was certainly one of them.

Verse 10, *"for the Son of Man came to seek and to save what was lost,"* is probably the key verse in all of Luke. The emphasis is on Jesus doing the acting. He made contact with Zacchaeus. He invited himself into Zacchaeus's home. He took out the old sinner's heart and gave him a new righteous heart.

Zacchaeus does not speak of his faith in Jesus as Savior, but he promised to give back what he had taken from taxpayers. This means his salvation was due to his act of restitution. Fact or fiction? Fiction! God did not reward Zacchaeus with salvation after he did a good deed. Rather, Zacchaeus's heart was changed by the miracle of salvation and that caused him to want to do a good deed. Only by putting his trust in Jesus could Zacchaeus have had such a complete change of heart.

 PHYSICIAN'S PERSPECTIVE—Does having a change of heart influence physical health? Luke the physician undoubtedly would answer yes! His opinion would be backed by personal observation as well as by statements in the Book of Proverbs. A heart made <u>joyful</u> by the assurance of sins forgiven makes the face glow. Knowing one is accepted as a child of God cannot help but lift one's spirits and give a hope that permeates every part of one's being.

Henry T. Blackaby and Claude V. King: Zacchaeus promised **restitution** to everyone he had deceived and stolen from. Zacchaeus, for the first time in his adult life, experienced love and forgiveness, grace and mercy—all in the presence of the Messiah. What society had considered to be a sinful occasion, that of Jesus staying with Zacchaeus, became an occasion of salvation. Jesus looked past the physical nature of Zacchaeus and looked into the

---

☞ **GO TO:**

Leviticus 6:5; Numbers 5:7 (plus one-fifth)

Luke 5:31–32 (call sinners)

FACT OR FICTION

☞ **GO TO:**

Proverbs 15:13, 30; 17:22 (joyful)

Exodus 22:1, 4, 7 (restitution)

restitution: *restoration of property previously taken away*

What Others are Saying:

---

soul of the man forsaken by society. Jesus saw someone who longed for the love of God and the chance to love other people. With Jesus, Zacchaeus stood tall.[2]

GIVE AND TAKE

Luke 19:11–15 While they were listening to this, he went on to tell them a parable, because he was near Jerusalem and the people thought that the kingdom of God was going to appear at once. He said: "A man of noble birth went to a distant country to have himself appointed king and then to return. So he called ten of his servants and gave them ten minas. 'Put this money to work,' he said, 'Until I come back.'

But his subjects hated him and sent a delegation after him to say, 'We don't want this man to be our king.'

"He was made king, however, and returned home. Then he sent for the servants to whom he had given the money, in order to find out what they had gained with it."

Meantime Living

Jericho was about seventeen miles from Jerusalem. The closer Jesus got the more people held their breath, hoping that at last Jesus would set himself up as king. Jesus told a parable to make clear what his followers should be doing while they waited for the kingdom of God to appear. His story had to do with a nobleman giving responsibility to his servants.

The nobleman, representing Jesus, was leaving for another country where he would be appointed king. He called in ten servants and gave them each a **mina**, which they were to invest during his extended absence and to give him a profit on his return.

Sadly, some of his subjects hated him so much they rejected him as king. These people represented the religious leaders and others of Israel who refused to recognize Jesus as the Messiah.

mina: unit of money thought to be about three months' wages

What Others are Saying:

Jack Hayford: The parable is based upon a historical event. According to the historian Josephus, after the death of Herod the Great, his son Archelaus went to Rome to be confirmed as king of Judea (v. 12). The Jews, however, sent a delegation to protest the appointment.[3]

Dana Gould: God entrusts believers with the gospel, and he wants them to multiply his message so the entire world will hear it. It is the obligation of believers to be faithful stewards of the message he has entrusted us until Jesus comes.[4]

> **Luke 19:16–19** "The first one came and said, 'Sir, your mina has earned ten more.'
> "'Well done, my good servant!' his master replied. 'Because you have been trustworthy in a very small matter, take charge of ten cities.'
> "The second came and said, 'Sir, your mina has earned five more.'
> "His master answered, 'You take charge of five cities.'"

KEY POINT

God is not a taskmaster, but he does require accountability.

Employee Evaluations

The king received reports from two of his servants who had been faithful in investing his money. The first servant had earned ten minas, a gain of one thousand percent. The king commended him and rewarded him with leadership over ten cities. The second servant reported that his mina had earned five more. The king rewarded him with leadership over five cities.

KEY POINT

The reward for faithful service is more responsibility.

R. Kent Hughes: The reward of Christ's faithful servants is an elevation of eternal intimacy with him. They will be his co-regents, viceroys, and confidants. What joy! Happily, the eternal reward is not rest but responsibility as we work with Christ in unimaginably vast new spiritual enterprises.[5]

What Others are Saying:

> **Luke 19:20–25** "Then another servant came and said, 'Sir, here is your mina; I have kept it laid away in a piece of cloth. I was afraid of you, because you are a hard man. You take out what you did not put in and reap what you did not sow.'
> "His master replied, I will judge you by your own words, you wicked servant! You knew, did you, that I am a hard man, taking out what I did not put in, and reaping what I did not sow? Why then didn't you put my money on deposit, so that when I came back, I could have collected it with interest?'
> "Then he said to those standing by, 'Take his mina away from him and give it to the one who has ten minas.'
> "'Sir,' they said, 'he already has ten!'"

Use It Or Lose It

Another servant had done nothing, so he returned the mina to the king with bitter words about his master. The king used the hateful explanation to expose the false servant who had not expected the master ever to return. If he had, he would have put the money in a bank to earn at least a little interest. The king took the mina away from him and gave it to the servant who had earned ten minas.

> **Luke 19:26–27** "He replied, 'I tell you that to everyone who has, more will be given, but as for the one who has nothing, even what he has will be taken away. But those enemies of mine who did not want me to be king over them—bring them here and kill them in front of me.'"

Settlement

Jesus' parable has a message for everyone. We all have the same job—to live for Christ. To his followers who serve him faithfully and look for his return, Christ has amazing rewards. To those who hide his investment and do not serve him, he has shame. And to those who reject him as king, he has eternal separation from him.

 MORE INFORMATION—Matthew 25:14–30 contains a story that is similar to the one in Luke. In Matthew's account the men are given differing and larger amounts, representing people of different abilities being given serious jobs. In Luke the amounts are the same and are small, showing that each of us has the same basic job. Matthew reports that the third servant was thrown out of the kingdom. That servant represents the people in the Jewish nation who did not want the king to reign over them. He was an enemy agent on the king's staff.

FACT or FICTION

When Jesus said *"to everyone who has, more will be given, but as for the one who has nothing, even what he has will be taken away,"* he meant that the rich get richer and the poor get poorer. Fact or fiction? Fiction. Jesus' story shows that those who make good use of their opportunities will receive more opportunities. Those who do not use the opportunities that are given to them will not be given more opportunities. Jesus was primarily speaking about spiritual opportunities, not material things. In the Christian life we must use the knowledge and insight God gives us, or we will lose it.

PRAISE PARADE

> **Luke 19:28–34** After Jesus had said this, he went on ahead, going up to Jerusalem. As he approached Bethphage and Bethany at the hill called the Mount of Olives, he sent two of his disciples, saying to them, "Go to the village ahead of you, and as you enter it, you will find a colt tied there, which no one has ever ridden. Untie it and bring it here. If anyone asks you, 'Why are you untying it?' tell him, 'The Lord needs it.'"
>
> Those who were sent ahead went and found it just as he had told them. As they were untying the colt, its owners asked them, "Why are you untying the colt?"
>
> They replied, "The Lord needs it."

KEY POINT

We cannot be neutral about Jesus.

MORE INFORMATION—Jesus' triumphal entry to Jerusalem was not an event that happened spontaneously. It was carefully planned by God. Up to this point, Jesus had avoided public acclaim. Though Luke does not do so, Matthew, Mark, and John give information that leads up to Jesus presenting himself as the Messiah in the event known as the triumphal entry.

- Jesus had raised Lazarus from the dead in Bethany. News of this exciting miracle had spread rapidly throughout Jerusalem. (John 11)

- Mary had anointed Jesus with costly ointment, an act considered inappropriately extravagant by some but defended by Jesus, who said plainly that she was anointing him for burial. (Matthew 26:10; Mark 14:6–9; John 12: 7–8)

- Crowds gathered to see Jesus and to learn more about Lazarus who had been miraculously raised from the dead. While many now believed in Jesus, religious leaders strategized behind the scenes how they might put Jesus—and Lazarus—to death. (Mark 14:10–11; John 12:9–11)

Amazing Preparation

Bethany was about two miles from Jerusalem. Jesus was now ready to enter the city, not as an itinerant teacher and healer from Nazareth but as the promised Messiah. On this one occasion he would arrive as their Anointed King!

He sent two disciples to borrow a donkey colt. The disciples must have been amazed that Jesus knew with absolute certainty that they would find *"a colt tied there, which no one had ever ridden"* and that the owners would be prepared to make the animal available to him. Luke does not tell us how Jesus knew all this. Some Bible scholars attribute his knowledge to his divine ability to see all things. Others assume he was counting on friends who would naturally make the colt available at his request. Still others think he must have made the arrangement with the owner in advance.

 MORE INFORMATION—Matthew, alone of the four Gospel writers, records that the disciples were instructed to bring a donkey and her colt. No one had ridden the colt before, so having its mother led along undoubtedly kept it calm. (See Matthew 21:1–7.)

Why Not A Horse?

☞ **GO TO:**

Zechariah 9:9–10
(prophecy)

In New Testament times a conquering king rode on a horse, a symbol of war. A donkey was a symbol of peace. Jesus deliberately fulfilled an Old Testament <u>prophecy</u> that the Messiah would ride on a donkey. He came, not as the military leader the people expected, but as the king of peace. He was their righteous, gentle king, who would some day remove war and bring peace.

> **Luke 19:35–38** They brought it to Jesus, threw their cloaks on the colt and put Jesus on it. As he went along, people spread their cloaks on the road.
>
> When he came near the place where the road goes down the Mount of Olives, the whole crowd of disciples began joyfully to praise God in loud voices for all the miracles they had seen:
>
> "Blessed is the king who comes in the name of the Lord!"
>
> "Peace in heaven and glory in the highest!"

A Noisy Celebration

As the crowds swelled they became caught up in the significance of Jesus' arrival on the donkey. They spontaneously threw their outer garments on the road, using a traditional way of welcoming a king. Their joyful shouts of welcome included expressions of <u>praise</u> from a **messianic psalm**.

 MORE INFORMATION—John 12:12–13 records that crowds who had come to Jerusalem for the Passover Feast went out to meet Jesus as the parade approached the city. They carried palm branches, which represented their great longing for Jesus to deliver them from Roman rule. As they joined the parade they shouted praises to the King of Israel!

> **Luke 19:39–40** Some of the Pharisees in the crowd said to Jesus, "Teacher, rebuke your disciples!"
> "I tell you," he replied, "if they keep quiet, the stones will cry out."

messianic psalm: *poem containing prophetic references to Christ the Messiah*

☞ **GO TO:**

Psalm 118:26 (praise)

Rock Music

The ever-present Pharisees approached Jesus and ordered him to take control of his followers and put an immediate stop to the praises. Did they feel the praise was misplaced? Probably. Or did they fear that the Romans would view the parade as a prelude to an uprising? If so, the Pharisees had a valid fear, especially since it was Passover and many visitors swelled the city.

Jesus responded that the exuberance of the crowd was so appropriate that if the people were silent, inanimate objects would take up the praise.

Larry Sibley: Whether they were critics or truth seekers, the Pharisees in the crowd were shocked by the honor the people accorded Jesus. Most likely they recognized enough scriptural allusions in the shouts of the crowd and Jesus' remarks to believe they had grounds on which to accuse him of blasphemy and heresy.[7]

What Others are Saying:

> **Luke 19:41–44** As he approached Jerusalem and saw the city, he wept over it and said, "If you, even you, had only known on this day what would bring you peace— but now it is hidden from your eyes. The days will come

> upon you when your enemies will build an embankment against you and encircle you and hem you in on every side. They will dash you to the ground, you and the children within your walls. They will not leave one stone on another, because you did not recognize the time of God's coming to you."

The Weeping King

As the parade moved toward Jerusalem, Jesus came to a ridge that gave a view of the city, which normally brought a surge of admiration and pride to a traveler. On this occasion, Jesus began to weep, not quietly as he had wept at <u>Lazarus's grave</u>, but aloud. In a heart-rending **lamentation**, Jesus mourned the destruction of the city because the people within it were unrepentant and would reject him. Roman soldiers fulfilled Jesus' prophecy in A.D. 70 when the city was destroyed.

PHYSICIAN'S PERSPECTIVE—Dr. Luke loved people, and he loved to show Jesus' love for people. All through his Gospel, Luke stressed Jesus' determined journey to Jerusalem. We would expect Jesus' parade through the city to be the climax of Luke's story, but it is not. Luke did not actually put his readers at the parade. (And all good writers know that the climax scene needs to make readers feel that they are actually seeing the events described.) Plus, Luke always said Jesus *was approaching* the city; he never said Jesus *arrived*. Instead, Luke's climax is Jesus' deep love highlighted by how he cried over Jerusalem and its people, a lament made all the more striking because of the contrasting joy in the city.

Jesus cried over Jerusalem, tears prompted by grief over the nation's coming judgment. He was ready to give his life for this people, but they did not want him as Savior-King, only as Conquering King. Judgment always follows rejection of Christ. Jesus repeated the word "you" ten times in two verses, showing that rejection and judgment are always personal.

☞ **GO TO:**

John 11:32–35
(Lazarus's grave)

lamentation: vocal expression of deep grief

Something to Ponder

TEMPLE BUSINESS

> **Luke 19:45–48** Then he entered the temple area and began driving out those who were selling. "It is written," he said to them, "'My house will be a house of prayer'; but you have made it 'a den of robbers.'"
>
> Every day he was teaching at the temple. But the chief priests, the teachers of the law and the leaders among the people were trying to kill him. Yet they could not find any way to do it, because all the people hung on his words.

Temple Headache

Luke gives a succinct account of what must have been a dramatic event (see GWLC2, page 150). Picture the scene: The temple court buzzed with activity. Jews from surrounding areas made a pilgrimage to Jerusalem for the yearly Passover celebration. Booths were set up for currency exchange. To pay their temple <u>tax</u>, visiting Jews were required to change their money to **tetradrachmas**. This gave the money changers opportunity to make a large profit from the exchange. They had a monopoly on the market.

Adding to the confusion were the sounds of sacrificial animals and doves, which temple officials sold to the pilgrims at greatly inflated prices. It was a lucrative business, to say the least.

The crass commercialism was an insult to God in the very place Jesus, as a twelve year old, had called his <u>Father's house</u>! Instead of worshiping God from pure hearts, the people were occupied with buying and selling, haggling energetically over their transactions, and robbing the poor who had come to worship. Enough already! Jesus took action and threw out the greedy merchants, <u>quoting</u> the Old Testament as he did so.

Matthew and Mark join Luke in including the incident of driving the merchants out of the Temple. John, however, records a cleansing of the Temple close to the beginning of Jesus' ministry. John made a mistake. Fact or fiction? Fiction. Because of the differences in the accounts and the Old Testament text quoted, it is certain that there were two actual cleansings of the Temple: one at the beginning of Jesus' ministry and one at the end (see GWLC, pages 107–109 and Matthew 21:13; Mark 11:15–19; and John 2:13–17).

☞ **GO TO:**

Exodus 30:11–14 (tax)

Luke 2:49 (Father's house)

Isaiah 56:7; Jeremiah 7:11 (quoting)

tetradrachmas: *shekels of Tyre; temple money*

FACT OR FICTION

FAST FORWARD

Does Jesus' cleansing of the Temple have anything to say to us today? We are warned to avoid anything that would detract from our focus on God and our desire to worship him. Any program or talent, any commercial venture in the name of religion, however seemingly legitimate, must not be allowed to come between us and God.

Poised To Pounce

The religious leaders were poised to pounce on Jesus and have him killed. But their hands were tied. Like it or not, they had to recognize that Jesus was surrounded by a growing crowd of fans who hung on his words and flocked to him for <u>healing</u>. The leaders waited for the right moment to make their move.

☞ **GO TO:**

Matthew 21:14
(healing)

Study Questions

1. What made Zacchaeus an unlikely prospect for Jesus' interest and concern, and how did Zacchaeus change as a result of his encounter with Jesus?
2. What does Jesus want us to learn from his parable of the ten servants?
3. Why did Jesus ride a donkey colt on his triumphal entry into Jerusalem?
4. Why did Jesus weep as he entered Jerusalem?
5. What prompted Jesus' anger so that he cleaned out the temple market?

CHAPTER WRAP-UP

- Jesus sought out Zacchaeus, a Jewish tax collector. Jesus changed his heart so that he was willing to make restitution far beyond what was required in Old Testament law. (Luke 19:1–10)

- Jesus told a parable of ten servants who were entrusted with their master's resources while he was away. The servants who were faithful were given more responsibilities. The servant who was unfaithful was relieved of his responsibility. (Luke 19:11–27)

- Jesus rode on a donkey colt when he made his triumphal entry into Jerusalem, signifying his peaceful conquering as the Messiah-King. (Luke 19:28–40)

- Jesus lamented over Jerusalem because the people rejected him and the city would be judged. (Luke 19:28–44)

- Jesus became angry at the commercial enterprises he found in the temple-market and cleaned house. (Luke 19:45–48)

LUKE 20: HOSTILE CHALLENGES

CHAPTER HIGHLIGHTS

- Bait about Authority
- Bait about Government
- Bait about Marriage and More

Let's Get Started

Jesus and the religious leaders in Jerusalem were on a collision course. While they were plotting his death, Jesus was calmly following the timetable set by his Father in heaven. They saw Jesus as guilty and were trying to hatch a plot to have him killed. Jesus, on the other hand, was preparing to <u>lay down</u> his life. He had stated that nobody would be able to take his life from him.

Although the leaders were desperate to stifle Jesus, they were not dummies. They knew the crowds loved Jesus. They didn't want to cause a riot by arresting Jesus for no apparent reason. Their only solution was to throw out some bait and try to trick him into publicly saying or doing something they could use as a reason to arrest him.

Luke uses a series of dialogues to highlight these challenges and to show how Jesus handily threw the questions back into the faces of his interrogators. Touché!

☞ **GO TO:**

John 10:14–18
(lay down)

BAIT ABOUT AUTHORITY

> **Luke 20:1–8** One day as he was teaching the people in the temple courts and preaching the gospel, the chief priests and the teachers of the law, together with the elders, came up to him. "Tell us by what authority you are doing these things," they said. "Who gave you this authority?"

> He replied, "I will also ask you a question. Tell me, John's baptism—was it from heaven, or from men?"
>
> They discussed it among themselves and said, "If we say, 'From heaven,' he will ask, 'Why didn't you believe him?' But if we say, 'From men,' all the people will stone us, because they are persuaded that John was a prophet."
>
> So they answered, "We don't know where it was from."
>
> Jesus said, "Neither will I tell you by what authority I am doing these things."

Official Posse Demands A Letter Of Recommendation

Jesus had taken initiative that proved he had authority when he rode into Jerusalem as a king. Then he had the nerve to drive the moneychangers and merchants out of the Temple. The religious leaders were miffed. They devised what they considered a brilliant question to trap Jesus. They gathered an official posse and demanded that he give his credentials and state who gave him the authority for his recent actions.

Jesus answered their question with a question about John the Baptist. Was his baptism authorized in heaven—meaning God— or by men? Now the religious leaders were trapped. If they answered that John's baptism was authorized in heaven, they would have to accept John's declaration that Jesus was the Messiah. If, on the other hand, they answered that John's baptism was merely from men, they would anger the multitudes who believed John's message.

The leaders could not answer Jesus, and Jesus chose not to answer them. Jesus refused to give more explanation to people who refused to accept the facts they already had. The way Jesus responded to the bait threw the religious posse for a loop.

 MORE INFORMATION—Both Matthew and Mark include this encounter with the chief priests and teachers of the law. Mark points out that these leaders understood that the people considered John the Baptist a prophet. (Check out Matthew 21:23–27 and Mark 11:27–33.)

Warren W. Wiersbe: The chief priests claimed their authority from Moses, for the Law set the tribe of Levi apart to serve in the sanctuary. The scribes were students of the Law and claimed their authority from the rabbis whose interpretations they studied. The elders of Israel were the leaders of the families and clans, chosen usually for their experience and wisdom. All of these men were sure of their authority and were not afraid to confront Jesus.[1]

> **Luke 20:9–12** He went on to tell the people this parable: "A man planted a vineyard, rented it to some farmers and went away for a long time. At harvest time he sent a servant to the tenants so they would give him some of the fruit of the vineyard. But the tenants beat him and sent him away empty-handed. He sent another servant, but that one also they beat and treated shamefully and sent away empty-handed. He sent still a third, and they wounded him and threw him out."

A Viny Tale

Jesus told a parable that would clearly define his authority. The setting for the story was a vineyard, something familiar to all his listeners both as a physical feature on the landscape and as a <u>symbol</u> of their nation.

The vineyard owner followed a common practice of leaving his vineyard in the hands of tenant farmers. He had every right to collect some of the harvest from his vines, but on three occasions the tenants badly mistreated the servants sent by the owner.

☞ **GO TO:**

Isaiah 5:1–7 (symbol)

R. Kent Hughes: The vineyard/Israel connection was so much a part of their national consciousness that the very temple in which Jesus was standing sported a richly carved grapevine, seventy cubits high, sculpted around the door that led from the porch to the Holy Place. The branches, tendrils, and leaves were of finest gold. The bunches of grapes hanging upon the golden limbs were costly jewels.[2]

> **Luke 20:13–16** "Then the owner of the vineyard said, 'What shall I do? I will send my son, whom I love; perhaps they will respect him.'
> "But when the tenants saw him, they talked the

> matter over. 'This is the heir,' they said. 'Let's kill him, and the inheritance will be ours.' So they threw him out of the vineyard and killed him.
>
> "What then will the owner of the vineyard do to them? He will come and kill those tenants and give the vineyard to others."
>
> When the people heard this, they said, "May this never be!"

Making A Painful Point

☞ **GO TO:**

Luke 3:22
   (dearly loved son)

Finally, the owner decided to send his <u>dearly loved son</u>, hoping the tenants would respect him. But the tenants saw this only as an opportunity to kill the heir and seize the vineyard for themselves.

To be sure his listeners did not miss his important point, Jesus asked what the owner of the vineyard would do to the evil tenants. Any reasonable owner would kill them and give the vineyard to more worthy tenants.

The people got the message! The vineyard was Israel, loved and cared for by God and responsible to bear fruit for him. But Israel had mistreated God's prophets and even now its leaders were plotting to kill his Son. Jesus was saying that unbelieving Israel would not be allowed in the kingdom, but Gentiles and people considered as outcasts would become the tenants.

KEY POINT

Jesus exposed the evil hearts of his critics.

The listeners were horrified and said, "God forbid!" They couldn't imagine that the privileges of the Jewish nation would be given to Gentiles. How dare God do such a thing!

 MORE INFORMATION—Matthew 21:33–44 and Mark 12:1–11 include this parable with more and varied detail. Jesus tells of the great care the owner gave his vineyard to make it safe and productive. Mark gives more detail about the murder of the son.

> **Luke 20:17–18** Jesus looked directly at them and asked, "Then what is the meaning of that which is written:
>
> "'The stone the builders rejected has become the capstone'?
>
> Everyone who falls on that stone will be broken to pieces, but he on whom it falls will be crushed."

Don't Get Stoned

Leaving the imagery of the vineyard, Jesus quoted from the Old Testament about a stone that was tossed away by stone masons that became the cornerstone—the most significant part of a building! If they didn't believe him, how would they interpret Psalm 118:22?

Further, Jesus said the stone had destructive power. People could reject Jesus but they would suffer both in this life and eternally. They <u>stumbled</u> over Jesus by not believing on him and they would be crushed.

 **GO TO:**

Isaiah 8:14–15 (stumbled)

William MacDonald: The Jewish builders had rejected Christ, the Stone. They had no place in their plans for him. But God was determined that he would have the place of preeminence, by making him the chief cornerstone, a stone which is indispensable and in the place of greatest honor.[3]

What Others are Saying:

Like a builder tossing aside a stone as unusable for his building, we may ignore Jesus Christ as totally irrelevant to our lives. But God has <u>appointed</u> Jesus head over all things. He has given Jesus the most exalted place. Someday we will all <u>bow</u> before him and confess that he is Lord.

 *Remember This . . .*

> **Luke 20:19** The teachers of the law and the chief priests looked for a way to arrest him immediately, because they knew he had spoken this parable against them. But they were afraid of the people.

 **GO TO:**

Ephesians 1:22–23 (appointed)

Philippians 2:9–11 (bow)

Hopping Mad

The religious leaders' blood pressure skyrocketed! They knew Jesus' parable had both established his authority as the Son sent from God and had pictured them as the murdering tenants rejected by God.

If only they could arrest Jesus and get rid of him—but they didn't want to start a riot and risk losing their privileges. Jesus' popularity with the crowds kept them from moving in on him.

BAIT ABOUT GOVERNMENT

> **Luke 20:20–22** Keeping a close watch on him, they sent spies, who pretended to be honest. They hoped to catch Jesus in something he said so that they might hand him over to the power and authority of the governor. So the spies questioned him: "Teacher, we know that you speak and teach what is right, and that you do not show partiality but teach the way of God in accordance with the truth. Is it right for us to pay taxes to Caesar or not?"

Send In The Spies

Frustrated, the religious leaders sent shameful spies to get Jesus to say something against the government that would warrant his arrest. If they couldn't catch him in religious gobbledygook, they would try to get him in trouble with the Romans. Notice the leaders weren't interested in discovering the truth. They wanted dirt. These spies used flattery to set Jesus up to give his opinion on whether it was right to pay taxes to the hated Romans.

> **Luke 20:23–26** He saw through their duplicity and said to them, "Show me a denarius. Whose portrait and inscription are on it?"
>
> "Caesar's," they replied.
>
> He said to them, "Then give to Caesar what is Caesar's, and to God what is God's."
>
> They were unable to trap him in what he had said there in public. And astonished by his answer, they became silent.

Look At The Physical Evidence

denarius: Roman coin worth about a day's wage for a workman

Jesus was not fooled for a minute. He asked them to show him a **denarius** and to identify the picture and the inscription on it (see illustration, page 263). They had to answer honestly. Jesus then told them to give to Caesar what was his and to give to God what was his. Jesus favored neither the people who wanted to revolt against Rome nor those loyal to Rome.

The trap sprang the wrong way! The spies slunk away in silence with their tails between their legs.

Denarius

A silver coin picturing on one side Tiberius Caesar, who ruled A.D. 14–37 and on the other side the Roman personification of peace.

Gilbert Bilezikian: For the people who lived in Palestine, the presence and the rule of the Romans were intolerable. But Jesus was careful not to appear anti-Roman. He acknowledged the presence of the Roman government and recognized their rights within the limits of their governmental function. But he also reminded the people that Rome could not take over that which belonged to God.[4]

The Jews bitterly resented having to pay taxes to the Roman government, which they regarded as **pagan**. *Jesus did not encourage them to oppose the government or to join the* **Zealots**, *who wanted to fight the Romans for freedom. Instead, he taught his followers to be respectful of government and to view themselves as citizens of God's kingdom who follow his rule of righteousness and love.*

Today we are called to be good citizens of our country, obeying its laws, paying the taxes, and respecting its leaders. We are also called to reach out in our country and around the world to win people to Christ and his kingdom.

BAIT ABOUT MARRIAGE AND MORE

Luke 20:27–33 Some of the Sadducees, who say there is no resurrection, came to Jesus with a question. "Teacher," they said, "Moses wrote for us that if a man's brother dies and leaves a wife but no children, the man must marry the widow and have children for his brother.

What Others are Saying:

FAST FORWARD

pagan: *heathen, against the true God*

Zealots: *party committed to violent overthrow of Romans*

KEY POINT

Jesus' followers should also be good citizens.

> Now there were seven brothers. The first one married a woman and died childless. The second and then the third married her, and in the same way the seven died, leaving no children. Finally, the woman died too. Now then, at the resurrection whose wife will she be, since the seven were married to her?"

How Many Angels Can Dance On A Pin?

The attempt to trap Jesus on a political issue failed. So now the **Sadducees** moved in to spar verbally with Jesus. They did not believe in any form of life after death, so they posed a ridiculous situation to entangle Jesus much the way kids love to debate how many angels can dance on the head of a pin. They didn't care about Jesus' answer. They just wanted to watch him wiggle.

First, they reminded Jesus that an <u>unmarried brother</u> was required to marry his brother's widow in order to carry on the family name and heritage. Then, they asked whose wife a woman would be if she actually married seven brothers and still had no children!

Sadducees: wealthy leaders opposed to Pharisees, and who denied the afterlife, angels, and spirits

☞ **GO TO:**

Deuteronomy 25:5–6 (unmarried brother)

What Others are Saying:

Leon Morris: [The Sadducees] were the conservative, aristocratic, high-priestly party, worldly-minded and very ready to cooperate with the Romans, which, of course, enabled them to maintain their privileged position. Patriotic nationalists and pious people alike opposed them.[5]

> **Luke 20:34–36** Jesus replied, "The people of this age marry and are given in marriage. But those who are considered worthy of taking part in that age and in the resurrection from the dead will neither marry nor be given in marriage, and they can no longer die; for they are like the angels. They are God's children, since they are children of the resurrection."

Bombing The Bluffers

Jesus called the Sadducees' bluff and launched a word bomb to silence them. Their clever what-if dilemma was a no-brainer. Marriage is for life on earth. After the resurrection, the relationships between husbands and wives would be on a different basis.

PHYSICIAN'S PERSPECTIVE—One of the duties of a physician is to care for the grieving spouse whose life companion has been snatched away in death. It would be a cruel blow to imply to the one in deep sorrow that there can be no reunion in heaven with the loved one. Luke was alert to note what Jesus did *not* say about the relationship of husbands and wives in heaven.

Jesus said that in the resurrection there will be no marrying. Therefore, couples will not even recognize each other after death. Fact or fiction? Look carefully at what Jesus did not say! Was he not suggesting something even better for all, including husbands and wives, who long for even a closer relationship after death?

FACT OR FICTION

Lawrence O. Richards: In the resurrection there is no marriage. But this does not mean husbands and wives are separated. It simply means that the intimacy we experience here on earth is a symbol of a reality we will experience in glory. The joy a married couple finds in their union will not be taken away, but will be multiplied, as we experience a closeness with others that is beyond us here and now.[6]

What Others are Saying:

> **Luke 20:37–40** "But in the account of the bush, even Moses showed that the dead rise, for he calls the Lord 'the God of Abraham, and the God of Isaac, and the God of Jacob.' He is not the God of the dead, but of the living, for to him all are alive."
>
> Some of the teachers of the law responded, "Well said, teacher!" And no one dared to ask him any more questions.

Chew On This

Jesus now turned to the real issue for the Sadducees, who did not believe in life after death. He pointed out that in the Old Testament Scriptures, which they professed to accept, God had <u>identified</u> himself to Moses as *"the God of Abraham, and the God of Isaac, and the God of Jacob."* These patriarchs had died many years before Moses, but God clearly indicates that they were alive with him.

Now there was silence in the temple court. Nobody dared to raise another question!

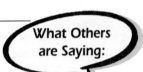 **GO TO:**

Exodus 3:15 (identified)

Personal Growth Study Bible: The Sadducees had such fun confounding the rival Pharisees with their hypothetical question ridiculing the belief in resurrection. But when they pulled out their old puzzle to trap Jesus, they were the ones left confused.

What stunned the Sadducees most was the proof that Jesus drew from Moses' writings, the only part of the Old Testament the Sadducees acknowledged as God's Word. The proof rested on the tense of a single verb! God did not say to Moses, "I *was* the God of Abraham." He said, "I am the God of Abraham." Clearly the verb tense implies that Abraham still lived. This means that belief in resurrection is not foolish, but assured.

Think for a moment. If Jesus had such confidence in the Word of God that he rested a basic doctrine on the tense of a single verb, how much confidence should we have in God's complete Word? Jesus trusted God's Word absolutely—so can we.[7]

Dallas Willard: To one group of his day, who believed that "physical death" was the cessation of the individual's existence, Jesus said, "God is not the God of the dead but of the living" (v. 38). His meaning was that those who love and are loved by God are not allowed to cease to exist, because they are God's treasures. He delights in them and intends to hold onto them. He has even prepared for them an individualized eternal work in his vast universe.[8]

> **Luke 20:41–44** Then Jesus said to them, "How is it that they say the Christ is the Son of David? David himself declares in the Book of Psalms:
>
> "'The Lord said to my Lord: "Sit at my right hand until I make your enemies a footstool for your feet."'
>
> "David calls him 'Lord.' How then can he be his son?"

Jesus Makes Their Heads Spin

The religious leaders, their spies, and the Sadducees had raised difficult questions. Jesus had silenced them with his wisdom. Now he raised an even tougher question—one that made their heads spin.

How can the Messiah be the son of David when <u>David called</u> the Messiah "my Lord"? In other words, how can Christ be both David's descendant and his Lord? This was outside Jewish thinking, for they held that the ancestor was always greater than any

☞ **GO TO:**

Psalm 110:1
(David called)

descendant. The people were silent because they could not accept the only possible answer: Christ was both God ("the Lord") and man (David's descendant).

> **Luke 20:45–47** While all the people were listening, Jesus said to his disciples, "Beware of the teachers of the law. They like to walk around in flowing robes and love to be greeted in the marketplaces and have the most important seats in the synagogues and the places of honor at banquets. They devour widows' houses and for a show make lengthy prayers. Such men will be punished most severely."

Now A Word Of Warning

Jesus spoke to his disciples, aware that the crowds were listening. He warned them about the **hypocrisy** of the teachers of the law who planned their daily lives around actions that would generate approval. These leaders wore long robes that showed their place in upper-class society. Common laborers could not work in such clothing. The teachers of the law made grand entrances at gathering places, so they could get the applause they desired. While they pretended to pray long caring prayers for defenseless widows, they actually plotted ways to make money from those defenseless women.

hypocrisy: false impression of desirable qualities

 PHYSICIAN'S PERSPECTIVE—Again Dr. Luke includes reference to widows. The blood in his caring heart boiled as he reflected on Jesus' insight into the plight of women who had no way to defend themselves against the manipulations of greedy religious leaders.

God has a tender heart for the defenseless. His heart goes out to women and children who live in fear and deprivation. He has entrusted others with the means to relieve their suffering. What are we doing about it?

Something to Ponder

Study Questions

1. Why did Jesus choose not to answer the religious leaders' question about his authority?
2. In what way was Israel like the tenant farmers in Jesus' parable?
3. What attitude does Jesus teach us to have toward government?

4. How did Jesus silence the Sadducees when he questioned them about the afterlife?
5. What hypocrisy did Jesus expose in the teachers of the law?

CHAPTER WRAP-UP

- When Jesus' critics questioned where he received his authority, he asked them whether John the Baptist's authority was from heaven or from man. (Luke 20:1–8)

- Jesus told a parable about tenants of a vineyard who beat the owner's servants and murdered his son. The tale made the religious leaders furious. (Luke 20:9–19)

- When questioned about paying taxes to Caesar, Jesus gave the principle that we are to be law-abiding citizens while remembering always that we belong to his kingdom of righteousness and love. (Luke 20:20–26)

- The Sadducees wanted to make sport of the Pharisees' belief that there is life after death. Jesus' reply confounded them because he proved from Moses' writings that Abraham, Isaac, and Jacob were alive in heaven. (Luke 20:27–44)

- The teachers of the law paraded around in expensive robes and attracted attention to themselves while they plotted ways to exploit the helpless. (Luke 20:45–47)

LUKE 21: WHAT MATTERS MOST

CHAPTER HIGHLIGHTS

- A Widow's Offering
- Sign Language

Let's Get Started

Jesus stood in the beautiful Temple as he spoke to the crowds and the critics who gathered to hear him. After observing the people who placed their offerings in the trumpet-shaped chests provided in the Women's Court, he left with his disciples.

It is easy to get so caught up in the here and now that we ignore the reality that lies beyond the visible. This was true of the disciples. They were impressed by the grandeur of the Temple. Jesus saw beyond the showmanship of the wealthy worshipers who dropped their large offerings in the chests, making an impressive clatter. He also saw beyond the marble and gold of the Temple to the horrible destruction that would come in a few years. As he spoke about what he saw, he pointed out what matters most. He told his disciples to be alert, to persevere to the end, and to be assured that he would remain faithful to them.

A WIDOW'S OFFERING

> **Luke 21:1–4** As he looked up, Jesus saw the rich putting their gifts into the temple treasury. He also saw a poor widow put in two very small copper coins. "I tell you the truth," he said, "this poor widow has put in more than all the others. All these people gave their gifts out of their wealth; but she out of her poverty put in all she had to live on."

Size Doesn't Matter

Jesus had pointed out the <u>evils</u> of the teachers of the law who made a show of their religion and attracted attention to themselves. They offered loud and long prayers, pretending to care about the needs of widows while they were making moves to defraud them!

Now he watched the wealthy approach the thirteen trumpet-shaped chests in the Women's Court of the Temple (see a diagram of the Temple, page 6). As they placed their offerings into the narrow opening at the top of the receptacle, their coins made an impressive clatter. The louder the sound, the more generous the giver! People nearby turned their heads to see what important person could afford to give such a large offering.

Then a poor widow approached. She carried two tiny coins, which barely made a clank as she placed them in the offering chest. She would have gone unnoticed by the throng, but Jesus pointed her out as having given more than the wealthy. They had given from their abundance; she had given her all. They had given to impress others; she had given to express her love to God.

Lawrence O. Richards: It's not how much we give, but our willingness to surrender all. Undoubtedly Luke purposely placed the ragged, humble widow beside the posturing, well-dressed politicians whose pretensions Jesus had just exposed. Luke wanted us to see others as God sees them. He wants us to realize that the mighty are seldom high on God's scale of values.[1]

 PHYSICIAN'S PERSPECTIVE—Dr. Luke's obvious care and concern for widows shines through in his Gospel account, and gives joy to God, who desires that the poor and defenseless be shown compassion.

In Bible times the plight of widows was desperate. They had no income, no way of earning a living, and had to depend on the dole of food distributed by the Temple. Even before God led the Israelites into the land of promise, he had expressed his tender concern for widows. He <u>defended</u> their cause and made it clear that widows were to be <u>treated justly</u> and be <u>provided for</u>. These provisions for the fatherless and widows were reinforced by the prophets.

GO TO:

Luke 20:46–47 (evils)

KEY POINT

While we look at how much we give to God, he looks at how much of ourselves we have made available to him.

What Others are Saying:

GO TO:

Deuteronomy 10:18 (defended)

Deuteronomy 27:19; Isaiah 10:1–4 (treated justly)

Deuteronomy 14:28–29; 24:19 (provided for)

James describes the essence of religion that is <u>pure and faultless</u> as watching out for the needs of orphans and widows. The early church took this responsibility so seriously that they appointed seven men known to be full of the Spirit and wisdom to serve the needs of widows who had been overlooked in the daily <u>distribution</u> of food.

Though government agencies and charities have taken over some of the services to people with needs, we each can still find ways to express God's love and care to needy individuals. We can show compassion personally to people in our communities. In addition, through donations to charities and faith-based ministries we can reach out to widows and orphans in other places.

FAST FORWARD

☞ **GO TO:**

James 1:27
(pure and faultless)

Acts 6:1–7 (distribution)

SIGN LANGUAGE

> **Luke 21:5–6** Some of his disciples were remarking about how the temple was adorned with beautiful stones and with gifts dedicated to God. But Jesus said, "As for what you see here, the time will come when not one stone will be left on another; every one of them will be thrown down."

Here Today, Gone Tomorrow

As Jesus left the Temple with his disciples, some of them commented on the beauty of the building and the generosity of those who had given to God for its construction. After all, the Temple had become one of the wonders of the Roman Empire!

Jesus' response must have sucked the breath out of the disciples' lungs. Workmen had labored on the <u>temple reconstruction</u> for forty-six years. Now Jesus said that not one of the huge foundation stones would be left in place. The Temple was going to be completely destroyed.

☞ **GO TO:**

John 2:20
(temple
reconstruction)

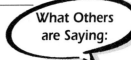

What Others
are Saying:

Howard Vos: The retaining walls of the Temple Mount rose 98 feet above the paved area at the foot of the mount. And in some places the lower courses of these walls, always planted on bedrock, go as far down as 65 feet below the street, making walls at such a point more than 165 feet high. Most of the stones in these walls weighed two to five tons. But in the southwest corner of the Temple Mount are stones that weigh about 50 tons apiece.[2]

> **Luke 21:7** "Teacher," they asked, "when will these things happen? And what will be the sign that they are about to take place?"

What's The Timetable?

As Jesus led the disciples to the Mount of Olives they could hardly wait to ask him questions about the future—questions about when Jesus' prophecy would be fulfilled and what clues would come in advance. People of all generations can identify with their curiosity about what the future holds. Jesus' response is called the Olivet Discourse.

 MORE INFORMATION—Matthew 24 and Mark 13 include Jesus' prophecy about the Temple and his Second Coming. In Matthew, Mark, and Luke Jesus answered three questions raised by the disciples:

- When will the Temple be destroyed?
- What will be the sign of your coming?
- What will be the sign of the end of the age?

In answering, Jesus did not address these questions in this sequence, nor did he attach specific dates to any of them.

> **Luke 21:8–11** He replied: "Watch out that you are not deceived. For many will come in my name, claiming, 'I am he,' and, 'The time is near.' Do not follow them. When you hear of wars and revolutions, do not be frightened. These things must happen first, but the end will not come right away."
> Then he said to them: "Nation will rise against nation, and kingdom against kingdom. There will be great earthquakes, famines and pestilences in various places, and fearful events and great signs from heaven."

Be Alert

First, Jesus warned that many men would appear claiming to be Christ. They would profess to have spectacular revelations, none found in the Bible.

Then Jesus predicted international unrest—wars, revolutions, and natural disasters. Some would be alarming, but Jesus assured his disciples that none would take God by surprise. They would come, but would not necessarily indicate the end time.

Daymond R. Duck: World leaders predicted a comprehensive peace in the Middle East by the year 2000, but the Bible teaches that there will be no peace until Christ returns. President Clinton is predicting there will be no more armies, just peacekeeping forces, but the Bible predicts a two hundred million-man army will invade the Middle East.[3]

What Others are Saying:

Some people have tried to pinpoint the date when "the end" will come, but their calculations always prove wrong. It's impossible to figure out that date. Fact or fiction? Fact! Jesus said that even *he* did not know nor did the angels—only the Father in heaven knows the <u>date and the hour</u>. (Learn more about the end times in GWPB.)

FACT OR FICTION

R. C. Sproul: Some people believe that, since we don't know when Jesus will come again, we ought not even think about the signs of the times—knowledge of such things was never intended for us. In the Olivet discourse, Jesus clearly suggests that we be vigilant and diligent and aware of what's going on around us.[4]

What Others are Saying:

☞ **GO TO:**

Matthew 24:36
(date and the hour)

Philip Yancey: I confess that, despite long hours of study in the prophets, I have no clearer understanding of what will happen next year, or in 2025. But I have a much clearer idea of what God wants to accomplish in my life right now. And I am gaining, gradually, the confidence to believe in the present what will fully make sense only when seen from the future.[5]

Luke 21:12–19 "But before all this, they will lay hands on you and persecute you. They will deliver you to synagogues and prisons, and you will be brought before kings and governors, and all on account of my name. This will result in your being witnesses to them. But make up your mind not to worry beforehand how you will defend yourselves. For I will give you words and wisdom that none of your adversaries will be able to resist or contradict. You will be betrayed even by parents, brothers, relatives and friends, and they will put some of you to death. All men will hate you because of me. But not a hair of your head will perish. By standing firm you will gain life."

Speechwriters Need Not Apply

Jesus prepared his followers for persecution. They would face hostile questioning and physical punishment from religious and government leaders. He assured them that they were not responsible to prepare in advance to defend themselves. At the precise moment they would need that defense, Jesus would give them irrefutable words, far better than any lawyer or speechwriter could provide.

Even if his followers were betrayed by family and friends, even if they were killed because of their loyalty to him, they would be safe, for Jesus promised they would <u>never perish</u>.

☞ **GO TO:**

John 11:25–26
(never perish)

What Others are Saying:

John Piper: The history of the expansion of Christianity has proved that "the blood of the martyrs is seed"—the seed of new life in Christ spreading through the world. For almost three hundred years Christianity grew in soil that was wet with the blood of the martyrs.[6]

> **Luke 21:20–24** "When you see Jerusalem being surrounded by armies, you will know that its desolation is near. Then let those who are in Judea flee to the mountains, let those in the city get out, and let those in the country not enter the city. For this is the time of punishment in fulfillment of all that has been written. How dreadful it will be in those days for pregnant women and nursing mothers! They will fall by the sword and will be taken as prisoners to all the nations. Jerusalem will be trampled on by the Gentiles until the times of the Gentiles are fulfilled."

Be Prepared

Jesus moved from long-range predictions to deal specifically with the disciples' question about when the Temple would be destroyed. He painted the picture in detail—every one fulfilled in A.D. 70, less than forty years later.

The Roman army moved in to surround Jerusalem. When war threatened in those days, the people who lived in the country grabbed a few belongings and headed for the protection of the closest walled city. History records that a million Jews who sought refuge inside Jerusalem died, either from starvation or from the carnage that followed when the army broke through the city walls.

Jesus' followers, now called Christians, heeded Jesus' warning, escaped to the mountains before the siege, and survived.

When the Temple was destroyed, Jews fled from the surrounding areas and scattered among many nations, exactly as Jesus had predicted.

The Romans who invaded Jerusalem were followed by other occupying nations, so that for almost two thousand years the Gentiles have trampled on the land of promise. *"The times of the Gentiles"* may refer to the period when Gentiles control the land of Israel. The Jews will regain control before Christ's Second Coming (see GWPB, page 271).

Jesus had wept over Jerusalem, knowing that their rejection of him would bring dire consequences. Now in foretelling the scope of the destruction, his heart overflowed with compassion for the human suffering that lay ahead, especially for the women and infants who would become victims. God takes <u>no pleasure</u> in the death of the wicked. He is <u>patient</u>, giving time for people to repent.

Remember This . . .

☞ **GO TO:**

Ezekiel 33:11 (no pleasure)

2 Peter 3:9 (patient)

> **Luke 21:25–28** "There will be signs in the sun, moon and stars. On the earth, nations will be in anguish and perplexity at the roaring and tossing of the sea. Men will faint from terror, apprehensive of what is coming on the world, for the heavenly bodies will be shaken. At that time they will see the Son of Man coming in a cloud with power and great glory. When these things begin to take place, stand up and lift up your heads, because your redemption is drawing near."

More Signs

Jesus promised to come again and spoke with vivid language of events that would indicate his return.

- Unusual signs in the sky and on earth will indicate Jesus' imminent return. Jesus did not give specific information for this as he had given for the destruction of Jerusalem, but he left no question that the upheaval will cause great consternation among people.

- Incredible distress will come on earth. Students of Bible prophecy call this the **Tribulation** (see GWDN, page 319; GWRV, page 101).

- Jesus will come in a cloud of glory.

Tribulation: seven years of God's judgment at history's end

Believers should welcome these signs because they announce Jesus' return and the final unfolding of believers' everlasting life with God.

R. Kent Hughes: The end will feature unnatural disasters. Cosmic portents—quakes in the heavens, terrestrial catastrophes, tidal disturbances, chaos—all these are part of his final appearing. This is apocalyptic language for violent change in the natural order and in human life. The result will be widespread despair and apprehension.[7]

> **Luke 21:29–33** He told them this parable: "Look at the fig tree and all the trees. When they sprout leaves, you can see for yourselves and know that summer is near. Even so, when you see these things happening, you know that the kingdom of God is near. I tell you the truth, this generation will certainly not pass away until all these things have happened. Heaven and earth will pass away, but my words will never pass away."

Be Assured

Jesus pointed to a fig tree, reminding his disciples that they could observe signs of new life in spring and know that summer was coming. The fig tree was important to the people, both for its fruit and the shade it provided, so it is understandable that people would watch for first signs of new growth. Similarly, people should be alert to signs of Jesus' kingdom.

When Jesus said *"this generation will certainly not pass away,"* he may have meant a span of several lifetimes, not one thirty- or forty-year period. Jesus promised that the physical aspects of the universe would wear out and disappear, but his words would remain forever. In essence he said, "Be assured. Keep trusting in me."

> **Luke 21:34–36** "Be careful, or your hearts will be weighed down with dissipation, drunkenness and the anxieties of life, and that day will close on you unexpectedly like a trap. For it will come upon all those who live on the face of the whole earth. Be always on the watch, and pray that you may be able to escape all that is about to happen, and that you may be able to stand before the Son of Man."

Time Keeps Slipping Into The Future

Jesus gave a warning that applies to all. Do not be fooled into thinking that life on Planet Earth will go on forever. It won't! Be careful not to be so involved with everyday life that you are caught unprepared when the end comes and <u>Jesus returns</u>. We prepare for what Jesus predicted by being alert and prayerful.

☞ **GO TO:**

Titus 2:11–13; 1 John 3:2–3 (Jesus returns)

What Others are Saying:

Elisabeth Elliot: Prayer is a powerful weapon. It is an indispensable weapon. It takes practice to wield it. It takes courage and time and spiritual energy.[8]

John Piper: If we follow Jesus it will lead us into severe conflict with evil. It will mean war. Evil will surround us and attack us and threaten to destroy our faith. But God has given us a transmitter. If we go to sleep it will do us no good. But if we are alert, as Jesus says, and call for help in the conflict, the help will come and the Commander will not let his faithful soldiers be denied their crown of victory before the Son of man. Thus repeatedly we see the same truth: we cannot know what prayer is for until we know that life is war.[9]

> A generation or two ago some Christians used to keep a motto on their wall that read, "Perhaps today." It was a reminder that Jesus could return any day, perhaps even today! If we took that thought seriously, what changes would we make in our lives today?

Something to Ponder

Jesus' Do-Not-Do List

We can summarize Jesus' Olivet Discourse with an eight-point do-not-do list.

1. Do not be fooled by false announcements. (21:8)

2. Do not be alarmed by wars and natural disasters. (21:9–11)

3. Do not panic if you're given a hard time by authorities, friends, and family. Tell them about me and count on me to give you the words to say. (21:12–16)

4. Do not give up even when everyone is down on you. (21:17–19)

5. Do not hesitate to run from Jerusalem when it is under attack. (21:20–24)

6. Do not be alarmed when natural laws in the universe seem to go awry. These are signs that I am coming soon. (21:25–31)

LUKE 21: WHAT MATTERS MOST

277

7. Do not worry that my word will let you down. I guarantee it won't. (21:32–33)

8. Do not become preoccupied with this life. Be on alert and prayerful so you will stick by me. (21:34–36)

> **Luke 21:37–38** Each day Jesus was teaching at the temple, and each evening he went out to spend the night on the hill called the Mount of Olives, and all the people came early in the morning to hear him at the temple.

Last Opportunity

Only a little time was left for Jesus' teaching ministry. He wanted to spend as much time as possible with the people. Every day he went to the Temple where people gathered to hear him. Every night he camped out nearby on the **Mount of Olives** where, no doubt, he spent precious hours talking to his Father in prayer.

Mount of Olives: site of Gethsemane, Jesus' ascension, and predicted return

Study Questions

1. Why was the widow's offering so significant?
2. What three questions did Jesus answer in his Olivet Discourse?
3. What eight things does Jesus say we should avoid doing in light of his return? Which ones most apply to you?
4. How did Jesus spend his time in his last week?

CHAPTER WRAP-UP

- At the Temple Jesus pointed out a widow who gave two tiny coins, and he said that she had given far more than others though they had poured in many large coins. (Luke 21:1–4)

- When Jesus' disciples commented on the beauty of the Temple, Jesus astonished them by saying that it would be destroyed. (Luke 21:5–7)

- In a lengthy discourse, Jesus spoke of war and natural disasters. He also warned of coming persecution. (Luke 21:8–19)

- Jesus spoke particularly of the destruction of Jerusalem and counseled believers to flee the city when armies came near. He gave additional warnings and assured followers he would remain faithful. (Luke 21:20–36)

- Jesus spent his last days teaching people in the Temple. In the evenings he went to the Mount of Olives. (Luke 21:37–38)

Part Three

BETRAYAL, DEATH, AND RESURRECTION

REVEREND FUN

I'm sorry ma'am, the resurrection of Jesus was a miracle, not a service of this cemetery.

LUKE 22: THE LONGEST NIGHT

Let's Get Started

Events moved toward the climax in which Jesus gave his life. Jesus' enemies formed plans for a coup when Judas agreed to betray Jesus in his nightly hangout. Jesus' last night as a "free man" was a long one that brought no relief when dawn came.

As we read Luke's account of Jesus' horrendous suffering, we recognize that Jesus was not a helpless victim. He knew what lay ahead for him, and he chose to give his life—for us.

JUDAS MAKES A DEAL

> **Luke 22:1–6** Now the Feast of Unleavened Bread, called the Passover, was approaching, and the chief priests and the teachers of the law were looking for some way to get rid of Jesus, for they were afraid of the people. Then Satan entered Judas, called Iscariot, one of the Twelve. And Judas went to the chief priests and the officers of the temple guard and discussed with them how he might betray Jesus. They were delighted and agreed to give him money. He consented, and watched for an opportunity to hand Jesus over to them when no crowd was present.

Pawn Puts King In Check

Many rival groups joined forces to nab Jesus. Prior to this point in the Gospel accounts, the Pharisees were the ones who sought ways to get rid of Jesus. In the verses above Luke says the *"chief priests and the teachers of the law"* were now hot on Jesus' trail. They had the legal and political connections needed to build a case against Jesus.

Enter Satan and his new buddy Judas. Judas, one of the Twelve, took the initiative to seek out the religious leaders and arranged to betray Jesus into their hands. He knew Jesus' habits and the places he hung out when no crowds were nearby to protest the arrest. Bible experts disagree about whether Judas was possessed by Satan or just influenced by him. In either case, Judas volunteered to be the satanic pawn to place the King in check.

The religious leaders licked their evil chops in anticipation and dished out the money.

MORE INFORMATION—Luke states simply that Judas took action to betray Jesus after Satan entered him. Matthew 26:14–15 and John 12:4–6 fill out the picture with valuable insights into Judas's character and motivation.

- Judas suffered from disillusionment. Some suggest he had joined Jesus' band, thinking that he could rise to a place of prominence in a political kingdom, which he hoped Jesus would institute. He disagreed with the way Jesus ran things. This group was going nowhere fast.

- Judas was dominated by love of money. As treasurer of the Twelve, he had been dipping into their limited funds. When he approached the religious leaders, proposing to hand Jesus over to them, he took thirty silver coins, the price of a slave.

KEY POINT

Satan, Judas (an "insider"), and religious leaders joined forces against Jesus.

☞ **GO TO:**

Exodus 21:32 (price of a slave)

What Others are Saying:

Warren W. Wiersbe: When Judas understood that Jesus would not establish the kingdom but rather would surrender to the authorities, he turned against him in bitter retaliation.[1]

George R. Bliss: That Satan entered into Judas, means that the devil, to accomplish his malignant purposes against our Lord, took advantage of the wickedness of Judas, to direct him as a serviceable tool.[2]

JESUS PREPARES HIS PALS

> **Luke 22:7–13** Then came the day of Unleavened Bread on which the Passover lamb had to be sacrificed. Jesus sent Peter and John, saying, "Go and make preparations for us to eat the Passover."
>
> "Where do you want us to prepare for it?" they asked.
>
> He replied, "As you enter the city, a man carrying a jar of water will meet you. Follow him to the house that he enters, and say to the owner of the house, 'The Teacher asks: Where is the guest room, where I may eat the Passover with my disciples?' He will show you a large upper room, all furnished. Make preparations there."
>
> They left and found things just as Jesus had told them. So they prepared the Passover.

Prearranged Private Meal

Aware that Judas had made plans to betray him to his enemies, Jesus made plans to partake of the Passover meal with his pals in private. He sent only Peter and John to a prearranged, secret location where they could prepare the meal.

The clue they would have to the location of this meal was meeting a man who would be carrying a jar of water. They were to follow him to his house. This man would stand out in the crowded

Male Water Carrier

A woman carried water in a large clay jug on her head. A man carried water in a goatskin bottle on his back as shown here.

streets, because in Bible times, women carried pitchers of water while men carried water in larger, heavier water skins (see illustration, page 283).

Luke refers to the Feast of Unleavened Bread as being called the Passover. According to God's instructions for celebrations, the Passover was to be observed on a specific day in the first month of the Hebrew religious calendar followed by a week of observing the separate Feast of Unleavened Bread (Deuteronomy 16:1–8; 2 Chronicles 30:1, 21). Luke was confused. Fact or fiction? Fiction! Josephus, the Jewish historian of early New Testament times, indicates that by Jesus' day the Jews had combined the two occasions into one longer celebration.

> **Luke 22:14–18** When the hour came, Jesus and his apostles reclined at the table. And he said to them, "I have eagerly desired to eat this Passover with you before I suffer. For I tell you, I will not eat it again until it finds fulfillment in the kingdom of God."
>
> After taking the cup, he gave thanks and said, "Take this and divide it among you. For I tell you I will not drink again of the fruit of the vine until the kingdom of God comes."

The Last Repast

Jesus had purposefully arranged to have the Passover meal in private with his disciples. He *eagerly desired* this because he had much to say to them and needed uninterrupted time to open his heart. (For a full account of Jesus' final teachings, see chapters 13–17 in GWJN.) He alerted them to the seriousness of the occasion by saying this was his last meal before his time of great suffering. Jesus also looked forward to the future when he would take his place beside God and would fellowship with all believers at the marriage supper of the Lamb (see GWRV, pages 282–284).

☞ **GO TO:**

Revelation 19:9 (marriage supper)

> **Luke 22:19–20** And he took bread, gave thanks and broke it, and gave it to them, saying, "This is my body given for you; do this in remembrance of me."
>
> In the same way, after the supper he took the cup, saying, "This cup is the new covenant in my blood, which is poured out for you."

The Lord's Supper

The <u>Passover</u> meal reminded the Jews of the Exodus when the Lord literally passed over the homes of the Israelites and spared the lives of their firstborn sons and not the lives of the Egyptians' sons. Now Jesus put a new perspective on elements of the meal he ate with his disciples. They were to eat this meal to remember him.

Jesus used bread and wine that was already on the table to institute a way of <u>remembering</u> him that is still used today. He broke the unleavened bread, shared it with his disciples, and asked them to think of his body, which would soon be broken for them. He took the wine and asked his followers to think of his blood, which would soon be poured out for their salvation.

Jesus introduced a way for his followers to remember him and his sacrifice for them. He pointed forward to his death. Early Christians followed his instructions, looking back with love and gratitude to his death (see GWLC2, pages 199–200; GWHN, pages 146–147).

Jesus' followers continue to remember him in what is called the Lord's Supper or Holy Communion today. Jesus asked his followers to remember him in this way until his <u>return</u>.

Lloyd John Ogilvie: And it is here, as we break this bread and drink of this cup that we tangibly experience the central truth of life—he was broken for us that our hearts might not be splintered by the fragmentation of a multiplicity of loyalties. As we become whole through his brokenness, everything in our life begins to revolve around the central loyalty to him and his kingdom. Worry is replaced by what the poet called "the deep mysterious joy of absolute subjection"—to him rather than to the things and persons of our lives.

And the cup of the new covenant—the very word indicates that there is now a new relationship. . . . When we drink of that cup, we know that we may go to him on the basis of his love and not on the basis of our adequacy.[3]

> **Luke 22:21–23** "But the hand of him who is going to betray me is with mine on the table. The Son of Man will go as it has been decreed, but woe to that man who betrays him." They began to question among themselves which of them it might be who would do this.

☞ **GO TO:**

Exodus 11:12–14 (Passover)

1 Corinthians 11:23–26 (remembering)

FAST FORWARD

What Others are Saying:

☞ **GO TO:**

1 Corinthians 11:26 (return)

KEY POINT

Remembering Jesus in the Lord's Supper reaffirms our relationship with him and with other believers.

Who's The Weakest Link?

Jesus broke into a moment of tender closeness with a stunning announcement. Within this group around the table, sharing Jesus' words about his death, was one who would be a traitor by betraying him. Jesus' use of the word "decreed" shows Luke's emphasis on divine orchestration of events. Jesus would not be a victim; he would be a victor.

Judas had concealed his evil intentions, covering his tracks so well that the disciples did not know that Jesus was speaking about him. Even though God was in charge of the events, Judas was still responsible for his actions. Jesus said, "Woe to him!" It was an expression of grief, like saying, "Uh oh! Bad things are gonna happen to him."

> **Luke 22:24–27** Also a dispute arose among them as to which of them was considered to be greatest. Jesus said to them, "The kings of the Gentiles lord it over them; and those who exercise authority over them call themselves Benefactors. But you are not to be like that. Instead, the greatest among you should be like the youngest, and the one who rules like the one who serves. For who is greater, the one who is at the table or the one who serves? Is it not the one who is at the table? But I am among you as one who serves."

Servant Leaders

Instead of assuring Jesus of their loyalty and their deep caring for the suffering that lay ahead for him, the disciples began to argue. Being top rung on Jesus' roster should have been the last thing on their minds, but they couldn't resist the impulse to be competitive and self-seeking. Perhaps they still thought Jesus was about to set up a kingdom on earth. Their argument broke the unity that Jesus spoke of only minutes before when he instituted the Lord's Supper.

Jesus had made the effort to arrange this private meal so that there could be an intimate sharing of hearts. But now the interruption came from within. How disappointed Jesus must have been! Jesus patiently dealt with their argument by pointing out that humble service is the badge of leadership. He had already modeled this by <u>washing</u> their feet, a task of a lowly servant.

☞ **GO TO:**

John 13:1–17 (washing)

Self-interest and competitive scrambling for recognition and promotion lie under the surface at all times unless we consciously give Jesus first place in our lives. It's a decision we must make daily.

Something to Ponder

W. Glyn Evans: The true servant surrenders pride. Jesus described himself as "one who serves," then illustrated what he meant by washing his disciples' feet. He did not allow his equality with the Father to prevent him from doing a servant's task.[4]

What Others are Saying:

Jesus said that worldly leaders like to exercise power over people while at the same time boasting that they are caring for the interests of the common man. In contrast, godly leaders are to <u>truly serve</u>. Their actions prove the purity of their motives.

Today we see political leaders who claim to keep the needs of the poor highest on their agendas. But for true service to the homeless and the victims of abuse and tragedy, look to the men and women who give of themselves without ever asking for titles, huge salaries and benefit packages, or even recognition. In God's sight faithful service in a humble place is the mark of true greatness.

FAST FORWARD

☞ **GO TO:**

1 Peter 5:3 (truly serve)

> **Luke 22:28–30** "You are those who have stood by me in my trials. And I confer on you a kingdom, just as my Father conferred one on me, so that you may eat and drink at my table in my kingdom and sit on thrones, judging the twelve tribes of Israel."

Forward Thinking

With unfailing understanding of their human frailties, Jesus pointed to the future. His disciples had forgotten that God was preparing a kingdom for them. In his kingdom they would have positions of authority. The verb "<u>judging</u>" is used here in the sense of "ruling," the way "judge" is used to mean "ruler" in the Book of Judges.

☞ **GO TO:**

Judges 2:16–18 (judging)

Jesus made a promise or a covenant with his followers. They would share a glorious future with him. There was no need to scramble for prestige and honor. There would be plenty of that for every faithful follower. But first, they must join him in humiliation and suffering (see GWRM, pages 119–120).

Luke 22:31–34 "Simon, Simon, Satan has asked to sift **you** as wheat. But I have prayed for **you**, Simon, that your faith may not fail. And when you have turned back, strengthen your brothers."

But he replied, "Lord, I am ready to go with you to prison and to death."

Jesus answered, "I tell you, Peter, before the rooster crows today, you will deny three times that you know me."

Overconfident Simon Says

Satan had it in for all the disciples. He was convinced they were wimps. "They will fold under pressure," he told God. "Let me test them and you'll see."

So Jesus warned Peter that he was about to be taken to the mat by Satan. This warning must have stunned the group as well as Peter, for he was their spokesman, one of the most loyal and enthusiastic of Jesus' disciples. Characteristically, he would have been the loudest in the argument they had just had. "I am the greatest!" he would have asserted.

Now Jesus was saying that he would surely fail, apart from his prayers for Peter. But when he repented, he would become an encouragement to the others.

Overconfident, Peter cried, "I'll go to the death for you, Lord!"

"Uh oh, no, you won't," Jesus said. Then he prophesied Peter's denial.

Satan has no rights. He <u>must ask</u> God for permission to bring trials into the lives of Christians. God wields supreme control over our circumstances, our testings, and the unseen world of spirit beings.

Remember This . . .

☞ **GO TO:**

Job 1:6–12 (must ask)

Luke 22:35–38 Then Jesus asked them, "When I sent you without purse, bag or sandals, did you lack anything?"

"Nothing," they answered.

He said to them, "But now if you have a purse, take it, and also a bag; and if you don't have a sword, sell your cloak and buy one. It is written: 'And he was numbered with the transgressors'; and I tell you that this must be fulfilled in me. Yes, what is written about me is reaching its fulfillment."

The disciples said, "See, Lord, here are two swords."

"That is enough," he replied.

Allies In Arms

Previously, when Jesus sent his disciples out to preach, he told them to carry <u>no provisions</u>. Now, things had changed. Jesus would be arrested and executed as a <u>transgressor</u>. His followers would be suspect. He advised them to be prepared, even to the point of carrying swords.

The disciples failed to understand the implications of what he was saying, and Bible scholars have also debated the point. Was Jesus saying Christians should take up arms? That seems unlikely, especially after the way Jesus responded to one disciple's literal interpretation of the words and his <u>sword swipe</u> in the garden of Gethsemane.

Was Jesus reversing his earlier teaching when he sent out the disciples as missionaries in Luke 9:1–3 and 10:1–4? This seems unlikely as well, although Jesus is making a contrast. Before the disciples had it easy; this time things would be tough. They would face difficulties, hardships, and they would have to do without certain things. They would even face death.

R. Kent Hughes: The Last Supper closed as a vast disappointment to Jesus. The Messiah had come so eagerly to the Upper Room and had taken the Passover bread and cup and instituted the Last Supper—only to see the evening disintegrate. Judas left to betray him, the disciples fell to infighting, Jesus prophesied failure for Peter and the rest, and his final words were misunderstood due to the disciples' abysmal spiritual dullness. In dismay, Jesus despaired.[5]

GARDEN PRAYERS

> **Luke 22:39–44** Jesus went out as usual to the Mount of Olives, and his disciples followed him. On reaching the place, he said to them, "Pray that you will not fall into temptation." He withdrew about a stone's throw beyond them, knelt down and prayed, "Father, if you are willing, take this cup from me; yet not my will, but yours be done." An angel from heaven appeared to him and strengthened him. And being in anguish, he prayed more earnestly, and his sweat was like drops of blood falling to the ground.

☞ **GO TO:**

Luke 9:3; 10:4
(no provisions)

Isaiah 53:12
(transgressor)

Matthew 26:51–52
(sword swipe)

What Others are Saying:

Agony In The Garden

Jesus left the upper room and led his disciples to the Mount of Olives where they had been spending the last several nights.

When Jesus entered the garden, he left his disciples, asking them to pray that they would withstand temptation. He then went to pray alone. The normal posture for prayer in that day was to stand and look toward heaven. Jesus' anguish was horrendous as he thought about what lay ahead. He knew he faced <u>death</u> as he would bear the sins of the world, actually <u>becoming sin</u> for us, and he faced his Father's <u>wrath</u> for that sin. This wrath, which was punishment for the sins he was bearing, meant that his Father would turn away from him, a separation that was far worse than physical death. He asked if it were possible to be spared this terrible pain, but affirmed that he wanted to do only his Father's will.

An angel came to him and strengthened him. Still he prayed even more earnestly so that *"his sweat was like drops of blood."*

☞ **GO TO:**

Romans 3:23 (death)

2 Corinthians 5:21 (becoming sin)

1 John 2:2 (wrath)

What Others are Saying:

Max Lucado: Never has he [Jesus] felt so alone. What must be done, only he can do. An angel can't do it. No angel has the power to break open hell's gates. A man can't do it. No man has the purity to destroy sin's claim. No force on earth can face the force of evil and win—except God.[6]

PHYSICIAN'S PERSPECTIVE—Dr. Luke is the only Gospel writer to include the description of Jesus' physical appearance as he prayed. As a physician he would be particularly sensitive to visible clues of internal distress.

What Others are Saying:

Warren W. Wiersbe: [Luke's] use of the word *like* may suggest that the sweat merely fell to the ground like clots of blood. But there is a rare physical phenomenon known as *hematidrosis*, in which, under great emotional stress, the tiny blood vessels rupture in the sweat glands and produce a mixture of blood and sweat.[7]

> **Luke 22:45–46** When he rose from prayer and went back to the disciples, he found them asleep, exhausted from sorrow. "Why are you sleeping?" he asked them. "Get up and pray so that you will not fall into temptation."

Not Standing By Their Man

In spite of Jesus' warning about what was ahead, in spite of his agony in prayer, the disciples did not stand by him. They fell asleep. Luke says they were depressed. Their self-centeredness added to Jesus' hardships. Jesus woke them up, urging them to pray that they would not yield to <u>temptation</u>. He knew what lay ahead for them.

☞ **GO TO:**

1 Corinthians 10:13 (temptation)

 MORE INFORMATION—Matthew 26:36–46 and Mark 14:32–42 give more details to Jesus' experience in the garden. All the disciples, except Judas who had already left the group, went to the garden with Jesus. He asked Peter, James, and John to go aside with him as he prayed to his Father. He confided to them, *"My soul is overwhelmed with sorrow to the point of death."* He asked them to stay by him as he prayed. However, they fell asleep. He prayed three times, and three times he found them asleep.

ARRESTING JESUS

> **Luke 22:47–51** While he was still speaking a crowd came up, and the man who was called Judas, one of the Twelve, was leading them. He approached Jesus to kiss him, but Jesus asked him, "Judas, are you betraying the Son of Man with a kiss?"
>
> When Jesus' followers saw what was going to happen, they said, "Lord, should we strike with our swords?" And one of them struck the servant of the high priest, cutting off his right ear.
>
> But Jesus answered, "No more of this!" And he touched the man's ear and healed him.

Kiss And Tell

Even as Jesus was speaking with his disciples, this Judas guy—that's how Luke describes him in Greek—appeared in the garden. He was accompanied by an armed crowd sent by the religious leaders. Judas had arranged to identify Jesus by a secret signal—a kiss! He could have used any other means of identifying Jesus, but he chose to use a sign of caring and love as a signal of betrayal. It was a horrible mockery.

☞ **GO TO:**

John 18:10 (Peter)

As the crowd grabbed Jesus and arrested him, <u>Peter</u>, true to his impulsive nature, whipped out his sword and cut off the ear of Malchus, a servant of the high priest. Peter wasn't aiming for the guy's ear! Malchus ducked to save his neck! Jesus immediately healed the man and put a stop to further violence.

> **Luke 22:52–53** Then Jesus said to the chief priests, the officers of the temple guard, and the elders, who had come for him, "Am I leading a rebellion, that you have come with swords and clubs? Every day I was with you in the temple courts, and you did not lay a hand on me. But this is your hour—when darkness reigns."

An Illegal Warrant

Jesus did not resist the arrest, but he did confront the religious leaders who arrived in the garden. Why had they come with an armed crowd to arrest him as if he were a rebel? Why had they not simply taken him when he was in the temple courts? Clearly, they were doing something illegal. They were cowards who used the darkness of night to conceal their dastardly deed. But he submitted to them because of God's plan for saving sinners.

PETER DENIES JESUS

> **Luke 22:54–60** Then seizing him, they led him away and took him into the house of the high priest. Peter followed at a distance. But when they had kindled a fire in the middle of the courtyard and had sat down together, Peter sat down with them. A servant girl saw him seated there in the firelight. She looked closely at him and said, "This man was with him."
>
> But he denied it. "Woman, I don't know him," he said.
>
> A little later someone else saw him and said, "You also are one of them."
>
> "Man, I am not!" Peter replied.
>
> About an hour later another asserted, "Certainly this fellow was with him, for he is a Galilean."
>
> Peter replied, "Man, I don't know what you're talking about!" Just as he was speaking, the rooster crowed.

Fingered In The Lineup

Peter and <u>another disciple</u> followed Jesus as he was led out of the garden and into the house of Annas, the power monger behind the official high priest, Caiaphas. The other disciples fled from the scene with heart-stopping fear. Peter deserves credit for at least tagging along. But he too was scared. As he sat in the courtyard, warming himself at a fire, he was identified three times as one of Jesus' followers. Three times he vigorously denied Jesus. Then a rooster crowed.

☞ **GO TO:**

John 18:15
(another disciple)

Michael Card: Immediately after being arrested Jesus was bound and taken to the <u>home</u> of Annas, who was in all likelihood the key conspirator behind the plot to have Jesus killed. The marketplace in the temple, which Jesus had twice destroyed, was called the Bazaar of Annas. It belonged to him. Caiaphas had married Annas's daughter. Annas had been high priest some fifteen years earlier but had been removed from office by the Romans. Jesus was held here while the members of the Sanhedrin, the Jewish ruling council, could be called together.[8]

What Others are Saying:

☞ **GO TO:**

John 18:12–23 (home)

> **Luke 22:61–62** The Lord turned and looked straight at Peter. Then Peter remembered the word the Lord had spoken to him: "Before the rooster crows today, you will disown me three times." And he went outside and wept bitterly.

The Eyes Have It

Meanwhile Jesus was probably being moved across the courtyard between the homes of Annas and Caiaphas. Just as the rooster crowed, Jesus' eyes met Peter's. Jesus looked at him with love and concern, not disgust or anger. Suddenly Peter knew that Jesus knew of his denials, and he remembered what Jesus had told him. Jesus said he would disown him three times. Regret flooded Peter's heart. He stumbled outside and bawled like a baby.

Max Lucado: [Peter] considered himself the MVA (most valuable apostle). Wasn't he one of the early draft picks? Wasn't he one of the chosen three? Didn't he confess Christ while the others were silent? Peter never thought he needed help until he lifted his eyes from the fire and saw the eyes of Jesus.[9]

What Others are Saying:

Remember This . . .

☞ **GO TO:**

Romans 8:34–35;
   Hebrews 7:25
   (praying)

Peter failed. He failed to tell the truth. He failed to keep his promise. He failed in his loyalty to Jesus. Yet he was not destroyed. Jesus had prayed for him. Even as he wept bitterly, Jesus had not rejected him.

Jesus' prayer for Peter was not a one-time act of mercy. Today Jesus is in the presence of his Father <u>praying</u> for you and me.

TAKING A BEATING

> **Luke 22:63–65** The men who were guarding Jesus began mocking and beating him. They blindfolded him and demanded, "Prophesy! Who hit you?" And they said many other insulting things to him.

Humiliation And Insults

Guards let loose on Jesus. They made sport of him and beat him. So he was a prophet? Prove it! They blindfolded him and demanded that he identify the person who hit him. Then they heaped even more insults on him.

If he had chosen to, Jesus could have played their game. He could have escaped from their beatings. He could have called ten thousand angels to destroy these measly soldiers.

MOCK JEWISH TRIAL

> **Luke 22:66–71** At daybreak the council of the elders of the people, both the chief priests and teachers of the law, met together, and Jesus was led before them. "If you are the Christ," they said, "tell us."
>
> Jesus answered, "If I tell you, you will not believe me, and if I asked you, you would not answer. But from now on, the Son of Man will be seated at the right hand of the mighty God."
>
> They all asked, "Are you then the Son of God?"
>
> He replied, "You are right in saying I am."
>
> Then they said, "Why do we need any more testimony? We have heard it from his own lips."

Trial Before The Sanhedrin

Throughout the night the religious leaders held meetings and discussions, trying to figure out how to formally charge Jesus. It wasn't legal for them to hold a trial at night. It wasn't even legal for them to give a verdict at night on the day of a trial. But why let a little thing like the law stop them? They were in a hurry.

As dawn broke over the city of Jerusalem, Jesus was taken before the **Sanhedrin**. Caiaphas led the "legal" proceeding. The group held no presumed-innocent-until-proven-guilty opinion; they had their minds made up. All they had to do was find Jesus guilty of some offense that would allow them to turn him over to the Romans to be put to death. The top issue on their list was Jesus' identity. Was he the Messiah? If they could get him to admit this, they could accuse him of making a false claim and being guilty of **blasphemy**. According to Jewish law, the penalty for blasphemy was death.

When they asked if he was the Messiah, he replied that they would not believe his answer. Then he went on to say that he would soon be seated at the right hand of the mighty God.

"Are you the Son of God?" they asked in unison.

Jesus replied that they were correct in saying so.

"Enough!" They had all the testimony they needed. Now they could turn him over to the Romans.

Sanhedrin: Jews' highest ruling council

blasphemy: treating God with contempt by reducing him to mere human level

☞ **GO TO:**

Leviticus 24:10–16 (penalty)

Study Questions

1. Why were the religious leaders so pleased when Judas offered to betray Jesus?
2. Why was it important for Jesus to have an uninterrupted Passover meal with his disciples?
3. What is the significance of the Lord's Supper?
4. What disturbing things did Jesus say at the Passover meal?
5. What did Jesus talk about with his Father in Gethsemane?
6. Describe Jesus' arrest, identifying the emotions of the key people involved.
7. What happened after Peter denied Jesus and the rooster crowed?
8. Where was Jesus taken through the night and how was he falsely accused and mistreated?

- Judas made a deal with the religious leaders to betray Jesus into their hands. (Luke 22:1–6)

- Jesus celebrated the Passover meal with his disciples, at which time he talked about the future and instituted the Lord's Supper. (Luke 22:7–20)

- Jesus reminded the disciples that greatness is revealed by humble service and prophesied Peter's denial. (Luke 22:21–38)

- Jesus prayed in Gethsemane, seeking strength for the suffering that lay ahead. His disciples slept. (Luke 22:39–46)

- Judas led an armed crowd into the garden and betrayed Jesus with a kiss. Jesus was arrested and led away for trial. (Luke 22:47–53)

- When Peter was questioned, he denied Jesus three times. (Luke 22:54–62)

- Jesus was mocked, beaten, and insulted. At daybreak he was led away to be questioned by the Sanhedrin. (Luke 22:63–71)

LUKE 23: A DARK DAY IN HISTORY

CHAPTER HIGHLIGHTS

- Mock Roman Trial
- The King Is Crucified
- Jesus Dies on the Cross
- The King Is Buried

Let's Get Started

We enter a darkened room. As we gradually become adjusted to the dim lighting, we discern some objects between the shadows. Suddenly someone opens the curtains and we are immediately horrified at the disgusting untidiness and dirt surrounding us. As we move to make a hasty exit, we begin to note some items of beauty and incredible wealth almost covered by the filth. We stop and ponder the scene.

This is the view that Luke gives us now. We have seen religious and political leaders throughout this Gospel. Now Luke pulls back the curtain and shows us what was lurking behind their shadows. He reveals the most horrendous view of men's hatred and cruelty. We can hardly bear to think of the pain Jesus endured. Yet, as we shrink from observing it, we begin to discern something more in Luke's account, something strikingly in contrast to the evil of men. We see the love of Jesus in giving his life, and we see the love of his Father in sending his Son to give his life—all for us.

 MORE INFORMATION—Jesus endured both religious and civil trials. Although all four Gospels contain accounts of the trials, it is difficult to piece together an exact order. Each writer focuses on different things. Matthew highlights human weakness. Mark tells about the key events. Luke emphasizes Jesus' suffering. John details Jesus' trials. Shown below are the most complete accounts.[1]

Religious Trials

Civil Trials

MOCK ROMAN TRIAL

Luke 23:1–7 Then the whole assembly rose and led him off to Pilate. And they began to accuse him, saying, "We have found this man subverting our nation. He opposes payment of taxes to Caesar and claims to be Christ, a king."

So Pilate asked Jesus, "Are you the king of the Jews?"

"Yes, it is as you say," Jesus replied.

Then Pilate announced to the chief priests and the crowd, "I find no basis for a charge against this man."

But they insisted, "He stirs up the people all over Judea by his teaching. He started in Galilee and has come all the way here."

On hearing this, Pilate asked if the man was a Galilean. When he learned that Jesus was under Herod's jurisdiction, he sent him to Herod, who was also in Jerusalem at that time.

Trumpeting Trumped Up Charges

After a night spent dishing out interrogation, humiliation, and physical abuse, the Sanhedrin was ready to have Jesus put to death. At that time, though, Jews were not allowed to impose a death penalty. Once they had given a guilty verdict, they were required to hand the offender over to Roman authorities.

When morning came, the whole angry pack of leaders marched their prisoner to Pontius Pilate, governor of Judea. They came up with crimes, completely false accusations, which they felt would merit severe punishment from the Romans. They accused Jesus of perverting the nation, opposing paying taxes to Caesar, and claiming to be a rival king—meaning that he was a political threat to Pilate and Roman rule. None of these charges had been brought against Jesus at his trial before the Sanhedrin.

While the religious leaders wanted Pilate to view Jesus as an insurrectionist, Pilate found Jesus innocent. The Jewish leaders protested, claiming that Jesus had stirred up the people from Galilee to Jerusalem.

Pilate was no dummy. He could sense the hatred of the group toward Jesus, and he jumped at the chance to ship this hot potato off to another official. Galilee was in Herod's jurisdiction. Pilate was off the hook—or so he thought.

MORE INFORMATION—All four Gospel writers include accounts of the events in this chapter. John 18:28–38 gives more details of Jesus' trial before Pilate. The religious leaders would not go inside Pilate's palace because they wanted to avoid ceremonial uncleanness before eating the Passover that day. So Pilate came outside to talk with them.

Pilate questioned Jesus about the accusation that he was king of the Jews. He learned that Jesus' kingdom is not of this earth. Based on the fact that Jesus' kingship was in no way a threat to Rome, Pilate found no reason to charge Jesus with any crime.

> **Luke 23:8–10** When Herod saw Jesus, he was greatly pleased, because for a long time he had been wanting to see him. From what he had heard about him, he hoped to see him perform some miracle. He plied him with many questions, but Jesus gave him no answer. The chief priests and the teachers of the law were standing there, vehemently accusing him.

Delighted To Meet You

Sending Jesus to Herod may have been considered something of a compliment from Pilate. Pilate could have handled the case since the supposed offenses had happened in his jurisdiction, but he chose to hand the baton to his least favorite colleague.

Herod, who had imprisoned and killed John the Baptist, was delighted to have a crack at Jesus. He had heard much about the teacher and miracle worker and hoped now to see Jesus perform a miracle.

Any prisoner in his right mind would have milked this opportunity for all it was worth. He would have performed a few pyrotechnics on the palace plants to please Herod, with the hope of being released. Not Jesus! Jesus refused to answer Herod's many questions and he pulled no miracles out of his sleeves. Jesus had never failed to answer sincere seekers, but Herod sought only sensationalism. Although the chief priests stood close by and agitated Jesus, he remained silent.

> **Luke 23:11–12** Then Herod and his soldiers ridiculed and mocked him. Dressing him in an elegant robe, they sent him back to Pilate. That day Herod and Pilate became friends—before this they had been enemies.

Here He Is! Mr. King!

Finally, Herod got bored. He did not take the charges against Jesus seriously. "What a jerk this guy is! Some king!" With no corner video stores, Jerusalem entertainment was often sparse, and Herod appreciated the chance for a diversion. He told the guards, "Have some fun and ship him back!" Returning the accused could have been viewed as returning Pilate's compliment. So, the former rivals became friends.

Robert L. Thomas: Because much of Jesus' public ministry had been in Galilee, Pilate thought he had found a way to avoid condemning an innocent person, but Herod did not pronounce Jesus guilty or innocent. Luke had contacts within Herod's household that enabled him to describe a phase of the trial not found in the other gospels, just as John had access to information about what happened at Annas' house.[2]

> **Luke 23:13–16** Pilate called together the chief priests, the rulers and the people, and said to them, "You brought me this man as one who was inciting the people to rebellion. I have examined him in your presence and have found no basis for your charges against him. Neither has Herod, for he sent him back to us; as you can see, he has done nothing to deserve death. Therefore, I will punish him and then release him."

Beat-And-Release Offer

Now Pilate was in a tough spot. He tried to reason with Jesus' accusers. Since neither he nor Herod had found anything in Jesus that deserved death, he offered to beat him (to appease his accusers) and then release him.

> **Luke 23:18–25** With one voice they cried out, "Away with this man! Release Barabbas to us!" (Barabbas had been thrown into prison for an insurrection in the city, and for murder.)
>
> Wanting to release Jesus, Pilate appealed to them again. But they kept shouting, "Crucify him! Crucify him!"
>
> For the third time he spoke to them: "Why? What crime has this man committed? I have found in him no grounds for the death penalty. Therefore I will have him punished and then release him."
>
> But with loud shouts they insistently demanded that he be crucified, and their shouts prevailed. So Pilate decided to grant their demand. He released the man who had been thrown into prison for insurrection and murder, the one they asked for, and surrendered Jesus to their will.

Don't Confuse Us With The Facts!

Pilate's suggestion met with fury. The religious leaders demanded that Pilate release Barabbas, an **insurrectionist** and murderer who was currently in prison. They insisted that Jesus be crucified.

Three times Pilate attempted to have Jesus released and each time the leaders insisted that Jesus be punished with death. The crowd got louder and louder. They didn't want to listen to the facts. Pilate feared a riot. Finally, he gave in. He released Barabbas and turned Jesus over to be put to death.

insurrectionist: person who revolts against government

 MORE INFORMATION—Matthew is the only Gospel writer who tells us what happened to Judas (Matthew 27:3–10). When he saw that Jesus was condemned to die, Judas was overcome with horror and remorse. He met with the chief priests and elders, confessing that he had sinned in betraying Jesus, who was completely innocent. Finding the religious leaders indifferent, Judas threw the thirty silver coins down and went out to hang himself.

Peter Marshall: The little man did not stop running until he was outside the city gates. A picture kept flashing before his eye— he brushed his hands before his eyes but it would not leave. It was Jesus' face at that moment when he, Judas, had kissed his cheek.

"Friend," he had said gently, "wherefore art thou come? Why have you done this?"

"Friend," that was what he had said. "Friend"—why have you done this?

It broke Judas' heart . . .

His plan had failed.

Everything was smashed . . . his dreams . . . his hopes . . . his life—everything.

There was nothing left —now.

Only one way out . . .[3]

MORE INFORMATION—Even though Pilate knew Jesus was innocent and did not deserve punishment of any kind, he allowed Jesus to be flogged and cruelly ridiculed. (See John 18:39–19:16.) He presented Jesus to the religious leaders as a king—wearing a crown of thorns and covered in a purple robe.

KEY POINT

Pilate had a high title but a low character.

Finally, when Pilate declared that he could find no basis for a charge against Jesus, the religious leaders declared that he must die because he claimed to be the Son of God.

Though this struck fear in Pilate, he still handed Jesus over to be crucified. As Jesus was led away to die he was charged with two "crimes": blasphemy (by the religious leaders) and claiming to be king and thus a rival of Caesar in Rome (by Pilate).

THE KING IS CRUCIFIED

> **Luke 23:26** As they led him away, they seized Simon from Cyrene, who was on his way in from the country, and put the cross on him and made him carry it behind Jesus.

A Forced Privilege

Prisoners who were being put to death by crucifixion were publicly humiliated by being required to carry the crossbar of their cross to the place of death. It was a heavy piece of wood. Jesus had endured a night of extreme emotional and physical torture, so it is not surprising that he did not have strength to carry the crossbar.

The Roman soldiers could pick any civilian to do any task. "Hey, you, there!" they said to Simon from **Cyrene**. "Carry this cross!" Simon was a traveler from Africa who had come to observe the Passover in Jerusalem.

Cyrene: modern Tripoli, North Africa

Simon could not have known the privilege the Roman soldiers had given him. For all time he is remembered as one who literally took up the cross and followed Jesus. Perhaps he was already a believer or perhaps after this encounter he became one, because Mark 15:21 mentions Simon's sons as though readers know them.

Something to Ponder

MORE INFORMATION

☞ **GO TO:**

Luke 14:27 (took up)

Crucifixion Events at Calvary[4]

Following is the order of events at Calvary from the combined accounts of the Gospel writers:

1. Jesus was offered drugged drink to lessen suffering (Matthew 27:34).
2. Jesus crucified (Matthew 27:35).
3. Jesus cries, *"Father forgive them"* (Luke 23:34).
4. Soldiers gamble for Jesus' clothing (Matthew 27:35).
5. Jesus mocked by observers (Matthew 27:39–44; Mark 15:29).
6. Jesus ridiculed by two thieves (Matthew 27:44).
7. One of the thieves believes (Luke 23:39–43).
8. Jesus promises, *"Today you will be with me in paradise"* (Luke 23:43).
9. Jesus speaks to Mary, *"Behold your son"* (John 19:26–27).
10. Darkness falls on the scene (Matthew 27:45; Mark 15:33; Luke 23:44).
11. Jesus cries, *"My God, my God"* (Matthew 27:46–47; Mark 15:34–36).
12. Jesus cries, *"I thirst"* (John 19:28).
13. Jesus cries, *"It is finished"* (John 19:30).
14. Jesus cries, *"Father into thy hands"* (Luke 23:46).
15. Jesus releases his spirit (Matthew 27:50; Mark 15:37).

> **Luke 23:27–31** A large number of people followed him, including women who mourned and wailed for him. Jesus turned and said to them, "Daughters of Jerusalem, do not weep for me; weep for yourselves and for your children. For the time will come when you will say, 'Blessed are the barren women, the wombs that never bore and the breasts that never nursed!' Then
> they will say to the mountains, "Fall on us!"
> and to the hills, "Cover us!"'
> For if men do these things when the tree is green, what will happen when it is dry?"

Don't Cry For Me, Jerusalem

Executions were public events, and the one this sad day probably drew an even larger number of spectators. The city was packed because of Passover, and Jesus had been a popular teacher. Reports of his miracles had circulated for three years. Pilate had feared a riot. What he got was a bunch of crying women. They mourned and wailed as if Jesus were already dead.

Characteristic of his selflessness, Jesus expressed his concern for them, not himself. "Don't worry about me, ladies," he said. "You're the ones who will have to deal with the consequences."

 PHYSICIAN'S PERSPECTIVE—Luke is the only Gospel writer to include the account of the women who followed Jesus weeping and wailing in their distress for him. These were kindhearted women from Jerusalem who, historians suggest, may have been professional mourners and were prepared to provide medications to ease the pain of the men being executed. Luke reports Jesus' counsel to them. Incredible suffering was ahead for them when God would fulfill prophecy by destroying Jerusalem in A.D. 70.

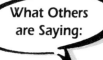

What Others
are Saying:

Robert C. Girard: He [Jesus] said, *"For if men do these things when the tree is green, what will happen when it is dry?"* (Luke 23:31).

This was a Jewish proverb meaning "If today God pours his wrath on his Son—an innocent 'green tree'—what will conditions be when he pours his wrath on the world that spurned his love and rejected his Son?"[5]

> **Luke 23:32–34** Two other men, both criminals, were also led out with him to be executed. When they came to the place called the **Skull**, there they crucified him, along with the criminals—one on his right, the other on his left. Jesus said, "Father, forgive them, for they do not know what they are doing." And they divided up his clothes by casting lots.

Skull: in Hebrew, Golgotha, *a hill with skull-like rock formations.*

Crime And Punishment

Crucifixion was an incredibly painful and humiliating form of execution (see GWLC2, pages 240–242). Two criminals were crucified with Jesus that day, one on either side of him. Unlike anyone who had ever been executed, Jesus prayed aloud, asking his Father to forgive his Roman executioners who had no idea of the enormity of the wrongs that were being done to the sinless Son of God that day. What love and grace!

Unaware of the significance of what was occurring, the soldiers followed their custom of dividing the clothes of the men being executed. Rather than cutting the one garment that remained, they gambled over it.

> **Luke 23:35–38** The people stood watching, and the rulers even sneered at him. They said, "He saved others; let him save himself if he is the Christ of God, the Chosen One."
>
> The soldiers also came up and mocked him. They offered him wine vinegar and said, "If you are the king of the Jews, save yourself."
>
> There was a written notice above him, which read: THIS IS THE KING OF THE JEWS.

Cruel Mockery

Onlookers began to mock Jesus. They reminded him that through his miracles he had helped others, now he could prove who he really was by saving himself from death.

Roman soldiers joined in the mockery. Even the notice that was nailed to the cross above his head was a mockery, for it identified Jesus, in Aramaic, Latin, and Greek, as king of the Jews.

> **Luke 23:39–43** One of the criminals who hung there hurled insults at him: "Aren't you the Christ? Save yourself and us!"
>
> But the other criminal rebuked him. "Don't you fear God," he said, "since you are under the same sentence? We are punished justly, for we are getting what our deeds deserve. But his man has done nothing wrong."
>
> Then he said, "Jesus, remember me when you come into your kingdom."
>
> Jesus answered him, "I tell you the truth, today you will be with me in paradise."

Cross Conversation

One of the criminals joined the mockery, gasping out insults at Jesus and challenging him to save the three of them—if he was the Christ.

The second criminal rebuked him, pointing out that both of them had done deeds deserving punishment, but Jesus had done nothing wrong. Then with amazing insight he asked Jesus to remember him when he established his kingdom. Jesus promised far more. He said on that very day he would be with Jesus in <u>paradise</u>.

☞ **GO TO:**

Revelation 2:7
(paradise)

JESUS DIES ON THE CROSS

> **Luke 23:44–45** It was now about the sixth hour, and darkness came over the whole land until the ninth hour, for the sun stopped shining. And the curtain of the temple was torn in two.

Unexplained Events

Unexpectedly at the sixth hour, noon, an eerie darkness came over the scene and remained for three hours. There is no record of an eclipse, but certainly the darkness was most unusual.

In Jerusalem the beautiful curtain that hung in the Temple was torn from top to bottom. The curtain separated the most holy place in the Temple, called the Holy of Holies, from the rest of the building (see illustration, page 61). No one could explain how or why this occurred. Only an act of God could take a heavy woven drape and rip it apart from top to bottom.

The curtain kept people from the holy place where God had promised to reside. Once a year the high priest was permitted to <u>enter</u> that Holy of Holies and offer blood for his sins and for the sins of his people. When that curtain was torn, it signified that Jesus' death provided the way that all people could actually enter God's presence.

Today we have the privilege of <u>direct contact</u> with God. Because Jesus has opened the way for us, we can come near to God, having our hearts cleansed by Jesus' sacrifice of his life for us.

> **Luke 23:46** Jesus called out with a loud voice, "Father, into your hands I commit my spirit." When he had said this, he breathed his last.

FAST FORWARD

☞ **GO TO:**

Hebrews 9:7 (enter)

Hebrews 10:19–22 (direct contact)

Volunteer Victory

Ordinarily, someone close to dying from crucifixion would not be able to speak anything more than a low groan. But Jesus spoke loudly, calling to his Father in prayer and committing his spirit into God's loving hands. His words mirror Psalm 31:5. Then he died, not in defeat as a victim, but in victory. He had accomplished what he had been <u>born to do</u>—and actually what he had planned to do from the <u>foundation</u> of the world! He voluntarily gave up his life.

☞ **GO TO:**

Mark 10:45 (born to do)

1 Peter 1:18–20 (foundation)

What Others are Saying:

Oswald Chambers: The only ground on which God can forgive sin and reinstate us in His favor is through the cross of Christ, and in no other way. Forgiveness, which is so easy for us to accept, cost the agony of Calvary.[6]

Larry Richards: At the cross an amazing transaction took place. Jesus took our sins on himself; his death took the penalty that our sins deserved. And, wonder of wonders, God then credited the righteousness of Jesus to us! With sin paid for, there was no longer a barrier between human beings and God. With Jesus' own righteousness credited to our account, we are welcome to enter God's presence.[7]

Our eyes brim as we read of Jesus' suffering—it was horrendous. We are aghast at the cruel and unjust way he was tried and killed. But never forget his words: *"I lay down my life— only to take it up again. No one takes it from me, but I lay it down of my own accord"* (John 10:17–18).

KEY POINT

If Jesus had not died, he could not be our living Savior today.

> **Luke 23:47–49** The centurion, seeing what had happened, praised God and said, "Surely this was a righteous man." When all the people who had gathered to witness this sight saw what took place, they beat their breasts and went away. But all those who knew him, including the women who had followed him from Galilee, stood at a distance, watching these things.

Awe-Filled Onlookers

A Roman centurion who had observed the whole execution was so filled with awe that he confessed audibly that without doubt Jesus was a righteous man. This caused him to praise God. Other onlookers were deeply impressed and left expressing their grief and consternation at what had happened.

 PHYSICIAN'S PERSPECTIVE—Luke makes special note of the role of women at the cross. He points out that those who knew and loved Jesus separated themselves from those who mocked him, and stood at a distance. In this group were women who had followed him from Galilee, including Mary, Jesus' mother, his mother's sister, the wife of Clopas, and Mary Magdalene.

THE KING IS BURIED

> **Luke 23:50–54** Now there was a man named Joseph, a member of the Council, a good and upright man, who had not consented to their decision and action. He came from the Judean town of Arimathea and was waiting for the kingdom of God. Going to Pilate, he asked for Jesus' body. Then he took it down, wrapped it in linen cloth and placed it in a tomb cut in the rock, one in which no one had yet been laid. It was **Preparation Day**, and the Sabbath was yet to begin.

Preparation Day: Friday

Borrowed Tomb For A King

Where were Jesus' disciples? We do not know. But one man, Joseph, approached Pilate and obtained permission to bury Jesus. Joseph was a wealthy member of the Sanhedrin, but Luke notes that Joseph had not voted to condemn Jesus. Perhaps Joseph's views were known and his fellow Sanhedrin members conveniently "forgot" to wake him up for the mock trial. Joseph took Jesus' body down from the cross, wrapped it in many yards of linen cloth, and placed it in a cave-like tomb, which was for a private family burial.

> **Luke 23:55–56** The women who had come with Jesus from Galilee followed Joseph and saw the tomb and how his body was laid in it. Then they went home and prepared spices and perfumes. But they rested on the Sabbath in obedience to the commandment.

Rushed Burial

The women who had stood at the scene of Jesus' crucifixion followed Joseph to the tomb where he laid Jesus' body to rest. There was no time to follow the proper burial customs, for it was time to observe the Sabbath laws of rest.

PHYSICIAN'S PERSPECTIVE—Again Dr. Luke highlights the role of women. When Joseph, a secret believer in Jesus, received permission to bury Jesus' body, Nicodemus, another secret believer, supplied myrrh and aloes to be bound in the lengths of linen wound around his body. This was not enough for the women. Their deep grief had to find some expression, so they planned to prepare more spices and perfumes to bring to the grave after the Sabbath.

Jesus had prepared his followers for his death, but he assured them that he would rise again. To avoid facing this as fact, Jesus' enemies have declared that Jesus did not really die on the cross. Jesus was merely unconscious. Fact or fiction? Fiction! Read on.

☞ **GO TO:**

John 19:39–40
(Nicodemus)

FACT OR *FICTION*

MORE INFORMATION—All four Gospel writers recorded details about Jesus' burial. They made it clear that Jesus had indeed died since the glorious truth of Jesus' resurrection required acceptance of his death. (See Matthew 27:57–61; Mark 15:42–47; and John 19:38–42.)

Something to Ponder

Why did Jesus die? He could have avoided it, but he did not. Why? *"God demonstrates his own love for us in this: While we were still sinners, Christ died for us"* (Romans 5:9). *"This is how God showed his love among us: He sent his one and only Son into the world that we might live through him. This is love: not that we loved God, but that he loved us and sent his Son as an atoning sacrifice for our sins"* (1 John 4:9–10).

Study Questions

1. Why did the religious leaders take Jesus to Pilate?
2. Why was Herod happy when Pilate sent Jesus to him?
3. Why did Pilate turn Jesus over for execution even though he was convinced that Jesus was innocent?
4. What crime was Jesus charged with by (a) the religious leaders, and (b) Pilate?
5. While groups of people watched the agonizing death process, what was happening unseen and spiritually as Jesus voluntarily gave his life on the cross? What does this mean to you?
6. What happened to Jesus' body after he died?

CHAPTER WRAP-UP

- The Jews took Jesus to Pilate for sentencing. They charged Jesus with undermining the nation, opposing payment of taxes to Rome, and claiming to be Christ, a king. (Luke 23:1–7)

- Pilate found Jesus innocent. Since Jesus was a Galilean, Pilate sent him to Herod, who ruled that province. When Jesus did not satisfy his curiosity, Herod sent him back to Pilate after allowing Jesus to be ridiculed and mocked. (Luke 23:8–12)

- Pilate gave in to the demands of the religious leaders and sentenced Jesus to death. (Luke 23:13–25)

- Jesus was crucified between two criminals. Groups of people gathered around the cross to watch the agonizing death process. (Luke 23:26–49)

- After Jesus died, Joseph, a secret follower of Jesus, went to Pilate and asked for Jesus' body. He laid it in his own tomb. (Luke 23:50–56)

LUKE 24: A BRIGHT DAY DAWNS

CHAPTER HIGHLIGHTS

- Rising Up from Being Down
- Three Is Not a Crowd
- Amazing Appearances
- Return to Sender

Let's Get Started

We look forward to a happy event with almost impatient expectancy, whether it's a graduation, a promotion, a wedding, or the birth of a longed-for child. The happiest event of all history was about to occur. It had been promised, even to the timing, but nobody really expected it to happen!

Jesus had told his disciples that he would die and that in three days he would <u>rise</u> from the dead. But after his death and burial, who stood outside the tomb in a countdown to be an eyewitness to his coming alive again? Nobody! All his followers were so confused and depressed, so crushed by grief, that they could not imagine how soon their mourning could be turned to joy.

Luke, in the closing chapter of his Gospel, gives a factual account of individuals who have firsthand experiences of meeting the risen Christ.

☞ **GO TO:**

Luke 18:31–34 (rise)

RISING UP FROM BEING DOWN

> **Luke 24:1–3** On the first day of the week, very early in the morning, the women took the spices they had prepared and went to the tomb. They found the stone rolled away from the tomb, but when they entered, they did not find the body of the Lord Jesus.

Devoted Fan Club

Observing the Sabbath law of rest must have been an ordeal for the women who were determined to express their love for Jesus by placing fragrant spices around his body. They couldn't wait for the Sabbath to be over. They may have rushed around Friday gathering ingredients or mixing potions. It was the least they could do! Finally, Sunday came. They got up while it was still dark. As dawn broke they were making their way to the tomb, worrying about how they would move the stone that covered the entrance to the tomb (see illustration below).

Imagine their amazement as they approached the tomb and found the stone rolled away. Imagine their shock and consternation at finding no body inside!

Soldiers who were guarding the tomb's sealed entrance reported that while they were sleeping, Jesus' disciples came and stole his body. The soldiers were telling the truth. Fact or fiction? Any soldier who fell asleep while on guard duty was <u>executed</u>. So why would these soldiers openly confess that they had fallen asleep? Further, if they were asleep, how could they report convincingly that they knew Jesus' disciples had broken the seal,

☞ GO TO:

Acts 12:19 (executed)

Tomb

Jesus' body was laid in a cave-like tomb such as this one. A large stone was rolled to cover the entrance.

rolled back the stone, and removed the body? If they knew this to be a fact, how could they explain that they did not do their duty in preventing the theft? The only reasonable answer is that the soldiers' report was pure fiction, a tale they were bribed to tell. (See Matthew 27:62–66; 28:11–15.)

MORE INFORMATION—Matthew 28:2–4 gives the true account of how the tomb was opened. The ground was shaken and an angel rolled back the heavy stone that covered the entrance so that Jesus' followers could see for themselves that Jesus body was not there. The guards who were charged with keeping the tomb sealed saw the angel and were terrified.

> **Luke 24:4–8** While they were wondering about this, suddenly two men in clothes that gleamed like lightning stood beside them. In their fright the women bowed down with their faces to the ground, but the men said to them, "Why do you look for the living among the dead? He is not here; he has risen! Remember how he told you, while he was still with you in Galilee: 'The Son of Man must be delivered into the hands of sinful men, be crucified and on the third day be raised again.'" Then they remembered his words.

Astonished By Two Angels

Suddenly two angels appeared, filling the astonished women with fear. The heavenly messengers reminded them of what Jesus had clearly told them. Their understanding had been clouded then, so that they had not really understood his <u>promise</u> that he would be raised from the dead on the third day.

☞ **GO TO:**

Matthew 16:21 (promise)

John 14:15–26 (Holy Spirit)

Something to Ponder

The angels made an excellent point. To understand what God is doing and to have our questions answered, we need to remember what Jesus has said. There may be much we do not understand in the Bible, but Jesus promised to send the <u>Holy Spirit</u> to teach us the truth and to clarify what Jesus has said. Understanding grows through careful study of the Bible and obedience to what is shown to us. (Check out GWMK for tips on studying God's Word.)

> **Luke 24:9–11** When they came back from the tomb, they told all these things to the Eleven and to all the others. It was Mary Magdalene, Joanna, Mary the mother of James, and the others with them who told this to the apostles. But they did not believe the women, because their words seemed to them like nonsense.

Serious Sorrow And Supposed Scuttlebutt

KEY POINT

Sorrow and doubt prevented the disciples from hearing the women's announcement.

The women hurried back to Jerusalem where the disciples and other followers of Jesus were grieving their loss. These women, who had been sharing their loss, were now bubbling with excitement as the good news tumbled out of their mouths. So full of sorrow were Jesus' disciples that they could not even take in the news. In fact, women's announcement seemed to them like hysterical nonsense.

What Others are Saying:

Darryl DelHousaye: The church of Jesus Christ, in honor of his rising from the dead on the first Easter, gathers every Sunday to celebrate the victory of her Lord over death, and the hope we therefore have. For He promises, "I am the <u>resurrection</u> and the life; he who believes in me shall live, even if he dies."[1]

☞ **GO TO:**

John 11:25–26
(resurrection)

> **Luke 24:12** Peter, however, got up and ran to the tomb. Bending over, he saw the strips of linen lying by themselves, and he went away, wondering to himself what had happened.

Peter's Checkup

KEY POINT

Peter ran to the empty tomb and went away wondering.

Peter heard the women—at least enough that he ran to the tomb to check out what they had reported. He looked in the opening and saw an amazing sight. There was no question where Jesus' body had been laid to rest. The strips of linen were there, the head covering was in its place, and the separate body covering was in its place. But the body was missing! He walked away scratching his head.

What Others are Saying:

William MacDonald: We are not told whether [the cloths] were unwound, or still in the shape of the body, but we are safe in presuming the latter. It appears that the Lord may have left the grave-clothes as if they had been a cocoon.[2]

THREE IS NOT A CROWD

> **Luke 24:13–18** Now that same day two of them were going to a village called Emmaus, about seven miles from Jerusalem. They were talking with each other about everything that had happened. As they talked and discussed these things with each other, Jesus himself came up and walked along with them; but they were kept from recognizing him. He asked them, "What are you discussing together as you walk along?"
>
> They stood still, their faces downcast. One of them, named Cleopas, asked him, "Are you only a visitor to Jerusalem and do not know the things that have happened there in these days?"

Rehashing The Happenings

The day of the resurrection two of Jesus' followers were walking from Jerusalem to Emmaus. As they went they rehearsed all that had happened while they were in Jerusalem. The painful sights and sounds were seared in their hearts. The events gripped them and their grief required an outlet.

Suddenly, they were joined by Jesus, who appeared to them as just another traveler. They were stunned when he asked them what they were talking about. How could he not have heard about the tragic events of the past few days?

Leon Morris: This charming story is one of the best loved of all the resurrection narratives. There is something very moving in one of the Lord's few appearances being given to these humble, quiet unknown disciples. The story, moreover, has something so vivid about it that some hold that it must have come from one of the participants, perhaps even that Luke himself was the unnamed disciple.[3]

What Others are Saying:

> **Luke 24:19–24** "What things?" he asked.
>
> "About Jesus of Nazareth," they replied. "He was a prophet, powerful in word and deed before God and all the people. The chief priests and our rulers handed him over to be sentenced to death, and they crucified him; but we had hoped that he was the one who was going

> to redeem Israel. And what is more, it is the third day since all this took place. In addition, some of our women amazed us. They went to the tomb early this morning but didn't find his body. They came and told us that they had seen a vision of angels, who said he was alive. Then some of our companions went to the tomb and found it just as the women had said, but him they did not see."

Spilling Their Guts

When Jesus asked what had happened, the two unburdened their hearts. They recounted their love for Jesus of Nazareth, the incredible injustice and cruelty of his trial and crucifixion, their shattered hopes that he would be the Messiah to rescue Israel, their amazement at the women's news—and their **unmitigated** sorrow because they had not seen Jesus.

Why did Jesus draw close to two obscure disciples? He read their hearts and knew their needs. He joined them and gave them opportunity to pour out their confusion and disappointment. He has not changed. He will draw close to us and listen as we tell him what troubles us.

> **Luke 24:25–27** He said to them, "How foolish you are, and how slow of heart to believe all that the prophets have spoken! Did not the Christ have to suffer these things and then enter his glory?" And beginning with Moses and all the Prophets, he explained to them what was said in all the Scriptures concerning himself.

Clues For The Clueless

Jesus must have shaken his head and said, "Guys, get a clue!" Then patiently he reminded them of the Old Testament Scriptures that foretold how the Messiah would come and suffer before he would arrive to establish his kingdom. The phrase *"all the Scriptures"* may mean that these two had focused only on the prophecies about the Messiah's glory and not his prior suffering. Jesus set them straight.

unmitigated: *not lessened or relieved*

FAST FORWARD

KEY POINT

Jesus opened the Scriptures to the two. He will do the same for us today.

GOD'S WORD FOR THE BIBLICALLY-INEPT

G. Campbell Morgan: Then he opened to them all the Scriptures as they applied to himself. From their standpoint we see these two, then, listening to a stranger interpreting to them the Scriptures which they thought they knew, but the deep meaning of which they had never apprehended. Moreover, they were listening to this stranger interpreting to them the events through which they had recently passed in the light of Messianic foretelling.[4]

> **Luke 24:28–32** As they approached the village to which they were going, Jesus acted as if he were going farther. But they urged him strongly, "Stay with us, for it is nearly evening; the day is almost over." So he went in to stay with them.
>
> When he was at the table with them, he took bread, gave thanks, broke it and began to give it to them. Then their eyes were opened and they recognized him, and he disappeared from their sight. They asked each other, "Were not our hearts burning within us while he talked with us on the road and opened the Scriptures to us?"

Tantalizing Tip-Off

As the two travelers approached the end of their journey, the stranger appeared to be going on. Traveling in the dark was too difficult and dangerous. "Have dinner and spend the night with us," they said. As they began to share the evening meal, they suddenly recognized who Jesus was. At that moment he disappeared.

What tipped off the men to Jesus' identity? Did they see his nail-scarred hands as he broke the bread? Did they recognize something in his voice and phrasing as he prayed? Did God simply choose that moment to allow them to see Jesus?

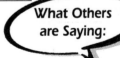

Something
to Ponder

Elisabeth Elliot: The two who sat with [Jesus] had not been pessimists. They had indeed had hopes. But what puny hopes theirs had been. In their wildest optimism they could not have dreamed of the glory they now saw. A resurrection, the ultimate contradiction to all of the world's woes, had taken place. They saw Jesus with their own eyes. What must their own words have seemed to them if they thought about what they had said: "We were hoping . . ."? They could not deny that those hopes had died, but what insane dreamer could have imagined the possibility that had become a reality here at their own supper table? Their savior had come back. He had walked with them. He was in their house. He was eating the very bread they had provided.[5]

> **Luke 24:33–35** They got up and returned at once to Jerusalem. There they found the Eleven and those with them, assembled together and saying, "It is true! The Lord has risen and has appeared to Simon." Then the two told what had happened on the way, and how Jesus was recognized by them when he broke the bread.

Not Running On Empty

There was not a moment to lose. The two hurried back to Jerusalem to share with Jesus' friends their most amazing discovery. They didn't finish their meal and they didn't care that it was getting dark. Their news couldn't wait. Jesus was indeed alive again!

When they arrived, they discovered their encounter with Christ was not unique. Peter had also seen the Lord. The disciples had not believed the women who went to the tomb, but now the truth sank in.

AMAZING APPEARANCES

KEY POINT
Jesus came to his fearful disciples and proved that he was indeed their risen Lord.

> **Luke 24:36–43** While they were still talking about this, Jesus himself stood among them and said to them, "Peace be with you."
>
> They were startled and frightened, thinking they saw a ghost. He said to them, "Why are you troubled, and why do doubts rise in your minds? Look at my hands and my feet. It is I myself! Touch me and see; a ghost does not have flesh and bones, as you see I have."
>
> When he had said this, he showed them his hands and feet. And while they still did not believe it because of joy and amazement, he asked them, "Do you have anything here to eat?" They gave him a piece of broiled fish, and he took it and ate it in their presence.

Not A Ghost In Sight

Suddenly Jesus appeared with them and greeted them. The group was taken aback, thinking they had seen a ghost. Assuring them of his identity, Jesus invited them to touch his hands and feet. Still they did not believe their eyes, so Jesus asked them for some food. He ate a piece of fish to prove that he was not a ghost.

Max Lucado: It was a moment the apostles would never forget, a story they would never cease to tell. The stone of the tomb was not enough to keep him *in*. The walls of the room were not enough to keep him *out*.[6]

PHYSICIAN'S PERSPECTIVE—We may wish Dr. Luke included more information about Jesus' resurrected body. We would like to know how Jesus could enter a <u>locked</u> room and how he could suddenly appear and disappear. His body was solid flesh and bones. He invited his disciples to touch his body and to look closely at the prints of the nails, which were evident on his hands and feet. He even ate.

Luke does not satisfy our curiosity. Instead, he leaves it up to us to focus on the fact that Jesus is alive today and we are to be witnesses to this truth.

Larry Richards: The Gospels report several incidents where Jesus brought the dead back to life. This was not resurrection, but resuscitation. In resuscitation biological life is restored. But the individual remains mortal, and must experience biological death again.

On the other hand resurrection is not a restoration of biological life. It is a transformation of the individual; a **transmutation** from mortality to immortality. The resurrected never again die, but live forever with the Lord. The resurrected are not subject to suffering or pain, or to the limitations that restrict mere men.

Christ entered into the glory of the resurrected life when he burst triumphant from his tomb.[7]

> **Luke 24:44–49** He said to them, "This is what I told you while I was still with you: Everything must be fulfilled that is written about me in the Law of Moses, the Prophets and the Psalms."
>
> Then he opened their minds so they could understand the Scriptures. He told them, "This is what is written: The

What Others are Saying:

☞ **GO TO:**

John 20:19 (locked)

What Others are Saying:

transmutation: change from one state to another

Christ will suffer and rise from the dead on the third day, and repentance and forgiveness of sins will be preached in his name to all nations, beginning at Jerusalem. You are witnesses of these things. I am going to send you what my Father has promised; but stay in the city until you have been clothed with power from on high."

Clue Review

Jesus then reviewed what he had told them. He opened their minds as he went over the Old Testament Scriptures that had foretold about his death and resurrection.

Then He gave them their assignment. They were to stay in Jerusalem until they received spiritual power to bear witness for him to all nations. The needed power would come in the person of the <u>Holy Spirit</u> at **Pentecost**.

 MORE INFORMATION

Events on Resurrection Day

1. Before sunrise, an angel rolls away the stone covering Jesus' tomb (Matthew 28:2–4).
2. Women discover the tomb is empty (Matthew 28:1; Mark 16:1–4; Luke 24:1–3; John 20:1).
3. Mary Magdalene leaves to give the news to Peter and John (John 20:1–2).
4. Other women who stay at the tomb see two angels who tell them Jesus has risen from the dead (Matthew 28:5–7; Mark 16:5–7; Luke 24:4–8).
5. Peter and John visit Jesus' tomb (Luke 24:12; John 20:3–10).
6. Mary Magdalene returns to the tomb; Jesus appears to her (Mark 16:9–11; John 20:11–18).
7. Jesus appears to Mary, mother of James, Salome, and Joanna (Matthew 28:8–10).
8. Guards are bribed into giving a false report instead of saying the angel rolled away the stone at the tomb (Matthew 28:11–15).
9. Jesus appears to Peter (1 Corinthians 15:5).
10. Jesus appears to two disciples on the road to Emmaus (Mark 16:12–13; Luke 24:13–32).

11. Two disciples tell the others that they have seen Jesus (Luke 24:33–35).

12. Jesus appears to disciples in a locked room (Luke 24:36–43; John 20:19–25).

RETURN TO SENDER

> **Luke 24:50–53** When he had led them out to the vicinity of Bethany, he lifted up his hands and blessed them. While he was blessing them, he left them and was taken up into heaven. Then they worshiped him and returned to Jerusalem with great joy. And they stayed continually at the temple, praising God.

Rising To The Occasion

Jesus led his followers out of the city where he blessed them. His actions remind us of a priest who blessed the people when he came out of the Temple and give Christians an image of Jesus as high priest today, interceding with God on their behalf (Luke 1:22; Hebrews 1:3; 4:14).

Then Jesus left the disciples. He returned to the One who sent him, his Father, and to his home in heaven. This time the disciples were not thrust into mourning. They worshiped him and returned to Jerusalem with joy. They stayed there to wait for the coming of the <u>Holy Spirit</u>, who would empower them to be Jesus' witnesses.

Luke's concise conclusion to his book emphasizes Jesus as the Son of God and shows what should be our logical response.

For the continuation of Luke's story we need to read the Book of Acts, which he also wrote for Theophilus (see also GWAC, page 4). The disciples were eyewitnesses to Jesus' resurrection. Their fears turned to joy, and after Jesus ascended to his Father, they became enthusiastic witnesses for him. Empowered by the Holy Spirit, they led many in Jerusalem to believe on Jesus, and thus the church was born.

Today Jesus has witnesses scattered around the world preaching the Gospel, teaching, ministering in acts of Christlike compassion to physical needs, preparing people from <u>every nation</u> to stand before Christ and sing his praises.

☞ **GO TO:**

Acts 1:8 (Holy Spirit)

FAST FORWARD

☞ **GO TO:**

Revelation 8:9 (every nation)

Study Questions

1. Who first learned that Jesus had risen from the dead?
2. What amazing discovery did two obscure disciples have as they left Jerusalem in confusion and disappointment?
3. How did Jesus convince his disciples that he was alive again and had a mission for them?
4. How did the disciples respond when Jesus left them to return to his Father?

CHAPTER WRAP-UP

- On the first day of the week women approached the tomb, bringing spices to lay on Jesus' body. They found the tomb empty. Angels announced that Jesus had risen from the dead. (Luke 24:1–8)

- The women reported the astounding news to the disciples, but they did not believe. Peter ran to the tomb, saw that it was empty, and left wondering. (Luke 24:9–12)

- Jesus appeared to two disciples as they walked from Jerusalem. (Luke 24:13–35)

- Jesus appeared to more disciples and opened their minds and hearts to the Scriptures. He commissioned them to be witnesses for him around the world. (Luke 24:36–49)

- When Jesus ascended to his Father in heaven, the disciples returned to Jerusalem with great joy and praises to God. (Luke 24:50–53)

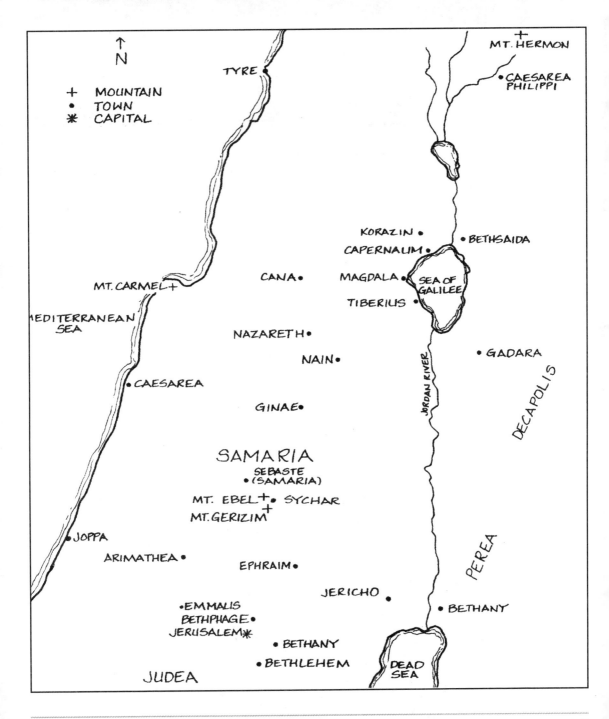

APPENDIX B—MAP OF JESUS' TRIAL AND CRUCIFIXION

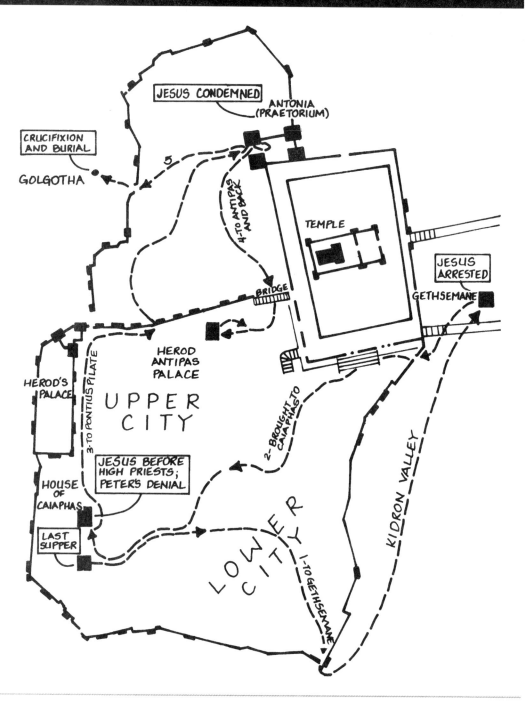

JESUS CONDEMNED

ANTONIA (PRAETORIUM)

CRUCIFIXION AND BURIAL

GOLGOTHA

5

4-TO ANTIPAS AND BACK

TEMPLE

JESUS ARRESTED

BRIDGE

GETHSEMANE

HEROD ANTIPAS PALACE

HEROD'S PALACE

3-TO PONTIUS PILATE

UPPER CITY

2-BROUGHT TO CAIAPHAS

KIDRON VALLEY

JESUS BEFORE HIGH PRIESTS; PETER'S DENIAL

HOUSE OF CAIAPHAS

LOWER CITY

LAST SUPPER

1-TO GETHSEMANE

APPENDIX C—THE ANSWERS

LUKE 1: VISITORS FROM HEAVEN

1. God sent the angel Gabriel on two separate occasions. First, to speak to Zechariah, as the priest offered incense in the Holy Place. Gabriel announced that Zechariah and Elizabeth would have a child. This child would be called John and would have the mission of preparing people to receive the long-awaited Messiah. Then Gabriel announced to Mary, a young virgin, that by the overshadowing of the Holy Spirit she would be the mother of the Messiah. (Luke 1:5–20; 26–38)

2. When Gabriel made his announcements to Zechariah and Mary, they both responded with fear. Zechariah raised a question, reflecting doubt that God could keep his promise to give him a son. Mary, on the other hand, raised a question for clarification but immediately submitted herself to whatever God willed for her. (Luke 1:11–19; 29–38)

3. John's unique mission would be to bring people back to the Lord and to prepare them to receive the coming Messiah. (Luke 1:14–17)

4. While Zechariah was unable to speak, he could not express further doubts about God's ability to keep his promise to send a son to him and Elizabeth in their old age. (Luke 1:18–20)

5. If we cannot accept and believe in the virgin birth of Jesus, we cannot accept and believe anything else that is recorded in the New Testament about who Jesus is and how he can be our Savior from sin.

6. Events connected with the birth of John led people to watch him for further evidences that the Lord's hand was on him: his birth to Zechariah and Elizabeth, who were past childbearing years, and the astounding way in which both Elizabeth and Zechariah confirmed that the baby's name would be John, though custom dictated that he should have been called Zechariah. (Luke 1:57–66)

LUKE 2: BIRTH AND BOYHOOD

1. God caused Caesar Augustus to decree a census. This required all Jewish males to return to their ancestral towns to be registered, which forced Joseph to go to Bethlehem, where Jesus was born. This fulfilled the prophecy of Micah. (Micah 5:2; Luke 2:1–7)

2. Jesus was born in a stable, which could have been a cave or an open courtyard in which animals were kept. He was born there because Mary and Joseph could not find space to stay in the inn. (Luke 2:7)

3. God chose to send his angel messenger to announce to humble shepherds that Jesus had been born. This was significant because many Bible students believe they were tending temple sheep which would be offered as sacrifices. Jesus had come to give his life as the Lamb of God. Thus, temple offerings would no longer be needed. (Luke 2:8–14)

4. Both Simeon and Anna recognized that the baby Mary and Joseph presented at the Temple was the promised Messiah. Simeon took the baby in his arms and praised God for allowing him the privilege of seeing the Savior who would bring salvation to the Gentiles as well as the Jews. Anna also recognized who Jesus was, gave thanks to God, and shared this good news with others in the Temple who were also looking for the Messiah. (Luke 2:25–38)

5. Jesus visited Jerusalem for the Feast of Passover when he was twelve years old. While there, he visited the Temple and entered a discussion with the religious leaders. They were amazed at his insights and the wisdom reflected in the questions he raised. When Mary asked why he had stayed at the Temple when they were anxiously searching for him, Jesus asked in return why they were searching for him. They should have known that he "had to be in my Father's house." This indicated his awareness that God in heaven was his real Father. Still, he returned to Nazareth with Mary and Joseph and submitted himself to live in obedience to them. (Luke 2:41–52)

LUKE 3: A DESERT CALL

1. John's God-given mission was to prepare the hearts of people to receive the coming Messiah. He preached repentance and turning to God, baptized the people in the Jordan River, and called for them to prove their change of heart by their everyday actions and attitudes. (Luke 3:1–14)

2. Personal answers will vary. What might John say to those who carelessly waste earth's resources, businesses that overcharge the poor so they can live in luxury, individuals who exploit the poor and the elderly with false offers and outright lies? (Luke 3:7–9)

3. Personal answers will vary. Everyone who professes to have turned to God is called to stand for justice for others and to share what they have in time, influence, and material resources with people who have needs. (Luke 3:10–14)

4. John's baptism signified repentance and turning to God, whereas Jesus would baptize with the Holy Spirit, creating inner cleansing and transformation. John considered himself so inferior to the Messiah that he was not worthy to assume the humble role of a slave by untying the thongs of Messiah's sandals. (Luke 3:15–18)

5. After John baptized Jesus, the Holy Spirit came on Jesus in the form of a dove, and a voice spoke from heaven confirming that Jesus was God's dearly loved Son, and was fully approved by God. (Luke 3:21–22)

6. Matthew traces Jesus' ancestry back through Abraham and King David, showing that as the legal son of Joseph, Jesus had the right to the throne of David. Luke, on the other hand, traces Jesus' ancestry through Mary back to Adam, the Son of God. In doing so, Luke confirms that Jesus was truly human, bearing our weaknesses. (Matthew 1:1–17; Luke 3:21–37)

LUKE 4: TEMPTATION AND TRIUMPH

1. The Holy Spirit led Jesus into the desert to be tempted because by this means Jesus proved his humanness and his complete commitment to God. The temptations prepared him for ministry. (Luke 4:1)
2. Jesus' forty days in the desert run parallel to the Israelites' forty years of wandering in the desert after the Exodus.
3. Jesus was tempted in the general areas of (1) not relying on God's promised provision and care, (2) seeking success apart from God's plan, and (3) testing God.
4. The people of Nazareth rejected Jesus because they refused to believe he was who he claimed to be unless he would perform miracles for them. Also, they became angry when he told them that God's grace extended to Gentiles as well as to Jews. (Luke 4:14–30)
5. Jesus proved his authority over evil spirits by commanding them to keep silent and by ordering them to leave their victims. (Luke 4:31–37)
6. Jesus showed compassion to people with physical needs by touching and healing them. (Luke 4:38–44)

LUKE 5: BREAKING THE RULES

1. Experienced fishermen knew better than to attempt to catch fish in deep water during the day. But when Simon obeyed, Jesus performed a miracle by providing a huge catch of fish. This led Simon to recognize Jesus' power and his own sinfulness. More than anything Jesus taught that day, the nets overflowing with fish convinced Simon and his three companions to leave all and follow Jesus. (Luke 5:1–11)
2. In healing the man with leprosy, Jesus showed compassion and divine power. In reaching out to touch the man, Jesus showed his disregard for Old Testament laws. In commanding the man not to tell others of his healing, Jesus wanted him to go directly to the priest to be pronounced clean. Possibly Jesus also wanted to delay the surge of crowds coming for healing once the news was out. (Luke 5:12–16)
3. Jesus raised questions by claiming to be able to forgive sins—an act that was not visually verifiable to his critics. He healed the paralyzed man, thus proving he had power both to heal and to forgive sins. (Luke 5:17–26)
4. The Jews in Jesus' day were prejudiced against their fellow Jews who represented the hated Roman government as tax collectors. Not only did Jesus refuse to condemn Levi, but he also called him to be a disciple. Jesus also accepted Levi's invitation to honor him at a banquet in Levi's spacious home where he socialized with Levi's friends and fellow tax collectors—all who were considered outcasts by the religious leaders. (Luke 5:27–32)
5. Jesus' critics observed that while their disciples and those of John the Baptist fasted and prayed regularly, Jesus' followers joined him in enjoying an active social life. Jesus replied that he had come to replace the old legalistic system with something much better. (Luke 5:33–39)

LUKE 6: JESUS, PH.D.

1. Jesus spoke out against man-made laws that turned observing the Sabbath into a burden. As Lord of the Sabbath, he showed that it should be a day of rest, delighting in God, and doing good to others. (Luke 6:1–11)
2. Jesus chose twelve men to be his disciples. A disciple is a learner who becomes like his master. An apostle is sent out to represent his master. (Luke 6:12–16)
3. Jesus pronounced his followers to be blessed when because of

their loyalty to him they experienced poverty, hunger, pain, and persecution. In contrast, people would be under judgment who enjoyed prosperity and popularity with no regard for heavenly values. (Luke 6:20–26)
4. Disciples who demonstrated God's love and generosity to the undeserving would be rewarded by becoming more like their Father in heaven. (Luke 6:27–36)
5. We will stand firm in times of temptation if our lives are built on the foundation of putting Jesus' words into practice. (Luke 6:46–49)

LUKE 7: JESUS, M.D.

1. The centurion was a Gentile who had learned to love the Jews so much that he had built a synagogue for them. Though he felt unworthy to approach Jesus directly, he sent Jewish elders to request that Jesus come to heal his dying slave. Then he sent friends to ask Jesus just to "say the word" of healing. He understood that Jesus' word would be effective because Jesus was under God's authority. Even Jews had not shown such understanding and faith. (Luke 7:1–10)
2. Jesus has great compassion for the poor, for all who suffer and grieve. He still has compassion for all who are in need of his touch. We convey his compassion when we reach out to people who hurt. (Luke 7:11–17)
3. John wrestled with doubt that Jesus was the Messiah whose coming he had announced. Jesus' reply was proof that he was fulfilling the prophecy of the Messiah. He had a blessing for John if he kept trusting, in spite of the disappointment that Jesus had not yet fully established his kingdom. (Luke 7:18–23)
4. John was great because he had the privilege of preparing people to receive Jesus. The "least" in his kingdom would have blessings that John only announced would be coming. (Luke 7:24–28)
5. Jesus' religious critics complained about the messengers: John was too severe and Jesus was too relaxed. Actually, they refused both messengers because they didn't want to hear the truth from anyone. (Luke 7:29–35)

LUKE 8: THE WAY OF JESUS

1. Women who had received Jesus' healing touch were especially devoted to him. They traveled with him and his band of twelve disciples, sharing their personal finances to provide practical assistance to them. (Luke 8:1–3)
2. The seed is the "word of God." The packed-down path represents people with hard hearts who are not open to the truth. The rocky soil represents people who accept the Word but reject it when they are tested. The thorny soil represents people who give more attention to this life than to eternal values. The good soil represents people who receive and obey God's message. (Luke 8:4–15)
3. Jesus is the light of the world. We who believe in him are like lamps shining in a dark world. Jesus' light also shines within us, exposing our secrets. If we conceal them instead of confessing and forsaking them, he will expose them. (Luke 8:16–18)
4. We become members of Jesus' spiritual family by hearing and obeying God's Word. (Luke 8:19–21)
5. Jesus wanted his disciples to trust him even when everything seemed hopeless and death was certain. He proved his authority to calm the tempest, thus proving to them that he was the Lord over creation. (Luke 8:22–25)
6. The woman was desperate for help. After twelve years of physi-

cal misery, being declared ceremonially unclean and spending money on doctors who could not help her, she took a daring step of faith—she touched the tassels of Jesus' cloak and was healed immediately. (Luke 8:43–48)

7. Though Jesus was delayed in arriving at Jairus's home, he encouraged Jairus to have faith and believe that his daughter would be restored to him. On arriving at Jairus's home, he found the mourning in progress. He was not deterred by the mockery of the group in the home, but took the parents and three of his disciples into the room and raised the girl from the dead. (Luke 8:40–56)

LUKE 9: WHO JESUS IS

1. The disciples realized they had been given power and authority by Jesus. Their preaching was effective and they were able to perform miracles of healing. They also experienced God's provision for their needs. (Luke 9:1–6)

2. Peter identified Jesus as the Christ of God, an insight he had received from God. Jesus cautioned the disciples not to talk about this truth. He had yet to suffer rejection, death, and resurrection. (Luke 9:18–22)

3. Having identified Jesus as the Christ of God, the disciples expected to share in his glory in some way. But the time was not yet. In the meantime, they needed to follow his standards of discipleship. They needed to deny themselves, take up their cross, and follow him. They should be willing to lose their lives in his service—and save their lives. And they were not to be ashamed of Jesus and his words. (Luke 9:23–27)

4. Jesus took Peter, James, and John with him up a mountain. As he prayed, he was changed so that his true glory shone brightly. Moses and Elijah appeared and talked with Jesus about his approaching suffering and death. God spoke from a cloud, confirming that Jesus was his son and the disciples should listen to him. (Luke 9:28–36)

5. Jesus knew the disciples were arguing about who was the greatest. So he brought a child to stand next to him. He pointed out that true greatness was reflected in their attitude toward a child—or anyone needing their care and protection. If they cared for a child they would be welcoming Jesus himself. Among the disciples, the one who was least, as a child, would be the greatest. (Luke 9:46–50)

LUKE 10: SIGNIFICANT DECISIONS

1. Jesus sent out seventy-two to precede him to Judea. On their return they reported great joy that even demons submitted to them. Jesus said that they should find even greater joy in the fact that their names were written in heaven. (Luke 10:1–20)

2. God chooses to reveal the truths of Scripture to only those who come with childlike hearts—humble and dependent on Him. He hides the truths from the wise who rely on themselves without any sense of need to depend on Him. (Luke 10:21–24)

3. The expert in the law hoped to trick Jesus into giving an answer that would be a basis for accusing him. Jesus responded with a question and a story. The expert learned that there was nothing he was capable of doing that would earn him eternal life. He simply could not truly love a neighbor because he did not totally love God. (Luke 10:25–37)

4. To fulfill the law, the expert in the law should express his love for God by being a neighbor to anyone who had need. (Luke 10:25–37)

5. Both Martha and Mary loved Jesus and welcomed him. Martha expressed her love by preparing an elaborate meal for Jesus,

wearing herself out to the point that she was frustrated and angry with Mary and Jesus. On the other hand, Mary left the kitchen to sit at Jesus' feet and listen to him. Jesus said Mary had chosen what was better because listening to him was more important than serving him without first hearing him. (Luke 10:38–42)

LUKE 11: CANDID CONVERSATIONS

1. Jesus' pattern for prayer included approaching God as Father, desiring that his name be honored, asking help to do his will and extend his kingdom throughout the earth, depending on him for everyday needs, trusting him to forgive our sins, as we are willing to forgive others, and asking him to keep us from yielding to temptation. (Luke 11:1–4)

2. Jesus pointed out that Satan would never weaken his kingdom by casting out his demons. (Luke 11:17–26)

3. While Jesus did not detract from Mary, he pointed out that when we hear God's Word and act on it, we are even more blessed. (Luke 11:27–28)

4. Jesus condemned those who insisted on a sign from heaven, saying that the Queen of Sheba and the wicked citizens of Nineveh had more faith than they did. He said they would get a sign: as Jonah was in the deep for three days, he would be buried for three days and would come alive again. (Luke 11:29–32)

5. Jesus condemned the Pharisees (1) for not showing justice and mercy to the poor, (2) for parading their self-righteousness and seeking praise from people, and (3) for spreading unbelief and false teaching. (Luke 11:42–44)

6. Jesus condemned the experts in the law (1) for burdening people with rules and not helping them, (2) for honoring the memory of God's prophets while harboring in their hearts the evil attitudes of their murderers, and (3) for not wanting the truth of Scripture and for keeping others from receiving it. (Luke 11:45–52)

LUKE 12: WISE WORDS

1. The yeast of the Pharisees is hypocrisy, pretending to be something that does not reflect the real person inside. Jesus warned his disciples that hypocrisy was a danger if they faked their relationship with him. (Luke 12:1–3)

2. Jesus gave an antidote to fear of enemies: They should fear not man but God, who has power over this life and the next. However, God loves and cares for his own as a loving Father. (Luke 12:4–12)

3. Greed blinds us to our duty to share our prosperity with others who have needs. Greed also keeps us from building treasure in heaven. (Luke 12:13–21)

4. Jesus' followers should seek his kingdom first, which includes taking care of the needs of others. As they do this, God will take care of their needs of food and clothing. (Luke 12:22–34)

5. Jesus gives his followers assignments to do while he is away. They need to be faithful in their duties, always on alert for his return. We need to do the same. (Luke 12:35–48)

6. Allegiance to Jesus must have first place in the hearts of his followers. Sometimes this causes divisions in family relationships when some members follow Jesus and some reject him. (Luke 12:49–53)

7. We observe signs of weather change. We also need to be alert and responsive to what Jesus teaches that impacts our lives forever. (Luke 12:54–59)

LUKE 13: GOING AGAINST THE GRAIN

1. People assumed that the victims of a massacre and the victims of an accident had been punished by God. Jesus pointed out that they were no more guilty than his listeners. Each person needed to repent and avoid eternal judgment. (Luke 13:1–5)
2. When Jesus healed a woman on the Sabbath, the synagogue ruler became furious and told people not to seek healing on the Sabbath. Jesus pointed out his hypocrisy. Sabbath laws allowed compassion for the needs of an animal. Was it not lawful to show compassion on a human? (Luke 13:10–17)
3. God's kingdom is like a tiny mustard seed and a small amount of yeast. Though both seem to be insignificant, in time both would grow and have wide influence. (Luke 13:18–21)
4. Jesus spoke of the narrow door as the only way to enter God's kingdom. Many in Jesus' day assumed that they would enter simply because they were descendants of Abraham, Isaac, and Jacob. Jesus pointed out that unless they accepted him and his teaching, they could not be part of the kingdom. The same applies to us today.(Luke 13:22–30)
5. Jesus thought about his goal of dying on the cross and of Israel's rejection of him. He knew the Jews faced terrible eternal consequences and that made him sad because he loved them. (Luke 13:31–35)

LUKE 14: RELATING TO PEOPLE

1. When Jesus healed the man with dropsy on the Sabbath, he silenced the Pharisees by saying they had more concern for an ox falling into a well on the Sabbath than they had for a man who was suffering from a disease. (Luke 14:1–6)
2. The guests at the Pharisee's dinner who pushed their way to the seats of honor showed that they were proud. The Pharisee who invited only those guests who could repay him showed that he did not care about social outcasts. God rewards those at the resurrection who show kindness and generosity to others. (Luke 14:7–14)
3. The Pharisees understood Jesus' parable about the banquet to picture God's kingdom. The law-abiding Jews thought they had a secure place there. But Jesus pointed out that when he came to invite them to commit themselves to the kingdom, they made flimsy excuses. The host sent his servant out to bring in the social outcasts and to go further and bring in even more guests. Jesus was saying that God would welcome those Jews whom the Pharisees considered unworthy and would expand his kingdom to include Gentiles. (Luke 14:15–24)
4. Jesus said that anyone who wanted to be his disciple must count the cost of total commitment to him. Jesus must come before every human relationship and the disciple must be willing to suffer and even give his life for his uncompromising loyalty to Jesus. (Luke 14:25–35)

LUKE 15: LOST AND FOUND

1. The Pharisees were critical of Jesus for welcoming sinners, whom they despised. Jesus told the parables to show that God loves and welcomes each sinner who comes to him. (Luke 15:1–2)
2. The shepherd tirelessly searching for the lost sheep pictures God's love for each lost person. He seeks us and rejoices when we come to him. (Luke 15:3–7)
3. The woman's search for the lost coin pictures God's search for people because they are precious to him. (Luke 15:8–10)
4. We are loved by God the Father but have chosen to go our own way and are indifferent to the pain we cause the Father.

When we turn to God in repentance, we are welcomed with love. (Luke 15:11–24)
5. We may pride ourselves in living according to God's rules but miss enjoying his perfect love and demonstrating it to others. (Luke 15:25–30)
6. The father loved both sons and longed to have a close relationship with them. He was quick to forgive the sinning son and longed for the older son to repent of his bitterness and self-righteousness and come home to his father's love. (Luke 15:31–32)

LUKE 16: MONEY MATTERS

1. When the dishonest manager was advised that he was facing an audit and certain termination, he called in the rich man's debtors and significantly reduced the amounts owed. In so doing, he bought the friendship of the debtors and guaranteed for himself their favor after he was without employment. Jesus taught that we can learn from his shrewdness by using our money to build his kingdom on earth. After death we will be welcomed in heaven by people who are there because we have invested in the spread of the Gospel. (Luke 16:1–9)
2. How we view and use what money we have reveals our character—whether we use it on ourselves for comfort in this life or faithfully invest it in Christ's kingdom. (Luke 16:10–15)
3. The Pharisees were blind to Jesus' teaching about the kingdom because they were preoccupied with money and their obsession to be highly regarded by others. (Luke 16:16–18)
4. In Jesus' parable of the rich man and Lazarus, we learn that we need to take God's Word seriously and act on it, because there are no second chances after death. We are responsible to use our resources for the relief of others' needs. (Luke 16:19–31)

LUKE 17: HEART ATTITUDES

1. Jesus has special love for children and new believers. Because he knows the influence we have on them, he warns that punishment awaits us if we cause "little ones" to sin. (Luke 17:1–3a)
2. When someone sins against us, we need to take the initiative to confront him. If he repents, we are to forgive him—even if he repeats the sin and the repentance again and again. (Luke 17:3b–4)
3. A disciple is called to do whatever the Lord asks of him. When he has done that, he is an "unworthy servant" because he has done only what was expected. (Luke 17:5–10)
4. Jesus healed ten lepers. One returned to thank him—a Samaritan and a "foreigner" to the Jews' concept of God. Jesus said his faith had healed him. (Luke 17:11–19)
5. While we wait we need to beware of false predictions of when and where he will return. We also need to beware lest we give priority to everyday concerns and not be prepared in our hearts for his appearance. (Luke 17:20–37)

LUKE 18: PEOPLE MAGAZINE

1. God loves us and listens to our prayers. Unlike the insensitive judge, he works for our good. Like the widow, we need to be persistent in our prayers and not give up. (Luke 18:1–8)
2. The Pharisee was proud of his outward religious acts. He felt superior to the tax collector. The tax collector came humbly with sincere repentance. He went home justified. (Luke 18:9–14)
3. We should welcome children and seek to lead them to Jesus, who loves them and can bring blessing into their lives. We need to be like children, who have open, trusting hearts that are willing to depend on God's love and care. (Luke 18:15–17)

4. The rich young ruler wanted eternal life but was not willing to give up his wealth and follow Jesus with an undivided heart. (Luke 18:18–30)
5. The disciples thought Jesus was going to set up Messiah's kingdom. Luke says, *"Its meaning was hidden from them."* (Luke 18:31–34)
6. Jesus does not discourage us from being bold in seeking him, though those around us may want to discourage us. (Luke 18:35–43)

LUKE 19: LOVED LITTLE PEOPLE
1. Zacchaeus was despised because he, a Jew, was a tax collector for the Roman government. After his encounter with Jesus, he volunteered to make restitution—going far beyond what was required in the Old Testament law. (Luke 19:1–10)
2. Jesus told a parable about ten servants who were entrusted to care for their master's resources while he was away. When he returned, he asked them to give account. Jesus has entrusted us to serve him loyally while he is away. Someday he will return and will ask us to give an account of our service. (Luke 19:11–27)
3. Jesus chose to ride into Jerusalem on a donkey colt. He fulfilled Zechariah's prophecy that he would ride on a donkey, thus signifying that he was coming as the righteous, gentle Messiah-King who would bring peace, in contrast to the conquering kings who rode on horses to signify their power and authority. (Luke 19:28–40)
4. Jesus wept as he lamented over Jerusalem because the people rejected him and were heading toward the unavoidable consequences of their sins. Within forty years the Roman army would level the city and destroy its people. (Luke 19:41–44)
5. When Jesus came to the Temple he found a market set up to make high profit from the out-of-town people who came to worship. The temple entrepreneurs cheated the visitors when they forced them to exchange their currency for the required Galilean shekels. They also forced the worshipers to buy sacrificial animals and doves at steep prices. (Luke 19:45–48)

LUKE 20: HOSTILE CHALLENGES
1. Jesus knew the evil motivation behind the question of his authority. He raised the question about John the Baptist, knowing that his critics could not answer it without falling into a trap. (Luke 20:1–8)
2. Like the tenant farmers who rejected the owner's servants, Israel rejected the prophets God had sent. Like the farmers, Israel was preparing to kill God's Son. (Luke 20:9–19)
3. Jesus' followers should be good citizens by respecting positions of authority and paying taxes while at the same time living as citizens of Christ's kingdom of righteousness and love. (Luke 20:20–26)
4. The Sadducees did not believe in life after death, so Jesus confounded them by proving from Moses' writings that God referred to Abraham, Isaac, and Jacob as alive in heaven. (Luke 20:27–44)
5. Jesus exposed the hypocrisy of the teachers of the law who wore expensive robes and made a show of greeting people. They prayed for widows while plotting to exploit them. (Luke 20:45–47)

LUKE 21: WHAT MATTERS MOST
1. In giving her two tiny coins, the widow gave her all. Others gave much more money, but kept plenty for themselves. The widow kept nothing for herself. (Luke 21:1–4)

2. Jesus answered three questions raised by the disciples: (1) When will the Temple be destroyed? (2) What will be the signs of your coming? (3) What will be the sign of the end of the age? (Luke 21:5–7)
3. Don' be fooled by imposters, don't be alarmed about wars, don't worry about what to say, don't give up, don't hesitate to run from Jerusalem, don't be alarmed when natural laws fail, don't worry that I will fail, and don't be preoccupied with this life. (Luke 21:8–36)
4. Jesus spent his time teaching in the Temple. In the evening he went to the Mount of Olives to pray and spend the night. (Luke 21:37–38)

LUKE 22: THE LONGEST NIGHT
1. The religious leaders couldn't arrest Jesus during the day because they feared a riot from the crowds that followed Jesus, and they did not know how to find him when he was alone with his disciples. Judas would lead them to Jesus. (Luke 22:1–6)
2. Jesus wanted to prepare them for what was soon to happen and to institute the Lord's Supper. (Luke 22:7–18)
3. The Lord's Supper is Jesus' way of helping us remember him, his death for us, and his promised return. We celebrate it today because Jesus asked us to do this until he comes back. (Luke 22:19–20)
4. At the Passover meal (1) Jesus announced that he would be betrayed by one of the Twelve. (2) The disciples argued about which of them was the greatest. (3) Jesus told Simon Peter that he would deny him. (4) Jesus warned his disciples that they would need to be resourceful after he was arrested. (Luke 22:21–38)
5. In Gethsemane Jesus went to pray alone. He was in anguish as he asked if it were possible to be spared the terrible suffering that lay ahead, but he would do his Father's will. (Luke 22:39–46)
6. Judas led an armed crowd into the garden of Gethsemane to arrest Jesus. Judas betrayed Jesus with a kiss, a cruel mockery. The disciples were terrified, but drew their swords to protect him. One disciple cut off the ear of a servant of the high priest. Jesus calmly healed him and put an end to any attempted violence. Throughout the arrest, Jesus remained calm and "in charge." (Luke 22:47–53)
7. Jesus' eyes met Peter's, and Peter was overwhelmed with regret and sorrow for his failure. He went out and wept bitterly. (Luke 22:54–62)
8. Jesus was taken to the high priest's house at night. No one read a charge against him. Later, soldiers mocked and beat him. At daybreak Jesus was led before the Sanhedrin for questioning. (Luke 22:63–71)

LUKE 23: A DARK DAY IN HISTORY
1. Under Roman law Jews were not permitted to execute criminals. The religious leaders sent Jesus to Pilate for sentencing for false charges. (Luke 23:1–7)
2. Herod had long wanted to meet Jesus. He welcomed the opportunity to see him, hoping to see Jesus perform a miracle. (Luke 23:8–12)
3. Pilate sentenced Jesus to death, knowing that Jesus was innocent, because he feared a riot if he didn't. He gave in to the demands of the religious leaders. (Luke 23:13–25)
4. Jesus was charged with two crimes. The Jews charged him with blasphemy because he claimed to be the Son of God and Pilate charged him with claiming to be king and thus a rival of Caesar in Rome. (Luke 23:1–25)

5. What observers could not see was the transaction that was taking place as Jesus took our sins on himself and thus made the way for us to be welcomed in God's presence. (Luke 23:26–49)

6. Joseph, a secret believer, obtained permission to take Jesus' body and lay it in a tomb, wrapped in linen cloth. Women went home to prepare spices and perfumes to place around the body after the Sabbath. (Luke 23:50–54)

LUKE 24: A BRIGHT DAY DAWNS

1. Women came early in the morning to place spices on Jesus' body. They worried how they could roll back the heavy stone that closed the entrance to the tomb, but found the stone rolled away and the tomb empty. Angels told them that Jesus was alive again and sent them to share the good news with Jesus' disciples. (Luke 24:1–12)

2. As two disciples went away from Jerusalem they were overtaken by Jesus, whom they did not recognize. As they poured out their confusion and disappointment to him, he opened their hearts as he explained the Old Testament Scriptures that showed that Jesus would die and come back to life again. Only as he shared a meal with them did he reveal his identity to them. (Luke 24:13–35)

3. Jesus appeared to the frightened disciples and convinced them that he was indeed alive again as he ate with them and showed them the nail prints on his hands and feet. He reminded them of what he had taught them and commissioned them to take the good news of the Gospel to all nations of the world. (Luke 24:36–49)

4. When Jesus ascended to his Father the disciples did not grieve. Instead, they returned to Jerusalem with great joy and praises to God. (Luke 24:50–53)

APPENDIX D—THE EXPERTS

Max Anders—Writer and Bible teacher; a founding member with Walk Thru the Bible Ministries and former pastor of a mega-church.

William Barclay—New Testament scholar and writer; professor of divinity and biblical criticism at the University of Glasgow; author of many books, including the multivolume *Daily Study Bible* commentary on all the New Testament books.

Bob Benson—Pastor, popular speaker, and executive with the Benson Publishing Company.

Paul N. Benware—Professor of Bible and theology at Moody Bible Institute.

Gilbert Bilezikian—Cofounder of Willow Creek Community Church and professor of Biblical Studies at Wheaton College.

Henry T. Blackaby—consultant to several mission boards; coauthor of the popular *Experiencing God* books.

George R. Bliss—Outspoken abolitionist; professor of Greek, librarian, and president of Bucknell University; pastor of a Baptist Church in the mid-1800s.

Darrell L. Bock—Professor of New Testament studies at Dallas Theological Seminary.

Frederick Buechner—Presbyterian pastor; author of more than thirty works of fiction and nonfiction.

Michael Card—Contemporary Christian author, composer, performer, and recording artist.

Oswald Chambers—Principal of Bible Training School, London; founder of two YMCA desert camps in Egypt during World War I where he ministered to British soldiers.

Darryl DelHousaye—Senior pastor of Scottsdale Bible Church in Arizona.

Daymond R. Duck—Best-selling author of *Revelation*, *Daniel*, and *Prophecies of the Bible* in the *God's Word for the Biblically-Inept*™ series.

Elisabeth Elliot—Popular seminar leader, best-selling author, and speaker on the radio program *Gateway to Joy*.

W. Glyn Evans—Minister-at-Large for the Conservative Baptist Association of New England, professor, and writer.

Stephen Fortosis—College professor and author.

Richard J. Foster—Best-selling author; founder of Renovare, an organization dedicated to church renewal, and professor of spiritual formation at Azusa Pacific University.

Robert C. Girard—Pastor for over forty years and a writer of adult education curriculum; author of *Life of Christ, Volumes 1 and 2* and *Acts* in the *God's Word for the Biblically-Inept*™ series.

Ken Gire—Author of more than a dozen best-selling books.

Gary A. Haugen—President of International Justice Mission, Washington, D.C., worked in the civil rights division of the U.S. Department of Justice, and was director of the United Nations genocide investigation in Rwanda.

Jack Hayford—Editor of the *Spirit-Filled Life Bible*; pastor of the Church on the Way; teacher; composer; author of more than twenty books.

Matthew Henry—Popular pastor in London during the 1700s; author of a six-volume set of Bible commentaries that is still widely respected.

R. Kent Hughes—Senior pastor at College Church, Wheaton, Illinois; author of a number of books, including titles in the *Preaching the Word* series.

Phyllis Kilbourn—Lived and worked with children caught in the civil war in Liberia, West Africa. A missionary and educator serving under WQEC International, she has become a leading advocate for the hurting children of our world.

Claude V. King—Coeditor of *The Experiencing God Study Bible*.

Peter Kreeft—Author and professor of philosophy at Boston College.

Lois LeBar—Before retirement, chair of the Christian Education Department, Wheaton College, Wheaton, Illinois.

Max Lucado—Pastor of Oak Hill Church of Christ in San Antonio, Texas; poet; artist; apologist; prolific writer of inspirational books.

William MacDonald—Bible teacher at Emmaus Bible School (now College) and author of commentaries on the Old and New Testaments.

Peter Marshall—Chaplain of the U.S. Senate from 1947–1949; pastor of New York Avenue Presbyterian Church, Washington, D.C.; his life story is told in the popular film *A Man Called Peter*.

G. Campbell Morgan—Bible teacher at the Westminster Bible School, London; conference speaker in America and Britain; author of numerous Bible study books.

Leon Morris—Anglican priest; former principal of Ridley College, Melbourne, Australia; author.

Henri J. M. Nouwen—Taught at University of Notre Dame, Yale, and Harvard; from 1986 until his death in 1996 was associated with L'Arche Community in France and Toronto.

Lloyd John Ogilvie—Chaplain of the U.S. Senate; former senior pastor of the First Presbyterian Church in Hollywood; writer; radio and television broadcaster.

John Piper—Senior pastor of Bethlehem Baptist Church, Minneapolis; author of best-selling books.

Derek Prime—Former pastor of the largest evangelical church in Edinburgh.

Larry (Lawrence O.) Richards—Theologian; Bible scholar; ecclesiologist; prolific author of more than 175 books, including Bible commentaries and reference works for pastors, church leaders, teachers, laymen, and youth; curriculum developer for various publishers.

Sue Richards—Wife of Larry; retired English teacher and women's Bible study teacher.

Randall D. Roth—Senior pastor of First Covenant Church of Oakland, California, and a founding board member of Concerts of Prayer International.

J. C. Ryle—Nineteenth-century bishop of Liverpool; author of more than one hundred tracts and pamphlets on doctrinal subjects and numerous books.

Charles C. Ryrie—Theologian; former professor of systematic theology at Dallas Theological Seminary; author of theological books and the notes for *The Ryrie Study Bible*.

Larry Sibley—Guest lecturer in practical theology at Westminster Theological Seminary; author.

Tom Sine—Consultant in futures research and planning and in developing a theology of mission for both Christian and secular organizations. He speaks widely at colleges, churches, and missions conferences and leads creativity seminars for a variety of Christian groups.

R. C. Sproul—Theologian, pastor, teacher, chairman of the board of Ligonier Ministries, and author of best-selling books.

C. Samuel Storms—Author, conference speaker, and pastor of Christ Community Church in Ardmore, Oklahoma.

Charles R. Swindoll—President of Dallas Theological Seminary; popular Bible expositor, radio preacher, and author of best-selling books.

Helmut Thielicke—Former professor on the faculty of the University of Hamburg, Germany; preacher at St. Michael's Church in Hamburg; author.

Robert L. Thomas—Editor of *The NIV Harmony of the Gospels*.

Howard Vos—Professor emeritus of history and archaeology at The King's College in Tuxedo, New York; author of more than twenty books; has traveled and studied extensively throughout the Middle East.

Jerry White—General director of The Navigators, an international discipleship ministry; author.

Warren W. Wiersbe—One of the evangelical world's most respected Bible teachers and author of more than one hundred books.

Dallas Willard—Professor at the University of Southern California's School of Philosophy; visiting professor at the University of Colorado; author of best-selling books.

Philip Yancey—Editor-at-large for *Christianity Today*; author of award-winning books.

Note: To the best of our knowledge, all of the above information is accurate and up to date. In some cases we were unable to obtain biographical information.

—THE STARBURST EDITORS

ENDNOTES

Introduction
1. Lois LeBar, *Education That Is Christian* (Westwood, NJ: Fleming H. Revell, 1958), 121.
2. Larry Sibley, *Luke: Gospel for the City* (Colorado Springs, CO: David C. Cook, 1988), 10.
3. Ken Gire, *The Reflective Life* (Colorado Springs, CO: Chariot Victor, 1998), 12.

Luke 1: Visitors from Heaven
1. Paul N. Benware, *Luke: Everyman's Bible Commentary* (Chicago: Moody Press, 1985), 9.
2. John F. Walvoord and Roy B. Zuck, eds., *The Bible Knowledge Commentary* (Colorado Springs, CO: Chariot Victor, 1985), 202.
3. J. C. Ryle, *Luke: The Crossway Classic Commentaries* (Wheaton: Crossway Books, 1997), 22.
4. R. C. Sproul, *A Walk with Jesus* (Geanies House, Fearn, Ross-shire GB, 1999), 15.
5. Darrell L. Bock, *Luke: The NIV Application Commentary* (Grand Rapids, MI: Zondervan, 1996), 55.
6. Gilbert Bilezikian, *Christianity 101* (Grand Rapids, MI: Zondervan, 1993), 63.
7. Charles C. Ryrie, *Basic Theology* (Colorado Springs, CO: Chariot Victor, 1987), 242.
8. Benware, *Luke: Everyman's Bible Commentary,* 31.
9. Sibley, *Luke,* 18.
10. Walvoord and Zuck, *The Bible Knowledge Commentary,* 205.
11. Ibid., 206.
12. Stephen Fortosis, *Great Men and Women of the Bible* (New York: Paulist Press, 1996), 106.

Luke 2: Birth and Boyhood
1. R. Kent Hughes, *Luke, Volume One* (Wheaton, IL: Crossway Books, 1998), 83.
2. William Barclay, *The Gospel of Luke,* Revised Edition, The Daily Study Bible Series (Louisville, KY: Westminster John Knox Press, 1975), 17.
3. Ryle, *Luke,* 39–40.
4. Frederick Buechner, *Peculiar Treasures* (San Francisco: Harper & Row, 1979), 157.
5. John Piper, *A Hunger for God* (Wheaton, IL: Crossway Books, 1997), 88.
6. Sproul, *A Walk with Jesus,* 41.
7. Leon Morris, *Luke: Tyndale New Testament Commentaries* (Grand Rapids, MI: Eerdmans, 1988), 102.
8. Oswald Chambers, *Still Higher for His Highest* (Grand Rapids, MI: Zondervan, 1970), 77.

Luke 3: A Desert Call
1. Hughes, *Luke, Volume One,* 111.
2. Bilezikian, *Christianity 101,* 159.

3. Benware, *Luke: Everyman's Bible Commentary,* 40.
4. Robert C. Girard, *Life of Christ, Volume 1: God's Word for the Biblically-Inept™* (Lancaster, PA: Starburst Publishers, 2000), 93.
5. Ibid., 62.
6. Lawrence O. Richards, *Illustrated Bible Handbook* (Nashville, TN: Thomas Nelson, 1997), 516.
7. Girard, *Life of Christ, Volume 1,* 43.
8. *The Zondervan NIV Matthew Henry Commentary* (Grand Rapids, MI: Zondervan, 1992), 226.

Luke 4: Temptation and Triumph
1. William MacDonald, *Believer's Bible Commentary* (Nashville, TN: Thomas Nelson, 1995), 30.
2. Sproul, *A Walk with Jesus,* 59.
3. Piper, *A Hunger for God,* 58.
4. Raymond B. Dillard and Tremper Longman, *An Introduction to the Old Testament* (Grand Rapids, MI: Zondervan, 1994), 66.
5. Derek Prime, *Jesus—His Life and Ministry* (Nashville, TN: Thomas Nelson, 1995), 44–45.
6. Warren W. Wiersbe, *Be Compassionate* (Colorado Springs, CO: Chariot Victor, 1988), 46.
7. Ibid.
8. John Piper, *A Godward Life* (Sisters, OR: Multnomah, 1997), 86–87.

Luke 5: Breaking the Rules
1. Hughes, *Luke, Volume One,* 161.
2. Larry Richards, *Bible Difficulties Solved* (Grand Rapids, MI: Fleming H. Revell, 1993), 235.
3. Philip Yancey, *The Jesus I Never Knew* (Grand Rapids, MI: Zondervan, 1995), 173.
4. Michael Card, *Immanuel: Reflections on the Life of Christ* (Nashville, TN: Thomas Nelson, 1990), 116.
5. Barclay, *The Gospel of Luke,* 62.
6. Yancey, *The Jesus I Never Knew,* 174–175.
7. Max Anders, *Jesus—Knowing Our Savior* (Nashville, TN: Thomas Nelson, 1995), 63.
8. Larry Richards, ed., *The Personal Growth Study Bible* (Nashville, TN: Thomas Nelson, 1996), 1247.
9. Wiersbe, *Be Compassionate,* 56.

Luke 6: Jesus, Ph.D.
1. Joy Davidman, quoted in Kathy Collard Miller, *Since Life Is a Game, These Are God's Rules* (Lancaster, PA: Starburst Publishers, 1999), 8; Joy Davidman, *Smoke on the Mountain* (Philadelphia, PA: Westminster Press, 1953), 16.
2. Richard J. Foster, *Seeking the Kingdom* (San Francisco: HarperSanFrancisco, 1995), 66.
3. Hughes, *Luke: Volume One,* 208.
4. Peter Kreeft, *Making Sense Out of Suffering* (Ann Arbor, MI: Servant Books, 1986), 142.

5. John Piper, *Desiring God* (Sisters, OR: Multnomah, 1996), 234.
6. Marcus Borg, *beliefnet,* "What Would Jesus Think of King's Protests? New scholarship about 'turning the other cheek,'" <http://www.belief.net/story/6/story_689_1.html> (22 August 2001).
7. Bock, *Luke: The NIV Application Commentary,* 191.
8. Benware, 60–61.
9. John Piper, *Future Grace* (Sisters, OR: Multnomah, 1995), 164.
10. Oswald Chambers, *Studies in the Sermon on the Mount* (London: Simpkin Marshall, Ltd., n.d.), 97.
11. Dallas Willard, *The Divine Conspiracy* (San Francisco: HarperSanFrancisco, 1998), 276.

Luke 7: Jesus, M.D.

1. G. Campbell Morgan, *The Great Physician* (London: Marshall, Morgan and Scott, 1937), 138.
2. Wiersbe, *Be Compassionate,* 73.
3. Bock, *Luke: The NIV Application Commentary,* 208.
4. Ibid., 215.
5. Charles R. Swindoll, *Hope Again* (Dallas: Word Publishing, 1996), 17.
6. Morris, *Luke: Tyndale New Testament Commentaries,* 158.
7. Sue and Larry Richards, *Every Woman in the Bible* (Nashville, TN: Thomas Nelson, 1999), 164.

Luke 8: The Way of Jesus

1. Richards, *Every Woman in the Bible,* 188.
2. Helmut Thielicke, *The Waiting Father* (New York: Harper and Row, 1959), 60.
3. Max Lucado, *Just Like Jesus* (Nashville, TN: Word Publishing, 1998), 42.
4. Kenneth L. Barker and John R. Kohlenberger III, eds., *NIV Bible Commentary,* vol. 2 (Grand Rapids, MI: Zondervan, 1994), 239.
5. Barclay, *The Gospel of Luke,* 105.
6. Wiersbe, *Be Compassionate,* 90–91.
7. Sproul, *A Walk with Jesus,* 161.
8. Lawrence O. Richards, *The Bible Reader's Companion* (Colorado Springs, CO: Chariot Victor, 1991), 659.
9. Barclay, *The Gospel of Luke,* 114.
10. Lawrence O. (Larry) Richards, *The 365 Day Devotional Commentary* (Colorado Springs, CO: Chariot Victor, 1990), 725.

Luke 9: Who Jesus Is

1. *Zondervan NIV Matthew Henry Commentary,* 243.
2. Hughes, *Luke, Volume One,* 324.
3. Jack Hayford, ed., *Spirit-Filled Life Bible, New King James Version* (Nashville, TN: Thomas Nelson, 1991), 1437.
4. Walter L. Liefeld, quoted in Kenneth L. Barker and John R. Kohlenberger III, eds., *Zondervan NIV Bible Commentary,* Volume 2: New Testament (Grand Rapids, MI: Zondervan, 1994), 244.
5. Wiersbe, *Be Compassionate,* 107.
6. Liefeld, *Zondervan NIV Bible Commentary,* 247.
7. Bock, *Luke: The NIV Application Commentary,* 283.
8. Jerry White, quoted in Robert Crosby, *More Than a Savior* (Sisters, OR: Multnomah, 1999), 55.

Luke 10: Significant Decisions

1. Morris, *Luke: Tyndale New Testament Commentaries,* 199.
2. Walvoord and Zuck, *The Bible Knowledge Commentary,* 233.
3. John Piper, *The Pleasures of God* (Sisters, OR: Multnomah, 2000), 271.
4. Piper, *Desiring God,* 279.
5. Willard, *The Divine Conspiracy,* 110.
6. Gary A. Haugen, *Good News about Injustice* (Downers Grove, IL: InterVarsity, 1999), 143.
7. Richards, *The Bible Reader's Companion,* 661.

Luke 11: Candid Conversations

1. Richard J. Foster, *Prayer: Finding the Heart's True Home* (San Francisco: HarperSanFrancisco, 1992), 135.
2. Willard, *The Divine Conspiracy,* 243.
3. Darryl DelHousaye, *Today for Eternity: 365 Powerful Daily Readings* (Sisters, OR: Questar, 1991), September 27.
4. Jack Hayford, ed., *Spirit-Filled Life Bible, New King James Version,* 1536.
5. Anders, *Jesus: Knowing Our Savior,* 30–31.
6. Ibid., 31.

Luke 12: Wise Words

1. R. Kent Hughes, *Luke, Volume Two* (Wheaton, IL: Crossway Books, 1998), 38.
2. Sproul, *A Walk with Jesus,* 228–229.
3. Wiersbe, *Be Compassionate,* 139.
4. Bock, *Luke: The NIV Application Commentary,* 344–345.
5. Leon Morris, *The Gospel According to St. Luke: Tyndale New Testament Commentaries* (Grand Rapids, MI: Eerdmans, 1974), 213.
6. Bob Benson, *"See You at the House"* (Nashville, TN: Generoux, 1986), 95.

Luke 13: Going against the Grain

1. Charles C. Ryrie, *So Great Salvation* (Colorado Springs, CO: Chariot Victor, 1989), 45.
2. MacDonald, *Believer's Bible Commentary,* 1423.
3. Lawrence O. Richards, *The Revell Bible Dictionary* (New York: Wynwood Press, 1990), 718–719.
4. Tom Sine, *The Mustard Seed Conspiracy* (Waco, TX: Word Books, 1981), 12.
5. Yancey, *The Jesus I Never Knew,* 160.

Luke 14: Relating to People

1. Richards, *The 365 Day Devotional Commentary,* 738.
2. C. Samuel Storms, *To Love Mercy* (Colorado Springs, CO: NavPress, 1991), 47.
3. Willard, *The Divine Conspiracy,* 109.
4. Thielicke, *The Waiting Father,* 185–186.
5. Hughes, *Luke, Volume Two,* 125.
6. Oswald Chambers, *My Utmost for His Highest* (New York: Dodd, Mead and Company, 1935), 184.
7. Benware, *Luke: Everyman's Bible Commentary,* 104.

Luke 15: Lost and Found

1. Bilezikian, *Christianity 101,* 149.
2. Phyllis Kilbourn, *Children in Crisis: A New Commitment* (Monrovia, CA: MARC Publications, div. of World Vision, 1996), 14.
3. Lawrence O. Richards, *The Teacher's Commentary* (Colorado Springs, CO: Chariot Victor, 1987), 685.
4. Walvoord and Zuck, *The Bible Knowledge Commentary,* 245.
5. Henri J. M. Nouwen, *The Return of the Prodigal Son* (New York: Image Books, Doubleday, 1995), 52.
6. Piper, *The Pleasures of God,* 189.
7. Max Lucado, *In the Grip of Grace* (Dallas: Word Publishing, 1996), 71.
8. Nouwen, *The Return of the Prodigal Son,* 71.

Luke 16: Money Matters

1. Barclay, *The Gospel of Luke,* 208.
2. Charles R. Swindoll, *The Quest for Character* (Portland, OR: Multnomah, n.d.), 117.
3. Richards, *The 365 Day Devotional Commentary,* 744.

Luke 17: Heart Attitudes

1. Ryle, *Luke: The Crossway Classic Commentaries,* 219.
2. Dallas Willard, *Hearing God* (Downers Grove, IL: InterVarsity, 1999), 11–12.

3. Barclay: *The Gospel of Luke*, 218.
4. DelHousaye, *Today for Eternity*, reading for November 26.
5. R. C. Sproul, *Almighty Over All* (Grand Rapids, MI: Baker Books, 1999), 184.

Luke 18: People Magazine
1. Warren W. Wiersbe, *Be Courageous* (Colorado Springs, CO: Chariot Victor, 1989), 62.
2. Richards, *Every Woman in the Bible*, 262.
3. Randall D. Roth, *Prayer Powerpoints* (Colorado Springs, CO: Chariot Victor, 1995), 12.
4. *Zondervan NIV Matthew Henry Commentary*, 285.
5. Sproul, *A Walk with Jesus*, 294–295.
6. Lawrence O. Richards, *The Bible Reader's Companion* (Colorado Springs, CO: Chariot Victor, 1991), 669.
7. MacDonald, *Believer's Bible Commentary*, 1439.
8. Barclay, *The Gospel of Luke*, 231.

Luke 19: Loved Little People
1. Storms, *To Love Mercy*, 178.
2. Henry T. Blackaby and Claude V. King, ed., *The Experiencing God Study Bible—New King James Version* (Nashville, TN: Broadman and Holman, 1994), 1541.
3. Hayford, *Spirit-Filled Life Bible*, 1554.
4. Dana Gould, ed., *Shepherd's Notes: Luke* (Nashville, TN: Broadman and Holman, 1998), 70.
5. Hughes, *Luke: Volume Two*, 234.
6. Barclay, *The Gospel of Luke*, 238.
7. Sibley, *Luke*, 66.

Luke 20: Hostile Challenges
1. Wiersbe, *Be Courageous*, 84.
2. Hughes, *Luke: Volume Two*, 255.
3. MacDonald, *Believer's Bible Commentary*, 1444.
4. Bilezikian, *Christianity 101*, 70.
5. Morris, *Luke*, 316.
6. Richards, *The Bible Reader's Companion*, 671.
7. Larry Richards, ed., *The Personal Growth Study Bible* (Nashville, TN: Thomas Nelson, 1996), 1351.
8. Willard, *The Divine Conspiracy*, 84.

Luke 21: What Matters Most
1. Richards, *The 365 Day Devotional Commentary*, 751.
2. Howard Vos, *Nelson's New Illustrated Bible Manners and Customs* (Nashville, TN: Thomas Nelson, 1999), 406.
3. Daymond R. Duck, *Prophecies of the Bible—God's Word for the Biblically-Inept™* (Lancaster, PA: Starburst Publishers, 2000), 170.
4. R. C. Sproul, *Now That's a Good Question!* (Wheaton, IL: Tyndale, 1996), 490.

5. Philip Yancey, *The Bible Jesus Read* (Grand Rapids, MI: Zondervan, 1999), 195.
6. Piper, *Desiring God*, 226.
7. Hughes, *Luke, Volume Two*, 302.
8. Elisabeth Elliot, *Keep a Quiet Heart* (Ann Arbor, MI: Servant Publications, 1995), 220.
9. John Piper, *Let the Nations Be Glad!* (Grand Rapids, MI: Baker Books, 1993), 46.

Luke 22: The Longest Night
1. Wiersbe, *Be Courageous*, 107.
2. George R. Bliss, quoted in *Shepherd's Notes*, 80.
3. Lloyd John Ogilvie, *The Cup of Wonder* (Wheaton, IL: Tyndale, 1976), 87.
4. W. Glyn Evans, *Don't Quit until You Taste the Honey* (Nashville, TN: Broadman Press, 1993), 50.
5. Hughes, *Luke, Volume Two*, 331.
6. Max Lucado, *The Final Week of Jesus* (highlights from *And the Angels Were Silent*) (Sisters, OR: Multnomah, 1994), 93.
7. Wiersbe, *Be Courageous*, 119.
8. Michael Card, *The Parable of Joy* (Nashville, TN: Thomas Nelson, 1995), 213.
9. Lucado, *In the Grip of Grace*, 125.

Luke 23: A Dark Day in History
1. Richards, *Illustrated Bible Handbook*, 537.
2. Robert L. Thomas, ed., *The NIV Harmony of the Gospels* (San Francisco: HarperSanFrancisco, 1988), 222.
3. Peter Marshall, *The First Easter* (Lincoln, NE: Chosen Books, 1959), 66, 69.
4. Richards, *Illustrated Bible Handbook*, 537.
5. Robert C. Girard, *Life of Christ, Volume 2* (Lancaster, PA: Starburst Publishers, 2000), 239.
6. Chambers, *My Utmost for His Highest*, 325.
7. Larry Richards, *The Bible—God's Word for the Biblically-Inept™* (Lancaster, PA: Starburst Publishers, 1998), 210.

Luke 24: A Bright Day Dawns
1. DelHousaye, *Today for Eternity*, reading for April 12.
2. MacDonald, *Believer's Bible Commentary*, 1457.
3. Morris, *Luke*, 367.
4. G. Campbell Morgan, *The Great Physician*, 318.
5. Elliot, *Keep a Quiet Heart*, 76.
6. Max Lucado, *Six Hours One Friday* (Sisters, OR: Multnomah, 1989), 72.
7. Richards, *The 365 Day Devotional Commentary*, 755.

INDEX

Boldface numbers refer to defined (What?) terms in the sidebar.

A

Aaron, 5, 6
Abba, **155**
Abijah, 5, 6
Abilene, 39
Abraham, 10, 18, **48**
  "daughter of Abraham," 184
  "God of Abraham," 265–266
  in heaven, 187
  Jews as children of, 41, 186–187
  Lazarus and the rich man, parable, 219–221
  in *Magnificat,* 15–16
  "son of Abraham," 245–248
Abraham's side, **219**
Abyss, **116**
Acts, Book of, 321
  Luke as writer, xiii
Adam, 47–**48**, 202, 223
Advocate, **235**
Aloes, 309
Altar, **6**
  Altar of incense, illustration of, 8
Anders, Max:
  on Jesus and religious leaders, 162
  on Jesus challenging Pharisees, 163
  on the Pharisees, 77
Andrew, 57, 84–85
  (*See also* Apostles; Disciples; the Twelve)
Angel(s):
  Annunciation, 11–12
  Gabriel, 5–10, 11–13
  Gloria, singing, 26
  Jesus, as strengthening, 289–291
  Jesus mentioning, 131, 169
  Joseph, appearing to, 17
  Joseph, warning, 33
  Mary, appearing to, 11–13

shepherds, appearing to, 26–28
  at temptation of Christ, 56
  at tomb of Jesus, 312–313
  Zechariah, visiting, 5–10, 13
  (*See also* Gabriel)
Animal(s)
  at birth of Jesus, 25
  Sabbath care of, 184
  (*See also* specific animals)
  Animal sacrifice, 29, 255
  doves or pigeons, 29
  lamb, 29
  sheep, 27
Anna, 31–32
Annas, 39, 293, 298
Annunciation, 11–13
Apostle(s), **4**
  Eleven, the, and resurrected Jesus, 314, 318–321
  twelve chosen, 84–85
  (*See also* Disciples; the Twelve; individual names; specific events)
Aramaic, xv
Arimathea, Joseph of, 308–310
Ark, 230
Ashes, 143
Attitude (*See under* Christians: right attitude)
Augustine, Saint, on truth, 61
Austere, **102**
Authority, **126**
  of God over Satan, 288
  salvation's greater value, 144
  seventy-two as given, 144
  of the Twelve, 125–126
Authority of Jesus, 257–258
  to heal, 123
  over death, 122, 123
  over demons, 117, 123–124
  over nature, 114–115, 123

B

Babies (*see* Birth; Boys; Children; Girls; Sons)
Babylon, wise men from, 33
Badger, **156**
Balaam, **19**
Banquet, great, parable of, 195–196
Baptism, **40**
  with Holy Spirit and fire, 43–44
  "I have a baptism to undergo," 177–178
  of Jesus, 45–47
  (*See also* John the Baptist)
Barabbas, 301
Barclay, William:
  on birth of a boy, 28
  on the bleeding woman, 120
  on Christian life, 251
  on cross and crown, 242
  on Jesus at sea, 114
  on sin, 75
  on the ten lepers, 227
  on the wily steward, 214
Bar mitzvah, 34
Barnabas, 5
Barren, barrenness, 5–10
Barren fig tree, parable of, 182–183
Bartholomew, 84–85
  (*See also* Apostles; Disciples; the Twelve)
Beatitudes, 86–88
Beelzebub, **113, 157**
  (*See also* Satan)
Beggar(s):
  blind, in Jericho, 242–243
  Lazarus, in parable, 218–221
Belief in God, xii
  and unbelief, 10–11
Believers (*see* Christians)
Benedictus, xiv, 18–19, 27
Benson, Bob, on Jesus, appeal of, 174

Benware, Paul N.:
  on good for evil, 89
  on John the Baptist, 44
  on Luke's purpose, 4
  on Mary and Elizabeth, 15
  on salt and discipleship, 199
Bethany, 151–152
  Mary and Martha, 149–150
Bethlehem:
  birth of Jesus in, 23–29
  Joseph, as hometown of, 24
  male babies killed in, 33
Bethphage, 251
Bethsaida, 127, 143
Betrothal, significance in Jesus' day, 17
Bible:
  Books in (*see* individual Books)
  composition of, xi–xii
  contradictions in, 48
  genealogies (of Jesus) in, 47–49
  God as source, xii
  languages and translations of, xv
  New International Version (NIV), xv
  quoted, discernment regarding, 55–56
Bible study:
  guidance for, xv, xviii
  value of, xi–xiii, xvii, 113, 313
Bible Knowledge Commentary:
  on betrothal customs, 17
  on God and infertility, 7
  on the Godhead, 145
  on the prodigal son, 207
Bilezikian, Gilbert:
  on God as love, 202
  on Roman rule in Palestine, 263
  on sin and repentance, 41
  on the virgin birth, 14

genealogy of, 47–49
as God and man, 266–267
God as father of, 34–35,
45–46, 66, 144–145, 294
Godhead, 145
as ideal human, 69
as King, 11–12
life of, Gospels as telling,
xii–xiii
ministry of (see
specific events, topics,
places, and names)
Second Coming of (see
Second Coming)
as Son of Man (see Son of
Man)
(See also Messiah; Savior;
specific topics and
events)
Jew(s), first-century:
Abraham as father of, 41,
186–187
and eternal life, 187
"king of the Jews," 33
religious elite of (see
Pharisees; Sadducees)
scattering of, 274–275
synagogue (see Syna-
gogue)
(See also specific topics
and events)
Joanna (wife of Cuza),
107–108
at tomb of Jesus, 311–314
Job, 184
John, Gospel of, xiii
(See also Gospels, the
four; New Testament;
specific events and
topics)
John (apostle), 57, 84–85, 121
"disciple whom Jesus
loved," 5
at Gethsemane, 291
at Lake of Gennesaret,
69–71
at the Transfiguration,
131–133
"whoever is not against
you is for you," 135–136
(See also Apostles;
Disciples; the Twelve)
John Mark (see Mark)
John the Baptist, 7, 126–127
angel announcing birth of,
5–10
appearance of, 40
authority of, 258
baptism by, 43–44
birth of, 17–20, 28
Christ, as thought to be,
43

desert, life in, 39–40, 101
disciples of, 77–78, 100–
101
fate of, 126–127
"His name is John," 17–18
Isaiah as predicting, 39–40
Jesus thought to be,
126–127, 129
locusts and honey, 40
as messenger, 40,
101–102, 218
ministry of, 39–45
mission of, 19
prayer, instructing
followers in, 153–154
role of, 7, 39–40, 43–44
soldiers and tax collectors,
ministry to, 41–42
Jonah, 160
Jordan River, 40
baptism of Jesus, 45–46
(See also John the Baptist)
Joseph, 11, 16–17
angel as warning, 33
(See also Birth of Jesus;
Mary; specific topics and
events)
Joseph of Arimathea, 308–310
Joy:
in Luke, Gospel of, xiv
pervading Jesus' ministry,
78
service, resulting from, 131
source of, 90, 144
Judas Iscariot, 84–85,
281–283, 285–286
fate of, 301–302
kiss of, 291
(See also Apostles;
Disciples; the Twelve)
Judas son of James
(Thaddaeus), 84–85
(See also Apostles;
Disciples; the Twelve)
Judea:
"flee to the mountains,"
274
Herod as king of, 5
John the Baptist born in,
14, 17–18
ministry of Jesus in, 65
Pontius Pilate as governor,
39, 298
seventy-two disciples,
141–144
Judgment:
"Do not judge," 90
judging others, 91
as personal, 254
Pharisee and tax collector,
parable, 235–236
Tribulation, 275

Judgment Day, 168
Justice, 233–235
Justified, **236**

K
Kilbourn, Phyllis, on children,
responsibility to, 204
King, Claude V. (see Blackaby,
Henry T., and Claude V.
King)
Kingdom divided against
itself, 158
Kingdom of God, 130–131, **142**
and earthly riches, 239
"easier for a camel to go
through the eye of a
needle," 239
narrow door to, 186–187
the Twelve, place in, 287
as within you, 228
(See also Eternal life;
Heaven)
King(s):
Christ as, xiii, 11–12, 65
"King of the Jews," 33,
298–299, 305
war, as planning, 198
(See also individual
names)
Kiss, of Judas, 291
Korazin, 143
Kreeft, Peter, on the point of
our lives, 87

L
Lackeys, **148**
Lake of Gennesaret, **69**
Lamb of God, 27
Lamb(s):
"lambs among wolves,"
141–142
marriage supper of, 284
Passover, 283
as sacrifice, 29
seventy-two disciples,
141–142
Lamb's Book of Life, 144
Lamentation, **254**
Lamp, 112, 161
Last Supper, 283–289
Law, lawyers:
"Beware of the teachers of
the law," 267
as enemies of Jesus, 165
Jesus as challenging,
163–164
(See also Enemies of Jesus)
Law of Moses, 319
Lazarus, 122, 149–150, 251, 254
Lazarus and the rich man,
parable, 218–221
Leadership, 286–287

LeBar, Lois, on knowing God,
xii
Legion, 115–118, **116**
Lepers, leprosy, 60, 72–74
Jesus as healing, 72–74
ten lepers, 226–228
Levi (see Matthew)
Levite, **146**
Life:
point of, 87
words of, xvii
Light, 112, 161
Lightning, 229
Light of the world, 112
Lilies, 173–**174**
Locusts, 40
Lollygagging, **142**
Longman, Tremper (see
Dillard, Raymond B., and
Tremper Longman)
Lord, 27
Lord's Prayer, 153–155
forgiving others, 224–225
Lord's Supper, 285
Lost coin, parable, 204–206
Lost sheep, parable, 202–204
Lot; Lot's wife, 230–231
Lots, **6**
Love, 89
brotherly, 113
of enemies, 88
and forgiven debt, 104–106
of God and others, 148
God as, 202
of God for people, xiv,
xvii, 120
godly, 89
good Samaritan, 146–148
human freedom and, 189
key to, 90
for neighbor, 145–146
for others, 88
showing, 147
Lucado, Max:
on grace, 209
on Jesus at Gethsemane,
290
on parable of the sower, 112
on Peter, 293
on resurrected Jesus, 319
Luke, xiii, 5
Luke, Gospel of, xiii–xiv, xiv,
xvii, 4
genealogy (of Jesus) in,
47–49
as for Gentiles, 4
historical context in, 39,
40
(See also Gospels, the four;
New Testament; specific
events and topics)
Lysanias (tetrarch), 39

Books by Starburst Publishers®

(Partial listing—full list available on request)

The **God's Word for the Biblically-Inept™** series is already a best-seller with over 100,000 books sold! Designed to make reading the Bible easy, educational, and fun! This series of verse-by-verse Bible studies, topical studies, and overviews mixes scholarly information from experts with helpful icons, illustrations, sidebars, and time lines. It's the Bible made easy!

Luke—God's Word for the Biblically-Inept™
Joyce L. Gibson

Luke tells the story of Jesus as a compassionate human who cares for women, the poor, and the oppressed. Written by a doctor, Luke is the longest of the Gospels. It reveals miracles and parables not found elsewhere. Discover the truth about common misperceptions of Jesus and his teachings and feel God's love reaching down to you through the touch of the Great Physician.
(trade paper)   ISBN 1892016478 $17.99

Acts—God's Word for the Biblically-Inept™
Robert C. Girard

An important book of history, Acts recounts the ascension of Jesus into heaven, the spread of Christianity throughout the Roman Empire, and the rapid growth of the church—despite the persecution of Paul and other apostles. A must-read for anyone interested in learning more about the early days of the church without getting bogged down in complicated language and confusing details.
(trade paper)   ISBN 189201646X $17.99

The Bible—God's Word for the Biblically-Inept™
Larry Richards

An excellent book to start learning the entire Bible. Get the basics or the in-depth information you are seeking with this user-friendly overview. From Creation to Christ to the Millennium, learning the Bible has never been easier.
(trade paper)   ISBN 0914984551 $16.95

Daniel—God's Word for the Biblically-Inept™
Daymond R. Duck

Daniel is a book of prophecy and the key to understanding the mysteries of the Tribulation and end-time events. This verse-by-verse commentary combines humor and scholar-ship to get at the essentials of Scripture. Perfect for those who want to know the truth about the Antichrist.
(trade paper)   ISBN 0914984489 $16.95

Genesis—God's Word for the Biblically-Inept™
Joyce L. Gibson

Genesis is written to make understanding and learning the Word of God simple and fun! Like the other books in this series, the author breaks the Bible down into bite-sized pieces making it easy to understand and incorporate into your life. Readers will learn about Creation, Adam and Eve, the Flood, Abraham and Isaac, and more.
(trade paper)   ISBN 1892016125 $16.95

Health & Nutrition—God's Word for the Biblically-Inept™
Kathleen O'Bannon Baldinger

The Bible is full of God's rules for good health! Baldinger reveals scientific evidence that proves the diet and health principles outlined in the Bible are the best for total health. Learn about the Bible diet, the food pyramid, and fruits and vegetables from the Bible! Experts include Pamela Smith, Julian Whitaker, Kenneth Cooper, and T. D. Jakes.
(trade paper)   ISBN 0914984055 $16.95

John—God's Word for the Biblically-Inept™
Lin Johnson

From village fisherman to beloved apostle, John was an eyewitness to the teachings and miracles of Christ. Now, readers can join in an easy-to-understand, verse-by-verse journey through the fourth and most unique of all the Gospels. Witness the wonder of Jesus, a man who turned water into wine, healed the blind, walked on water, and raised Lazarus from the dead.
(trade paper)   ISBN 1892016435 $16.95

Life of Christ, Volume 1—God's Word for the Biblically-Inept™
Robert C. Girard

Girard takes the reader on an easy-to-understand journey through the Gospels of Matthew, Mark, Luke, and John, tracing the story of Jesus from his virgin birth to his revolutionary ministry. Learn about Jesus' baptism, the Sermon on the Mount, and his miracles and parables.
(trade paper)   ISBN 1892016230 $16.95

Life of Christ, Volume 2—God's Word for the Biblically-Inept™
Robert C. Girard

Life of Christ, Volume 2, begins with events recorded in Matthew 16. Read about Jesus' transfiguration, his miracles and parables, triumphal ride through Jerusalem, capture in the Garden of Gethsemane, and his trial, crucifixion, resurrection, and ascension. Find out how to be great in the kingdom of God, what Jesus meant when he called himself the light of the world, and what makes up real worship.
(trade paper)   ISBN 1892016397 $16.95

Mark—God's Word for the Biblically-Inept™
Scott Pinzon

The shortest of all the Gospels, Mark focuses on Jesus' actions. Telling the story of the adult Jesus from the time of his baptism by John the Baptist to his crucifixion and

resurrection, readers will learn about the Book of Mark in simple, vivid terms that will bring it to life like never before!
(trade paper)   ISBN 1892016362 $17.99

Men of the Bible—God's Word for the Biblically-Inept™
D. Larry Miller
Benefit from the life experiences of the powerful men of the Bible! Learn how the inspirational struggles of men such as Moses, Daniel, Paul, and David parallel the struggles of men today. It will inspire and build Christian character for any reader.
(trade paper)   ISBN 1892016079 $16.95

Prophecies of the Bible—God's Word for the Biblically-Inept™
Daymond R. Duck
God has a plan for this crazy planet, and now understanding it is easier than ever! Best-selling author and end-time prophecy expert Daymond R. Duck explains the complicated prophecies of the Bible in plain English. Duck shows you all there is to know about the end of the age, the New World Order, the Second Coming, and the coming world government. Find out what prophecies have already been fulfilled and what's in store for the future!
(trade paper)   ISBN 1892016222 $16.95

Revelation—God's Word for the Biblically-Inept™
Daymond R. Duck
End-time Bible prophecy expert Daymond R. Duck leads us verse by verse through one of the Bible's most confusing books. Follow the experts as they forge their way through the captivating prophecies of Revelation!
(trade paper)   ISBN 0914984985 $16.95

Romans—God's Word for the Biblically-Inept™
Gib Martin
The best-selling *God's Word for the Biblically-Inept™* series continues to grow! Learn about the apostle Paul, living a righteous life, and more with help from graphics, icons, and chapter summaries.
(trade paper)   ISBN 1892016273 $16.95

Women of the Bible—God's Word for the Biblically-Inept™
Kathy Collard Miller
Finally, a Bible perspective just for women! Gain valuable insight from the successes and struggles of such women as Eve, Esther, Mary, Sarah, and Rebekah. Interesting icons like "Get Close to God," "Build Your Spirit," and "Grow Your Marriage" will make it easy to incorporate God's Word into your daily life.
(trade paper)   ISBN 0914984063 $16.95

• **Learn more at www.biblicallyinept.com** •

An Expressive Heart: Stories, Lessons, and Exercises Inspired by the Psalms
Edited by Kathy Collard Miller
An intimate book of inspirational lessons from the best-selling editor of the *God's Abundance* collection. Each selection includes a passage from the poetic Book of Psalms, an inspirational story, lesson, quotation, and idea for personal journaling with room to write. The Psalms provide an unmatched guide for anyone who wants to know God better, and *An Expressive Heart* will help you say what's on your heart.
(trade paper)   ISBN 1892016508 $12.99

A Growing Heart: Stories, Lessons, and Exercises Inspired by Proverbs
Edited by Kathy Collard Miller
The profound truths of Proverbs provide wisdom for making good choices in life. Each selection includes a verse from Proverbs, an inspirational story, teaching, quotation, and an idea for journaling with room to write. Lessons will guide the reader on topics such as discipline, friendship, love, parenting, wealth, and work.
(trade paper)   ISBN 1892016524 $12.99

Cheap Talk with the Frugal Friends
Angie Zalewski and Deana Ricks
A collection of savvy tips and tricks for stretching the family dollar from celebrity thrifters, Angie Zalewski and Deana Ricks, known as the Frugal Friends by their radio and television audiences. This book features twenty-nine chapters on various topics, including automotive, beauty care, cleaning products, dating, decorating, entertainment, medicine, pet care, and sporting goods. Includes advice on eliminating credit card debt, making extra money, and organizing the home. Finally, a practical way to save money with without compromising convenience or lowering lifestyle standards!
(trade paper)   ISBN 1892016583 $9.99

Stories for the Spirit-Filled Believer
Edited by Cristine Bolley
It's one thing to know that God is real. It is quite another to have profound and on-going experiences that confirm that belief. In this awesome collection of stories, Cristine Bolley compiles the real-life testimonies of believers who have heard God's voice and responded. This volume includes stories from today's most dynamic charismatic personalities: Oral Roberts, Beth Moore, T. D. Jakes, Joyce Meyer, and more. Each selection contains a Scripture verse, true story, and a prayer. Sure to inspire readers to listen for God's voice in their own lives.
(trade paper)   ISBN 1892016540 $13.99

God Things Come in Small Packages: Celebrating the Little Things in Life

Susan Duke, LeAnn Weiss, Caron Loveless,
and Judith Carden

Enjoy touching reminders of God's simple yet generous gifts to brighten our days and gladden our hearts! Treasures like a sunset over a vast sparkling ocean, a child's trust, or the crystalline dew on a spider's web come to life in this elegant compilation. Such occasions should be celebrated as if gift wrapped from God; they're his hallmarks! Personalized Scripture is artfully combined with compelling stories and reflections.
(cloth)   ISBN 1892016281 $12.95

God Things Come in Small Packages for Moms: Rejoicing in the Simple Pleasures of Motherhood

Susan Duke, LeAnn Weiss, Caron Loveless, and Judith Carden

The "small" treasures God plants in a mom's day shine in this delightful book. Savor priceless stories, which encourage us to value treasures like a shapeless, ceramic bowl presented with a toothy grin; a child's hand clinging to yours on a crowded bus; or a handful of wildflowers presented on a hectic day. Each story combines personalized Scripture with heartwarming vignettes and inspiring reflections.
(cloth)   ISBN 189201629X $12.95

God Things Come in Small Packages for Friends: Exploring the Freedom of Friendship

LeAnn Weiss, Susan Duke, and Judy Carden

A heartwarming combination of true stories, paraphrased Scripture, and reflections that celebrate the simple yet cherished blessings shared between true friends. This series combines the beauty of gift books with the depth of devotionals. Includes reflective meditation, narrative vignettes detailing powerful moments of revelation, and encouraging scripture passages presented as letters to a friend.
(cloth)   ISBN 1892016346 $12.95

God Things Come in Small Packages for Women: Celebrating the Unique Gifts of Women

LeAnn Weiss, Susan Duke, and Judy Carden

Women will experience God's love like never before through wonderfully paraphrased Scripture, true stories, and reflections, which celebrate the unique character of women. Includes reflective meditation, narrative vignettes detailing powerful moments of revelation, and encouraging scripture passages presented as letters from God.
(cloth)   ISBN 1892016354 $12.95

The Weekly Feeder: A Revolutionary Shopping, Cooking, and Meal-Planning System

Cori Kirkpatrick

A revolutionary meal-planning system, here is a way to make preparing home-cooked dinners more convenient than ever. At the beginning of each week, simply choose one of the eight preplanned menus, tear out the corresponding grocery list, do your shopping, and whip up each fantastic meal in less than 45 minutes! The author's household management tips, equipment checklists, and nutrition information make this system a must for any busy family. Included with every recipe is a personal anecdote from the author emphasizing the importance of good food, a healthy family, and a well-balanced life.
(trade paper)   ISBN 1892016095 $16.95

God Stories: They're So Amazing, Only God Could Make Them Happen

Donna I. Douglas

Famous individuals share their personal, true-life experiences with God in this beautiful new book! Find out how God has touched the lives of top recording artists, professional athletes, and other newsmakers like Jessi Colter, Deana Carter, Ben Vereen, Stephanie Zimbalist, Cindy Morgan, Sheila E., Joe Jacoby, Cheryl Landon, Brett Butler, Clifton Taulbert, Babbie Mason, Michael Medved, Sandi Patty, Charlie Daniels, and more! Their stories are intimate, poignant, and sure to inspire and motivate you as you listen for God's message in your own life!
(cloth)   ISBN 1892016117 $18.95

Treasures of a Woman's Heart: A Daybook of Stories and Inspiration

Edited by Lynn D. Morrissey

Join the best-selling editor of *Seasons of a Woman's Heart* in this touching sequel where she unlocks the treasures of women and glorifies God with Scripture, reflections, and a compilation of stories. Explore heartfelt living with vignettes by Kay Arthur, Elisabeth Elliot, Emilie Barnes, Claire Cloninger, and more.
(cloth)   ISBN 1892016257 $18.95

Seasons of a Woman's Heart: A Daybook of Stories and Inspiration

Edited by Lynn D. Morrissey

A woman's heart is complex. This daybook of stories, quotes, Scriptures, and daily reflections will inspire and refresh. Christian women share their heartfelt thoughts on seasons of faith, growth, guidance, nurturing, and victory. Includes Christian writers Kay Arthur, Emilie Barnes, Luci Swindoll, Jill Briscoe, and Florence Littauer.
(cloth)   ISBN 1892016036 $18.95

Stories of God's Abundance for a More Joyful Life

Compiled by Kathy Collard Miller

Like its successful predecessor, *God's Abundance*, this book is filled with beautiful, inspirational, real-life stories. Those telling their stories of God share Scriptures and insights that readers can apply to their daily lives. Renew your faith in life's small miracles and challenge yourself to allow God to lead the way as you find the source of abundant living for all your relationships.
(trade paper)   ISBN 1892016060 $12.95